WARSHIP 1997–1998

WARSHIP 1997–1998

Edited by David McLean and Antony Preston

CONWAY
MARITIME PRESS

Frontispiece
HMCS Bonaventure *is moved out of the fitting-dock at the Royal Navy's Aircraft yard, Sydenham, Belfast, on 27 February 1957 (Rudnicki/MARCOM Museum). The history of this Canadian aircraft carrier is the subject of the fourth article in Thomas G Lynch's four-part series* The Canadian Naval Aviation Experience *(see page 95).*

© Brassey's (UK) Ltd 1997

First published in Great Britain in November 1997 by
Conway Maritime Press,
an imprint of Brassey's (UK) Ltd
33 John Street
London WC1N 2AT

British Library Cataloguing in Publication Data
A record of this title is available on request from the British Library.

ISBN 0–85177–722–8

Project editor: Andrew Brown
Jacket design by Peter Champion
Typesetting in Plantin and page make-up by M Rules
Printed and bound in Great Britain by the
University Printing House, Cambridge.

CONTENTS

EDITORIAL

Readers of *Warship 1996* need not be alarmed by the Publisher's decision to number this latest edition 1997–1998. The reason is merely the need to acknowledge that *Warship* appears later in the year than it used to, and is certainly not a device to skip an issue; next year's volume will cover 1998–1999.

Every effort has been made to choose a wide variety of periods, nationalities and topics. The periods covered range from the mid-nineteenth century to today. *Warship* does not exist to deal with the latest naval technology, but where appropriate we will record what is likely to be a significant milestone in warship development, such as the *Visby* class 'stealth' corvette. It is almost impossible to understand the *rationale* of a design without reading its history and gaining an understanding of the major influences such as the threat, cost and industrial capability. This does not stop critics, however, from asking the perennial question, 'What idiot designed that ship?' The same can be said of tactics: analysis of the pressures on a senior commander is ultimately more revealing than any statistical comparison of rival fleets' weapons and speeds.

The temptation to trawl through Royal Navy topics has to be controlled, although the richness of the Royal Navy's heritage makes it difficult to avoid. A recent review criticised *Warship 1996* for being a sort of 'Beezer Book for Boys over 35', dealing with what the reviewer dismissed as a 'rag-bag of mainly technical descriptions of long-dead warships'. That is, of course, an unavoidable drawback of a publication dedicated to warship history, but as editors we can only hope that our choice from the manuscripts submitted strikes a reasonable balance between unusual items of technical interest and the perennially popular. In recent years there have been a small number of features dealing with operational matters and even personalities. This is deliberate, because we believe that technical history is strongly influenced by operational experience, even in peacetime. The careers of great warship designers such as Sir William White and Sir Stanley Goodall are inseparable from the designs created by them. However, we cannot be allowed to forget that you, the readers, are the ultimate judges of what ought to be covered in *Warship*.

When *Warship* was first published we had the ambitious aim of raising the standard of warship history (as opposed to general naval history), to get away from the widespread habit of giving equal credence to all published statistics, with no questions asked. As the first editor of *Warship*, I am naturally delighted to see how the lusty infant has grown in the intervening years. In a sense, this has created its own problems; all the standard 'easy' subjects have been covered, leaving the more obscure items to the end. However, our contributors have done us proud. Colin Jones' description of the 1869–70 cruise of the Flying Squadron gives an insight into a Royal Navy coming to terms with the new technology of the mid-nineteenth century. The impact of that advanced technology on tactics had to be absorbed at a time when the Crimean War and the American Civil War taught ambiguous lessons at best.

R D Layman looks at the role of kite balloons in the US Navy, one of the early developments in naval aviation. Although lacking the glamour of aircraft and airships, the humble kite balloon offered a short cut to improved reconnaissance for the fleet. Layman's knowledge of the early faltering steps to naval air power is unsurpassed.

Warships that 'might have been' continue to fascinate ship historians, and in this issue we have two features. Peter Brook looks at the designs offered by the famous Armstrong shipyard on Tyneside, which dominated the naval export market in the nineteenth and early twentieth centuries. George Moore looks at a different angle, the development of Royal Navy cruiser designs from 1939 until 1942, when the last traditional cruisers took shape.

David Brown looks at the career of Sir Stanley Goodall, arguably the only Director of Naval Construction to rank with Sir William White. But, unlike White, Goodall was deeply involved in two world wars, two periods of ultra-rapid technical advance. He was clearly a powerful influence with a strong personality, but obviously commanded great loyalty from his staff. When reading the Ship's Cover for HMS *Vanguard* some years ago I was impressed by Goodall's loyalty to his subordinates. When in 1944 (I think) he was asked by the Naval Staff to investigate the possibility of converting the new battleship to an aircraft carrier, Goodall replied angrily that his constructors and draughtsmen had been working under great pressure to complete the ship for the final offensive against Japan. Morale in the department would be badly affected by what could be taken as a casual attitude at Board level. If the Staff were serious about the change of policy, then the DNC's department would loyally obey orders, but they would need convincing that it was more than a passing whim!

John Jordan has written another chapter in his examination of French naval designs between the two world wars, looking at the 8,000-ton cruisers of the early 1920s. Keith McBride looks at similar-sized ships, the Royal Navy's *Leander* and *Amphion* classes (the latter better known as the Australian *Sydney* class). Thomas Lynch brings his chronicle of Canadian naval aviation to an end with the story of HMCS *Bonaventure*, a most elaborate modernisation of the original *Colossus* class light fleet carriers.

No matter how advanced real and protected designs may be, the purpose of warships is to 'go in harm's way', or to put it another way, all warships run the risk of being sunk. Peter Kelly looks at the tragic loss of the small anti-aircraft cruiser HMS *Curacoa*, rammed by the liner *Queen Mary* in 1942. The tragedy was compounded by the fact that the *Queen Mary*, packed with thousands of troops, could not be allowed to pick up survivors in case a U-boat was loitering in the area. The authorities decided to censor all mention of the story until the end of the war in 1945, a decision which must have aroused strong feelings among the relatives of those lost in the *Curacoa*. In 1942, however, it must have seemed less controversial; no newspaper coverage would bring back the dead, and the story might have 'given comfort to the enemy' at a time when the Battle of the Atlantic was still in the balance. The parallel of the loss of American LSTs off Slapton Sands in April 1944 comes to mind (see *Warship 1996*).

Pierre Hervieux examines the chequered careers of the captured Italian torpedo boats and a solitary Yugoslav destroyer which fought under the German ensign in 1940–45. David Miller examines the strangely tortuous process of scuttling the surrendered *Kriegsmarine* U-boats in 1945–46. M W Williams' description of the sinking of the German submarine minelayer *UC–55* by HMS *Tirade* is a vignette of the naval war in home waters in 1917. Neither the event nor the protagonists were of outstanding significance, but naval history of the First World War is so often centred on Jutland and the success

of the U-boats that the remainder of the conflict is a closed book to most students. The sinking of *UC–55* occurred during that hard slog in 1917–18 which resulted in the defeat of the U-boats and, finally, the Imperial German Navy itself.

A related comment appears in 'Warship Notes', with a description by Keith McBride of the recent discovery of the wreck of the destroyer HMS *Pheasant*, lost off the Orkneys on 1 March 1917. The Army Sub-Aqua Club carried out a methodical search and exploration in 1994–96, for which they must be congratulated. The conclusions do not challenge the official verdict in 1917 that the *Pheasant* struck a mine, possibly a British one, although there is a remote possibility that she was torpedoed. This would not be the only occasion in two world wars when a Board of Enquiry thought that being sunk by a torpedo seemed somehow more 'dignified' than hitting a mine. With the discovery of the wreck of HMS *Racoon* last year, all sixty-seven Royal Navy destroyers lost in 1914–18 are now accounted for. Such a scale of loss seems light when compared with the Second World War, but 'torpedo boat destroyers' (TBDs) were the workhorses of the anti-submarine war. These two items contain very useful descriptions of standard wartime destroyer designs (although the 'M' design was prepared before 1914). Royal Navy destroyers performed so well in 1914–18 that the main features of the final 'V & W' design were universally adopted by other navies.

The Review section is unchanged since last year, with detailed notes and letters from readers, book reviews, a summary of the important naval events since the summer of 1996 and Warship Gallery. The choice of images in the latter is eclectic, but it gives some idea of the wealth of the Conway Picture Library.

Antony Preston
David McLean

RULING THE WAVES

The Royal Navy Flying Squadron's world cruise in 1869–70 produced a powerful impression of British military power. **Colin Jones** looks at the stately progress of the squadron and its implications.

Policy and the Projection of Power

It was one of the perennial problems faced by the Royal Navy in fulfilling its responsibilities in a far-flung empire to ensure that sufficient force was available where and when required. This frequently led to the stationing of squadrons of ships on foreign stations for show as much as for action, and a government looking for savings might well look closely at the benefits achieved from this policy in relation to the costs incurred. Thus in 1868 the new government of William Gladstone decided that the Navy could weather some cuts, and the reduction of the strength on foreign stations was the policy which seemed the most attractive. On the several distant stations, Hugh Childers, the new First Lord of the Admiralty, arranged for ships to be brought home and paid off. Between 1868 and 1870 the East Indies station was reduced from 11 to 6 ships at a saving of 779 men; the Cape and the West Africa stations were combined and reduced from 18 to 13 ships at a saving of 637 men; the China station was reduced from 35 to 27 ships at a saving of 1,390 men; the Pacific station was reduced from 12 ships to 10 at a saving of 775 men; and the Australia station was reduced from 5 to 4 ships at a saving of 322 men. The savings amounted to almost 4,000 men.

The self-governing colonies were being encouraged to provide for their own defence, and Victoria, for one, was enthusiastic in taking up the offer, acquiring for its infant navy the obsolete battleship *Nelson*, which arrived in February 1868, and the monitor *Cerberus*, launched at Jarrow in December of the same year. Two monitors were also being built for India, but nowhere else was a local naval force raised. In the case of the North America station, as well as China and the Pacific, the presence of an ironclad of the Royal Navy was considered to be important, whatever else might be sacrificed.

To ensure that the shield of British power would still be visible, Childers arranged for the worldwide reductions to fund a cruiser squadron, which could be sent at short notice to any trouble spot. It would be able to augment any local force significantly, but in the absence of any war at this time, it was seen as an ideal training vehicle for blue-water sailors. It would provide familiarity with the navigation of many seas, it was stated, and with the hydrography of the principal harbours of the empire. For the other nations whose navies had a stake in distant waters, it would be seen as an expression of Britain's continued might, as well as the length of its reach. It supported the arguments put by Captain Colomb in his publications that only overall naval mastery could properly protect the lines of commerce of the empire. On this occasion, Childers told Parliament, it would be visiting every distant station except North America, India and the Mediterranean. So it was that the Flying Squadron set out to flaunt the White Ensign in the furthest regions. The *Army and Navy Gazette* called it 'one of the most interesting voyages undertaken since the days of Cook'. As Bandsman William Haynes, aboard the *Phoebe*, wrote in a long narrative poem which became a full-length book,

> With a fleet of blue jackets round the world we can run,
> And keep down aggression with Childers' Squadron.

In January 1869 the squadron was placed under the command of one of the Navy's rising stars. At 44 years of age, Rear-Admiral Geoffrey Phipps Hornby was the most junior admiral on the list, most recently having served as commodore of the West Africa squadron aboard the frigate *Bristol*. He was seen as the man who could best accomplish the voyage around the world of Britain's special cruiser squadron. His new flagship was the frigate *Liverpool*. To his men, Hornby was universally 'Uncle Geoff'. His very presence seemed to be 'command personified'. At sea he insisted on everyone working hard, and in getting the best from the sailing of the ships. In port, a little relaxation was permitted.

The Ships

As the squadron left Plymouth on 19 June 1869 it comprised the frigates *Liverpool*, *Liffey*, *Bristol* and *Endymion*, and the corvette *Scylla*. The other corvette, *Barrosa*, was late with engine repairs and joined two weeks later in Funchal. She had taken aboard the crew of the corvette *Cadmus*, which had been prevented from sailing with the squadron because of her grounding, at speed and in fog, on rocks at Salcombe. The *Bristol* was to leave the squadron at Bahia to return to Britain with her cadets. She was replaced by the *Phoebe*, from Halifax. The *Phoebe*, which had already been two years away from home, was to lose almost one in five of her men by desertion in the course of the cruise, far the greatest number of any of the squadron.

The three older frigates *Liverpool*, *Liffey* and *Phoebe* were all armed with six 64pdr MLR, four 7in 6.5ton MLR and twenty 8in 65cwt BL smooth bores as well as two 12pdr and one 9pdr boat guns. The *Endymion* was admired as the very latest of her type. Her airpump trunk

The frigate Endymion, *completed in 1866, was the last of the wooden frigates to be built. The Duke of Edinburgh was offered her command, but preferred the* Galatea. *(CPL)*

engines had originally been intended for the frigate *Ister*, which had been laid down in 1860 but subsequently cancelled. They could develop 2,800hp, compared with the 1,940 of the *Liverpool*'s horizontal direct-acting engines, but although she had originally been acknowledged as a fast ship, an ill-judged change in her weights had 'clogged her sailing'. She was armed with three 7in 100pdr Armstrong breech loaders, four 8in Somerset 6.5ton rifles and fourteen 7in 68pounders. Economy decreed that sail would be used most of the time, but recourse could always be had to 'the mariner's friend', the screw. The engines of the *Endymion* let her down on her departure from Melbourne and she had to be towed through the South Channel by the *Liffey*. The *Liverpool* and *Liffey* both carried a steam launch. In the event that the main boilers were closed down, the engines of these launches could supply power for the 'Keyham donkey' pumping engine.

Quality under sail was important, and in this the *Liverpool* was admitted to be almost as dull as the *Endymion*. Nothing, it seemed, would improve her, though retaining a heavy press of sail in strong wind was the usual solution. The upper masts were given extra backstays and gaff outriggers to make sure that they would take the strain. Her best point was with a strong breeze just before the beam.

HMS *Barrosa* was much admired and fast under sail. 'She was of yacht-like lines, with a long low hull, rather like the racing China tea clippers'. As the squadron's poet put it, she 'steals along like a snake when the sea it is green'. She was armed with seventeen 71cwt Palliser converted 64pdr rifles, but the absence of a topgallant forecastle, while it provided space for a pivot gun, made her wet. She had, as they said, a reputation as a 'diving bell'. Although all of the ships had been active, the *Barrosa* was one of the few to have seen action, against the forts at Shimonoseki in Japan in September 1864. Her sister ship *Orpheus* had been tragically wrecked in New Zealand in 1863. The *Scylla* was the smallest of the squadron, with an armament of sixteen 64pdr MLR 'shunt-rifled guns'. She had also been in Japan in 1864, detailed to protect base facilities at Nagasaki during the bombardment.

The figure-head of the *Barrosa* was 'a fine looking lady' similar to that of the *Phoebe*. The *Liverpool* had to be content with a gentleman.

In all, the squadron came with a total complement of some 2,680 men and boys, ranging from 565 in the *Phoebe* to 275 in the *Barrosa*. The captain of the *Phoebe* was John Bythesea, who had gained the new order of the Victoria Cross as a lieutenant aboard the frigate *Arrogant* when he daringly captured the Russian mail and despatches before Bomarsund in the Baltic in 1854. He had also invented a type of cot for himself which would not be affected by the rolling of the ship.

The Voyage Out

The departure of the squadron had in it a little of a yet-to-be-written Gilbert and Sullivan opera as, while the frigates searched for a wind near the Eddystone, the Commander in Chief, Sir William Martin, came out with 'a large multitude of ladies' in the steam tender *Princess Alice* to see them off. Here, as elsewhere, 'All the ladies love the shipping'. At Bahia there was another humorous event, when the captain of one ship mistook the *Phoebe* for his own in a fog and not only insisted on going aboard, but on having his cutter hoisted also. Discipline decreed that no-one would question his orders, though his subsequent embarrassment must have lasted for some time. The word in the squadron was that he realised it was not the right ship when he saw the wrong nightcap lying on his pillow.

At Funchal there were the ironclads *Warrior* and *Black Prince*, preparing to tow the new floating dock to Bermuda. They were the visible presence of British power in the Atlantic, but from this point on, the Flying Squadron was on its own. Also, it had a prearranged timetable to meet.

The first major port was Rio de Janeiro, where the squadron was much later than was expected and missed the celebrations put on for its arrival. Nevertheless, it was greeted by two Brazilian warships, the paddle frigate *Amazonas* and the turret ironclad *Lima Barros*, and was inspected with great interest by the Emperor, with much firing of royal salutes and warlike demonstrations. To show off the men at general quarters, manning and arming of boats and a *feu de joie* of rockets were a necessary demonstration of British efficiency, as the Emperor's own warships had only recently eliminated the last enemy vessels in their war in Paraguay. The British ships would also be seen by the Spanish admiral aboard the frigate *Blanca*, then in port. At Rio the *Endymion* had her bottom scraped by divers and was much improved in sailing as a result. They then moved on to Argentina where, on leaving Montevideo, Hornby demonstrated his seamanship by taking the ships out under sail in very difficult weather. The French Admiral, watching from the stationary deck of the frigate *Circé*, was very impressed.

From there it was a voyage to Cape Town, and a thorough refit at the Simon's Bay base. The base was quite cleared out of stores. Indeed, the demands made by the squadron when it reached Australia earned it the nickname of 'the hungry six'. Ships were sent in turn to Table Bay to give leave, and there was a one-day sailing race against the station flagship, the corvette *Rattlesnake*.

The fleet left the Cape on 16 October 1869, and, like six racing clippers, ran the great circle to Melbourne through the Roaring Forties. The ships were roughly handled in the Southern Ocean. There were fogs, gales and snowstorms; sometimes the ships came close to collision, but always they were made to perform at their peak. Thirteen knots was not unusual, and the whole squadron averaged between 10 and 11 knots for an entire week. The *Endymion* proved still too slow and the *Scylla* too fast, and both parted company with the squadron. As a result, the *Scylla* was ordered to remain outside Port Phillip Heads to wait for the laggard. While they waited for the tide, they were able to admire the *Great Britain* steaming out of Port Phillip and then crowding on all sail for a fast passage home.

On Friday, 26 November they came through the Heads on a southerly gale, with the big waves rolling on the Rip and the four ships under double-reefed topsails, courses and topgallant sails. Then they made a magnificent spectacle as they raced up to Hobson's Bay. Midshipman William Creswell, aboard the *Phoebe*, noted that:

> The wind freshened and it was the flagship's best sailing point. She carried everything she could stagger under and we were all heeling to it like yachts. The water was smooth and now and again the muzzles of our lee main deck guns skimmed the tops of the waves. I remember our pilot was

The Liverpool *fires a salute as the squadron changes tack.*

an immense man, considerably over six feet, broad and stout. He told us it was the fastest run he had ever made from the Heads to our anchorage in Hobson's Bay.

The Victorian flagship *Nelson* fired a salute of thirteen guns, to which the *Liverpool* replied with seven. The men of the squadron voted Melbourne 'the finest city in the southern hemisphere', and 158 decided for themselves that it would provide a better home than the Queen's cruisers.

As a return of Melbourne's hospitality, a naval review was to be held, in company with the *Nelson* and gunboat the *Pharos*. It was expected to involve a mock attack on the Hobson's Bay forts, and to show how ideal was Port Phillip for naval evolutions. In the event, with the press of people wanting to come aboard, it became a simple sail and a few manoeuvres, just for show. It was a Saturday and a public holiday had been proclaimed. The Premier and all of Cabinet, and others to whom 'invitations were somewhat too prodigally issued', some 2,000 in all, went aboard the *Nelson* for the manoeuvres. If the 100 men of the Naval Brigade had wanted to fire the guns they would have been hard pressed. As it was, the catering was utterly inadequate. The *Nelson* was, in fact, overwhelmed by non-invited guests who stated, 'Aren't we a free people and isn't this our ship?' The Governor and his party went on the *Liverpool*, and all the other ships had their 500 or so guests. In addition, every Melburnian who could get

aboard a steamer or a sailing boat did so. It is estimated that 30,000 people were afloat, as the warships made up two columns under plain sail. *Scylla*, the fastest, had constantly to shorten sail to keep station with the others. The *Nelson*, under steam with just a jib set, was worked up to 10 knots and 'answered her helm like a yacht'. As she passed the excursion steamers there was much cheering and climbing in the rigging.

The weather, however, was far from kind. Creswell put it this way:

All went well, a beautiful day, guests poured on board by the boatful, we weighed anchor and made sail with a light fair wind down the Bay. Then at lunch time it clouded over and poured in the manner specially provided for naval outdoor entertainments. It did not interfere with lunch arrangements, but the rest of the day it poured. There was nothing to be done but sail back. The wind failed us and we had a late return to our anchorage in Hobson's Bay. A few remained to an impromptu dance.

He also noted that, for the people, 'the navy provided social delights additional to anything so far within their ken'. The captain of the squadron's cricket team was 'foot-sore by day and heart-sore by night'. His team had beaten Brazil convincingly, but he tended to be the loser in subsequent matches. A speculative coal merchant was noted

The Victorian battleship Nelson, *under steam, accompanies the sailing evolutions of the Flying Squadron on Port Phillip on 4 December 1869. Despite the artist's impression, the* Nelson *at this time mounted thirty-seven guns, compared with the thirty of the big frigates, twenty-one of* Endymion, *seventeen of* Barrosa *and sixteen of* Scylla. *The artist has shown the* Nelson *flying a white ensign of doubtful legality. Soon afterwards the colony was granted its own ensign, which was raised on the* Nelson *on 9 February 1870. (LaTrobe Collection, State Library of Victoria)*

The Flying Squadron is greeted by the steamer Thetis *as it approaches Sydney Heads on 12 December 1869. The* Liverpool *is flying a signal for the ships to form in line ahead. (Illustrated Sydney News)*

to have bought up a great supply in the hope of selling it at a good profit to the squadron. He was most put out when Hornby told him he had no need of coal.

On 7 December the squadron sailed in a strong gale, under short canvas, for Sydney, which it reached five days later. It surged into Port Jackson under royals, and then demonstrated its smartness by coming rapidly to anchor in North Harbour, from where it proceeded to Farm Cove the following day under steam in view of the press of boats on the waterway. The government steamer *Thetis* was there to welcome it, flying the pennant of the Commodore of the Australian Station. There were huge crowds, as it was a Sunday, though there were inevitably some long-faced gentlemen who deplored it as 'the occasion of a large amount of Sabbath desecration'.

After that, the squadron went to Hobart Town, then Lyttleton, Wellington and Auckland. Every city saw its deserters, though none ever came near to matching the attraction of Melbourne. The *Barrosa* was subsequently sent back from Hobart and rejoined in Wellington, but only four deserters were recovered. Hornby had noted that such losses would weigh against a further visit by a similar force, but local police declined to support the pursuit, despite the rewards offered. As the newspapers coyly put it, 'a striking contrast exists between our ordinary life and habits and those of the navy'. Typical of the plaudits heaped on the squadron was a description in *The Empire* of 'those stately ships coming quietly through the water,

with all their deadly armament, as it were, slumbering, but ready to pour out its terrific fire if need were'.

In Sydney, a regatta was organised against the men and boats of the corvette *Challenger*, flagship of the station. The locals had a secret weapon, in the shape of a cutter built by a local boatbuilder, John Cuthbert. This boat, built of local cedar, proved its legendary speed to the great satisfaction of the men of the *Challenger*, but an immediate order produced another boat from the same builder, which the *Phoebe* took with it. The *Challenger* sailed for Auckland on the day the squadron left Sydney, and met them again in Wellington, where the two Cuthbert boats were pitted against each other in a thrilling race. This time the men of the squadron were victorious.

In view of the monotonously frequent query put by Sydney people to any of their visitors, some of the ships' officers were prepared. They had a painted banner which read, 'We are the officers of HMS—, we are on a party of pleasure and we think very highly of your harbour.'

At Lyttleton, Hornby had insisted that the squadron come up to its anchorage under sail, a lengthy beat. At one stage when the *Liverpool* should have given way to another ship he signalled 'I am on the starboard tack'. Ships on the starboard tack have right of way, and though he was palpably on the port tack, no-one would deny his signal.

After more than three months on the Australia station, the squadron sailed from Auckland for the northern Pacific on 9 February. The last twelve deserters in this port took the racing cutter. The boat was recovered but the men never. Creswell commented that they probably later became pillars of the community.

The Voyage Home

Whereas the first half of the voyage was to some extent a working up of the ships and the crews for extended ocean sailing, the second half had some more serious aspects. After almost two months' sailing from Auckland, they arrived in Japan at Yokohama on 6 April 1870. It was a tedious voyage, with the expedient of three of the ships getting up steam to tow the other three for four days near the equator. Here the *Barrosa* left to join the local squadron and the corvette *Pearl* joined to accompany them home. The *Pearl* had seen action against the Kagoshima forts in 1863 but, like the Old *Superb* in the song, she now 'was barnacled and green as grass below'. Her sudden transition from a station ship to a member of a crack cruiser squadron was something of a shock to her well-padded officers, who subsequently had to devise a system for scraping her bottom while at sea.

It was a critical time in the history of Japan, a country which had finally achieved unification as a modern nation state only in June 1869. At the end this had been achieved by a civil war whose final actions had been naval battles between a rebel squadron and the ships of the Emperor. Not one of the Japanese vessels had been nearly as large or as efficient as these British ships, but the implication was plain. National security, both within and without, demanded a modern navy. Modern navies, needless to say, tended to need both British hardware and British expertise.

Hornby was anxious to make a good impression. The British squadron moved to Yedo (now Tokyo), where it was visited by the Japanese notables, who watched the evolutions on the big ships and the cannonade of the boats in covering a mock landing, and who no doubt compared the squadron most favourably with similar American visitors. The US sloop *Oneida* had been run down and sunk by a liner just off Yokohama Bay just two months before. At all events, a young man named Heihachiro Togo was soon to be sent away to England to learn just how it should all be done. He was later to win a battle as great as Trafalgar against Russia. As a first instalment on the hardware, the Japanese government bought the Royal Navy corvette HMS *Malacca* for its infant navy. Having learned at school that Yedo was 'the largest town in the world', the officers of the squadron expressed the opinion that it did not really compare with London.

From Japan, the squadron crossed the Pacific to the naval station at Esquimalt in British Columbia. British Columbia had been the scene of some tension over a period, with the difficulties over the demarcation of the border with the United States in the San Juan Islands, and the threat of raids by the Fenians. Indeed, Hornby himself had been involved in holding the line some years earlier while local tempers ran hot. In 1869 the Childers administration had put further expansion of the base on hold to save money and it had ceased to be station headquarters.

At Esquimalt the squadron lay in the bay with the station ironclad *Zealous* and its three smaller consorts as an embodiment of naval force at a place whose limitless profusion of pine trees gave it the semblance of being at the end of the earth. The *Zealous* was armed with twenty 7in MLR, and so, except for her armour, was not noticeably superior to the frigates. The ironclad was there mainly because there was no gun battery to protect the base. Here, officers of a classical bent were delighted to note, the squadron would leave behind the *Scylla*, but it would be replaced by its sister ship, *Charybdis*. This last ship was not, in fact, leaving the station, as she was just on passage to Valparaiso, where the squadron was to be joined by the local station ship *Satellite*. The maintenance of ships on this station was awkward, in view of the absence of large dry docks. In 1868 even the new dock at Mare Island, near San Francisco, could not take a ship as large as an ironclad, and anyway, this might well be in enemy territory during a war. The only large dock in the Pacific region was far away at Melbourne, but then was still under construction.

For the United States, the great philosophical push of the time was 'Manifest Destiny', which included a kind of commitment to continental rule. It had justified a war with Mexico some years before. With the purchase of Alaska from the Russians in March 1867, would the remaining imperial enclave be left intact? Secretary of State Seward had even suggested that British Columbia should be ceded to the US in settlement of the *Alabama* claims. For the people of the colony there had been a question of the political future, whether to remain separate, to join the Canadian confederation, or even to become part of the United States. The British government firmly supported the option of union with Canada, and the presence of those black ships and their chequered gunports was a reminder that strength was available if necessary, and that the empire was willing to use it. Yet there was never a question of the use of the big guns. The ships themselves, for those two weeks in May 1870, were symbol enough. The election for members of the colonial legislature in November returned supporters of a union with Canada in all seats, and British Columbia became a province in 1871.

Officers of a sporting bent would know that this harbour was unique in being a place where salmon would rise to a lure in salt water. There was a grand regatta in Esquimalt, at which Midshipman Creswell, in the *Phoebe*'s racing cutter, triumphantly beat two other Sydney-built boats belonging to the *Scylla*. Hornby would have smiled. 'Precision under sail will lead to precision under steam, which otherwise cannot be learnt without great expense', was his opinion. The ships were pressed so hard that there was always something broken. The gun vessel *Boxer* was sent to bring back the makings of a new main yard for the *Phoebe* from a lumber camp – a 13-ton tree. The squadron then sailed on, via Honolulu, which was yet to feel the force of Manifest Destiny, to Chile. At Honolulu the *Endymion* collided with the *Phoebe* and lost her head gear. Tahiti had been on the original itinerary, but it was bypassed owing to local disturbances.

At Valparaiso, although it was again Pacific station headquarters, the reception by the English community was very lukewarm. The local people remembered with some pain the bombardment of the city by the Spanish fleet in March 1866. They had expected some form of insurance against such events by the presence of the British and American warships, but these had acted like true neutrals and had just sailed away. Austrian and French ships were present, nervous for news about the crisis in Europe. The corvette *Donau*, also on the last leg of a round-the-world cruise, flew the flag of Rear-Admiral Baron von Petz, who had flown his broad pennant in the *Kaiser* at Lissa. He had left Pola in May 1869 and was concerned that, with war between France and Prussia, Russia might seize the chance to even some scores with his country. The main issue for Britain was whether it would have to send troops to maintain the integrity of Belgium. At Valparaiso the squadron refitted, and news of the outbreak of the Franco-Prussian War speeded their departure.

The squadron sailed on 28 August and made a passage direct for home, calling only at Bahia, where they learned of the current state of the war and the surrender of the French emperor, as well as the tragic loss in the Channel of the new ironclad *Captain*. Typically of the experience of other station ships, the *Satellite* had difficulty keeping up with the squadron. In the great trade route of the central Atlantic, the squadron chased several vessels, always anxious for news from home and of the progress of the war. The newspapers, even though over a month old, were the best information available, but the commander of a cruiser could never have too much news, at a time when any foreign man-of-war could conceivably be an enemy. In the doldrums, three ships in steam again towed the three others. They arrived back at Plymouth after seventeen months away, on 15 November 1870. They had covered 53,022 miles.

The Value of It All

To those who were there, the most obvious benefit was in the training of the men for extended blue-water operation aboard cruisers. Too often, station ships lay at their moorings and their efficiency deteriorated. The Americans had recently shown the havoc which could be wreaked in wartime on trade by just such vessels, if they were well handled. John Jellicoe, who commanded the Grand Fleet in the First World War, and who served in a similar cruiser squadron in 1874–75, believed that sail was invaluable for the training of body and mind. Also, in view of loss of the *Captain* in September 1870, it could be seen that, whatever damage there might be to spars and sails, these were ships which were not likely to capsize and lose their men and their guns in any sort of a blow. Hornby himself went straight from the squadron to the committee of inquiry into the *Captain* disaster.

On the other hand, Admiral Ballard, who served as midshipman and sublieutenant in another squadron in 1880–82 observed,

> Our ships should be so disposed that the naval forces of other Maritime Powers on distant stations should be matched by British forces of at least equal strength in the same general locality, and, as even the Flying Squadron could not be in two places at once, its cruises about the

world produced a situation in which we were unnecessarily strong wherever it happened to be at the moment although not strong enough in other areas.

The French navy rejected the concept of flying squadrons until 1902.

The other major benefit was in the influence the squadron had in the north Pacific, in providing the inspiration for the creation of a strong Japanese navy, and for, however quietly, ensuring that the western coast of Canada remained part of the empire. In this last point it fulfilled the strategic requirement which was implicit in its existence.

Even to some of its contemporaries there was, however, one thing missing. The men aboard the ships were trained to sail them like racing machines, but they were not trained to any great extent to fight. Creswell, aboard the *Phoebe*, noted of one of his officers, 'He was one of the cult looked down upon at that time, a gunnery man, not a seaman'. A young Percy Scott was at this very time observing the lip-service that the officers aboard the frigate *Forte* paid to the required quarterly expenditure of powder and shot. It was to be some time in the future when Admiral Hornby promulgated his rules for the conduct of squadrons in battle, and another generation before Scott managed to reform the attitude of the Royal Navy to its big guns.

The voyage of the Flying Squadron has an echo in more recent history. The theory which it demonstrated was usually seen thereafter as a viable option in the application of naval power. The building of a naval base at Singapore in the 1920s was predicated on the swift despatch of a powerful squadron from home waters to augment local forces in the confrontation of a possible enemy. By 1941, however, the times had so changed that the squadron which was sent was overwhelmed, and in short order, by the power of militant Japan. It was only then that it was realised that the world for which the Flying Squadron was created had vanished forever.

Sources

The Times (London)

The Argus (Melbourne)

The Australasian (Melbourne)

Sydney Morning Herald

JB, *The Cruise Round the World of the Flying Squadron 1869–1870*, Potter, London, 1871

John Bach, *The Australia Station*, New South Wales University, Sydney, 1986

G A Ballard, 'Admiral Ballard's Memoirs', series in *The Mariner's Mirror*, 1975–77

Glyn Barratt, *Russian Shadows on the British Northwest Coast of North America 1810–1890*, University of British Columbia, Vancouver, 1983

Admiral Sir William Creswell, *Close to the Wind*, Heinemann, London, 1965

Mrs Fred Egerton, *Admiral Sir G. Phipps Hornby G.C.B.*, Blackwood, Edinburgh, 1896

Barry M Gough, *The Royal Navy and the Northwest Coast of North America 1810–1914*, University of British Columbia, Vancouver, 1971

William Haynes, *My Log*, privately published, Devonport, 1871

KITE BALLOONS IN THE US NAVY 1915–22

A little-known aspect of US naval aeronautics was the use of kite balloons at sea during and for a short time after the First World War. **R D Layman** and Stephen McLaughlin touched upon this venture in *Warship 1992*. Now, after further research, Layman gives a fuller account.

On the blustery day of 13 August 1918, Ensign Charles E Reed, US Navy Reserve Force, was swaying in the basket of a kite balloon towed by the sloop HMS *Flying Fox*[1] off Bantry Bay in Ireland. The balloon was being hauled down by Reed's American deck crew, as the ship steamed at 15 knots into a 30mph wind, and had reached a low altitude when it began to swing violently. It dipped into the water, then rose again. Reed shouted for the vessel to stop, but the request, relayed to the bridge, was refused, and some sharp words were exchanged between Americans and Britons. The balloon's gyrations grew wilder; it again skimmed the sea and, rising once more, scraped over the ship's deck, tearing out a portion of railing, and came down in the sea to port. The vessel then did stop, and Reed was twice spotted in the water and his parachute seen afloat. A boat was lowered but had to return when it began to fill with water from an undiscovered leak. Reed was not seen again.

A board of inquest convening on 17 August on the submarine tender *Bushnell*, after hearing testimony from Reed's deck crew, concluded that 'his death was occasioned by an act of duty in which he was engaged . . . and was not the result of his own misconduct'.

Genesis

This fatality was the result of the US Navy's first excursion into a field of aeronautics it had ignored since the early years of the American Civil War, when both the Union and the Confederacy employed spherical balloons from surface craft during riverine operations.

The decades since had seen the development of the kite balloon, whose greater stability made it superior for observational purposes. Balloons had been raised experimentally by French, Italian, Swedish and German ships, and a few were used operationally by Russian vessels during the war with Japan. Shipboard employment of kite balloons by the Royal Navy began in 1915, and it was the British experience that induced the US Navy (USN) to order two of the type from the Goodyear Tire & Rubber Co.

The first was accepted on 22 December 1915. Early in 1916 it was sent to Pensacola, Florida, for testing aboard the armoured cruiser *North Carolina*, but was badly damaged in a storm and required lengthy repair. Tests were finally conducted by the battleships *Nevada* and *Oklahoma* in November.

Reports on the experiments were mixed. On the debit side, a balloon revealed the location of the ship lofting it and could hamper the vessel's manoeuvrability, while its highly combustible lifting gas, hydrogen, could pose a hazard.[2] But its use for extending range of vision, with the potential of spotting for gunfire, was obvious. As a result, two more kite balloons were ordered, and under a new system of USN aircraft designation these first four were given the serial numbers *A-59*, *A-151*, *A-160* and *A-161*.

One of them, probably *A-151*, was tested aboard the armoured cruiser *Huntington* (ex-*West Virginia*) at Pensacola during June 1917 (for a photograph see *Warship 1992*). It was still with the cruiser three months later when she sailed to escort six troopships bound for France (the United States now being at war with Germany). On 17 September it was aloft with Lieutenant (jg) Henry W Hoyt in its basket when a sudden squall sent it into the sea. Ship's Fitter 1st Class Patrick McGunigal leaped into the water and saved the balloonist, for which he received the war's first Medal of Honor.

Procurement and Personnel

Once having accepted balloons, the US Navy, exhibiting the zeal of the convert, started acquiring them with the prodigality that American armed services often display after becoming enchanted with an innovation. By the time of the Armistice the Navy had a reported total of 215 of them (sources differ, and apparently no official count exists). Of these, at least 117 were manufactured in the United States, including 65 by Goodyear and 29 by its rival Goodrich Tire & Rubber Co. The remainder came from America's allies.

Early US balloons were inferior to their European counterparts, which were based on a highly successful design of French *Captaine d'Aerostiers* Albert Caquot. Consequently, all but the earliest US balloons were of the Caquot type. Of the American-manufactured craft, the

Sloop HMS Flying Fox *in Bantry Bay in 1918, photographed from the American balloon she is towing. It is possible this photograph was taken by the ill-fated Ensign Charles E Reed. (US Naval Historical Center)*

A typical US naval kite balloon of the First World War, probably preparing to go aloft, with two observers in the basket. Date and location unknown. (US Naval Institute)

main types were the Goodrich Type M and Goodyear Type C, both of 33,000cu ft capacity, and the Goodyear Type R of 37,000cu ft.

Only forty-eight of these, however, went to the overseas balloon bases established by the USN – at Berehaven (Castletownbere) to the west of Bantry Bay (to which the unfortunate Ensign Reed was assigned) and at La Trinité, Brest, and La Pallice in France. Brest, on which work began in June 1918, became the largest.

The number of personnel assigned to balloon service cannot be determined, but it was certainly in the hundreds. Few, however, were officially certified naval aviators. The great majority came from the hordes of eager young men who rushed to join the Naval Reserve Flying Corps in the hope of becoming aeroplane pilots. That hope was soon dashed for those who, hastily commissioned as ensigns (a few rose to lieutenant junior grade), were shunted off to learn the ropes (quite literally) of kite balloon control and management. As one of them many years later expressed their chagrin:

> It was in October of 1917 that twenty-three of us blithe young rookies found ourselves at Goodyear's balloon flight school in Akron, Ohio. We had . . . enrolled and had waited anxiously for active duty orders (which) would send us to Pensacola, Fla. where we would become intrepid airplane pilots. But this was not to be. Just when our numbers came up, the Navy needed balloon pilots and here we were . . . doomed to fly balloons.[3]

Operational Use

The original *raison d'etre* of the British shipboard balloon was for the directing of naval gunfire against shore targets, a function it performed usefully during the Gallipoli and the East African littoral campaigns. With the conclusion of those operations its value diminished. Balloons were used for a time to spot for bombardments of the Belgian coast, but that became too dangerous in the face of strong German defences, while advances in aerial wireless communications made it possible for aeroplanes from land bases to perform this task with less risk. Eventually all but one of the five merchantmen that had been converted into balloon ships were turned to other uses.

For warships, however, the shipboard balloon retained an advantage: much more secure and rapid telegraphic or telephonic communication with the surface. This held potential value for spotting gunfire against enemy vessels, as well as providing aerial eyes for ships at distances from shore that aeroplanes could not reach or in weather in which they could not function.

Thus by the end of the war twenty-two British capital ships had been equipped with balloons. The US Navy followed suit. Balloons were operated by the battleships *Nevada*, *Oklahoma* and *Utah* from August to mid-October 1918 while they were stationed at Berehaven to guard against the off-chance appearance of German surface raiders. Their balloons were maintained by the Casteltownbere base in Berehaven.

Battleship Nevada *at Guantanamo in March 1919 with the same type of balloon she operated while stationed at Bantry Bay the previous year. (US Naval Institute)*

The balloon of the battleship New York *falling in flames after being struck by lightning while the King and Queen of Belgium were visiting the ship in 1918. (Author's collection)*

Other battleships equipped with balloons were *New York*, flagship of the vessels constituting the Grand Fleet's 6th Battle Division, and *Arkansas* of the same unit. The USS *New York*'s balloon was destroyed by lightning (a frequent hazard) while King Albert and Queen Elizabeth of Belgium were visiting her in 1918. Fortunately it was unmanned. Balloons were either supplied or were to be supplied to the *New Mexico* and *Pennsylvania*, and the pre-dreadnoughts *New Jersey*, *Rhode Island* and *Vermont* (which did not leave home waters during the war), but plans to provide a balloon for the flagship of each battleship division were not carried through.

By the time the United States entered the war the main concern of the allied navies had become the defeat of the U-boat. Balloons entered the anti-submarine campaign in mid-1917, at the behest of Admiral Sir David Beatty, with North Sea sweeps by balloon-towing destroyers. Although a balloon observer could spot a surfaced U-boat at distances considerably greater than were possible from the surface, these needle-in-a-haystack searches were not very successful, with only one definite and one probable submarine kill achieved.

Balloons proved more valuable after the adoption of mercantile convoy; their observers could direct escorting warships toward a U-boat that was using its surface speed to reach position for submerged attack, forcing it down before it could strike. A disadvantage was that the presence of a balloon enabled a submarine to detect a convoy, but to judge from the small number of vessels lost from convoys having balloon escort, the deterrent effect more than compensated – although in the absence of statistics it cannot be quantified.

By the end of the war scores of British anti-submarine craft, including destroyers, sloops, trawlers, P-boats and drifters, had been fitted to loft balloons.

American use of balloons in the anti-submarine role was apparently instigated by Admiral William S Sims, Commander of United States Naval Forces Operating in European Waters. A memorandum from the Office of Naval Operations to Captain Noble E Irwin, Director of Naval Aviation (undated, but probably written during or shortly after March 1918), stated: 'About three months ago a cable was received from Admiral Sims by Operational Material, asking to have twelve (12) destroyers fitted with Kite Balloon Winches as early as possible, and sent across.'

The paper identified twelve destroyers selected 'because they were at that time in such a state of completion that the fitting of Kite Balloon Winches would not delay their construction'. All were of the 1,090-ton flush-deck, four-funnel *Wickes* class. However, the memorandum continued:

No steps have been taken to make them suitable for Kite Balloon operation. They have high mainmasts located well aft, and for this reason it will be impracticable to use them for Kite Balloon operation until some alterations have been made . . . All destroyers of future programs are in a similar situation, except that the destroyers after No. 185 [*Bagley*] have smaller mainmasts, but are still unsuitable for Kite Balloon operation.

Mainmasts did indeed pose a problem for ships operating balloons. Since it was impracticable to tow a balloon except from the stern, there was always the danger that its mooring line could foul the mast. For this reason several British balloon sloops had their mainmasts removed and a few French pre-dreadnoughts and armoured cruisers had theirs reduced in height.

This problem was apparently solved later, for by November 1918 six of the destroyers on the list of twelve had been, were being or were to be fitted with winches: the *Fairfax, Bell, Stringham, Bagley, Sigourney* and *Taylor*. So were two others of the class, the *Kennison* and *Kilty*, that had not been on the list, as well as two of the later *Clemson* class, the *Shubrick* and *Bailey*, plus the much older *Perkins*, which was awaiting the removal of her mainmast.

Observers changing position in the basket of a balloon towed by an American battleship of the Grand Fleet's 6th Battle Squadron in the North Sea in 1918.
(US Naval Historical Center)

Several ships in other categories were also designated to receive winches. One that did was the minesweeper *Robin*, but it is unlikely that she made use of it when later she helped to clear the North Sea Barrage. Also chosen were the ocean-going tug *Chemung* (ex-*Pocahontas*), employed for a time as a minesweeper, and the submarine chasers *SC-123* and *SC-238*. It may be conjectured that these two were intended to join the sub-chasers that in 1918 reinforced the Otranto Barrage, where the Australian destroyers *Huon, Yarra* and *Parramatta* had employed balloons in anti-submarine operations. In August 1918 the Coast Guard cutter *Comanche* (ex-*Windom*, dating from 1896 and a Spanish–American War veteran), based at New Orleans, was ordered to Pensacola to have a winch installed for balloon use in projected coastal convoy escort duty, but it cannot be ascertained whether this was done.

Aside from the battleships mentioned above, it seems that the only US warships to operate balloons in European waters were five destroyers based at Brest: the *Benham, O'Brien, Cushing, Ericsson* and *Winslow*, all of the *Cassin* class, that were completed during 1913–15 and among the first destroyers sent overseas. Much of their work was experimental; but there were at least four escort missions, the first a five-day cruise by the *Cushing* that started on 1 August 1918. Beginning on 14 August the *Ericsson* spent 100 hours at sea, maintaining balloon observation for a total of 64 hours.

This paucity of operational use was mainly because the USN's balloon programme, like so many other aspects of American efforts in the First World War, came to fruition too late. Had the conflict continued there is little doubt but that many more destroyers and other craft would have operated balloons. It also seems certain that several destroyers laid down during the huge wartime construction programme were given winches, but inadequate documentation makes it impossible to determine how many. (And so forgotten did the balloon become that, when in 1939 the *Kennison* and *Kilty* were being surveyed for recommissioning after seventeen years in reserve, the purpose of their winches baffled the inspecting officers.)

The balloon programme was further retarded by a problem developing over winches. Initially, four types were installed on various ships – the steam-powered Lidgerwood and Mumford, electrically powered Lawrence-Scott, and a petrol-powered Ford model produced by the Lidgerwood Manufacturing Company. The steam Lidgerwood was eventually chosen to become standard, but was later found to have technical defects. It was to be replaced by the Mumford, but their manufacturer stated it would be unable to supply them in adequate number until December 1918. Consequently, balloon work was halted or not undertaken on all but a few vessels.

Balloon Vessels in Coastal Patrol

During the Spanish–American War and again in the First World War the USN acquired a large and motley collection of vessels for coastal patrol and other auxiliary duties; many were private yachts or other civilian craft purchased, leased or volunteered by their owners. Several were chosen

The yacht Xarifa *in US Navy service in 1918. She has been armed but the mainmast has not yet been removed to facilitate balloon operation. (US Naval Historical Center)*

The yacht Mohican, *which operated a balloon in 1918, being refitted at New York in 1919 for return to her owner. (US Naval Historical Center)*

for the operation of balloons; some were so equipped, being so, or scheduled to be as of late October 1918.

One such was *Gloucester* (ex-*Corsair*), formerly the yacht of industrial and financial mogul J Pierpont Morgan; acquired in 1898, she took a conspicuous part in the Battle of Santiago and was retained by the Navy.

Others in the yacht category included vessels named *Ranger*, *Sultana*, *Rambler* and *Harvard*, most of which, like *Gloucester*, had winches installed, but too late to make use of them.

Some of these ships were oddities, such as *Xarifa* (ex-*Ophelia*, ex-*Xarifa*). This elegant clipper-bowed, sail-cum-auxiliary steam yacht was built in Britain in 1894, transferred to American ownership around 1911 and acquired by the USN in August 1917. She operated a balloon for patrol around New York harbour for a time in 1918, but only after a delay caused by the search for a derrick able to remove her 81ft, 18in-diameter mainmast. *Xarifa* was unusual as apparently one of only three vessels in USN service ever to bear a name starting with the letter X, and almost certainly unique as the last primarily sail-propelled ship to have operated an aerial device of any kind.

Another curious vessel was the excursion boat *Commander*, a little motorship leased by the Navy on 17 September 1917 and first employed in helping to fit out submarine chasers. Equipped with a Ford winch and twenty cylinders of hydrogen, she took aboard a balloon in July 1918 and was subsequently based at the Rockaway Beach, Long Island, Naval Air Station. She patrolled the New York harbour and Long Island Sound areas until November. *Commander*, nearly 80 years old in 1997, is still afloat, operated as an excursion-dinner cruise boat by Hudson Highlands Cruises & Tours, of Highland Falls, New York. She has been re-engined but retains in large part her 1917 appearance. She is not only one of the very few vessels of the First World War era to remain functional, but without doubt the last from that period to have had an aeronautical association.

Another ship used for balloon service in the New York area, beginning on 23 August 1918, was the yacht *Mohican*. Her duties, according to her entry in the *Dictionary of American Naval Fighting Ships*, were 'at times directing the heavy maritime traffic in the lower bay and at others aiding ships in distress due to fire or collision' – work continuing until her return to her owner in early 1919.

Destroyers fitting out at the New York Shipbuilding Corporation at Camden, New Jersey, 5 June 1919. The third vessel from the left, believed to be the Herbert, *has what may be the cover for a balloon winch on her aft deckhouse. (National Archives)*

Towing and Handling

USN balloon-handling techniques followed the procedures of the Royal Navy. The balloons were inflated ashore (where they were maintained and repaired) before going aboard ship. Once the mooring cable was attached to the winch the balloon was kept aloft, where it could remain for long periods. This relieved the ship of the necessity of storing hydrogen or housing equipment for its generation. Gas leakage causing loss of buoyancy was inevitable, but a very gradual process.

The balloon therefore required lowering only to permit the observer to enter or leave the basket. A technique was devised to permit this to be done without the balloon's touching the deck:

> This made use of a very simple arrangement, namely, a length of rope and a pulley. The pulley was tied up in the balloon's rigging above the basket. The pilot snapped one end of the rope into the chest ring of his parachute harness. It passed up through the pulley and down to the [ship's] deck where four or five husky sailors were holding it. The pilot waited for a 'smooth' when he was above the deck. He then bailed out and was lowered aboard.[4]

The lighter-than-air tender Wright, *a cover over her balloon well, at Hampton Roads, Virginia, 2 October 1922, pending conversion to a seaplane tender. (National Archives)*

Entry to the basket could be gained by reversing this same process.

Although a balloon's ascent and descent were governed primarily by the winch, considerable manpower was needed to control its staying and steadying lines at low altitudes above deck. A report from the battleship *Arkansas*, dated 2 May 1918, stated 'For the proper handling of a kite balloon . . . at least 66 men are required exclusive of the regular . . . winch operators'.

Service aloft could be dangerous. Lightning could pose a peril, mooring lines could break, and, despite the kite balloon's intrinsic stability, it could be severely buffeted in bad weather. Balloonists were usually supplied with parachutes, but parachuting into the sea, where survival depended on quick rescue, was a daunting prospect.

Despite all these hazards, Ensign Reed was apparently the only fatality among USN balloonists. However, two others, Ensigns C E Baunch and R B Marshall, had a close call on 14 July 1918 during the first manned ascent from *Commander* near Rockaway Beach. They were aloft at 350 feet when a thunderstorm approached and the balloon, Goodyear Type R No. A-2711, was hauled down. Three minutes after the ensigns touched deck and the balloon was allowed to rise again into a 40mph wind, the mooring cable broke; the balloon soared rapidly to more than 4,000 feet and was swept away.

Tactical Thought

From the number of ships being equipped or intended to be equipped with kite balloons in late 1918, it is obvious that the USN was taking them seriously as weapons in the war against the U-boat. This is also borne out by a memorandum, 'Kite Balloons in Escorts', issued by Sims's Planning Section, dated 15 October 1918, for circulation to 'all ships and air stations'. It was reissued the next month by the Office of Naval Intelligence as a confidential publication.

It is a well-thought-out analysis and discussion, with detailed recommendations of how balloons should best be used – in what positions and at what distances balloon ships accompanying convoys should be placed, how they should manoeuvre, and how balloon observation could best be carried out during dawn, daylight, dusk and night hours under varying conditions of visibility. But this manual came too late – the war ended before its instructions could be digested and put into practice.

Postwar Developments

The USN's new-found romance with the balloon continued for a short time after the war. In February 1919, when the Atlantic Fleet assembled at Guantanamo Bay, Cuba, for annual exercises, six of its battleships were assigned balloons. They were maintained by the minelayer *Shawmut*, flagship of the newly formed Fleet Air Detachment, and also depot ship for six flying boats.

About the same time it was decided to acquire three or four vessels as combination seaplane tenders and balloon ships. The choice fell upon incomplete hulls that had been under construction by the American International Shipbuilding Corporation as Army transports. However, when these were inspected it was found that all but one had advanced so far to completion that reconstruction to a new design would be prohibitively costly. Consequently, the one which was to have been named *Somme* became the USS *Wright*, commissioned on 16 December 1921 as the only USN vessel ever to bear the designation AZ (lighter-than-air tender) with a large after-deck well to shelter a balloon.

The End

Although balloons would soon become safer when hydrogen was replaced by helium, as was later done in naval airships,[5] accidents could still happen. And in March 1921 one did, as the Atlantic Fleet was conducting gunnery practice off Guantanamo in rough weather. A balloon towed by the battleship *Oklahoma* lost buoyancy and fell into the sea. One tethered to the battleship *Florida* gyrated wildly and broke its mooring line. *Oklahoma*'s balloonist was saved by a flying boat but one of that craft's crew was killed when struck by a propeller. *Florida*'s balloon drifted off after throwing its occupant to his death.

This disaster went a long way toward dooming the balloon in the USN. It was not, however, the decisive reason. Strong doubts about its continuing usefulness had already arisen. Advances in aircraft technology and aerial wireless were beginning to prove that aeroplanes could perform reconnaissance and gunfire-spotting more efficiently and at much greater distances; the shipboard catapult was showing promise; the collier *Jupiter*, renamed *Langley*, was being turned into a flight-deck aircraft carrier; plans were tentatively afoot for the conversion of incomplete battle cruisers into carriers. The Atlantic Fleet's commander, Admiral Henry B Wilson, pronounced balloons 'neither practical nor useful'.

As a result of all this, the curtain was rung down on the kite balloon. *Wright*'s career as an AZ was cut short; she lofted a balloon for the last time in July 1922 and was turned into a pure seaplane tender.

The kite balloon would reappear in the US Navy during the Second World War in the form of the barrage balloon,[6] but after 1922 its days as a manned observation craft were over.

Notes

1. *Flying Fox* belonged to the '24' class, so designated because it consisted of twenty-four vessels. These were built to a symmetrical design intended to confuse submarines as to the direction in which they were steaming. It is highly doubtful that any U-boat commander was ever deceived.
2. Hydrogen was used in the overwhelming majority of military manlifting balloons from the 1790s until after the First World War. The current popularity of hot-air ballooning as a sport causes many present-day writers ignorant of aeronautical history to label any or all balloons of earlier eras incorrectly as 'hot air'.
3. Allan L Morse, 'Tribute', unpublished manuscript, 1981.
4. Ibid.

5   Helium was costly until American research during the First World War developed methods of extracting it inexpensively in large volume. This breakthrough, however, came too late to permit its use in lighter-than-air craft in the conflict.

6   These unmanned craft, sent up to deter aeroplanes, were first used by Italy and later by Britain during the First World War. Their ubiquity in this defensive role during the Second World War causes many modern-day writers to believe that that was the only function of balloons in the earlier conflict. Many barrage balloons were lofted by surface vessels during the later war – an unexplored area of aeronaval history.

Sources

Documents in the National Archives, Washington, DC:
    Testimony at board of inquest hearing, 17 August 1918, into the death of Ensign Charles E Reed.
Memorandum from Office of Naval Operations to Captain Noble E Irwin, undated.
Report from Lieutenant (junior grade) John R Brophy to Officer in Charge, Repair Section, Material Department, 3rd Naval District, 22 October 1918.
Report on conditions at kite-balloon stations from Ensign Fred Stoppel to Intelligence and Planning Division, US Naval Forces Operating in European Waters, 20 June 1918.
Letter from commandant, 8th Naval District, New Orleans, to commandant, Pensacola Naval Air Station, 11 August 1918.
'Suggestions for drill for Kite Balloon crew and stations for handling same' from USS *Arkansas*, 2 May 1918.
Report from Ensigns C E Bauch and R B Marshall to Bureau of Construction and Repair, 14 July 1918.
'Kite Balloons in Escort', memorandum from commander, US Naval Forces in France, to all ships and air stations, 15 October 1918. Printed as Office of Naval Intelligence publication No 45, November 1918.
Roy A Grossnick (ed), *Kite Balloons to Airships . . . the Navy's Lighter-than-Air Experience*. Government Printing Office, Washington, DC, nd.
Adrian O Van Wyen and Lee M Pearson, *United States Naval Aviation 1910–60*. Government Printing Office, Washington, DC, 1960.
Archibald D Turnbull and Clifford L Lord, *History of United States Naval Aviation*. Yale University Press, New Haven, 1949.
Adrian O Van Wyen (ed), *Naval Aviation in World War I*. Government Printing Office, Washington, DC, 1969.
Harold Blaine Miller, *Navy Wings*. Dodd, Mead, New York, 1937.
Office of Chief of Naval Operations, Naval History Division, *Dictionary of American Naval Fighting Ships*. Government Printing Office, Washington, DC 1959–81.
John D Alden, *Flush Decks and Four Pipes*. Naval Institute Press, Annapotas MD, 1965.
Paul Silverstone, *U.S. Warships of World War I*. Ian Allan, London, 1970.
Gordon Swansborough and Peter M Bowers, *United States Navy Aircraft since 1911*. Funk & Wangall, New York, 1968.
Garland Fulton, 'Kite Balloons Afloat', *American Aviation Historical Society Journal*, Vol 8, No 4, 1963.
Jean Wort, 'M/V Commander', *Sea History*, No 75, Autumn 1995.
R D Layman and Christopher C Wright, 'Ask INFOSER', *Warship International*, Vol 18, No 2, 1981.
Noel C Shirley, 'History of U.S. Naval Aviation in World War I, unpublished manuscript.

Acknowledgements

The author is grateful for research assistance by Lieutenent Colonel Edward S Milligan, US Army (ret); Noel C Shirley, League of World War I Aviation Historians; Captain John Wort, Hudson Highlands Cruises & Tours, Inc; the late Rear-Admiral George van Deurs, US Navy (ret), and the late Dr A D Topping, Lighter-than-Air Society.

ARMSTRONGS' UNBUILT WARSHIPS

The Tyneside firm Sir W G Armstrong, Whitworth & Co. Ltd built many warships for export, but **Peter Brook** takes a closer look at the ships which never got beyond the drawing board.

Designs of warships never built or greatly modified before construction offer a fascinating insight into naval architects' ingenuity subjected to customer requirements, together with the play of market forces. Unfortunately, drawings of abandoned, or much modified designs are uncommon but one important though relatively little used source is 'Design Portfolio No. 3' produced by the great Tyneside firm of Sir W G Armstrong, Whitworth & Co. Ltd, which spans the years 1909 to 1914; this is now held by the National Maritime Museum, Greenwich. This large volume contains many pages of drawings, some coloured, of battleships, coast defence battleships and cruiser battleships, an early name for battlecruisers. Most have brief specifications and there are as well outline specifications, but with no accompanying drawings, of smaller vessels such as armoured cruisers, cruisers, destroyers and river monitors. Most interesting of all are a large number of preliminary drawings for the *Rio de Janeiro* which were used by the late David Topliss to illustrate his article on that famous ship.[1]

In addition to these early twentieth-century drawings there is one other Armstrong design in the form of a blueprint of a ram cruiser dating from 1881 held in the Rendel collection of the Tyne and Wear Archive Services. There is no title to this plan and the only details given are length, beam and depth, although freeboard and draught may be easily measured. I propose to look first at this ship, design 10190, which I have labelled '*Improved* Tsukushi', before moving to Portfolio No. 3. Details of the original *Tsukushi* as built are given for comparison.

	Improved **Tsukushi** Design 10190, 12 Feb 1881	**Tsukushi**
Dimensions (ft)	230 pp×37×17	210 pp×32×15
Freeboard (ft)	17 forward, 8 aft	6 forward, 6 aft
Armament	2–10in BL 6–4.7in BL	2–10in BL 4–4.7in BL

George Rendel, Armstrongs' chief naval architect 1867–1882.

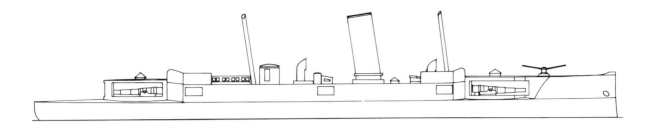

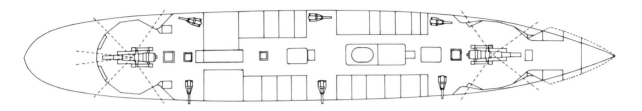

Improved Tsukushi. *This is based on a blueprint held by Tyne and Wear Archive Services. Inadvertently it was used as an illustration of* Tsukushi *as built on pp 98–99 of* Warship 1996. *(Drawn by Ian Sturton)*

Apart from the increased dimensions, which allowed an extra 4.7in gun on each side, there was a permanent forecastle which meant that the forward 10in gun, mounted in a fixed turret, had no ahead fire but had a broadside arc of training on each side of 90°, compared with *Tsukushi*'s 70°. The after big gun had an 80° arc on each side but did have a very limited traverse aft of 14°. Clearly the armament was meant primarily for broadside fire. Other points of difference included the installation of an electric generator in an 'electric room', a spur ram bow and increased freeboard, particularly forward. The underwater deck was strongly curved, extending from stem to stern with the steering engine beneath it.

Argentine Battleships

In response to the Brazilian dreadnought building programme inaugurated in 1905, and also because of border problems with Brazil, Chile and Uruguay, Argentina determined to build two dreadnoughts and in 1908 issued sketch outlines specifying trial displacement, number of main guns, secondary armament, armour thickness, propulsive details and a 21-knot speed. Fifteen firms responded, including Armstrongs, Vickers, Blohm and Voss, and three American firms: Cramps, Newport News and Fore River. The commission responsible for ordering the battleships then selected the best features from each submission, modifying the guidelines for competing firms, then repeating the whole process a second time, a procedure which aroused much ill feeling because the shipyards taking part believed that their trade secrets had been

Josiah Perrett, Armstrongs' chief naval architect 1903–1916.

looted. In the end two American firms, Fore River Shipbuilding Co. and New York Shipbuilding won the order.[2] Armstrongs produced four alternatives for Argentina with design 611 being smaller than 610 with only ten 12in guns but this design was never sent, while design 612 managed to accomodate twelve 12in guns on a

comparatively short ship by placing the cage mast amidships in place of the derricks. Design 623 had a 12in waterline belt. In fact, this design closely resembled the ships as completed, the *Rivadavia* and *Moreno* although 623 had its cage mast amidships and was 28ft longer than the completed pair.

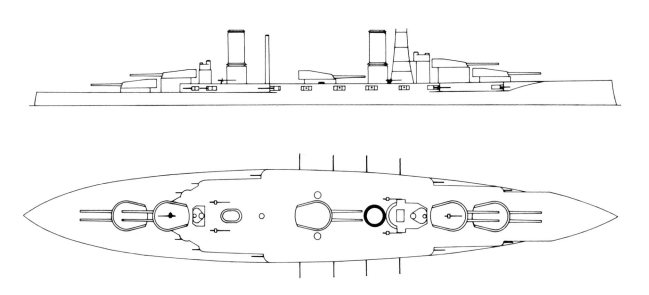

Design 611, battleship for Argentina. (Drawn by Ian Sturton)

Design 612, battleship for Argentina. (Drawn by Ian Sturton)

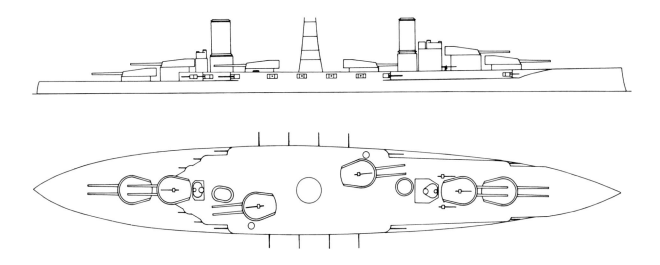

Design Number	610	611	612	623
Date	25 Oct 1909	25 Oct 1909	25 Oct 1909	n.k.
Dimensions	610pp (642oa) ×90×27	550pp (582oa) ×90×27	570pp (602oa) ×90×27	580pp (613oa) ×94×27
Displacement (tons)	27,500	24,500	25,500	28,500
Armament	12–12in, 50 cal 12–6in, 50 cal 12–4in, 45 cal 2–21in TT	10–12in, 50 cal 12–6in, 50 cal 12–4in, 45 cal 2–21in TT	as 610	as 610
Armour	belt 10–6–5–4in middle belt 9–6–5–4in citadel 4in bulkheads 9–6–4in CT8in director tower 8in observer tower(aft) 9in barbettes 9in	as 610 CT12in forward 9in aft director tower 8in	as 610	belt 12–6–5–4in upper belt 9–6–5in citadel 6in bulkheads 9–6in aft 9–4in forward barbettes 12in
Decks	forecastle over citadel 2in upper outside citadel 1.5in armoured 1.5in on flat, 2in slopes magazine and shell room protection 0.5–1.5in	as 610	as 610	as 610
Machinery	turbines 21 kts	as 610	as 610	as 610
Coal (tons)	1,000–4,000	1,450–4,000	as 610	1,800–4,500
Oil (tons)	260	240		70–300
General	6 turrets, A&B superimposed forward, P&Q en echelon amidships, X&Y superimposed aft, long forecastle extending to X turret, single cage mast forward	long forecastle All guns on centreline, A&B superimposed forward, Q amidships X&Y superimposed aft	as 610 but cage mast amidships	as 610 but cage mast amidships

First-Class Cruiser Designs for Japan: Designs 636 and 636A

These designs are undated but were probably prepared early in 1910. They are smaller and very inferior versions of *Kongo*.

The two designs were identical except that 636 had a forecastle deck with 4ft more freeboard and with the 6in guns 4ft 8in higher above the waterline. Despite this, displacement and dimensions were the same.

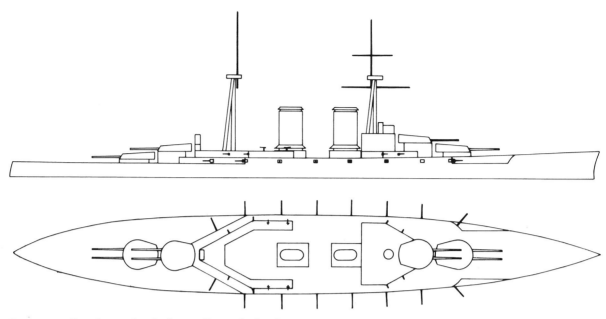

Design 636, first-class cruiser for Japan. (Drawn by Ian Sturton)

Dimensions	575pp (610oa)×83×27
	freeboard forward: 636A=17; 636=21.3
Displacement (tons)	*c.* 20,000
Armament	8–12in–50 cal in twin mountings
	16–6in–50 cal in upper deck armoured citadel
	8–12pdr QF
	4–3pdr QF 3–21in TT 2 broadside and 1 stern submerged
	height of guns above wl (ft)
	636: A=31, B=40, X=31 Y=22
	636A: A=27, B=36, X=33.5, Y=24.5
	6in guns: 636=18.5, 636A=13.7
Armour	belt 8–6–2in (aft)
	upper belt–main to upper deck–6in
	citadel–upper to forecastle deck–6in
	screen–6in
	barbettes 8in where unprotected by armour, 2in inside citadel
	CT 10in
	tube 6in
	director tower 3in
	forecastle deck over citadel 1in
	main, fore and aft 1in
	middle deck amidships 1in
	lower, fore and aft 1in
Machinery	turbines, water tube boilers of approved type
Speed (kts)	26
Coal (tons)	1,000–2,500

Portuguese Battleship Designs

In 1911 Portugal had a tiny navy[3] and no obvious need for a larger one, but in February and March 1911 Armstrongs produced designs for two coast defence battleships. Design 691 was a reasonably balanced design but 694 could only carry six 12in guns on a displacement of 11,750 tons by accepting a speed of 14 knots with natural draft and an unrealistic 17 knots with forced draft. In 1912 the dreadnoughts were dropped from the programme.[4]

Design Number	691	694
Date	23 Feb 1911	20 Mar 1911
Dimensions (ft)	420×78×25	360×78×25
Displacement (tons)	14,500	11,750
Armament	4–14in, 50 cal	6–12in, 50 cal
	12–6in, 50 cal	12–4in, 50 cal
	4–21in submerged TTs	
Armour (in)		
belt	9–6–4	9–6–4
middle belt	7–5–3	6–5–4
bulkheads	2–4–3	3–6
barbettes	9–4–2	9–4–3
CT	9	7
observer tower	7	7
deck	upper, over citadel 1	upper, over citadel 1.5
	main, fore & aft, 1	main, 1–1.5
	middle, 1.5	middle, 1–1.5 aft
	lower, 1.5	lower, 1
	wing bulkheads in way of	magazine protection 1
	magazine protection 1.5	
Machinery	turbines & water tube boilers	turbines or vertical triple
		expansion & water tube boilers
Speed (kts)	20	17 FD 14 ND
Coal (tons)	750/1,000	500/1,250
	turrets mounted fore and aft	

Later in the year two more designs, 702 and 708, were produced but for larger ships which were no longer described as for coast defence. Unfortunately, there are no plans for 708 but she would have had her four twin turrets on the centre line with A/B and X/Y turrets superimposed.

Design Number	702	708
Date	12 Apr 1911	27 May 1911
Dimensions (ft)	510 pp (547 oa)×83×24.5	500 pp (530 oa)×84×27
Displacement (tons)	19,750	19,500
Armament	10–12in, 45 cal	8–13.5in, 45 cal
	20–4.7in, 50 cal	14–6in, 50 cal
	4–3in, 50 cal	8–3in
	2–21 TTs submerged	2–21in TTs
Armour		
belt	234–102mm fore	9in–6in–4in and aft
middle belt	178mm	7in
upper belt	153mm	battery 7in
bulkheads	76mm	
barbettes	234–127–76mm	9–3in
CT	254 (tube 76mm)	12in
spotting tower	153–76mm	
director tower	76mm	
decks		
upper over citadel	31.7mm	forecastle over citadel 1.5in
	main outside citadel, 31.7–25.4mm	main forward 1.5–1in, aft 1.5in
	protective.25.4mm amidships,	protective forward, 1in, aft 3in.
	38–25.4mm forward, 76–38mm aft	platform deck over magazines, 1in
	magazine and shellroom bulkheads, 38mm	magazine and shellroom bulkheads, 1in
Speed (kts)	21	21
Fuel (tons)		
coal	700–2,000	800–2,500
oil	800	—

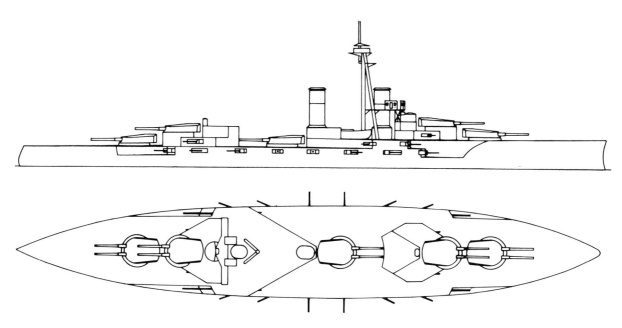

Design 702, battleship for Portugal. (Drawn by Ian Sturton)

Cruiser Battleships and Battleship Designs for Greece

In 1912 Armstrongs prepared a 'cruiser battleship' design for Greece in response to a request for a design for a 13,500-ton ship mounting six 14in and eight 6in guns with a speed of 21.5 knots and to be ready in 26 months. Armstrongs' preliminary design, 743, was prepared in June 1912, but in July the order went to the German firm of Vulkan. Doubts had been raised by some of the British firms submitting tenders as to whether the original design could produce a satisfactory ship (Armstrongs required an extra 1,450 tons to meet the specifications). By

Design 741, cruiser battleship for Greece. (Drawn by Ian Sturton)

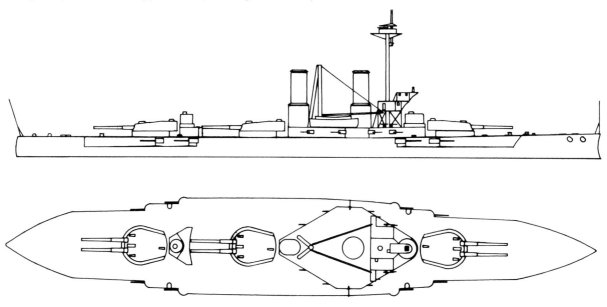

December the German firm produced a modified design for a ship of 19,500 tons mounting eight 14in and twelve 6in guns, heavier armour and a speed of 24 knots.[5] This, the *Salamis*, was never completed but her turrets and 14in guns, which were made in the United States, were acquired by Great Britain in 1914 and used to arm the monitors *Abercrombie*, *Havelock*, *Raglan* and *Roberts*. At the end of 1913 the Turks purchased the *Rio de Janeiro*, which spurred the Greeks to order another dreadnought and presumably design 779 was in response to this, but the order went to France for a replica of *Lorraine*. Because of the outbreak of the First World War the Greek ship was never completed.[6] A further design, 779A, was prepared on 16 February 1914 but no details were given.

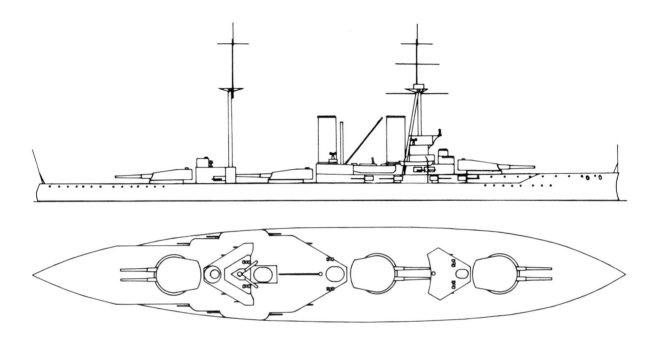

Design 779, battleship for Greece. (Drawn by Ian Sturton)

Design Number	**Cruiser Battleship** **741**	**Battleship** **779**
Date	17 Jun 1912	12 Feb 1914
Dimensions (ft)	450pp(486 oa)×77.5×26.5	500pp×83×26
Displacement (tons)	14,950	18,500
Freeboard (ft)	20 bow, 16 stern	26 bow, 16 stern
Armament	6–14in, 8–6in	6–15in, 45 cal, 8–6in
Armour (in)	no details	belt 9–6–3
		middle belt 9–6
		upper belt 6
		battery 6
		barbettes 9–7
Speed (kts)	21.5	24
Fuel (tons)		coal 800–2,500
		oil 750
General arrangement	flush decked, all guns mounted on midline, one bow turret, one amidships, one aft	as 743 but fore turret mounted on forecastle deck

Stock Designs for Battleships

The four designs below are all described as stock designs. The arrangement of 740's armament would have been similar to that mounted in the Japanese battleship *Fuso*. Design 764 was described as an improved *Malaya* carrying two extra 15in guns. Design 768 mounted a heavy armament of eight 15in guns in an unusual arrangement of a triple turret fore and aft and one twin turret amidships while the design of 9 September 1913 sacrificed one gun aft but with improved forward fire by having two superimposed twin turrets forward and one triple turret aft.

Portfolio No. 3 contains more drawings and even more specifications for battleships, some designed for specific countries others prepared as stock designs. They include a 12,500-ton armoured cruiser with eight 10in guns, a 15,000-ton battleship with six 12in, another of 17,000 tons and eight 12 in, and a 'training battleship' for China of 7,500 tons mounting two 12in in single turrets with a speed of 17 knots. Between 1910 and 1911 Armstrongs produced nine designs of battleships for Turkey ranging from 16,650 to 23,000 tons and armaments going from eight 12in to ten 13.5in.

The last designs in the portfolio are for an improved *Malaya* and for a 'Stock Design'. The first was based on her namesake but mounting five twin 16in gun turrets on the centreline and with a speed of 25.5 knots if oil fuel was to be used. These two represent a giant leap forward in naval design, but even if they had been accepted by the Admiralty they could not have been laid down before the outbreak of war.

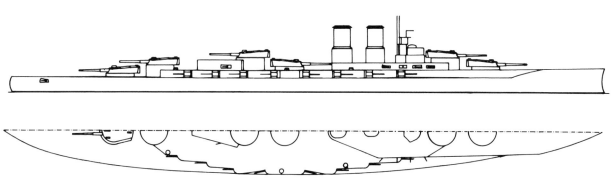

Design 740, stock battleship. (Drawn by Ian Sturton)

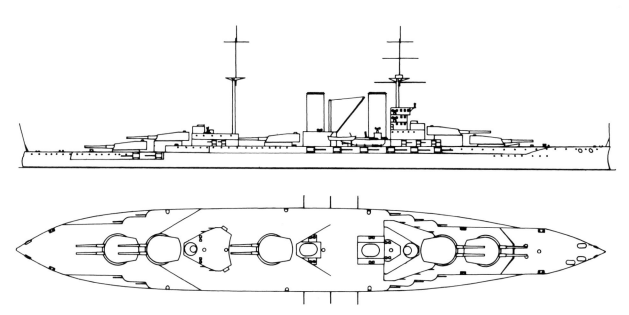

Design 764, stock battleship. (Drawn by Ian Sturton)

Design Number	740	764 and 764A	768	no number
Date	Apr 1912	11 Apr 1913	14 Aug 1913	9 Sep 1913
Dimensions (ft)	650pp(685oa)× 96×31.25	630pp(669oa) ×95×28.5	540pp×89 ×28	530×88×27 ×27
Displacement (tons)	31,500	31,500 764A: 32, 500	not given	not given
Armament	12–14in, 45 cal 16–6in, 50 cal	10–15in, 45 cal 16–6in, 45 cal 764A: 20–6in 10–3in 4–3in AA	8–15in 16–6in	7–15in 16–6in
	4 submerged broadside 21in TT		4–21in TT	
Armour (in)	belt 12–4 middle belt 9 upper belt 7 barbettes 12–9–5 CT 12	belt 13 middle belt 13–6–4 citadel 6 barbettes 10 (764A: 12)	belt 11–6–4 middle belt 8 citadel 6 barbettes 9–7–6–3	belt 11–4 middle belt 8 citadel 6
Decks (in)	forecastle 1.5 upper 1.5 main 1.5–1	no details given	forecastle 1 upper 1 main 1.25	deck 2–1
Speed (kts)	23	24–25		
Fuel (tons)	coal 1,000–4,000 oil 1,000	oil 800–2,500	oil 650–2,500	oil 600–2,500
Notes	12in belt extended from 4.5ft above to 4.5ft below wl 6 twin turrets, all on centreline, A/B superimposed, P/Q amidships superimposed, Q higher than P X/Y aft, superimposed	5 twin turrets all centreline, A/B superimposed, Q amidships, X/Y aft superimposed	3 turrets, 2 triple, fore and aft, 1 twin amidships	3 turrets 2 twin, forward, superimposed, one triple aft superimposed

Acknowledgements

I am most grateful to the staff of the National Maritime Museum, based at the Old Brass Foundry, Woolwich (most especially to the late David Topliss) for allowing me access to Portfolio No. 3, and also to Miss R Rendel and the helpful staff of the Tyne and Wear Archive Service, Newcastle. I owe a special debt to Dr Ian Sturton for the meticulous care that he has devoted in preparing the illustrations.

Notes

1 David Topliss, 'The Brazilian Dreadnoughts 1904–1914', *Warship International*, 3/1988, pp 240–89.

2 R L Scheina, *Latin America. A Naval History 1810–1987*. Naval Institute Press, Maryland, 1987, pp 82–4.

3 An ancient but modernised battleship, five protected cruisers – mostly small, a dozen or so gunboats of varying ages, a destroyer and four torpedo boats.

4 *Brasseys Naval Annual 1912*, p 66. *ibid*, 1913 p 73.

5 See University Press Paul G Halpern, *The Mediterranean Naval Situation 1908–1914*. Harvard University Press, Cambridge, MA, 1971, pp 324–7.

6 Ibid, pp 342–9.

CRUISERS FOR THE ROYAL NAVY:

The 1939–42 Programmes

The classic cruiser was obsolescent by the end of the Second World War.
George L Moore examines the Royal Navy's wartime efforts to build large cruisers.

The evolution of the cruiser in the months before the outbreak of the Second World War and during the first three years of the war had an air of relative stability, orders proceeding in a logical manner with existing designs being perpetuated, albeit with some modifications. The underlying story, however, told a very different tale with plans projected and then thwarted largely by the strategic and industrial situation with which the Admiralty was faced. The aim of this article is to give an insight into the evolution of the Royal Navy's quest for cruisers at this momentous time.

In 1939 the number of cruisers required was one hundred under the New Standard Fleet requirements. The cruiser had two essential functions in prewar plans: commerce protection, for which large trade-route cruisers were the mainstay, and attendance on the battle fleet, which included supporting destroyers, the duty of the small fleet cruisers. The aim was to have fifty-five vessels operating with the fleet, the remainder protecting the trade routes.[1] The Admiralty were, however, prepared to accept eighty-eight cruisers if the cost proved too high which, had peace prevailed, was probably an inevitable outcome. The target date for implementation was as late as 1949. The number of effective cruisers built, being built and ordered for the Royal Navy at the beginning of 1939

showed the scale of the shortfall to be faced. There were only fifty-six, a figure which included the 1938 programme, three *Hawkins* and two 'E' class.[2] Building at the close of 1938 were two *Belfast*, ten *Dido* and nine *Fiji* class. The tentative long-term new construction programme as at July 1938 was four 8,000-ton cruisers in each of the years 1939, 1940 and 1941,[3] a programme which would not have made up the shortfall in even a reduced target if it were extrapolated to 1949.

The 1939 Programme

The naval estimates for the year were being considered in January. At the instigation of Plans Division a debate was begun on the relative proportion of large trade-route cruisers and small fleet cruisers which should be included in the building programme. An outline design designated K34 was prepared which was effectively a cross between the two types (Table 1). The cost was expected to be about £2,000,000. The design was circulated in January and February and a prominent feature was the absence of any aircraft.

The Assistant Chief of Naval Staff felt the design to be well balanced in every respect save that of protection,

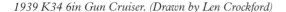

1939 K34 6in Gun Cruiser. (Drawn by Len Crockford)

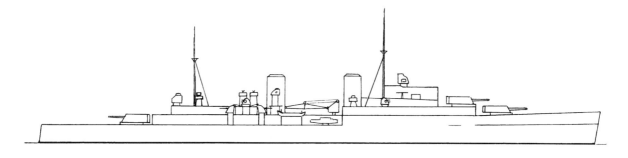

Table 1: *K34* AND FIJI *COMPARISON*

	K34	*Fiji*
Length (wl) (ft)	520	550
Breadth (extreme) (ft)	58	62
Displacement (standard) (tons)	7,350	8,170
Draught (fwd) (ft)	15.5	15.5
(aft) (ft)	17.5	17.5
Shaft horsepower	77,000	80,000
Propellor shafts	4	4
Speed (standard condition) (knots)	32.5	32.5
Oil capacity (tons)	1,600	1,700
Endurance (miles)	4,000	8,000
	at 20 knots	at 16 knots
Guns (in)		
	9–6	12–6
Rounds per gun	150	150
	8–4	8–4
Rounds per gun	150	150
	4–2pdr	4–2pdr
	(4-barrelled)	(4-barrelled)
(Stowage arranged for 200 rounds per gun for 6in and 4in and 1,800 rounds per barrel for 2pdr)		
Torpedoes	8	none quoted
Fixed heavy-type catapult	–	1
Walrus aircraft	–	3
Depth charges	6	6
Weights (tons)		
General equipment	500	525
Aircraft equipment	–	130
Machinery	1,370	1,440
Armament	900	1,010
Armour and protection	1,180	1,290
Hull	3,400	3,775
Total	7,350	8,170

Armour and protection (in) [identical in K34 and *Fiji*]
Vertical
    Ship's side abreast magazines and shell rooms   3.5
    Machinery spaces and control position   3.25
    Bulkheads   2 and 1.5
    Gun supports   1 and 0.75
    Turrets – fronts   2
    Turrets – sides and rear   1
Horizontal
    Decks over magazines, shell rooms
    machinery spaces and control position   2
    Turret roofs   2
    Bullet-proof plating   0.375
    Steering-gear protection   1.25–1.5
    Cable tubes and steering-gun controls   0.5

No torpedo tubes were quoted in the *Fiji* data when they were compiled in the spring of 1939 because to do so would have resulted in a further excess over the planned displacement of 8,000 tons (standard) which was a political objective of the government at that time for the maximum displacement of cruisers. The outbreak of the Second World War saw the demise of this constraint and two triple torpedo tubes were fitted to the *Fiji* class before completion.

Source: ADM 1 24224. Proposed New Nine gun 6in cruiser 1939

where he wanted a 4.5in belt. The logic behind this reasoning was the perception that the extra depth of armour would give better protection against shells from the German 5.9in gun. K34 had a 3.5in belt, the scheme being based on the *Fiji*. Other detailed matters were a concern to him, such as blast protection, location of pom-poms and vulnerability to a single hit (war experience with the *Dido* class showed up the latter weakness). The Deputy Chief of Naval Staff saw her as having no advantage over the *Fiji* save that of cost, and 25 per cent less armament. At the same time he also saw her as a well-balanced ship which could be improved with more protection. Another idea to emerge was 'a better protected *Dido*'.

At the end of February, Sir Stanley Goodall, the Director of Naval Construction, gave his views. He strongly defended the level of protection incorporated in K34, pointing out that when the *Fiji* design was being discussed by the Sea Lords in 1936 they were unanimous that a reduction of speed and protection was to be preferred to a reduction in armament. He considered the level of protection much superior to that of the *Leander* class, and that of the *Fiji*, on which K34's protection scheme was based, to be surpassed only by *Belfast*. He pointed out that increasing the belt to 4.5in would increase the cost to £2,060,000 as against £2,165,000 for a *Fiji*. Displacement would rise to 7,850 tons. A *Dido* with *Fiji* protection would displace about 6,600 tons and would cost about £1,800,000. This was felt to be too high a price for the weight of armament carried at that time. He made a final key point: 'If the 1939 cruisers are to be new designs instead of repeat *Fijis*, it will not be possible to invite tenders until December, which involves ordering all four in March 1940; at present it is proposed to order two in August 1939.'

In March the First Sea Lord fully agreed with the DNC's judgement that the *Fiji* was a better ship than a revised K34. The Controller also supported the *Fiji* against both K34 and the proposed version with better armour protection. On 16 May the Director of Plans drew up a paper prior to a Sea Lords' meeting which was to discuss the issue. He felt that the new design failed as a trade-route cruiser as it 'does not incorporate the maximum fighting power and endurance which can be attained within the existing treaty limit of 8,000 tons. As a fleet cruiser it appears to fail in that it is unnecessarily large for fleet work and too expensive in money and men to enable us to fulfil the essential requirements of numbers'. He said that a change in policy appeared particularly inopportune at that time because the denunciation of the Anglo-German Treaty had left the upper limit for cruiser construction in considerable doubt. He went on that 'we may find it necessary to embark on a programme of 8in cruisers for trade route purposes'. For the small fleet type of cruiser (*Dido*) the Director of Plans was 'strongly in favour of adhering to a type which mounts a HA/LA armament'. He anticipated them replacing the AA ships in later years.

At the Sea Lords meeting on 19 May it was decided that the cruisers of the 1939 programme should be repeat *Fijis*.[4] Four ships were indeed planned, the first two in the programme were to be built at Portsmouth and Devonport Dockyards, with instructions to commence work being given on 1 August and machinery being ordered on 9 August; the second pair of ships were to be ordered on 7 March 1940.[5]

The outbreak of war on 3 September 1939 resulted in a major revision of these plans. The order for the second pair of *Fijis* was expedited with *Bermuda* (John Brown) and *Newfoundland* (Swan Hunter) being ordered on 4 September. Six *Dido* class cruisers were also ordered on the same day: *Argonaut* (Cammell Laird), *Bellona* (Fairfield), *Black Prince* (Harland & Wolff), *Diadem* (Hawthorn Leslie), *Royalist* (Scotts) and *Spartan* (Vickers Armstrong: Barrow). All the cruisers were to be completed between August 1941 and June 1942.[6] The Treasury did not immediately sanction the whole programme, initially withholding approval for two of the *Dido* class. Prewar plans had envisaged four *Dido* class cruisers would be ordered when war broke out. The new First Lord of the Admiralty, Winston Churchill, was prepared to support the inclusion of six *Didos* in the programme provided they could be finished by the end of 1941.[7] All the *Didos* proceeded, but delivery dates for the cruisers ranged between August 1942 and January 1944. Churchill was not convinced that the two *Fijis* should go ahead and he wanted their construction given further consideration. The Controller pointed out that arrangements had been made two months earlier to order the two ships in an emergency and that capacity had been allocated with several firms and subcontractors, cancellation would cause considerable confusion and the question of compensation could arise.[7] The *Fijis* also proceeded and the First Lord's desire to substitute them with *Southamptons* was thwarted.[6] (Presumably he wanted to build repeat *Belfasts*.) The diary of Sir Stanley Goodall mentions on 13 September that a repeat *Belfast* could go to Harland and Wolff, Belfast, an entry one assumes related to the First Lord's ideas.[8] The two cruisers ordered from the Royal Dockyards were cancelled on 28 September, this action freeing some medium-calibre gun-making capacity to enable 5.5in howitzers to be produced at the rate of about sixty per annum, delivery starting May 1940.[9] This action effectively fulfilled Churchill's wish for further consideration of the *Fiji* programme.

The 1939 and 1940 Heavy Cruiser Designs

As foreshadowed when the 1939 cruiser requirements were being discussed, the Controller soon sought sketch designs for new heavy cruisers. Six designs designated 'A' to 'F' were produced (Table 2); a further design designated 'G' seems to have been added later. The sketch designs were submitted to the Controller on 12 June 1939, twelve days after the instructions had been received by the Director of Naval Construction.

The sketches illustrated various combinations of speed, armour and main armament. The designs were clearly constrained by the 10,000-ton treaty limit. No drawings have been found but some designs (including 'A') had the forecastle deck carried through to the stern to compensate for accommodation space lost through the

Table 2: *1939 Heavy Cruisers: Sketch Designs, June 1939*

	A	B	C	D	E	F	G
Guns (in)	9–8	9–8	8–8	8–8	8–8	8–8	8–8
	8–4	8–4	8–4	8–4	8–4	8–4	8–4
2pdr (4 barrel)	4	4	2	2	2	2	2
Triple torpedo tubes	2	2	2	2	2	2	2
Hangars	2	2	2	2	2	2	2
Speed (kts)	32	30	32	30	32	30	30
Standard horsepower (000)	80	58	80	58	80	58	58
Protection (in)							
Deck	2	2	2	2	2	2	[see note]
Side	5	5	5	5.5	5	6	
Weights (tons)							
Hull	4,700	4,700	4,700	4,700	4,700	4,700	4,650
Equipment	630	630	630	630	630	630	630
Armament	1,660	1,660	1,493	1,500	1,467	1,484	1,566
Protection	1,850	1,820	1,930	2,000	1,820	1,980	2,140
Machinery	1,445	1,120	1,445	1,120	1,445	1,120	1,120
Air equipment	160	160	160	160	160	160	160
Standard displacement (tons)	10,445	10,090	10,358	10,110	10,222	10,074	10,256

Notes:

A and B: three triple 8in; C and D: four twin 8in, E, F and G: two triple and one twin 8in. Design G: protection: deck 2in, sides 5in, except decks over magazines 3in and sides (magazines) 7in. Length (wl) about 580 ft, beam about 66ft (B and E are quoted as being 26ft longer; G: length 570ft)

Source: ADM229 22, DNC records (PRO)

reduced length. An aircraft hangar would have been fitted. One problem to be solved was the difficulty in fitting in a requirement for two eight-barrelled multiple AA mountings. To overcome this, the mounting of all the main armament forward was considered, but this feature does not appear in any of the studies. The 8in gun would have been the Mark V then at a very early stage of development.[9]

On 15 June the decision was made to go ahead with Design 'A' which it was felt would give a better ship all-round. It was estimated that it would take three years to build. The Director of Naval Ordnance was now against the 'old fashioned' twin 8in gun![8]

The return of Winston Churchill as First Lord of the Admiralty in September 1939 soon saw his active mind firing off ideas. On 6 September he asked the Director of Naval Construction to give him a legend of a 14,000- or 15,000-ton cruiser carrying 9.2in guns with good armour against 8in projectiles, a wide radius of action and superior in speed to any *Deutschland* or German 8in cruiser.[10] The first shot at meeting this request resulted in a ship carrying twelve 9.2in guns in three quadruple mountings (Table 3). This interpretation of the requirement was short-lived. On 30 September the DNC submitted his answer to the requirement to the Controller in the form of armoured cruisers with a main armament of 9.2in or 8in guns. No drawings were made at this time and in the absence of designs for triple 9.2in and triple 8in mountings some details were necessarily approximate only

(Table 3). The cost of the vessels was put at £5.5 million each and they were expected to take at least four years to complete.[12] The appearance of these new designs did not mean the immediate death of the 10,000-ton 8in cruiser since the diary of Sir Stanley Goodall records progress being made with this project early in October.[8]

The large 9.2in and 8in cruiser project was debated by the Naval Staff in October and November 1939. The realistic point was made that if these ships were built then they would be unlikely to be ready to take part in the war and that if 8in or 9.2in guns were selected then the vessel would be nearer 22,000 tons than 10,000 tons. It seemed likely that three of these ships would cost as much as two battleships; it was considered a far better buy to have the battleships for capital ships would be effective against anything whereas this cruiser would be effective against only her few opposite numbers and smaller vessels. Attention was drawn to the four 15in turrets already carried which would yield a good capital ship earlier than the Royal Navy could get any of the 9.2in or 8in cruisers. Design of a 15in battlecruiser, later the battleship *Vanguard*, was already in hand and it was then expected that she could complete in the spring of 1944. It was also pointed out that further ships of this type could be completed by this date if a similar number of 'R' class battleships were laid up from autumn 1942. An 8in-type armoured cruiser could be completed by the summer of 1944, and a 14in or 16in capital ship could be built by the winter of 1944

Table 3: *HEAVY CRUISERS 1939/40*
8IN/9.2IN GUNS

	9/39	2/40	2/40
Length (wl) ft	700	720	720
Beam (ft)	84	84	84
Draught (ft)	23.5	24	24
Displacement (tons)	–	21,500	21,500
Shaft horsepower (000s)	154	160	160
Speed (kts)	33	33.5	33.5
Endurance (miles)	10,000	9,000	9,000
	(at 16 kts)	(at ?)	(at ?)
Guns	12–9.2in	12–8in	9–9.2in
	4 quad	4 triple	3 triple
	12–4.5in	12–4.5in	12–4.5in
	6 twin	6 twin	6 twin
	16–2pdr	16–2pdr	16–2pdr
	2 × 8	2 × 8	2 × 8
Aircraft	3	2	2
Catapult	1	1	1
Armour (in)			
Belt	7	7	7
Deck	4	4	4
Cost (£m)	–	5.5	5.5

Source: 9/39 Lillicrap Work Book, via D K Brown (held at NMM); 2/40 ADM 138 624, 'Ships Cover – Armoured Cruiser Designs to Carry 8in or 9.2in Guns' (NMM)

provided work on the armament could start immediately. A 9.2in-type armoured cruiser could not be completed before early 1945. New gunpits for the manufacture of the 9.2in guns would have had to be built, whereas the 8in vessels could be produced at existing but adapted facilities. The only advantage perceived in the 9.2in gun over the 8in gun was that 'foreign armoured ships [heavy cruisers] were probably vulnerable to plunging fire [from a 9.2in gun] but not vulnerable to plunging 8in fire'. The conclusion by the Director of Plans, written on 12 November 1939, was that 'unless production difficulties are insuperable we should lay down a number of 15in Battlecruisers, at the earliest possible date, IN ADDITION to our full programme of 16in Capital Ships. If this is impossible, 9.2in or 8in armoured cruisers must be built, the choice

depending largely on the time required for design and production'.[12] No further work seems to have been done on these ships after the production of this report; the only subsequent mention found is in the Ships Cover, where a table is set out, dated 27 February 1940, which gives basic particulars of the design.[13] There are, however, no changes in any details and it seems likely that the information was produced so that comparisons could be made with new designs then in the early planning stages.

The 1940 Programme

The Sea Lords discussed the content of this programme on 3 January 1940. The Controller indicated that it was possible to lay down five *Belfast* and five *Dido* class annually. The question of 8in cruisers was raised, including the very large 20,000-ton ships, which were soon eliminated from the discussion. The general opinion was that the Royal Navy should have cruisers comparable to the new German 8in *Hipper*, which the Director of Naval Construction pointed out was most certainly of 12,000 tons and not 10,000 tons. The DNC was instructed to set out the characteristics of two new types: 15,000-ton 8in gun cruiser and a 12,000-ton (nominally 10,000-ton) 8in gun cruiser with armour similar to the *Hipper*'s. The meeting decided that we should not go on building the 10,000-ton 8in gun cruisers of the existing design which were accordingly cancelled. Proposals for the construction of five *Belfast* and five *Dido* class ships were approved.[1]

On 22 January the DNC produced a preliminary investigation of the two 8in cruiser designs which was accompanied by outline prints (Table 4). The larger of the two had machinery spaces much more extensively subdivided and it was this factor which accounted for the heavier displacement since the length to be protected was considerably greater. The costs were approximately estimated at £3.5m and £4.5m, with the ships taking about four years to complete.

Details of the new programme were forwarded by the First Sea Lord to the First Lord on 23 January. By this time the programme had evolved to two *Belfast* to be ordered immediately at a cost of £5.32m. The ships were to be laid down in May 1940 and completed in November and December 1942. There were some amendments in the design, the principal one being an increase in beam of two feet.[8] Three *Dido*s were also to be ordered, the cost

1940 8in Gun Cruiser, 12,500 tons. (Drawn by Len Crockford)

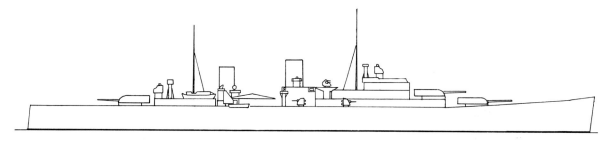

Table 4: *8IN CRUISERS, JANUARY 1940*

Length (wl) ft	610	670
Beam extreme (ft)	72	77.5
Draught (ft)	18.5	20
Shaft horsepower	96,000	125,000
Shafts	4	4
Speed (standard) kts	32.5	33
(deep) kts	31	31.5
Oil (tons)	2,200	2,500
Guns	9–8in	9–8in
	8–4in	12–4in
	16–2pdr	16–2pdr
Aircraft	2	2
Catapult	1	1
Armour (in)		
Abreast magazines, machinery, control position	5	6
Bulkheads	3	4
Gun supports	3in and 2in	4in and 3in
Turrets	5 front	6 front
	2 side	2 side
	2 rear	2 rear
Decks over magazines	3	3
Decks over machinery	2.5	2.5
Turret roofs	3	3
Weight (tons)		
General equipment	770	800
Machinery	1,755	2,300
Armament	1,615	1,700
Armour and protection	2,400	3,300
Hull	5,960	7,400
Standard displacement (tons)	12,500	15,500

Source: ADM 138 624, 'Armoured Cruiser Designs to Carry 8in or 9.2in Guns (held at NMM)

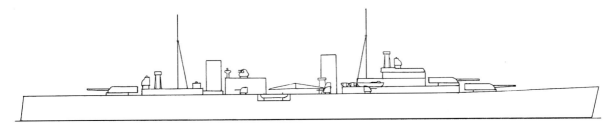

1940 8in Gun Cruiser, 15,500 tons. (Drawn by Len Crockford)

being £6.215m; the ships were to be laid down in June 1940 with the first ship completing in August 1942 and the remaining two in November. Five new 8in ships were also to be built, orders being placed in November 1940 with the first three being laid down in January 1941 and the last two in April 1941. Completions were planned for December 1943 and then March, May, June and November 1944. The first group of three mountings was expected to be ready for erection in June 1943. The cost of the 8in cruiser programme was £22.5m. It was, however, appreciated that the 8in cruisers could only be built if *Conqueror* and *Thunderer* did not proceed. On 26 January the Controller proposed that the 15,000-ton 8in design be preferred.[1]

Meanwhile the First Sea Lord, Admiral of the Fleet Sir Dudley Pound, in a memorandum to the First Lord of the Admiralty Winston Churchill expressed his concerns about the capital ship situation. He did admit that at some point in the war it might be necessary to stop building these very expensive ships but he did not feel that this time had yet come. Although not stated in the memorandum, the potential for conflict with Japan was a particular concern at that time. Not only were the four *Lion* class ships wanted but two 15in battlecruisers as well. To achieve this aim he was prepared to sacrifice two aircraft carriers and all the cruisers written into the plans.[1] There is a poignant entry in Sir Stanley Goodall's diary which aptly summed up his views and no doubt his frustrations: 'I was horrified that First Sea Lord wants still more Capital Ships: he is willing to give up anything to get them'.[8] An early draft of the Cabinet Paper produced in February 1940 confirmed the progress of the four *Lion* class and a new battlecruiser; it was also stated that 'The laying down of a second ship exactly similar may have to be undertaken early next year.' The reason for the 15in ships was 'to cope with the super-pocket-battleships and heavy 12in gun cruisers now being built in Japan'. British intelligence concerning Japanese programmes was inaccurate at this time and as late as March 1942 reference was being made to 'enlarged pocket battleships and small battlecruisers' at least one of which was said to be complete.[14] The final Cabinet Paper saw the First Sea Lord's ambitions somewhat trimmed back. Further progress was to be made with *Lion* and *Temeraire* and the future of *Conqueror* and *Thunderer* was to be reviewed in the Autumn. The plan to order *Vanguard* was confirmed but no mention was made of a possible second ship. The comment on Japanese building plans was also deleted in the final document. The reason for the absence of aircraft carriers and cruisers was now stated to be the need 'to provide for the most urgent and very large small-craft programme.'[1]

This point marked the end of the 1939/40 phase of heavy cruiser development. The 9.2in gun ships had gone for good while the next heavy cruisers were a completely new design with little relationship to the 1940 12,500-ton and 15,000-ton ships on which very little work was done since they survived for less than two months.

It is known that names were allocated to the 1940 heavy cruisers but the detailed record has not been found. One ship was named *Bellerophon* according to a note in the *Fiji* class Ships Cover.[15]

The Anti-Aircraft Cruiser

Eight sets of destroyer machinery were being constructed by Metropolitan Vickers for the Russian Navy, presumably as a result of a prewar order. On 29 February 1940 the Controller asked whether it would be feasible to use these turbines in a new class of destroyer but nothing seems to have come from this proposal. In early April 1940 the Controller's ideas had changed and consideration was now being given to using the machinery in an AA ship. There were clearly going to be problems to resolve since the propulsive efficiency would be reduced in the new design, which would operate at a lower speed than a destroyer. The units comprised only main turbines, condensers and gearing which meant that boilers and shafting would need to be manufactured. It was also unlikely therefore that the ships would be finished any earlier than if the whole project had started with a clean sheet. The manufacture of some of the units must have been well forward because the issue of the holding of material in Britain was raised in early April.[12]

By the end of April an outline of the AA cruiser design was given to the Controller, accompanied by prints. No drawings have, however, been found. By early May two ships were being considered. It was pointed out that the situation concerning the machinery was rather delicately balanced since Metropolitan Vickers were holding the machinery only pending further instructions from the Admiralty and that it had not been requisitioned. In the meantime there were Russian inspectors in Britain who were causing some anxiety to the security people. Work continued with Design 'C', the only particulars of the ship found[8] (Table 5). By 4 June it had been decided not to build the ships with the Russian machinery. The project was not then dropped because consideration was given to building the AA cruisers with either 'L' class destroyer *Dido* or the fast minelayer type of machinery.[12] The beginning of July saw the end of the project when the Controller instructed the DNC to 'set aside for the present'.[8] It was never resurrected, the deteriorating war situation now being the prime consideration.

Table 5: *ANTI-AIRCRAFT SHIP, DESIGN 'C'*

Length (ft)	470
Beam (ft)	54
Draught (deep) (ft)	17.25
Shaft horsepower	48,000
Propellor shafts	2
Speed (standard?) kts	28.75
(deep) kts	28
Guns	8–4.5in (4 twin)
	2–UP
	16–2pdr (2 × 8)
Torpedo tubes	2 triple 21in
Standard displacement (tons)	5,800

Source: D K Brown

Torpedo Cruiser

Another idea to emerge towards the end of February 1940 was the torpedo cruiser which was probably again inspired by Churchill. The basic particulars produced on 26 February illustrate a rather bizarre and expensive vessel (Table 6). A general arrangement drawing was made but it has not survived. What was wanted were a low freeboard, protected hull, six bow torpedo tubes and eighteen torpedos, one four-barrelled pom-pom and a speed of 35 knots. The hull had 1in plating over the sides and bottom with 2in plating on the curved (turtle) upper deck. The latter plating extended five feet below the waterline. The very powerful machinery would have taken up 260ft of the 400ft length. A large complement was needed to work the machinery installation and accommodation would have had to be to submarine standards, mainly in the superstructure above the protected deck. Investigations showed that it was impracticable to meet the requirements on a displacement of less than 4,900 tons.[11] The result seems to have been an expensive ship both to construct and operate to perform a role that was unclear but which, from the nature of the armament, could have been undertaken by the far more versatile destroyer. Nothing further was heard about this project until 15 September 1940 when Churchill asked what had happened to the armoured ram he had asked DNC to design.[10] No response has ever been found.

The Aftermath of the Fall of France

The crisis bought about by the evacuation of British forces from France and the resultant increase in the German threat to the United Kingdom quickly resulted in the suspension of three *Fiji* class cruisers *Ceylon*, *Uganda* and

HMS Bellona *as completed in 1943. (WSS)*

Table 6: TORPEDO CRUISER, FEBRUARY 1940

Length (ft)	400
Beam (ft)	47
Draught (ft)	17
Freeboard (about) ft	8
Armament	6 bow torpedo tubes (18 torpedoes) 4–2pdr (1 × 4)
Speed (about) kts	35
Shaft horsepower	120,000
Propellor shafts	2
Endurance (at 12 kts) miles	3,700
Estimate of weights (tons)	
Hull (ex-ballast)	2,660
Protection	425
Armament	80
Equipment	100
Machinery	1,700
	4,965

Source: Lillicrap Work Book, via D K Brown (held at NMM)

Newfoundland and the *Dido* class cruisers, *Black Prince, Royalist, Spartan, Diadem* and *Bellona*. The reasons given were, first 'to reduce the amount of new work in hand at various firms in order that earlier warships urgently needed may be accelerated and conversion repairs undertaken more rapidly', and secondly 'to reduce the requirement for materials'.[12] Work on developing existing and new cruiser designs did not stop in the period of suspension and on 8 August 1940 four propositions were put forward by the DNC at the instigation of the Controller. These were: 1. The three suspended *Fiji*s to have armament like *Dido* with improved deck and splinter protection. The armaments would be available from: 2. Three of the suspended *Dido*s which would have armament like *Scylla* (ie 4.5in twin as main armament.) 3. The remaining two *Dido*s could have improved splinter protection if mountings were reduced from five to four. 4. A cruiser mounting nine 6in guns with good protection and machinery like *Fiji*s appeared possible on 10,000 tons.[16]

One problem to be overcome was that progress was such that scrapping existing work would have been difficult and particularly in the case of the *Fiji*s.[16] Options 1 and 2 were clearly ruled out, presumably for this reason but the three *Fiji*s were fitted with three 6in mountings rather than the four planned. An enhanced AA armament and other improvements could then be accommodated. The five suspended *Dido*s proceeded to a revised design with four 5.25in mountings instead of the five planned, thus fulfilling option 3. Detailed differences were also worked in, particularly a lower bridge and upright funnels as a consequence of the removal of Q turret. Construction was suspended between June and October 1940.[17] Development of the new 6in cruiser design also now began to progress.

The 1940 Supplementary Programme

In early September 1940 the supplementary programme came forward for consideration. Initial drafts indicate that four cruisers were planned which would be *Dido* and *Fiji* class ships, although in what proportion was undecided. The First Sea Lord however recommended that 'improved *Belfast* cruisers, 10,000 tons, nine 6in, should be built instead of four new *Fiji* or *Didos*'.[18] Three specifications were drawn up (Table 7), the type being described as a heavy deck *Fiji*. The engines and boilers were identical to those installed in *Fiji*.[19] Plans Division, in a memorandum dated 29 August, saw the ships as having a displacement of 10,000 tons, nine 6in and twelve 4in guns, 4 quadruple pom-poms, 3in deck armour with 2.5in protection for machinery spaces. Speed was expected to reduce by half to three-quarters of a knot. Completions were expected in March, June, September and December 1944, provided that the sketch design was approved by October 1940 at the latest. The only difficulties were expected to be the provision of 4in guns and the pom-poms.[20] The programme presented to the War Cabinet included the four cruisers which were expected to be laid down in March 1941.[1] The cost of the programme was assessed as £10.6m, or £2.65m for each ship.[21] This compared with £2.75m which was the estimated cost of a *Fiji* in April 1941.[22] The programme was duly approved by the Cabinet. There were, however, soon doubts about the type of cruiser wanted because as early as October 1940 the Controller described the design and the type of vessel as under consideration with the position to be reviewed in January.[23] In December 1940 the balance of opinion was still largely in favour of building 6in cruisers, largely to avoid problems at any naval limitation conference which might be held at the end of the war. The experience of 1922 was influential in this thinking since an 8in cruiser race had resulted from the retention of the *Hawkins* class. The existence of these ships with a displacement of 9,750 tons and an armament of 7.5in guns had been the factor in negotiations which led to the fixing of cruiser limits at 10,000 tons and 8in guns in the Washington Treaty.

The 1941 Programme

At the turn of the year the First Sea Lord held a conference which discussed future cruiser requirements. Opinion was now in favour of laying down four 8in cruisers on the grounds of maintaining our strength for eventualities in the Far East. It also seems to have been agreed that a total of seven cruisers should be inserted in the 1941 programme, a figure which included the 1940 supplementary programme vessels. The overall requirement remained at one hundred ships, which the Director of Plans broke down into sixty heavy and forty light cruisers. His personal definition of a heavy cruiser was a vessel with nine 6in guns or a heavier armament rather than the usually accepted 8in armament.

Uncertainty clearly remained because on 15 January 1941 the Commander-in-Chiefs Mediterranean, Home Fleet and Force H were sent details of three types which were under consideration and asked for their views (Table 8). The C-in-C Mediterranean wanted 8in and 6in cruisers in the ratio of 1 to 3, a heavier armoured deck, increased speed in 6in cruisers, if necessary at the expense of aircraft, and a reduction in target area by which he presumably meant the superstructure. He also stressed the need for manoeuvrability. The Senior Officer Force H wanted 8in cruisers, which he considered the minimum calibre required to take advantage of RDF ranging, increased deck armour at the expense of side armour and possibly one 8in turret. Increased speed was wanted at the expense of endurance. The C-in-C Home Fleet stressed that numbers were important and hence he would prefer 6in cruisers, accepting that they would be outranged at longer ranges. Designs should be based on our needs and not follow the example of other powers. He also felt it better to counter enemy air attack with AA weapons rather than by adding weight to passive

Table 7: *6in Cruiser, September 1940: Heavy Deck* Fiji

Length (pp) ft	568	571	603
(wl) ft	580	583	614
Beam (ft)	70.5	70.5	72.5
Displacement (standard) tons	11,280	11,400	12,816
Shaft horsepower	80,000	80,000	80,000
Propellor shafts	4	4	4
Speed (standard displacement) kts	31	31	30.75
Guns	9–6in	9–6in	12–6in
	12–4in	12–4in	12–4in
	16–2pdr (4 × 4)	16–2pdr (4 × 4)	16–2pdr (4 × 4)
Torpedo tubes	6	6	6
Aircraft	2	2	2
Armour (in)			
Side	4.5	4.5	4.5
Deck	3	3	3

Source: D K Brown

Table 8: *Cruiser Designs considered in January 1941*

	A	B	C
Displacement (standard) tons	8,650	14,000	15,000
Length (ft)	550	635	650
Main armament	9–6in	12–6in	9–8in
Catapult	1	1	1
Aircraft	2	2	2
Speed (deep and clean) kts	31	31.5	31.5
Endurance (miles) at 16 kts	8,000	11,000	12,000
Armour (in)			
Belt	3.5/3.25	4.5	4.5
Deck over machinery	2	2	2
Deck over magazine	2	4	4
Estimated completion date	3/44	3/45	12/45

AA armament not less than 8–4in in each design with close-range armament according to the size of ship.

Note:
Design A was an improved *Fiji*; Design B was a large 6in cruiser probably based on *Belfast* (also known as Design Y); Design C was developed into the 1941 heavy cruiser design. Basic characteristics had been evolved only for Designs B and C at this date.

Source: ADM 1 11344 'Construction of New Cruisers including *Fiji* and *Dido* classes 1941' (PRO)

protection. The First Lord, A V Alexander, now entered the debate. He wanted ships which would complete in time for the present war; he also felt that if the United States came in then 8in cruisers would be less necessary.

By 5 February the way ahead was becoming clearer. The initial thought was to lay down two *Fiji*s and one *Dido* with four 8in ships to be laid down in the autumn. The First Sea Lord essentially agreed, except that he wanted three *Fiji*s now (building a *Dido* at John Brown had been considered[24]). In order to get ships quickly it was essential that an existing design was used otherwise there would have been a delay of between six and eight months while a new class was produced.[25]

The 1941 New Construction Programme produced for the Cabinet in April and presented by the First Lord confirmed the plan to build three improved *Fiji*s. The other four ships were to be 8in cruisers because, as stated in the paper, the 8in gun was the smallest calibre for accurate RDF range-taking, a reiteration of the view of the Commander of Force 'H', and, secondly, because of the avowed intention of the United States to continue 8in cruiser production. The supply of armour plate would, however, not allow building to start immediately and the situation was to be reviewed in the autumn. The cost of the 8in cruiser programme was now estimated to be £14m or £3.5m per vessel compared with £2.75m for an improved *Fiji*.[22]

The three improved *Fiji*s were: *Swiftsure* (Vickers Armstrong–Tyne), *Minotaur* later renamed *Ontario* on transfer to the Royal Canadian Navy (Harland and Wolff) and *Bellerophon* later renamed *Tiger* (John Brown). The principal changes built into the new ships were an increase of one foot in the beam of sixty-three to give improved stability, elimination of a 6in gun mounting and the aircraft hangars to improve anti-aircraft capability. A twin 4in mounting replaced the triple 6in turret in X position.[17]

The 1941 Heavy Cruiser

Development of the new heavy cruiser started at the end of February 1941.[9] A fresh start was made and in order to save weight the hull was designed to 6in cruiser standards, which were largely based on the *Southampton* class. The provisional staff requirements called for a ship with nine 8in and sixteen 4in guns; 4.5in guns would have been preferred if they could have been worked into a light cruiser hull. The Director Tactical and Staff Duties described the decision to build these ships as a 'snap one' in a letter to Sir Stanley Goodall which is in the Ships Cover.[13] Sir Stanley for his part had earlier told the Naval Staff to 'make up their minds' at what must have been a frustrating meeting on 19 December 1940.[9]

On 25 March four design options were sent to the Controller (Table 9): option ii was chosen because of the ability of sixteen 4in guns to produce a greater volume of AA fire and the perceived simplification of maintaining a four-cornered command system to control the AA defensive armament. The larger 4.5in gun would have been preferred but the resulting increase in displacement precluded this route forwards. Development of the design proceeded during the year and hull models were tested at the Admiralty Experiment Works at Haslar in June 1941. The displacement had now risen to 16,850 tons (standard) by October it was up to 16,930 (standard). On 12 October design work was stopped on the instructions of the Controller.[13] In spite of a clear reduction in the level of priority given to the class, development proceeded again and on 11 November an order was placed for gun mountings for one ship[13] the 1941 Supplementary Programme stating that a vessel of this class would be laid down in 1942.[26] By December the displacement had reached 17,500 tons with the ship now being designed to look as far as possible like a *King George V* class battleship to confuse the enemy.

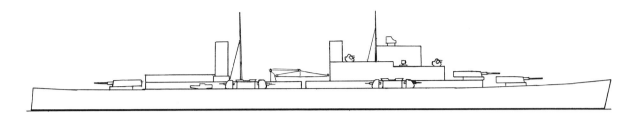

1941 8in Gun Heavy Cruiser. (Drawn by Len Crockford)

Table 9: *HEAVY CRUISER DESIGNS, MARCH 1941*

	i	ii	iii	iv
Length (pp) ft	636	656	643	635
(wl) ft	650	670	657	644
Beam (ft)	80	80	80	79
Displacement (standard) tons	16,100	16,500	16,200	15,800
Draught (amidships) ft	22.5	22.5	22.5	22.5
Shaft horsepower	110,000	110,000	110,000	110,000
Propellor shafts	4	4	4	4
Speed (standard) kts	32.25	32.25	32.25	32.5
(deep) kts	30.75	30.75	30.75	31.0
Oil (tons)	3,500	3,500	3,500	3,400
Endurance at 16 kts (miles)	12,000	12,000	12,000	12,000
Armament	9–8in	9–8in	9–8in	9–8in
	8–4.5in	16–4in	12–4in	8–4in
	16–2pdr	16–2pdr	16–2pdr	16–2pdr
Torpedo tubes	6	6	6	6
Catapult	1	1	1	1
Depth charges	15	15	15	15
Weights				
General equipment	670	700	685	660
Aircraft equipment	160	160	160	160
Machinery	2,050	2,050	2,050	2,050
Armament	2,000	2,000	1,930	1,860
Armour and protection	4,000	4,180	4,060	3,940
Hull	7,220	7,410	7,315	7,130
	16,100	16,500	16,200	15,800

Armour, all vessels (in): sides 4.5; bulkheads 2.5, 2; gun supports 3–1.5; turrets (front) 4.5 (sides and rear) 2, decks over 8in, 4.5in or 4in guns 4; over machinery and control positions 2; turret roofs 2.

Source: ADM 138 624 Armoured Cruiser Designs to carry 8in or 9.2in guns (held at NMM)

One feature now sought was to site the foremast as near as possible to the vertical fore funnel. Costs must have been a concern because on 11 February 1942 the Director of Gunnery Division was asking about the characteristics of a ship mounting two twin 8in turrets. The immediate reply was that if the hull was based on *Fiji* weights, the armament being four 8in and eight 4in guns, then the displacement would have been 11,140 tons. Nothing further was heard about this idea. As a result of the intensification of the war, work was suspended on the ship design on 17 February. Work was then suspended on design and manufacture of the new Mark V 8in guns on 29 July 1942.[13] This was effectively the end of the project but it was not finally abandoned until June 1943 when the consensus at a Sea Lords' meeting was that 'nothing should be built between the Small Cruiser and the battleship.[27]

In May 1941 following the inauguration of the Ships' Names Committee, the King approved the renaming of *Effingham* to *Cornwallis* and *Benbow* to *Albemarle*.[28] Not all the related papers can be found so the names of the other two ships are not confirmed. The likelihood is that they were named *Blake* and *Hawke*, names which were given to two later cruisers. It was a practice at this time to transfer names which had been approved from ship to ship as plans for new vessels were changed.

The 1941 Supplementary and the 1942 Programme

Consideration of the make-up of the 1941 Supplementary Programme commenced in October. Goodall was in favour of building more *Fiji* class vessels but he did point out that a new design was needed.[9] The key feature wanted was improved endurance. To obtain any worthwhile benefit displacement would rise to 10,000 tons. Machinery would be as fitted in *Fiji*, armament nine 6in, eight 4in guns (twin mountings) and six 21in torpedo tubes. Little work was done to advance this project because it ranked fourth in the DNC's priority list after the new destroyer ('Battle' class), aircraft carrier (*Ark Royal*) and 8in cruiser.[23] The pressure on design resources is best illustrated by the decision taken in January 1942 to subcontract the design of a fighter support ship (later designated an intermediate carrier, later still called a light fleet carrier) to Vickers Armstrongs. The first ideas which were to lead to this ship emerged in October 1941.[23] The Supplementary New Construction Programme was placed before the Cabinet in November 1941 and the construction of three modified *Fiji* class was approved. Also approved at this meeting was the construction of three 8in triple turrets for a new heavy cruiser which was to be laid down as early as possible in 1942.[26] The new ships were *Superb* (Swan Hunter), *Defence* (Scotts) and *Tiger* later *Bellerophon* (Vickers Armstrong–Tyne).[17] With the entry of Japan into the war in December 1941 the requirement for new ships became pressing. In the memorandum setting out the basis of the new year's programme it was made clear that the requirements were urgent, with the result that all effort was to be devoted to the building of improved *Fiji* class ships. The Naval Staff wanted seven vessels but the capacity existed for only six to be undertaken and this only if the planned 8in cruisers were suspended. The construction of 6in ships was also expected to alleviate the armour supply situation which was tight owing to the diversion of naval capacity to the production of armour for tanks. The new cruisers were expected to be completed between the end of 1944 and the end of 1945.[29] The programme was presented to the Cabinet in April 1942 and duly approved, construction of the 8in cruiser being ruled out.[30] Two of the ships were ordered quite rapidly, J1496 (Stephens) and *Blake* (Fairfield). The remaining four were to be ordered from Fairfield, Hawthorn Leslie, Vickers Armstrong–Barrow and Cammell Laird. The only major design change was an increase in beam to 64ft to further improve stability.

The 1942 programme also contained the first four orders for intermediate (later light fleet) aircraft carriers. In January 1942 Sir Stanley Goodall made the prophetic comment in his diary that 'these ships could only be built at the expense of something else'.[9] The course of the war particularly in the Pacific resulted in a sweeping review of the programme. In August 1942 it was decided that a further nine intermediate carriers should be ordered at the expense of four cruisers and other new naval and merchant ship construction. Other ships were to be delayed. The result was the cancellation of J1496, which was about to be laid down, the Hawthorn Leslie, Vickers Armstrongs and the second Fairfield ships, while the order for the Cammell Laird ship was to be deferred for six months.[31] Fairfields were to arrange for any useful material assembled for J1496 to be transferred for incorporation in *Blake*.[32]

There were, however, misgivings in the Cabinet at the loss of the cruisers, although the new carriers were approved. The committee formed to look into the matter recommended the reinstatement of one cruiser and *Hawke* was duly ordered from Portsmouth Dockyard thus increasing the cruiser programme from two to three vessels. Other facilities found at Harland and Wolff (two slips) and Devonport Dockyard were allocated to intermediate carriers, taking the programme to sixteen ships which the committee decided must have priority over cruiser construction. The Portsmouth slip incidentally could not take a carrier without major modifications being made. Building large ships on the south coast was a new departure since the fall of France, made feasible by improved air defences.[33] The Cammell Laird ship was destined never to be ordered. When formulating the 1943 programme in November 1942 it was decided not to order the ship so that the yard's efforts could be concentrated on carriers and fleet destroyers. The target number of cruisers wanted had now been reduced to fifty.[34]

Building the Cruisers

We now look at the progress of the construction programmes.[35] The production of cruisers throughout the war was subject to continuing delays. We have already seen how the crisis precipitated by the fall of France led to the suspension of three *Fiji* and five *Dido* class ships. The

HMS Superb *in October 1953. (CPL)*

only cruisers ordered in 1939 where construction was not suspended were *Argonaut* and *Bermuda*. They still failed to meet the completion dates expected when they were ordered by twelve and six months' respectively. The completion dates of the suspended ships were delayed between seven months for *Newfoundland* and twenty-eight for *Bellona*.[36] The cause of these delays was partly the priority given to production for the Army and the RAF as deliberate Cabinet policy. The need to concentrate on repairs to both merchant ships and warships also had its effect, as did the dislocation caused by bombing to both the shipyards and the homes of the workers.[37] Another problem highlighted in December 1940 was the departure of workers from firms engaged on Admiralty work for positions elsewhere. Fairfields were short of eighty fitters at this time.[16]

The case of *Bellona* seems to be a special one. In February 1941 the transfer of the ship from Fairfields to John Brown was considered but finally ruled out. Work on her, however, seems to have stopped again for some ten months.[24] The reason for the delay was presumably to enable work to be pressed forward on the carrier *Implacable* which was then scheduled to complete by the

end of 1943.[36] She would have competed for the same resources at this time for both ships were on the slipways.

The expansion of the intermediate-carrier programme in August 1942 was a defining moment which not only resulted in the immediate cancellation of four ships but also in planned delays to four other cruisers. *Superb* (Swan Hunter), *Blake* (Fairfield), *Tiger* (Vickers Armstrong–Tyne) and the Cammell Laird ship were immediately affected. No delays were expected in the completion of *Minotaur* (Harland and Wolff), *Swiftsure* (Vickers Armstrong–Tyne) and *Defence* (Scotts).[31] Paradoxically Scotts were the only firm building cruisers not engaged in carrier construction, yet the *Defence* proved to be one of the worst delayed ships. The firm had deep internal troubles including a lack of fitting-out facilities and labour, labour unrest and doubts on management efficiency, which were highlighted in December 1942 at a Controller's new construction and repair meeting.[38]

In December 1942 it was decided that the delayed *Tiger* would not be laid down until mid-1944 in order to give priority to destroyer and aircraft carrier construction. It was decided to send armour and materials already assembled to Portsmouth for incorporation in the *Hawke*.

Table 10: *CRUISERS AUTHORISED 1939–42*

	Builder	Job No.	Ordered	Laid down	Launched	Completed
1939 Programme						
one ship	Portsmouth	?	1.8.39	cancelled 9.39		
one ship	Devonport	?	1.8.39	cancelled 9.39		
Bermuda	John Brown	J1568	4.9.39	30.11.39	11.9.41	21.8.42
Newfoundland	Swan Hunter	J4124	4.9.39	9.11.39	19.12.41	20.1.43
1939 War Programme						
Argonaut	Cammel Laird	J3864	4.9.39	21.11.39	6.9.41	8.8.42
Bellona	Fairfield	J1679	4.9.39	30.11.39	29.9.42	29.10.43
Black Prince	Harland & Wolff	J3942	4.9.39	2.11.39	27.8.42	20.11.43
Diadem	Hawthorn Leslie	J4117	4.9.39	15.12.39	26.8.42	6.1.44
Royalist	Scotts	J1103	4.9.39	21.3.40	30.5.42	10.9.42
Spartan	Vickers–Barrow	J3780	4.9.39	21.12.39	27.8.42	10.8.43
1940 Supplementary Programme						
Benbow			not ordered	suspended 2.42	abandoned 6.43	
Blake?			not ordered	suspended 2.42	abandoned 6.43	
Effingham			not ordered	suspended 2.42	abandoned 6.43	
Hawke?			not ordered	suspended 2.42	abandoned 6.43	
1941 Programme						
Bellerophon	John Brown	J1593	19.5.41	1.10.41	25.10.45	1959
Minotaur	Harland & Wolff	J3370	27.5.41	20.11.41	29.7.43	25.5.45
Swiftsure	Vickers–Tyne	J4373	19.5.41	22.9.41	4.2.43	22.6.44
1941 Supplementary Programme						
Defence	Scotts	J1137	18.12.41	24.6.42	2.9.44	1960
Superb	Swan Hunter	J4545	18.12.41	23.6.42	31.8.43	16.11.45
Tiger	Vickers–Tyne	J4513	18.12.41	not laid down	cancelled 28.2.47 as 'new' *Minotaur* class	
1942 Programme						
Blake	Fairfield	J11710	13.5.42	17.8.42	20.12.45	1961
one ship	Stephens	J1496	7.4.42	not laid down	cancelled 8.42	
one ship	Fairfield		not ordered		cancelled 8.42	
one ship	Hawthorn Leslie		not ordered		cancelled 8.42	
one ship	Vickers–Barrow		not ordered		cancelled 8.42	
one ship	Cammell Laird		not ordered		cancelled 11.42	
one ship	Portsmouth	D279	13.10.42	1.7.43	cancelled 23.10.45	

Note:
Original names quoted, for changes see text

Work on the armour was well advanced with the deck armour being nearly complete. Work had not started on the armour for *Hawke*. *Bellerophon* (John Brown) was also suspended at this time with priority being given to the building of the *Vanguard*. Construction of the cruiser was not expected to resume until the battleship had been launched.[38] It was decided in January 1943 to increase the beam of *Bellerophon* to 64ft as there would be no wastage of labour or material other than some two hundred tons of armour which could be used for other purposes.[39]

In August 1943 the transfer of the contract for *Tiger* to Portsmouth Dockyard was considered. She would have followed *Hawke* which was scheduled to be launched in June 1944 on the slip. The aim was to free capacity so that an order for ten 'U' class submarines could be built at Vickers.[27] The cruiser order remained in place. Progress with the *Defence* was a cause of real concern and in August 1943 Goodall in his capacity as Assistant Controller–Warship Production (he was still DNC) visited the yard to investigate matters. On the day he arrived the riveters, carpenters and shipwrights had gone on strike and morale within management was clearly at a low ebb. Many of the labour problems arose from an attempt to accelerate work on *Defence*. The firm was asked to supply a list of labour requirements and to consider the whole building programme. Submarine construction was given priority but the launch date for the cruiser was set for April 1944 with completion wanted by July 1945.[46] February 1944 still saw *Vanguard* with priority over *Bellerophon* the former being expected to launch in December 1944.[41] A shortage of labour continued to affect progress on the cruisers an additional diversion of resources being caused by the transport-ferry (LST3) programme which had priority over virtually everything else.[41] A good illustration of the problems faced was the situation at Swan Hunter when in August 1944 fifty electricians were required for work on *Superb* but only four were available, other new construction with higher priority having preference. In February 1945 both *Tiger* (now renamed – previously *Bellerophon*) and *Blake* were delayed by a lack of labour although the completion dates (May and June 1946[36]) remained in place pending clarification.[42]

The 1944 programme included five cruisers of a new design and it was decided that the *Tiger* (later *Bellerophon*) should be the sixth member of this new class, a decision confirmed in the 1945 New Construction Programme.[43] This ship gave her name to the *Tiger* class in March 1943 when it was decided to fit Mark XXIV mountings instead of Mark XXIII mountings in *Bellerophon*, *Blake*, *Defence*, *Hawke* and *Tiger* subject to no delays in completion.[15] The advantage of the Mark XXIV mounting was its 60ft elevation. The XXIII mounting only had a 45ft elevation.

There was a confusing series of name changes caused by the need to rename *Tiger* following the decision to build her as a unit of the 1944 cruiser class. Initially *Blake* was renamed *Tiger*, but following strong representations by Admiral Blake, the chairman of the Ships' Names Committee, she was named *Blake* again. *Tiger* then became *Bellerophon* (1944 class) a name particularly wanted by the Committee while *Bellerophon* became *Tiger*.[15] *Defence* was renamed *Lion* in 1957.[44]

Later Developments

Not all the war-built cruisers served in the Royal Navy. In December 1943 the Cabinet agreed to a gift of two to the Royal Canadian Navy. At that time the ships were expected to be *Minotaur*, then expected to complete in June 1944, and *Superb* due to complete in August 1944.[45] In the event delays in the completion of *Superb* resulted in her being replaced by *Uganda*. In May 1944 the possibility of two ships being manned by the Royal Australian Navy was considered. *Defence*, then expected to complete in September 1945, and *Blake*, due in October 1945, were the two ships considered at that time.[46] In February 1945 the Australian government made a formal request for the transfer without payment of one *Colossus* class carrier and one or two *Tiger* class cruisers.[47] The two ships being considered were then *Mauritius*, available in September 1945, and *Defence*, said to be scheduled to be ready in March 1946.[48] By December 1945 the matter was in abeyance and nothing came of the idea.[49]

The chequered history of these cruisers continued after the war. *Hawke* was cancelled and broken up on the slip, while in November 1946 it was decided to take *Defence* to Devonport where she was to be taken in hand after the completion of the carrier *Terrible* (later *Sydney*). In the end the contract with Scotts was cancelled and she became a unit of the Reserve Fleet. *Tiger* and *Blake* were finally laid up in September 1947 at their builders who were responsible for maintenance. When the situation of the ships was reviewed in September 1947 it was calculated that no *Tiger* class cruiser could complete before mid-1951 at the earliest.[15] A major review of the armament started in November 1947 which was to lead to the completely revised vessels which were finally and belatedly completed at great cost between 1959 and 1961.

HMS Lion *(ex-*Defence*). The Royal Navy's only 'rebuilt' heavy cruiser. Her reconstruction was implemented when the 1939 heavy cruiser was being designed. (CPL)*

When *Defence* was completed in 1960 by Swan Hunter, her new contractors, and *Blake* in 1961 by her original builders, no fewer than nineteen years had elapsed between authorisation and completion. *Tiger* took eighteen years. This rather unusual performance reflects the great period of change which enveloped the building of cruisers authorised under the 1939–1942 programmes. At the start of the war the cruiser was a unit of prime importance in support of the Fleet, the protection of trade and as a back-up for destroyers in confined waters. By 1942 the aircraft carrier had taken over the cruiser role in most aspects and the strength of new destroyers such as the 'Battle' class meant that they could operate without the need for cruiser support. Old ideas and plans, however, took a very long time to die away.

Notes

1	ADM 205	5	First Sea Lords papers
2			Roskill, Naval Policy between the Wars, Vol 2
3	ADM 1	9762	1938 Naval Expenditure 1937–41
4	ADM 1	24224	1939 Proposed new 6in cruiser.
5	ADM 265	1	Engineer in Chief 1938–40: Miscellaneous Correspondence and Papers
6	ADM 205	2	First Sea Lords papers
7	ADM 167	105	1939 Board minutes and memoranda
8			Diary of Sir Stanley Goodall. Notes by D K Brown. Original in British Library
9	ADM 229	22	Director of Naval Construction: Reports etc, Jul 1939–Jun 1940
10			The Second World War
11			Lillicrap Work Books (NMM)
12	ADM 229	23	Director of Naval Construction Reports, etc. Jan 1940–Jun 1940
13	ADM 138	624	Armoured Cruiser Designs to carry 8in or 9.2in Guns
14	ADM 199	1935	First Lords Records and Reports
15	ADM 138	567	*Fiji* class
16	ADM 229	24	Director of Naval Construction Reports etc. Jun 1940–Mar 1941
17			*The Design and Construction of British Warships 1939–45* Conway Maritime Press
18	ADM 167	109	1940 Board Minutes and Memoranda
19			D K Brown RCNC
20	ADM 1	10850	1940 New Construction Programme
21	ADM 167	108	1940 Board Minutes
22	CAB 66	16	War Cabinet Memoranda WP Series
23	ADM 229	25	Director of Naval Construction: Reports etc. Mar 1941–Mar 1942
24	ADM 229	15	Director of Naval Construction Correspondence Jul 1940–Mar 1941
25	ADM 1	11344	1941 Cruiser Construction: Review of Policy and Long-term Requirements
26	CAB 66	20	War Cabinet Memoranda WP Series
27	ADM 229	30	Director of Naval Construction Reports etc. Jun 1943–Aug 1943
28			The Royal Archives, Moore, 'Warship Names', *Warships*, No. 126
29	ADM 116	4601	1940–42 New Construction Programme
30	CAB 66	24	War Cabinet Memoranda WP Series
31	ADM 167	116	1942 Board Memoranda
32	ADM 1	12156	1942 Orders for 10 Intermediate Aircraft Carriers
33	CAB 66	28	War Cabinet Memoranda WP Series
34	ADM 205	21	1942 Board Memoranda
35			Moore, 'The Royal Navy's 1944 Cruiser', *Warship 1996*, p78
36	ADM 209		Various (Blue Lists) also at Naval Historical Branch
37	ADM 167	115	First Sea Lords Papers
38	ADM 229	27	Director of Naval Construction Reports etc. Aug 1942–Dec 1942
39	ADM 229	28	Ibid Dec 1942–Mar 1943
40	ADM 229	31	Ibid Aug 1943–Oct 1943
41	ADM 229	33	Ibid Jan–Mar 1944
42	ADM 229	36	Ibid Aug 1944–Mar 1945
43	CAB 66	67	War Cabinet Memoranda WP Series
44			*Jane's Fighting Ships 1959–60*
45	CAB 66	43	War Cabinet Memoranda WP Series
46	ADM 205	38	First Sea Lords Papers
47	CAB 66	65	War Cabinet Memoranda WP Series
48	ADM 205	52	First Sea Lords Papers
49	ADM 205	49	First Sea Lords Papers

Acknowledgements

My thanks are due to David K Brown, RCNC, for information, assistance and for permitting me to use his copy of Sir Stanley Goodall's diary. I would also like to thank the staff of: The Naval Historical Branch, National Maritime Museum, Public Record Office and the Royal Archives for all their assistance.

SIR STANLEY V GOODALL, KCB, OBE, RCNC

David K Brown looks at the illustrious career of the Second World War Director of Naval Construction, one of the Royal Navy's most talented naval architects.

In his younger days, Goodall was presented with a rather turgid draft by his assistant and responded by writing 'If you will attend to the rest, I will endeavour to impart the enthusiasm'. This enthusiasm, so obvious in everything he did, helped him to design many successful ships and, as Director of Naval Construction, to create much of the Royal Navy of the Second World War.

Early Life and Career

Stanley Vernon Goodall was born on 18 April 1883 and was educated at Owens School, Islington. He intended to become a naval engineer officer but soon after he began his training at the RN Engineering College, Keyham, in July 1901, he decided to transfer to the Royal Corps of Naval Constructors (RCNC). He graduated from the RN College Greenwich in 1907 with one of the highest marks ever achieved and excellent records in tennis[1] – which he played until late in life – and in rugby.

His first, brief appointment was to Devonport Dockyard where he said that he learnt to write good English from the manager A E Richards. He was then moved to the Admiralty Experiment Works, Haslar, where he learnt the value of ship-model testing from Edmund Froude, son of the founder. Froude, too, believed in precise, if rather pedantic, English. The young Goodall also learnt the limitations of science. The new 'Tribal' class destroyers had a clause in the construction contract offering the shipbuilder a bonus for exceeding the specified speed and a penalty for failing to reach it. This exposed a then little-known effect of shallow water as in some depths ships would exceed their deep-water speed while other depths would cause a dramatic reduction in speed. This led to a series of legal actions as builders and the Admiralty made conflicting claims.

The Admiralty carried out a large number of model tests and ship trials and Goodall was briefed to attend court to explain the effect of shallow water. *Cossack* was run on three measured miles and, taking the Skelmorlie mile with 40 fathoms as correct, there was a slight loss at all speeds on the 16-fathom Chesil mile. The 7-fathom Maplin mile gave more dramatic effects with a bonus of at least one knot at 33 knots, while at power for 22 knots there was a penalty of at least 3 knots, accompanied by a very large stern trim. However, the builder's counsel pointed out that since the contract did not specify a particular mile this work was irrelevant and their ship had exceeded the contract speed on 'a mile'. In 1908, Goodall married Helen, daughter of C W Phillips of Plymouth.

A painting of Sir Stanley presented to him by his staff in 1938. It now hangs in the headquarters of the Royal Institution of Naval Architects. (RINA)

Cruiser Design

By 1911, Goodall was back at the Admiralty and was put in charge of the new *Arethusa*[2] class light cruiser, an unusual responsibility for one so junior. On completing the design work he was questioned by the Assistant Director, Whiting. Goodall was able to satisfy him on most points but had to admit that she would not get her design speed, mainly because the shaft rpm of her ungeared turbines was too high for good propeller performance. Geared turbines were under development which would solve this problem but were not seen as fully proven in 1911. In May or June 1914, Goodall visited the German cross-channel steamer *Königin Louise* to inspect her hydraulic transmission, an alternative means of reducing shaft speed. He also noted, with interest, that she was already fitted with sponsons for minelaying;[3] she was sunk on the first night of the war laying mines off Harwich.

The *Arethusa*s were fairly successful but were a little wet and their mixed armament of 6in and 4in was rather light; in later light cruisers an all-6in armament was adopted. Goodall tells how the size of the blast screen for open, superfiring mounts was determined; a pit was dug in front of the muzzle of a gun at Whale Island and covered with thick planks. A gun's crew was put in the pit and the gun above fired. One plank after another was removed until the tough CPO in charge cried enough. One extra plank was put back and this gave the size of the blast screen for superfiring mounts in the later 'C' and 'D' class cruisers.

Before the war, the annual dinner of the RCNC would end with a light-hearted sketch by the younger officers. Goodall achieved some fame for a performance based on the heated arguments then raging over the merits of hollow or full waterlines called 'Hollow or Full Lines for Thames River Boats', the first of his many skits on technical subjects.

At the outbreak of war Goodall was the lecturer at the RN College, a prestigious post, but was recalled to work on the *Repulse* and, later, the *Courageous* in the battle-cruiser section under Attwood. After Jutland he assisted S Payne in a study of the damage to surviving ships, attempting to explain the cause of sinking of the ships which were lost. Unfortunately, their report cannot be found (except for a fragment), but Goodall made it clear that he did not accept the idea that weak protection was to blame but attributed the losses to exposed charges. As a result of this investigation, he was appointed to a committee looking at the design of better shells.

Goodall in the United States

For a short time Goodall worked on ship production, particularly on the inspection of submarines, but when the United States entered the war he was sent to Washington as Assistant Naval Attaché working within the Bureau of Construction and Repair under Admiral D W Taylor.[4] Goodall was to work on some US Navy (USN) designs but his main task was to act as a line of communication between British and American design teams.

HMS Aurora *of the* Arethusa *class, Goodall's first design. (Author's collection)*

His views on American designs were summarised in a paper read in Portsmouth after the war[5] which was closely based on his official reports.[6] Goodall's comments seem impartial though he concentrated on things which he did not like. He said that the most noticeable feature of US battleships was their lattice, cage masts. Goodall went into the foretop of the *New Mexico* during the firing trials and thought that the vibration was acceptable. He was concerned over the difficulty in modifying a cage mast after its completion and attributed the serious accident to *Michigan*'s mast to modifications. He was also concerned that damage to the deck might cause a mast to fall – as happened during postwar bombing trials with the *Alabama*.

The triple turrets were smaller and lighter than British twin turrets, which delighted him as a naval architect. However, he thought they were very cramped and the way in which shells were moved on to the rotating structure was dangerous. Overall, he doubted whether the rate of fire from the US triple was any better than from an RN twin. There were a number of tests of armour made in both countries with rather inconclusive results.[7] Goodall was impressed with the value of sloping armour as introduced in *Hood* by Attwood and tried, unsuccessfully, to persuade the USN to adopt it in the *South Dakota* class (BB 49). He claimed that a 10° slope would enable armour to be reduced by 20 to 25 per cent in resisting a 15in shell at 12,000 yards.

Goodall reported extensively on the novel turbo-electric machinery fitted in US battleships. *Hood* developed two and a half times as much power for the same weight of machinery as *New Mexico* and needed only one-third of the space. The great advantage claimed for the US system was the improved subdivision; each of the eight boilers was in a separate space; there were three turbo-generator rooms and an electric motor room. However, there was a single switchboard room, high in the ship and not well protected, on which all propulsion depended.[8] Goodall also noted that there were many windows low down in the bulkheads.

'Before I had any personal experience of American ships I held the view that in matters affecting comfort our ships came second. I no longer hold this view.' Goodall liked the clear, open mess decks, though he thought that they lacked any comfort. His severest criticism was of the heads which were smelly and open, lacking any privacy. He also regretted the lack of a bar in the wardroom.

Goodall spent a good deal of time comparing the weights of British and US ships, which was not easy since the weight groups were differently defined. Overall, the *Lexington*, as originally designed as a battlecruiser, did not seem very different from that of a similar British hull though he thought *South Dakota* was rather heavy. He spent some time on the structural problems of the *Omaha* class, working with Hovgaard (Goodall was concerned that Hovgaard was a captain in the USN though not then an American citizen). By August 1918 Goodall was much involved in aircraft-carrier design, which would lead to the *Lexington*. He handed over the designs of *Hermes*, *Argus* and *Eagle* and wrote a lengthy paper on his (British) views on carriers.[9] Goodall's reports[10] deal with many other topics for which there is insufficient space here. There was a great deal of correspondence on the then novel electric arc welding. The United States was perhaps ahead on the more theoretical aspects but the United Kingdom was well ahead in application. Many in both countries – including Goodall – saw the day of the all-welded ship to be close.

Goodall benefited greatly from this experience; directly with the receipt of the MBE and the US Navy Cross for his work, but even more from working in a different background, at a higher level than usual for a still fairly junior officer. He also made a number of friends whom he would meet again in the next war.

Postwar Battleships

Goodall returned to the Admiralty to work on battleship design under Attwood. His first task was an evaluation of the surrendered German battleship *Baden* which was carried out in his usual impartial style.[11] The machinery, he wrote '. . . would be described by a naval architect as "compactly arranged" and by a marine engineer as "very congested"'. He noted that the design stresses were some 25 per cent higher than those allowed in similar British ships, which led to some expensive detail work. Though she was closely subdivided, there were a large number of penetrations which could lead to a spread of flooding.

His studies of USN and German designs gave him a broad basis for the next generation of British designs. The Royal Navy's battlefleet was ageing, worn out and many ships were armed with 12in guns. New battleships and battlecruisers were planned[12] under Attwood, for whom Goodall had great respect, culminating in Goodall's magnificent 'G3' battlecruiser. She would have displaced 53,910 tons, carried nine 16in guns, had 14in side armour and 8in deck protection. Her design speed was 32 knots though there is a note in the file, signed by Goodall, betting the DNC (d'Eyncourt) the sum of five shillings that none of the class would reach this speed. Though four of these ships were ordered, they were cancelled under the Washington Treaty.

That treaty did permit the RN to build two modern battleships, limited to 35,000 tons. These two ships incorporated many of the 'G3''s features, in particular, their short, heavily protected citadel with engines aft; but they were relatively slow ships at 23 knots. The battleship section was still the most prestigious post and carried with it membership of some important committees. Goodall received a Board Commendation for his work on the Naval Anti-aircraft Committee and was involved with torpedo tube design and with the provision of dry docks. With regard to the last, it was suggested that docks be built in the principal dockyards with dimensions of 1200ft × 150ft × 45ft over the sill.

In 1925 Goodall went to Malta Dockyard where he was in charge of battleship refits. There is mention[13] of problems in setting the floating dock to work. No records survive from this period but there are indications that, for the one time in his career, the pressure was off and his tennis improved.

Rodney was designed by Goodall and Attwood after the Washington Treaty. She is seen here off Normandy in 1944. (IWM A23978)

Destroyers

In 1927 Goodall was promoted to Senior Constructor and returned as head of the destroyer design section. The first postwar designs were in hand, much updated versions of the excellent wartime 'V & W' class. Goodall's more radical design with a streamlined bridge, only two boilers and a single funnel was rejected.[14] Goodall strongly supported a plan to boost one of the 'B' class to higher power and run trials at a very light displacement in order to counter the exaggerated speed claims of some foreign builders. There were a number of problems, real and imaginary, which led Goodall to utter the words 'I will impart the enthusiasm.' The scheme came to nothing when it was found that the boilers did not give as much steam as had been hoped.

L T Carter, who was Goodall's assistant on destroyers, remembers him as full of fun and a popular leader of the department's concert party. Cancellation of four of the 'C' class was a sour note. Goodall, like many of his generation, maintained that defence should be 'above politics'. He fought hard and successfully for the new, large ship tank at Haslar and, when it was completed, won a further battle to retain the older, smaller tank.[15]

In 1930 Goodall became Chief Constructor in charge of the major refits of the older battleships and also ran weapon trials on some of those about to be discarded.

Assistant Director

Goodall became Assistant Director of Naval Construction in 1932[16] with responsibility for a mixed bunch of ships and tasks including battleships, river gunboats and protection against bombs and shells and the testing of armour. The Washington Treaty permitted an increase of up to 3,000 tons in the displacement of existing battleships to improve protection but funds were very scarce and it was often undesirable to put one or more of the Navy's scarce battleships out of commission for years. He and the head of the protection section, Dudley Offord, were particularly concerned over the hazard of the above-water torpedo tubes in HMS *Hood*. He was awarded the OBE in 1934, which he regarded as an insult to one of his rank and he tried, unsuccessfully, to refuse the award.

In February 1936 Lord Strabolgi wrote an article attacking the Admiralty for its alleged failure to test the effect of bombs on battleships. It was decided that the First Lord should reply in the House of Lords and Goodall was asked to draft the response. In fact he drafted four papers – one that he would like to use, a more diplomatic version for the minister, a further paper giving the minister some background material, not to be divulged and, lastly, some more secret notes for his own benefit. Goodall began by pointing out that there had been numerous trials and he had been associated with most of them,

Crusader *designed by Goodall in the late 1920s. (Author's collection)*

and the fact that such a generally well-informed critic as Lord Strabolgi had not heard of them was a great tribute to the discretion of the officers involved. Major trials involved the ex-German *Baden*, HMS *Monarch* and HMS *Marlborough*, while test sections were fitted to the monitors *Gorgon* and *Roberts*.

The first lesson was that it was difficult to hit an anchored ship, even in ideal weather conditions, so most trials of penetration were carried out on shore by firing the bomb from a howitzer against a vertical target. Bombs would then be placed within a target ship and detonated electrically. In the 1920s much of the work concentrated on the protection of boiler uptakes while in the 1930s attention focused on the 'B' bomb to be dropped ahead of a moving ship and explode under the bottom. A very large float, Job 74,[17] was built to test the protection of the *Ark Royal* and *King George V* full scale. Goodall wondered whether, despite its size, the RAF would actually be able to hit it. His paper was passed to the Air Ministry for comment and, while they accepted what he had written on ships, they disputed the value of AA fire since a radio-controlled Queen Bee drone had flown low over the fleet for two hours at 85mph without being hit. However, the RAF could not guarantee to sink enemy battleships in all conditions and hence the country still needed battleships to deal with those of the enemy.

The Director of Naval Construction, Sir Arthur Johns, was a sick man and Goodall began to appreciate that he had a good chance of replacing him. He realised that his knowledge of submarines was limited and persuaded Johns to put the design section under his direction. Johns

had spent most of his career on submarine design and warned Goodall of the responsibility – 'After an accident I have not been able to sleep for two or three nights wondering if anything I had forgotten was the cause.' Almost immediately, he found structural problems revealed in the deep dive of HMS *Severn*. Goodall also lobbied hard among his many friends. Finally, the Deputy Director (Bryant) summoned Goodall and told him that he did not want the top post. There was still a little time for humour such as the spoof paper 'Hard Chine Horse', a mechanical horse for the cavalry which circulated at high level. It is probable that Goodall's health was deteriorating and this, combined with his increasing responsibility, led to fewer light-hearted moments. Every six months he set out in his diary his intentions for the following six months and, at the end of that period, he would review his achievements against those intentions.

Director of Naval Construction, July 1936

The essential passage of the lengthy 'Terms of Reference' for the DNC read 'He is the principal technical adviser to the Board of Admiralty, and the final authority on the design of warships and other vessels of HM Navy, and will be directly responsible to the Controller for all matters of design, stability, strength of construction, weights built into the hulls of ships, armour, boats, masting and all nautical apparatus for all ships whether building in HM Dockyards or by contract.'

Goodall saw his responsibility in a very personal light.

'In the Navy List after the name of each ship is a column headed – By Whom Designed. In that column is the name of the Director of Naval Construction. That fixes the individual responsibility for the ship, mark you, not for part of the ship!'[18]

He set out the principal problem of warship design in the 1930s in a paper to the Institution of Naval Architects.[19] The size and hence the protection of battleships was limited by naval treaties, while there was no such limit on the growing power of bombs, shells and torpedoes, a point he was later to press strongly at the inquiry into the loss of the *Prince of Wales*. There were demands for improved torpedo protection, for thicker armoured decks, for more anti-aircraft guns and for the carriage of aircraft, all demanding in weight and space. Goodall seems to have favoured scrapping the older *Royal Sovereign* class (and the carrier *Furious*) as a drain on resources but was not yet ready to see the end of the battleship. He was vexed by the campaign led by Captain Ackworth for a large number of very small, coal-fired 'battleships' which appealed to the prime minister.

On taking up his post, Goodall found that the Controller, Admiral Henderson, had been dealing direct with Forbes, the head of the carrier section, during Johns's illness. Forbes was appointed to Malta, as Goodall was not having any threat to his authority, though for some years he was to tell successive Controllers that Forbes was the best choice for his successor as DNC. Goodall was always aware of the need to have a successor ready: by September 1940 Lillicrap emerged as the favourite though Forbes was still his second choice.

As Assistant Director, Goodall had led the preliminary design work on the *King George V* class, rather surprisingly rejecting the engines aft arrangement as impracticable in a fast ship – though the G3 was much faster. Job 74 was exposed to bombs[20] and underwater explosions. The *Ark Royal*, designed by Forbes, had a considerable amount of welded structure which was of concern because of its novelty. The first all-welded British warship, *Seagull*, was designed by a young assistant constructor, Baker,[21] and, because of opposition to welding in industry, was built in Devonport Dockyard. The welded ship proved quicker and cheaper to build, lighter and stronger in service and Goodall's support for welding was strengthened.

Occasional sea trials provided a welcome break from the strains of office. His diary says of the destroyer *Jersey* 'she's a little beauty' – a comment with which few would disagree.[22] He enjoyed the trials of the fast motor torpedo boats designed by Vosper and Scott Paine though he expressed some doubts as to their operational value. He was a keen advocate of the Denny-Brown active fin roll stabiliser which he had installed in the sloop *Bittern* for trial. Subsequently, such stabilisers were fitted to a number of sloops and destroyers, though their full value was not realised until postwar developments in control theory emerged. The award of the CB in 1937 and the KCB in the New Year's Honours List of 1938 made up for the earlier, insulting OBE. In March of that year the RCNC mess presented him with a portrait of himself.[23]

There were plenty of problems; the depression had closed the works of many armour manufacturers and supply was a major problem, partly resolved[24] by a large purchase from Czechoslovakia. In the last days of peace Goodall was distressed by the deaths of two Controllers, Henderson and Backhouse, for whom he had a considerable regard. Two of the ninety-nine men drowned in the submarine *Thetis* were constructors, adding a personal loss to Goodall's worries over the cause of the disaster – 'Reggie and RB died, both great Controllers, and we lost Bailley and Hill in the *Thetis*'. He fought hard for awards to his staff and every Honours List led to a diary entry complaining that insufficient recognition had been given.[25] It was noticeable that constructors serving in uniform were treated much more generously than those in civilian posts.

There was an interesting correspondence in July 1939 with ACNS in which Goodall asserted that two *London*s were 'a match for *Deutschland*'.

War, the Early Years

The Director had to monitor the progress of each of the many designs within his department and would formally sign the building drawings accepting personal responsibility. It is clear that the frequency of his visits to any one section was closely matched to the degree of trust he had in the head of it. Such visits were not mere formality as most diary entries conclude with the words 'gave decisions'. On one occasion the destroyer section was ready for him and gave him a pro forma on which he was invited to tick either the 'yes' or 'no' boxes; he found an alternative solution on one point. One of the most trusted colleagues was Pengelly, head of the battleship section, running the *King George V* design and guiding the *Vanguard*; there is a note at the top of a page of his notebook 'DNC came in this morning, I told him he was wrong'. Later that day Pengelly notes that Goodall came back to say that he realised he was wrong. Early in 1939 Goodall showed the draft of a paper to the Institution of Naval Architects (INA) on the *Ark Royal* which he had drafted to Lillicrap who read it and said '"NO" – I revised the final copy'. Goodall was always willing to take criticism from bright assistants who could justify their argument – 'Watson a valuable critic though I think him wrong'.

At the beginning of the war Churchill was First Lord (Minister) and Fraser was Controller and, though Goodall had great respect for both, they could be irritating. Churchill's imaginative brain threw up many novel schemes, all of which had to be investigated, wasting the time of busy men and of Goodall in particular. There was Churchill's Baltic scheme – Operation 'Catherine',[26] the trench-digging machine known as 'Nellie', a torpedo cruiser, the Seadrome and many schemes for very large cruisers with 8in or 9.2in guns.[27] 'Nellie' did provide the opportunity for Goodall to make his first flight from Bristol to Lincoln, which he described as noisy and boring. The *Actaeon* net defence was used to a limited extent and saved a few ships but it is doubtful whether it was cost effective. Novel projects throw an unusual load on the man at the top since there is no existing section to deal with the work. The First Sea Lord (1SL), Pound, caused a different problem – 'I was horrified that 1SL wants still more capital ships; he is willing to give up anything to get them.'

Another scheme was that to raise the wreck of the *Graf Spee* and bring it back to the United Kingdom. An assistant constructor, Ken Purvis, went out and bought the wreck[28] but it was beyond salvage. He brought back several samples of armour and welding.[29] Goodall was careful to be absolutely fair and never displayed any sign of favouritism. However, there are several indications in his diary that he thought very highly of Purvis[30] but like a Victorian parent, 'Whom the Lord loveth, he chastiseth'.[31] On one occasion Purvis was sent for and blasted for failure to be polite to his seniors; on another occasion a senior naval officer complained of Purvis's rudeness but, after investigation, Goodall noted that he was right to be rude! There are many diary entries on the need to encorage initiative by young men while, conversely, one ageing man is described as 'an unenthusiastic slug'.

Goodall took his duties as Head of the RCNC very seriously, pressing frequently for the Corps to be brought into the Royal Navy. He personally carried out the highly marked viva examination of final-year constructor students at the RN College, noting one year '— promising, rest indifferent to poor'. The promising student was to become a distiguished head of the Corps himself.

The move of the DNC and his staff to Bath raised many problems since Goodall no longer had the direct contact with Board members: ' . . . freaks have the ear of the Board and I do not.' The lack of early technical input to decision-making meant that many blind alleys were laboriously explored, let alone the waste of time incurred by the slow and uncomfortable wartime trains between London and Bath. The situation was only remedied in October 1942 when Goodall and a small staff returned to Whitehall. Goodall noted that he would stop going into the office on Sundays in London as travelling took too long – though he was furious when he could not get a typist on Saturday afternoon.

The continual high-speed steaming in wartime led to a number of technical problems. The big 'Town' class cruisers had a structural weakness amidships where the strength deck was stepped down close to the point at which the armour deck was also stepped. The smaller *Dido*s had a problem with 'A' barbette, while the riveted shell of many destroyers leaked and contaminated the boiler feed water, and leaking decks made life a misery for their crews. After the German occupation of western Europe there were many foreign ships serving with the RN and there were problems in deciding whether they should be brought to RN standards of stability and strength or refitted to their original, usually lower, standards. Perhaps the last of Goodall's spoof papers, the *Soemba* docket, which circulated at high level, dealt with this problem in flippant style. The problem came to a head when the small, modern French destroyer *Branlebas* broke in half in a moderate gale and examination of her sisters showed their stability to be too poor to permit the necessary structural stiffening.

The biggest design error ever made in the Admiralty came to light when the first of the 'Hunt' class completed. The position of the centre of gravity was much higher than calculated and many changes had to be made to the early ships of the class. Goodall felt he was to blame as head of the department and had carried out the final checks on the design.[32] ''Hunt' class stability my first big mistake which was overcome without spilling too much gravy.' He had had a feeling that the stability was inadequate and had made some changes but he failed to realise quite how bad the problem was.

There were also plans to move the department to Canada should the Germans invade England and an officer was sent out to make preparations. A list of essential records was produced, headed with the model resistance data contained in the ISO – K books initiated by Edmund Froude.

Air raids caused loss of sleep at headquarters – Goodall's diary records twelve warnings in January 1941 alone – and there were interruptions for fire fighting, Home Guard and other home defence tasks, all essential but all taking energy away from the real job and there was even a petition from wives of the staff objecting to their husbands sharing the fire-watching task with female staff. (There were some real sexual problems which Goodall had to handle.) There were difficult decisions on when to take shelter and when to risk working on after warning was given. Air raids on shipyards caused loss of production capacity, particularly at Harland and Wolff, Belfast. There was a further, substantial loss of production due to the black-out, taking shelter and repairs to damaged homes. *MTB-501* was destroyed in an air raid on Gosport and Goodall grieved in his diary 'My pet'. He was pleased that the cavitation tunnel at Haslar for which he had fought was proving its worth in developing better propellers for such fast craft. He was always interested in ship tank work and commented at length on Gawn's historic paper to the INA in 1941, while his occasional visits to Haslar gave him great pleasure.

The range of problems which came to his desk was enormous and the diary entry which follows gives some idea of a typical day (12 May 1941):

> Air raid warning. A thick day. Cleared up points for New Construction, Repairs and Conversion meeting [a monthly review conducted by Controller]. Sent papers to Director of Dockyards re fire in *Cormorin*. Went into 8inch cruiser/carrier, endurance of *Abdiel*, preparatory work on quick replacement of damaged caissons. Talk with Pringle [Director of Electrical Engineering] and Director of Contract Work re supplying power to blitzed shipyards. Design of destroyer with full AA armament ('Battles') sent paper to Director of Naval Ordnance. Liaison officer with Free French called with CO *Le Triomphant*, said I could not advise as this ship was theirs but habitability was below our standards.

Air raid warnings, even when bombs did not fall, interrupted sleep on many nights, contributing to general weariness. The phrase 'a thick day' or even 'a very thick day' occurs all too often in the diary. He normally worked seven days a week but there are occasional entries in which, exceptionally, he notes taking a whole day off on Sunday – 'Lovely'. Overwork may have contributed to his rather frequent, minor illnesses such as colds.

The year 1941 began badly with the loss of the *South-ampton*, which exposed weakness in fire fighting. However, there was good news, too. The *Lightning* and *Fiji* classes were liked in service – there are several diary entries praising John, the constructor in charge of *Fiji* – as were the three classes of submarine. There were some heated arguments over the alleged wetness of the *Javelins*, said to be worse than the 'Tribals'. The constructor with destroyers, Harrison, did not think there was any great difference, though he politely disagreed with Goodall's paper on seakeeping.

The 'Flower' class corvettes were built in large numbers since there was no alternative anti-submarine (A/S) vessel design, although a twin-screw corvette, later the 'River' class frigate, was under development. Goodall rejected criticism of the 'Flowers', saying that there was a dead set against corvettes, which the Navy did not like. 'Moral is, don't try and force cheap ships on the Navy, which as Winston says, "always travel first class"' – though late in 1940 it was decided to give them bigger bilge keels. There was a bitter argument with a weapons department developing an ahead-throwing weapon, as their optimistic designers thought a 5lb charge would be sufficient to breach a submarine pressure hull; after much argument they agreed first to a 20lb and eventually a 30lb charge. Though the 'Hedgehog' was quite successful in service, even the 30lb charge was on the light side. Goodall took an enthusiastic interest in the first escort carrier *Audacity*, converting at Blyth.

The loss of the *Hood* distressed Goodall greatly as he had been responsible for the prewar plans to improve her protection which were not carried out. Talking to Thursfield, a well known naval writer, he pointed out that pitting the *Hood* against *Bismarck* was like taking White's old *Majestic*s to Jutland. The inquiries into the loss and re-evaluation of *Bismarck* were time consuming. A Soviet report of July 1941 gave the first accurate information on her size and equipment and this was backed up by reports from her survivors. Goodall thought that her advantages were all functions of her size; having studied the old *Baden*, he found *Bismarck*'s plans very familiar.[33] The year closed with the loss of *Ark Royal* followed by that of *Prince of Wales* and *Repulse*.

Goodall was worried that the welded torpedo protection of *Ark Royal* could have contributed to her loss but a re-examination of the Job 74 report and interviews with survivors reassured him – Goodall would usually interview survivors of important sinkings and damage incidents himself using his long experience of weapon trials to read the right lessons. Once the United States entered the war, he studied their damage reports too.

War Weary

'The truth is that everybody has been overworked for more than 6 years and calling for still further effort hasn't the response it had 6 years ago.' (Diary, 26 August 1942)

Hibiscus, one of the 'Flower' class corvettes that were designed by Smith's dock and strongly supported by Goodall when they were attacked as cheap and nasty. (IWM A5513)

The design of the King George V *class was started by Goodall as Assistant Director and approved by him as DNC. He was very upset by the Bucknill inquiry into the loss of the* Prince of Wales *(seen here) as he thought he was being made a scapegoat for her loss. (IWM A3897)*

Goodall had certainly overworked for six years and on the anniversary of his appointment he wrote '6 years as DNC and fed up'. The first problem was the Bucknill inquiry into the loss of *Prince of Wales*, which Goodall believed, seemingly with good reason, was set up to make him the scapegoat. He objected, without success, to the terms of reference which asked that any other losses should be enquired into but refused to consider the many examples of survival from serious damage. He also thought that he ought to have been a member of the committee. The first Bucknill report had to be withdrawn when it was shown to have errors of fact. Goodall still objected to the second version and was upset that it was issued without his objections.[34] He was, however, wrong in suggesting that she was hit by seven or eight torpedoes with 867lb warheads.[35]

During 1942 some admirals were beginning to see the carrier as the capital ship of the future. At a deputy First Sea Lords' meeting on 14 September 'it was decided that the carrier should be the core of the fleet of the future'. Goodall noted 'Hurrah'; it was interesting that he, who had made his name as a battleship designer should so strongly welcome the change. Only rarely did he put forward his own views on fleet structure, but in June 1942 he had written:[36] '. . . but it is advocated that the most important units of the fleet should be armed with aeroplanes rather than big guns.'

Production also suffered from weariness. There are many entries criticising bad management in the shipyards and, less often, labour, together with a smaller number praising the few men, usually the younger ones, who were doing well. At one meeting a distinguished shipbuilder criticised labour which drew Goodall's diary comment 'Satan rebuking sin!', though on another occasion he wrote 'Labour is *not* playing up as Bevin in his broadcasts makes out.' He felt that some of his own ageing senior officers were dragging their heels on the introduction of welding and put a young constructor, John, in charge, who soon merited the comment 'a treat to see a keen man getting on with it'. Changes to a design once work[37] had started always infuriated him: 'These alterations are maddening and have a bad effect on the morale of men.' On one set of proposed changes to the 'Battle' class destroyers he remarked:

1. No, unless corresponding weights can be surrendered.
2. Is not impractical, but has many objections and was not part of the Staff Requirements.
3. Out of the question without a complete redesign.
4. Existing arrangements are considered sufficient.
   PS I hope you get my point. This design has been prepared to meet Staff Requirements. It was very fully discussed before the Sketch Design was approved. If the Staff Requirements are now different, the Board must rule that all the work so far done is to be thrown overboard and we are to start again. SVG.

There was a major inquiry into the excessive profits made by shipbuilders which took a great deal of time and added to Goodall's irritation, particularly as the report seemed to blame him and his department.[38] Another irritation comes up repeatedly as in the following: 'Dealt with paper accumulation, the curse of this job, since so much time goes on committees and interviews.' The bombing of Bath disrupted work with a big, unexploded bomb outside the offices in the Spa Hotel. The Deputy Director, Bryant, who had planned the move to Bath, was killed while fire fighting in the raid.

The 'Battle' class destroyers had been designed after the losses off Crete with an exceptional (by British standards) light AA armament. The design was a difficult one but proved successful. They were much criticised by senior naval officers (especially Cunningham as First Sea Lord) for their size and Goodall was infuriated that 'the naval staff are the limit, having decided that the present 'Battles' are too big they draw up requirements for a ship which is bound to be much bigger and they want much more stuffed in.'

There was a similar problem with cruisers in which the big USN 6in cruisers were much admired by officers who complained that the modified *Fiji*s of about 9,000 tons were too big. *Bismarck* and *Prince of Wales* had shown the vulnerability of big ships to hits in the area of the propeller and rudder. For the 1943 cruiser design, Goodall attempted to overcome this problem: 'I should like the following scheme considered. About ¾ of the total power

to be developed on two shafts driving propellers at the stern . . ., the remaining ¼ to be developed driving propellers at the bow.' A model was made and tested at Haslar but the bow propellers were almost useless as most of the power they developed merely increased the drag on the hull through friction. A similar scheme was considered for *Lion* and when Goodall saw the model, he wrote 'Horrid is the first impression'.

A very big programme of frigates ('Loch') and corvettes ('Castle') was planned. They were designed for prefabrication using many structural steel works. Goodall fully supported the plan but put his finger on the main problems that there were too few men on outfit work, particularly electrical fitters (these ships had far larger electrical installations than earlier designs) and doubted the ability of management to cope. Two special fitting-out yards were created but, even so, the problems he foresaw were to delay the programme considerably.

In March 1942 Goodall was able to visit the Home Fleet and discuss the success and occasional problem of 'his' ships with the operator. He came back full of ideas for detail improvements. About this time he wrote an excellent and lengthy paper[39] on the work of Sir Charles Parsons, his only recreation in wartime apart from an occasional game of tennis.

One success story was the opening of the structural research establishment at Rosyth (NCRE). There had been a lot of pressure to improve protection against underwater explosions but most thought that a test site was all

A view of Camperdown, *'Battle' class, in original condition. This class was attacked as being too big and expensive but the requirement ensured that the next class would be even bigger. (WSS)*

that was needed. Goodall was insistent that a proper research facility was a necessary component and that it should be under DNC's control. He took a keen personal interest in the establishment selecting the Superintendent (Dudley Offord, RCNC) and the Chief Scientist (King). Offord told the writer that Goodall did all the setting up himself and handed over the keys to Offord together with a private letter full of good advice.

New carriers were a matter of considerable – though reasoned – debate on the rival merits of open or closed hangars. Forbes came back from the United States full of ideas, 'thinks our closed hangar is right and armour should be on the flight deck but we should have accommodation just below the flight deck and 3 bigger lifts; also believes a double hangar is necessary. In size we must think big both for ships and aircraft.' *Ark Royal*'s bow rudder did not work very well; the new carrier (*Malta*) was to have five propellers and two rudders aft. *Habbakuk*, an aircraft carrier to be built of reinforced ice, wasted further effort.

Goodall reached his sixtieth birthday on 18 April 1943, noting '60 today.[40] To my joy I now feel that I am free. I have always felt that I undertook to serve until I was 60'. He gave considerable thought to retirement which he discussed both with his wife and with Controller. He told the latter that he wanted to go six months before the Controller wanted him to go! More seriously, he saw Lillicrap as his obvious successor and wanted him to have a good five years as Director. He retired as DNC on 21 January 1944, remaining Assistant Controller, responsible for warship production and as an 'elder statesman'. He was punctilious in seeking Lillicrap's approval for major decisions. His retirement as DNC was marked by a formal lunch from the Board at which he was surprised that the First Sea Lord (Cunningham) saw the aircraft carrier as a passing fad and that the battleship would return – the diary notes 'we are poles asunder'.

The Fleet Train to support the task force in the Pacific was a major problem as the fast cargo ships and tankers which were needed were scarce and also needed to supply the United Kingdom and liberated Europe. There were political pressures to do it on the cheap and, in his view, too much effort was put into refitting ancient warriors which would never fight again, such as *Valiant*. Interviewing one naval officer returning from a spell with the USN, Goodall wondered '. . . to what extent is he like me after my spell in the USA in the last war ie swept off my feet by American enthusiasm'.

Perhaps his only professional failing was insufficient delegation, leaving too many problems on his own desk. When he was away from his office almost all papers were held for his return rather than being dealt with by his deputy. He did leave a great deal to men such as Pengelly, whom he trusted, but felt that others needed closer supervision. I feel sure that he could have found a bright young man to run a special projects group, taking much of the effort on freak ideas while office problems, such as fire watching, should have been solved at a much lower level. However, these are trivial points when weighed against his real achievement in creating the fleet of the Second World War. The three volumes of *Design and Construction*

of British Warships 1939–1945 (Conway 1995–6) form his professional monument.

Home life was depressing as his wife's health was failing and there were frequent flying-bomb explosions near their home, which they had to leave when the house was damaged. After Hiroshima he took great exception to two sermons in which the vicar suggested science was to blame for evil weapons. Goodall believed that atomic bombs were no more evil than conventional weapons and that Christians had the right to defend themselves. He challenged the vicar to a public debate, an offer which was not taken up.

His diary was primarily for office reference and there were few personal entries. The death of his brother and wife were briefly noted and, surprisingly, there was an entry one day 'Saw three daffodils on the way to work. Beautiful.' Sir Stanley's nephew, H R Jarman, says that though he was an autocrat in the office, it was Lady Nell who ruled the house. It was a happy marriage and she guarded him carefully; alcohol was bad for his ulcer and not allowed in the house but, a few days after her death, Sir Stanley went out and bought a bottle of sherry which lasted him a month. On VJ day there was a gathering of senior staff at the Admiralty to mark the end of the war. Goodall remembered a similar meeting on 3 September 1939, noting that he was the only person present at both.

After retirement he continued an active life leading technical work for the Welding and Ship Research Associations, as Prime Warden of the Worshipful Company of Shipwrights, Vice-President of the Institution of Naval Architects and the Institution of Professional Civil Servants.

He died on 24 February 1965 at his home on Wandsworth Common. He was survived by the late H R Jarman, nephew, whose assistance in this article is gratefully acknowledged.

On retirement, he had given a series of lectures to constructor students concluding ' . . . my first love was ships: man's finest creation. Looking back I feel I have cause to be thankful that I have been able to devote my working life to that love.'

Sources

A principal source is the Goodall papers held in the British Library as Additional Manuscripts ADM 52785–52797. His farewell lectures to the Constructors' course at the Naval College are held in the RCNC collection in the National Maritime Museum.

Notes

[1]   He presented the Goodall Cup to the RCNC for tennis which is still competed for.

[2]   While serving later in the USA, Goodall lectured on the design of the *Arethusa* to US constructor students and when his speaking notes turned up, the present author adapted them for an article in *Warship International*, 1/1983 (Toledo).

[3]   She was sunk while laying mines on the first night of the war (5 August 1914).

[4]   Taylor was trained at Greenwich and was a pioneer of ship model testing in the USA.

[5]   *Engineering*, 1922.

6   Those readers who have worked for government departments, in any country, will not be surprised to learn that much of his early correspondence was concerned with the difficulty in getting repayment for his travel expenses.

7   It seems possible that the US shells were better.

8   *Saratoga*, with a similar machinery arrangement lost all power when hit by a single torpedo in 1942 due to flooding of the switchboard.

9   N Friedman, *US Aircraft Carriers*. Annapolis. 1983.

10   Now held in the PRO.

11   *Trans INA*, 1921.

12   Campbell, *Warship 1–4*. Conway Maritime Press, London, 1977.

13   Sir Eustace H W Tennyson d'Eyncourt, *A Shipbuilder's Yarn*, Hutchinson, London, 1951.

14   Ships Cover, 'A' class. National Maritime Museum.

15   Recently closed by the DRA.

16   Goodall's diaries in the British Library begin at this date and form a major source for the later years. Unattributed quotations come from these diaries, identified by date.

17   Job 74

18   Retirement lecture, R N College.

19   S V Goodall. 'Uncontrolled weapons and warships of limited displacement', *Trans INA*, 1937.

20   During the war it was used as an air raid shelter.

21   D K Brown, 'Sir Rowland Baker', *Warship 1995*. Regrettably, my two heroes, Goodall and Baker did not get on well together. Goodall inspecting Baker's design for the LCT(2) noted, sourly, that he did not believe Baker's speed estimate. Goodall was always fair and the next day's entry read 'checked Baker's figures; he was right.'

22   He thought her beauty was spoilt by the conspicuous galley chimney and later ships from *Juno* had the chimney inside the main funnel.

23   This painting now hangs in the headquarters of the RINA.

24   The late delivery of gun mountings delayed so many ships that armour manufacture was able to catch up (forthcoming article in *Warship International*).

25   It should be remembered that honours for civil servants were far more numerous then than today and, by those standards, Goodall was correct in complaining.

26   D K Brown, 'Operation Catherine', *Warship 40*. Planning meetings were in the late evening; the second such meeting drew the diary entry 'WSC not himself tonight'; the next that he was 'wopsy'.

27   G Moore, 'Cruisers for the Royal Navy' the 1939–1942 Programmes', *Warship 1997–1998*.

28   It is believed that British Steel is the present legal owner of the wreck.

29   M K Purvis is writing the inside story of the *Graf Spee* 'salvage' attempt.

30   Purvis was later to win fame, first for his work on *Pluto*, then for the *Leander*s and *Sheffield*s

31   Before Purvis left, Goodall took him out to dinner and warned him to avoid night clubs!

32   It is a complicated story which cannot be fully covered here, See J English, *The Hunts*. World Ship Society, Kendal, 1987.

33   A paper dated 7 April 1942 contained in ADM 52793 in the PRO.

34   I am inclined to think that Goodall over-reacted to the Bucknill inquiry, perhaps because of his weariness.

35   The most accurate account of the damage is contained in W H Garzke and R O Dulin, *Battleships: Allied Battleships in World War II*. NIP, Annapolis, 1980.

36   ADM 22926, 'The Capital Ship of the Future.'

37   Work in the sense of detailed drawings, even worse if shipbuilding had started.

38   The profits were certainly excessive but the explanation offered in the report is far from convincing.

39   There is mention of assistance from a then young constructor called Stevens. I spoke to him years later and asked if he had drafted the complete paper but he replied that Goodall gave him a complete draft and he merely inserted a few figures from the records.

40   D K Brown, *A Century of Naval Construction*, Conway Maritime Press, 1983, gives the remainder of this quotation.

THE GERMAN NAVY FROM VERSAILLES TO HITLER

George Paloczi-Horvath examines the complex history of the German Navy's struggle to rebuild its strength after the disastrous end to the First World War and the crippling provisions of the Versailles Treaty.

'The naval disarmament provisions of the Versailles Treaty were very onerous, and it was really too much to expect us to accept them passively and do everything in our power to carry them out in all respects.'
Grand Admiral Erich Raeder, Struggle for the Sea

The *Vorläufige Reichsmarine* or 'interim Imperial [German] Navy' was established by the new German Republic on 16 April 1919. Its definitive successor, the *Reichsmarine*, came into being on 31 March 1921, lasting fourteen years until its infamous successor, Hitler's *Kriegsmarine*, was established on 21 May 1935.

Despite the early abandonment of the title *Vorläufige*, throughout its life the *Reichsmarine* was still an 'interim' navy, in that it could do little more than train and prepare for wars for which it was hopelessly ill-equipped. Nevertheless, new construction authorised during its life provided the foundation of the navy which went to war in 1939, a navy which had been training for war against much more powerful foes since the early 1920s.

The armistice which the German government's new leaders sought in November 1918 had a grievous impact on the wounded pride of many officers in the German Navy. Never mind that mutinous crews had rebelled against the insanity of proposals for a last desperate sortie against the British Grand Fleet to salve the honour of a High Seas Fleet which had not seen major action since Jutland; the issue for officers such as Vice-Admiral Ludwig von Reuter and superiors such as the *Vorläufige Reichsmarine*'s first commander Vice-Admiral Adolf von Trotha was honour as an end in itself.

The result was von Reuter's order on 21 June 1919 for the scuttling of the ships interned at Scapa Flow, thereby avoiding the inevitable eventual order to hand them over to the victorious Allies, with whom Germany was negotiating a peace treaty. The scuttling of fifty ships was a severe breach of the armistice and accordingly made harsh treatment even more certain under the Versailles Treaty which Germany was obliged to sign on 28 June 1919.

The Versailles Treaty Limitations

The main naval limitations of Versailles were contained in Section II of Part V (Articles 181–197) of the treaty, although other articles were also relevant to the German Navy. The first of these articles (181) read as follows:

After the expiration of a period of two months from the coming into force of the present Treaty the German naval forces in commission must not exceed: 6 battleships of the *Deutschland* or *Lothringen* type, 6 light cruisers, 12 destroyers, 12 torpedo boats or an equal number of ships constructed to replace them as provided in Article 190. No submarines are to be included. [Note: The '*Lothringen*-type' ships are generally known to historians as *Braunschweig* class ships.]

Article 182 obliged Germany to maintain minesweepers 'as fixed by the governments of the Allied and Associated Powers' in order to complete minesweeping prescribed by Article 193. Article 183 set the personnel limits of the future German Navy at 15,000, including 1,500 officers with no reserves and including coast defence forces.

The key Article 190 laid down the rules on replacements for the surviving tonnage and read as follows:

Germany is forbidden to construct or acquire any warships other than those intended to replace the units in commission provided for in Article 181 of the present Treaty. The warships intended for replacement purposes as above shall not exceed the following displacement:

Armoured ships	10,000 tons
Light cruisers	6,000 tons
Destroyers	800 tons
Torpedo boats	200 tons

Replacements were allowed after existing battleships and

cruisers were twenty years old and existing destroyers and torpedo boats were fifteen years old. Once again, the ban on submarines was reiterated: 'The construction or acquisition of any submarine, even for commercial purposes, shall be forbidden *in Germany* [author's emphasis].

In March 1920 the Allied powers allowed the *Reichsmarine* to retain in reserve two more pre-dreadnought battleships than had been hitherto permitted, plus two more light cruisers, four more destroyers and four more torpedo boats. While this was a significant relaxation of the treaty on paper, in practice it was not, as the *Reichsmarine* had great problems operating the originally permitted fleet. Throughout much of the 1920s only four battleships could be kept in commission at one time.

It will be apparent that there was nothing in the language of the *naval* provisions of the Versailles Treaty which actually forbade Germany from doing what it eventually did: set up companies in foreign countries to design and build submarines for service overseas, thereby providing Germany with valuable experience in naval design and construction.

However, in a memorandum probably written on 12 April 1922, the armaments magnate Gustav Krupp admitted that the entire clandestine Krupp-organised Ingenieur-Kantoor voor Scheepsbouw (IvS) shipbuilding operation in The Hague – where surreptitious work on U-boats was taking place – would be a violation of the Articles 168, 170 and 179. Krupp's interpretation of these articles was a strict one, as the language is specific in what it disallows, but is *not* specific in disallowing what actually took place.

Article 168 read: 'The manufacture of arms, munitions or any other war material, shall only be carried out in factories or works the location of which shall be communicated to and approved by the Governments of the Principal Allied and Associated Powers, and the number of which they retain the right to restrict.' There is nothing here about not setting up companies abroad.

Article 170 read: 'Importation into Germany of arms, munitions and war material of every kind shall be strictly prohibited. The same applies to the manufacture for, and export to, foreign countries of arms, munitions and war material of every kind.' Clear enough, but again the IvS operation did not break this rule.

Article 179 read:

> Germany agrees, from the coming into force of the present Treaty, not to accredit nor to send to any foreign country any military, naval or air mission, nor to allow any such mission to leave her territory, and Germany further agrees to the appropriate measures to prevent German nationals from leaving her territory to become enrolled in the Army, Navy or Air service of any foreign Power, or to be attached to such Army, Navy or Air service for the purpose of assisting in the military, naval or air training thereof, or otherwise for the purpose of giving military, naval or air instruction in any foreign country.

Germany's actions in the Netherlands and elsewhere which involved civilians did not break these rules; but some acts most certainly did, as some people involved were actually naval personnel in civilian guise.

Article 185 dealt with vessels to be surrendered; Article 186 dealt with warships to be broken up under Allied supervision and Article 187 with the handover of no fewer than thirty-two auxiliary cruisers. Article 192 forbade naval exports; Article 193 prescribed the required minesweeping (see above).

Article 194 stipulated voluntary engagement for German Navy personnel – twenty-five consecutive years for officers and warrant officers and twelve consecutive years for petty officers and men. No men were to be engaged other than those discharged because of the expiry of their terms of service. This number was not to exceed 5 per cent per annum of the total personnel numbers laid down by Article 183. The 5 per cent discharge rule applied to the 15,000 total personnel allowed and to each category: the 1,500 officers and warrant officers and the 13,500 petty officers and men. Therefore the discharge and engagement of no more than 750 men a year was allowed, including seventy-five officers and warrant officers. The same Article also stipulated that officers should remain in the service until the age of forty-five, though this did not prevent the future Grand Admiral Karl Doenitz from considering retirement in order to make more money. Article 194 also forbade officers and men in the mercantile marine from receiving any training in the Navy.

Article 195 restricted coastal armaments in the North Sea and the Baltic, including Heligoland, while 196 permitted certain coastal guns but nothing with a calibre greater than those already in existence. The earlier Article 167 controlled coastal gunnery ammunition stocks, only 500 rounds per gun for weapons larger than 105mm, and 1,500 rounds for 105mm guns and smaller. Article 198 forebade the retention of German naval air forces, though a hundred seaplanes and 1,000 personnel were allowed to be kept to search for mines until 1 October 1919.

William Manchester's history of the arms maker Krupp says that after Versailles the company was confined to making 'just enough cannon, gun mountings, ammunition hoists, mechanical firing devices, and armour as might be needed to replace rusting equipment in Weimar's small fleet.' One final point on the treaty: there is nothing in its language which specifically forbade Germany from equipping the eventual replacements for her old battleships with guns larger than 280mm (11.02in). But some *Marineleitung* staff assumed calibres larger than 280mm might be unacceptable, while some historians have wrongly assumed that Versailles forbade larger calibres.

Implementation of the Treaty

The Versailles Treaty was no more than paper without effective implementation and to accomplish this the Allies established the Inter-Allied Commissions of Control (IACC) under Article 204. The IACC included an Inter-Allied Naval Commission of Control (IANCC) headquartered in Berlin, with three subcommissions and sundry district committees. The IANCC was headed by Britain's Admiral Charlton, and the scope of its work was mostly confined to overseeing the breaking up of ships which were not allowed to be retained (Article 186) and the demobilisation of German Navy personnel. Article 209, which established the IANCC, also called on Germany to furnish all documents and designs as the Allies might require.

One scholar (Petersen) argues that the IANCC led a relatively 'non-controversial existence', despite being unable to prevent what he called 'substantial undetected German violations, including concealment of weapons, illegal recruitment and training, and proscribed research and development at home and abroad'. The latter is really a moot point, as has been described.

The IACC began operations on 10 January 1920 and from then until April 1922 Germany was consistent in trying to have the Commission brought to an end. Even so, the Germans went to some lengths to convince the Allies that they were sincerely implementing the treaty: Chancellor Karl Josef Wirth even writing in May 1921 that the German government was 'determined' to implement the treaty. From April 1922 the IACC and the IANCC were wound down and the Allies even suggested to the Germans that the IACC be replaced by a 'commission of guarantee'.

From 1920 to 1925 there were fewer and fewer IACC/IANCC inspections of suspect installations. Despite extensive evidence of breaches of the Versailles Treaty's provisions, the mood of bitterness in Germany – particularly during the Franco-Belgian occupation of the Ruhr – and the Allies' weariness led the Conference of Allied Ambassadors to announce on 25 November 1925 that agreement had been reached with Germany on disarmament issues and the IACC would be dissolved when its tasks were completed. In the event, the final departure of the remaining elements of the IACC took place in February 1927. The IACC was fairly toothless and there were no surprise inspections at one key group of installations. Its movements in Essen, where Krupp's factories were located, were always telegraphed ahead to the company if a visit was planned.

From that point on, ensuring Germany's observance of the Versailles Treaty became the responsibility of the League of Nations, which never exercised its right under Article 213 to investigate German violations. It will therefore be appreciated that while Versailles prevented the emergence of a German fleet which was anything like the size of its forebear, it proved impossible to police the treaty effectively in the face of continuing vociferous German opposition to the IACC's work, opposition which was always expressed in aggrieved terms coupled with protestations that Germany was fully implementing the treaty's provisions. In his study of German rearmament between the wars, Barton Whaley observes that the IACC's departure 'only meant that design, testing and training could proceed under thinner, less hampering cover'.

The Surviving Navy

What ships were left to Germany after Versailles? The battleships were all pre-dreadnoughts, comprising five

Braunschweig class vessels – *Braunschweig, Elsass, Hessen, Preussen* and *Lothringen* – plus three *Deutschland* class ships – *Hannover, Schlesien* and *Schleswig-Holstein*.

The *Braunschweig* class ships were launched in 1902–04 and the *Deutschland* class in 1905–06. *Preussen* and *Lothringen* were disarmed and used as tenders in 1918–19 (for F-boats in 1919) and were in reserve in 1922, though *Lothringen* was used for fleet duties from 1922 to 1926. *Braunschweig* was in service from December 1921 to January 1926 and was stricken in 1931; *Elsass* served from February 1924 to February 1930, both being scrapped with *Lothringen* in March 1931. *Preussen* was stricken in April 1929 and broken up in 1931. Meanwhile *Hessen* served from January 1925 to November 1934, was stricken in 1935 but was rebuilt as a target ship. *Hannover* served from February 1921 to March 1927 (1931 according to Erich Gröner) and *Schleswig-Hostein* from February 1926 to September 1935, during which time she was designated the *Reichsmarine*'s Fleet flagship. *Schlesien* served from March 1927 onwards.

These ships were all originally coal-burners, displaced around 13,000 tons (standard) and were armed with two twin 280mm (11.02in) turrets fore and aft, plus fourteen 170mm (6.7in) guns. *Schlesien* and *Schleswig-Holstein* were extensively refitted in 1932 and 1936, respectively with the middle funnel) plus the installation of eight new oil-fired boilers. Both survived to see action in the Second World War, the latter firing the war's opening shots at Poland's Westerplatte fortress at 4.30am on 1 September 1939.

Most of the cruisers were even older than the battleships. They comprised six 2,617-ton *Gazelle* class, fourth-rate light cruisers (*Niobe, Nymphe, Thetis, Amazone, Medusa* and *Arkona*) and two larger *Bremen* class cruisers (*Hamburg* and *Berlin*) which displaced 3,220 and 3,241 tons, respectively. The *Gazelles* were launched between 1899 and 1902 and the surviving *Bremens* were both launched in 1903. The *Gazelles* were armed with ten 105mm 40cal and two submerged 450mm torpedo tubes, while the *Bremens* were rearmed in 1920 with ten 105mm (*Hamburg*) or eight 105mm (*Berlin*), plus two 500mm above-water torpedo tubes.

Niobe was only ever in reserve and *Nymphe* was in reserve in 1922, the former being sold to Yugoslavia in 1925. *Nymphe* serving from 1924 to 1929 and *Amazone* from 1923 to 1929 (Gröner: 1930). *Thetis* served between 1922 and 1924 and was stricken in March 1929. *Arkona* served in 1919–20 and 1921–23, and *Medusa* in 1920–24 – both were stricken in 1920–30, though they were raised for use as floating anti-aircraft (AA) batteries in 1942. Of the *Bremens*, *Berlin* was lengthened by a new bow in 1921–22, serving from 1919 to 1921 and then again from 1922 to 1929. *Hamburg* served briefly in 1919 and then again from 1920 to 1927. She was also notable for putting down a Communist uprising in Hamburg in October 1923.

The balance of the fleet comprised an assortment of destroyers to make the dozen allowed to Germany, these being *V1–V6* (excluding *V4*), plus *G6–G8, G10* and *G11, S18, S19* and *S23*. These had all been launched between 1911 and 1913, displacing 650 to 670 tons. Utterly obsolete, the *Reichsmarine* always called them *Torpedoboote*. All

The battleship Schlesien *in* Reichsmarine *service with her crew turned out. The photograph was taken after the major refit which saw her two forward funnels trunked into one in order to clear smoke from her fighting top and rangefinders.* Schlesien *survived to fight in the Second World War. (CPL)*

were reboilered in 1921–23 and given new 105mm 45 cal guns. The 'G' series vessels were lengthened; displacement in these and the other vessels rising by 15 per cent in *Reichsmarine* service. Most were scrapped in the late 1930s or earlier.

In 1922 the *Reichsmarine* had twenty of what the Allies called 'torpedo boats' in commission, though seven were in reserve and more were allowed in reserve for cannibalisation. These vessels originally displaced between 533 and 700 tons, that of the last size (*T175*) being an exception in having a higher displacement than ships classed as destroyers by the Allies. The torpedo boats were all built from 1906 to 1911 and *T151–158*, *T185*, *T190* and *T196* were modernised in the early 1920s. Of these, *T151–158* and *T190* served the *Kriegsmarine*. The rest were scrapped in 1927–32, though *T108–111* (ex-*G7–8*, *G10–11*) also survived to serve the *Kriegsmarine*.

Otherwise Germany maintained an unarmed minesweeping force at Allied insistence to implement Article 182 of the treaty. There were thirty-eight minesweepers when the IACC began work in 1920 and thirty-seven in 1922, all being of 1916–19 vintage and displacing 515 to 690 tons (Breyer records thirty-three minesweepers serving between 1919 and 1932). All survived into the Second World War and beyond. Otherwise, in 1920 the

IACC/IANCC found that the German Navy also had on strength the gunnery tenders *Drache* and *Hay* and five other gunnery tenders. There were also eighteen picket vessels (later reduced to eight), eight fishery protection ships, two accommodation ships, four survey vessels, one sailing ship and sundry minor craft.

Reichsmarine *Leadership and Policies*

Given that the period 1919 to 1924 may be characterised as one of extreme instability in Germany, it is remarkable that the country was able to maintain any kind of navy in the circumstances. Many right-wing sailors in the *Marinefreikorps* were fighting their left-wing brothers in arms, both Communist and radical Socialist. The *Marinefreikorps* was later split between the *Brigade Rode* and the *Brigade Loewenfeld* and upon these formations' dissolution former naval personnel joined the *Brigade Erhardt*. The personnel in these formations were, of course, too busy fighting to man the fleet, but they were still included in the personnel totals stipulated by the Versailles Treaty.

On 13 March 1920 the *Brigade Erhardt* occupied Berlin in Wolfgang Kapp's abortive *putsch* against the treaty's conditions, in which *Reichsmarine* commander von Trotha was anything but neutral. Navy opponents to the Kapp *putsch* either took control of their vessels or declared themselves neutral in Kiel and Wilhelmshaven. A general strike now took hold. (Doenitz commanded one torpedo boat keeping watch on larger ships and their rebellious crews in Kiel.) On 17 March the rising collapsed with Kapp's resignation in the face of the general strike's popularity. (It is worth recalling that it was only because the swastika was the emblem of the *Brigade Erhardt* that Hitler decided to adopt it for his party.)

The Kapp affair led direct to the establishment of a Socialist government which then sought those responsible. A special *Reichstag* committee was appointed to establish the Navy's degree of complicity. Some 172 officers, including von Trotha, either retired or were removed. On 31 May, the anniversary of the *Skaggerak Schlacht* (The Battle of Jutland), according to Doenitz's biographer Padfield: 'those officers deemed to have taken no part in the affair were formally reinstated – at the expense of the deck officers who were struck from the Navy list as a class. This was a significant moment for the Navy and the nation; the government had graphic warning of where the true loyalty of the officers lay, and it was not with the Republic, yet they reinstated the corps almost *en bloc*.' The reason was a mixture of two factors: continued violent resistance by the Communists in the Ruhr and the Republic's unwillingness to weed out the old guard.

Von Trotha's replacement, Vice-Admiral Paul Behnke, had been recalled from retirement by Minister of Defence Otto Gessler in October 1920 and fared rather better with those in power in Berlin. Behnke then set about laying the foundations for a new navy. Under Behnke's leadership, Erich Raeder, the future chief of the *Reichsmarine* (from 1928) and of the *Kriegsmarine* (1935–43), continued his inexorable rise, despite being suspected of 'unconstitutional activities' during the Kapp *putsch*. Thereafter Raeder was relegated to the naval archives for two years, writing a history of German cruiser squadrons during the First World War; in July 1922 he was reinstated as a Rear-Admiral and was appointed to the key role of Inspector of the *Bildungsinspection,* or Training Department.

Before Behnke's appointment as Chief of the *Seekriegsleitung* (literally, Sea War Leadership, though generally rendered in English as Supreme Naval Staff), some of his work had already been done for him by Rear-Admiral Wilhelm Michaelis. In a September 1920 memorandum, Michaelis set forth the aims of the new *Reichsmarine*. It is significant that these were set by the Navy itself, not by the government; they were as follows:

1. The imposition of authority and the laws of the state in coastal areas;
2. The control of territorial waters along the German coast;
3. The prevention of piracy in German waters;
4. The defence of the coasts against annexation by other coastal states nearby;
5. The control of coastal seaplanes, especially those to East Prussia;
6. The performance of courtesy visits 'to demonstrate the standards of efficiency and the attitudes of the whole nation';
7. The provision of security against a blockade by smaller Baltic countries;
8. The performance of so-called 'cultural duties' such as hydrographic survey, fishery protection and oceanography.

These aims were wholly consistent with what was within the *Reichsmarine*'s limited powers. In the following year *Vorläufige* was dropped from the *Reichsmarine*'s title as it became the fully fledged navy of the Republic, albeit one charged with defending a *Reich* or 'empire' which no longer had its kaiser. The year 1921 was also significant for the laying down of the first replacement warship for the new Navy: the light cruiser *Emden*, of which more later. The winter of that year was also notable for the first torpedo-boat exercises which secretly practised how future U-boats might mount surface attacks at night on enemy shipping.

Karl Doenitz learned much from these manoeuvres and already his superiors appreciated that to cut France off from its friend Poland and fight a blockade of German ports Germany needed U-boats. The mounting of co-ordinated surface attacks by night, even by torpedo boats, involved keeping track of an enemy at the edge of visibility and then pressing home a strike in twilight or after darkness. These were effectively prototype 'wolf-pack' tactics, as practised to such deadly effect in the Second World War. One of the first intellectual appreciations of the potential of such tactics seems to have been a paper by *Kapitänleutnant* Wassner in July 1922, which argued that during the First World War U-boat surface attacks were the most successful forms of attack and lone U-boat operations uneconomic against convoys. Padfield quotes Wassner's paper as saying that: 'in future it will be essential for convoys to be hunted by sizeable numbers of U-boats acting together'. Surface-ship exercises to practise U-boat tactics continued throughout the period to 1935, and the real submarines, built to German designs, were used for trials in Finland and elsewhere.

One further event in 1921 deeply influenced *Reichsmarine* policy: the Franco-Polish military pact, under which France was to assist Poland in the event of war with either Russia or Germany. Soon the *Marineleitung* learned of the pact's provisions, specifically of Article 7 which pledged France to defend the short Polish coast and to land French troops to aid the Poles. The French promised a squadron comprising two armoured cruisers, four cruisers, four destroyers, three submarines and a minelayer.

The *Marineleitung* now further refined *Reichsmarine* priorities in the light of the Franco-Polish pact. These were now defined as:

1. To hinder an enemy landing (for which the *Marineleitung* complained that all significant points between Schleswig-Holstein and the Oder's estuary were either undefended or almost defenceless);
2. The establishment of naval supremacy in the Baltic and the maintenance of links between East Prussia and

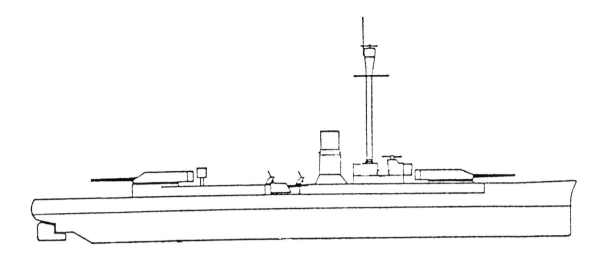

Design II/10 *represented the first effort by the* Marineleitung *to come up with ideas for the replacement of Germany's pre-dreadnought battleships. The concept resembles a coast defence monitor, albeit a powerfully armed one. Armed with four 381mm (15in) guns in two twin mountings, this design was rejected, like many others which followed. (Author's collection)*

Germany west of the Polish corridor – the protection of links with other north European states was also deemed important;

3. The protection of economically important trade in the North Sea.

Conflict scenarios under consideration by the *Marineleitung* in 1922–23 included a Russian–Polish war in which France helps Poland, Britain and Denmark are neutral, but Germany is not because she refuses permission to allow French troops to cross German soil to aid Poland. Another scenario was a war with both France and Denmark. Notably, no consideration was given to war with Britain and the most potent threats in German eyes at this time were the French *Danton, Courbet* and *Provence* class battleships with 342.9mm (13.5in) and 305mm (12in) main armament.

Behnke's stewardship of the Navy was also significant for the contacts established with Krupp to circumvent the Versailles Treaty's limitations. An agreement was signed between the Defence Ministry and Krupp on 25 January 1922 which, according to a Krupp memorandum, constituted 'the first steps jointly taken by the *Reichswehrministerium* and Krupp to circumvent, and thereby break down, the regulations of Versailles which strangle Germany's military freedom'. Already in the previous year Krupp had started clandestine military work in Sweden, developing a close relationship with Bofors.

Between 1920 and 1922 Krupp further developed its relationship with Dutch industry, purchasing – via the Krupp-owned holding company Siderius AG – Dutch shipyards, including IvS, which were to become so prominent in German rearmament.

During the early 1920s the German Navy performed its

first overseas visits since the war, although scarce funds restricted these to north European ports. The balance of Behnke's stewardship of the Navy included the design and laying down of the first replacement torpedo boats of the '1923 type' and the continuation of plans to evade the Versailles restrictions. Manchester says of the Jutland veteran Behnke: 'Unlike the flamboyant Tirpitz he was quickly forgotten by his countrymen, and in 1937 he died in obscurity, unhonoured by his Fuehrer. Yet Behnke, together with Krupp and Seeckt, had made the early Nazi triumphs possible.'

The *Reichsmarine*'s lack of cash to fund new construction and Germany's difficulties with the payment of reparations prompted one remarkable scheme to generate the money. Between 1925 and 1927 *Reichsmarine* warships were involved in a project proposed by the chemist Fritz Haber to extract the gold present in seawater. The scheme failed because the concentration of gold was much lower than had been originally estimated.

The Road to the Panzerschiff

The story of how Germany came to build the *Panzerschiff*, or armoured ship, *Deutschland* (which the British described as a 'pocket battleship') is a complex one, lasting from 1920 to 1928. The benchmarks in terms of likely opposition were the aforementioned French battleships. Under Behnke's leadership between 1920 and 1923, two designs were produced, one for a 381mm-armed (5in) coast defence ship (Design II/10) and one for an inadequate 210mm-armed (8.3in) heavy cruiser (Design I/10). In 1924–25 a better coast defence ship and a better heavy cruiser were designed under the leadership of Behnke's

The ancient light cruiser Arkona, *which with five similar vessels were all that the Versailles Treaty allowed the* Reichsmarine's *cruiser flotilla.* Arkona *served during the 1920s. She was stricken in 1929 but saw service as a floating AA battery in the Second World War. (CPL)*

successor, Vice-Admiral Hans Zenker, who took over on 1 October 1924. Both vessels were rejected for the same reasons as before: the coast defence ships could not deal with French cruisers and the heavy cruiser-like ships could not cope with French battleships.

This logjam prompted efforts to square the circle and produce a 10,000-ton ship able to deal with both battleship and cruiser opposition. The first was Design II/30 in 1925, with three twin 305mm (12in) turrets, the two aft in an asymmetrical superfiring arrangement similar to that later adopted for Germany's 'K' class cruisers. A new departure adopted for this and all future battleship replacement designs was a diesel powerplant comprising a triple-shaft 24,000shp arrangement giving a speed of 21 knots. Armour protection was as good as in Design II/10, but secondary armament at three 105mm (4.1in) AA guns and two underwater 533mm torpedo tubes was weak. Design IV/30 rearranged the main guns with all three 305mm turrets forward, and a better secondary armament of two twin 150mm aft, plus three 105mm AA. But armour was sacrificed to accomplish this. In Design V/30 two triple 305mm turrets were placed fore and aft, with secondary armament of six 150mm and three 88mm AA. Side armour, at 200mm (7.9in), was better than before, but this and all the previous designs since II/30 (judged the 'least unfavourable') were still rejected for their inadequate endurance.

The *Marineleitung* meeting of 15 May 1925 now considered a new design with II/30 as the baseline, but fitted with two twin 305mm able to achieve a rate of fire of one

per barrel every 25 seconds. This ship had both the requisite combat power and endurance. The two variations on this theme comprised Design VI/30 with two turrets fore and aft and Design VII/30 with both forward. Both had two twin 150mm turrets and three or two (VII/30) 88mm mountings. Armour protection was 250mm (9.8in) and triple-shaft diesels would have made 21 knots.

These were useful exercises, but it was felt that the Allies would object to 305mm guns, so they were reduced to 280mm (11.02in) in Designs I/28 and II/28 with triple turrets in the former and twins (both aft) in the latter. Other armament comprised four 150mm (two twins) and six or four (II/28) 88mm. The planners knew that time was pressing for a definitive design, as in 1925 the Versailles Treaty already permitted the first new replacement vessel, provisionally named *Ersatz Preussen* (the *Braunschweig* class battleship *Preussen* was completed in 1905).

Two more designs were now produced, Design I/35 for a 19kt coast defence ship with one triple 350mm (13.65in) and two twin 150mm aft, and the cruiser-like 24kt Design VIII/30 with two twin 305mm and six 150mm. But in August 1925 the decision to lay down *Ersatz Preussen* was delayed for another year, which meant that no steel could be cut until 1927 at the earliest. The indecision was seemingly ended after the 1926 fleet manoeuvres proved that the fleet needed a vessel combining cruiser and battleship qualities. This realisation spawned Designs I/M 26 and II/M 26 which were similar

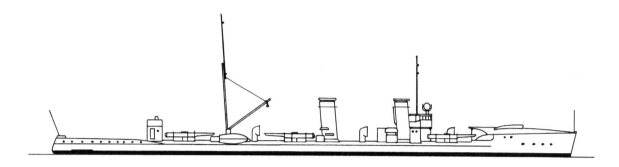

The torpedo boat VI *was one of a group built between 1911 and 1913 and by the 1920s was utterly obsolete. Nevertheless, she was among the dozen 'destroyers' allowed to the* Reichsmarine *by the Versailles Treaty. She and her sisters were reboilered in 1921–23 and given new 105mm 45 cal guns. (CPL)*

The light cruiser Emden *completed in 1925 was the first new major warship commissioned by the* Reichsmarine. *Based on a First World War design, and lacking the twin 105mm (5.9in) turrets which were originally intended for her, she was a less-than-satisfactory vessel but still provided valuable training experience. (CPL)*

The 'destroyer'-like appearance of the torpedo boat Greif *belied the fact that these little vessels were in no sense an equal of contemporary destroyers in other navies. However, most of the torpedo boats built under the* Reichsmarine *served with distinction in the Second World War. (CPL)*

to what became *Deutschland*. Both had two triple 280mm and eight 120mm AA, the latter differing only in its six 37mm AA and a higher aft tower.

This apparent resolution was shortlived though, as by June 1927 the conservative Zenker had asked for yet another four designs, from which a winner was finally chosen. The losing contenders were Type A, another coast defence ship with four 381mm; Type B1, a variant of A with six 305mm; and Type B2, as B1 but with thinner 200mm armour and a higher 21kt speed.

The winner was Type C, with six 280mm guns in two turrets, 100mm armour and a 26–27kt speed. With a range of 35,000m, Type C's 280mm guns could easily outrange the *Voltaire*'s guns' 23,000m range. Secondary armament comprised eight single 150mm and, initially, only three 88mm. Assessment of material in the German military archives in Freiburg suggests that the final debate was skewed in Type C's favour.

But the *Reichsmarine* was not out of the woods yet, as construction of the first *Panzerschiff* was a major issue in the 1928 elections, with both the Social Democrats and the Communists opposing the procurement on economic grounds. *Deutschland*'s keel was finally laid down on 5 February 1929 at the Deutsche Werke, Kiel. She was launched in May 1931 and was completed in April 1933, three months after Hitler came to power. By this time, two more such ships, *Admiral Scheer* (*Ersatz Lothringen*) and *Admiral Graf Spee* (*Ersatz Braunschweig*) were under construction at the Wilhelmshaven navy yard.

Though nominally supposed to have been squeezed within the 10,000-ton limit thanks to a combination of welded construction, diesel propulsion and other measures, *Deutschland*'s actual displacement was much greater. Gröner records a standard displacement of 10,600 tons, a 'designed' displacement of 12,630 tons and a maximum displacement of 14,290 tons. *Die Deutschen Kriegschiffe* says her fully armed displacement was recorded as 14,503 tonnes in November 1937.

New Cruisers

Before *Deutschland*, the *Reichsmarine* commissioned relatively few major warships. The first was the coal-fired

The light cruiser Königsberg *in* Reichsmarine *service (note the ensign aft). Note the triple 500mm (later 533mm) torpedo tubes visible amidships and aft of the ship's boats. (CPL)*

light cruiser *Emden* in 1925, which replaced the *Gazelle* class cruiser *Niobe*. She too managed to break the Versailles Treaty's 6,000-ton cruiser displacement limit, weighing in at 6,990 tonnes fully armed. Laid down in Wilhelmshaven in 1921, *Emden* was originally intended to be armed with four twin 150mm turrets, but these were forbidden by the IANCC, so she was instead fitted with eight single 150mm from existing stocks, allowing a broadside of six. Other armament as designed comprised two, later three 88mm and initially four 500mm torpedo tubes. Strikes delayed construction and she was not regarded as a particularly impressive vessel on completion, though she bore a proud name and took part in extensive training cruises.

After *Emden* Germany completed four more light cruisers between 1929 and 1931 to replace the cruisers *Thetis*, *Medusa*, *Arkona* and *Amazone*. Three were the so-called 'K' cruisers – *Königsberg*, *Karlsruhe* and *Köln* – all laid down in 1926 in Wilhelmshaven and at the Deutsche Werke, Kiel in *Karlsruhe*'s case. They were completed in 1929 and 1930 (*Köln*). They were radical improvements on *Emden*, in that they were oil-fired and diesel-powered and armed with nine 150mm guns in three triple turrets,

plus four 88mm AA and twelve 500mm torpedo tubes (four triples; 533mm from 1934).

Once again, considerable licence was taken with their declared displacements: 7,500 tons fully loaded for *Königsberg*, 7,700 tons for *Köln* and as much as 8,350 tons for *Karlsruhe*. As with *Deutschland*, their alleged ability to meet the 6,000-ton limit was ascribed to the wonders of welded construction and lighter diesel propulsion – hogwash swallowed by many observers. The fourth, similarly armed light cruiser built under Weimar, *Leipzig*, was laid down in Wilhelmshaven in 1928 and was completed in 1931. She differed visually from her predecessors in having one rather than two funnels; standard displacement was 6,515 tons and 8,250 tons full load. (Her sister *Nürnberg* (*Ersatz Nymphe*) was launched in December 1934 and commissioned into the *Kriegsmarine* in November 1935.) Not all of these cruisers were entirely successful vessels though: the 'K' cruisers construction was not quite strong enough for the rigours of world cruises. Their combined diesel and steam engines operated separately, providing a 10kt cruising speed on diesels and a 32kt turbine 'dash' speed.

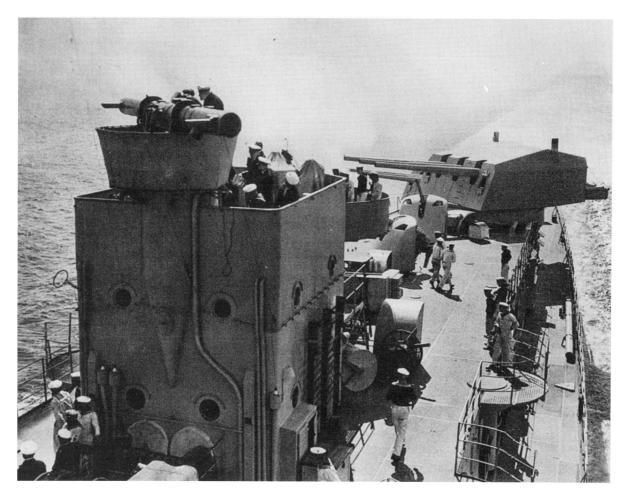

The light cruiser Königsberg *at gunnery practice. Visible are her two after triple 150mm (5.9in) mountings and two 88mm AA guns. Note the asymmetrical positioning of the two 150mm mountings, common to all the 'K' cruisers and note also the early model 88mm mounting. (CPL)*

Torpedo Boats, Schnellboote *and Other New Construction*

During this period no destroyers as such were completed for the *Reichsmarine*. The *Möwe/Wolf* class were based on the similar First World War *H145* type of 1917–18 vintage. The six *Möwe* class torpedo boats were laid down in 1924 and 1925 and were completed in 1926–28. As destroyer replacements, they were supposed to displace 800 tons standard, but in fact weighed in at 924. Armed with three 105mm guns and six 500mm (533mm after 1931) torpedo tubes, these 33kt vessels were classified as *Torpedoboote Typ 23* by the *Reichsmarine* which, like its successor, never called them destroyers. The *Möwe*s were followed by six similarly armed, *Typ 24 Wolf* class torpedo boats completed between 1927 and 1929. (Germany's first genuine new destroyers, the 1934 type *Z–1* to *Z–4*, displaced 2,223 tons standard; though designed under

Weimar to breach totally Versailles' limitations, they were not completed until 1937.)

The *Schnellboote* – which the Allies later erroneously called E-boats – were the product of early research into fast motor torpedo boats in the late 1920s. Two such were built in 1928, the *Narwal UZ(S).18* and the so-called K-boat *UZ(S).12*. Both these Thornycroft-type boats were failures and the next effort, a round bilge boat by Lürssen, was the first 39-ton S-boat, commissioned in August 1930 in total secrecy as the *UZ(S).16* – a designation later changed to *W.1* (*Wachboot* – Guard Boat). This vessel was much more successful and in 1932 Lürssen built four more S-boats, *S.2* to *S.5*, but with a greater displacement at 45 tons. Armament of these mahogany/light metal construction boats comprised two fixed torpedo tubes, one 20mm gun and one machine gun.

The other surface warships to be built for the *Reichsmarine* were two fishery protection vessels *Elbe* and *Weser*, commissioned in 1931; the gunnery training ship

The gunnery training ship Bremse *was a curiosity which was originally conceived with a more warlike appearance than this view shows and was even regarded as a* de facto *small light cruiser by some. Funnel caps and the large foremast with rangefinders have been removed to reduce topweight (and pacify political worries).* Bremse *took part in the invasion of Norway in 1940. (CPL)*

The end-result of all the frustrating design efforts of 1920–28 was design 'C', which became the Panzerschiff *(armoured ship)* Deutschland. *The theory behind her impressed the outside world: a ship which could outrun a battleship and outgun any cruiser (although not battlecruisers). In the event* Deutschland *saw service as a commerce raider in 1939, but did not engage in any fleet actions under her second name* Lützow. *She was reclassified – rather more accurately – as a heavy cruiser in 1940. (CPL)*

Bremse, completed in 1932; and sixteen motor minesweepers (*R1–16*) of 1929–34 vintage. *Bremse* prompted worry in the German foreign ministry, at whose behest her original appearance (a cruiser-like funnel top and mast) was altered. Armed with four 127mm guns, she was in fact the trials ship for *Deutschland*'s diesels.

U-Boats

Germany never stopped working on U-boat design and kept her hand in via foreign companies set up for the purpose, notably IvS. Her first own first coastal submarines to be built since 1918, the Type II AU-boats *U–1* to *U–6* built in 1934–35, were direct descendants of the German-designed Finnish submarine *Vesikko*. They displaced 252 tons surfaced and 303 tons dived and were armed with three 533mm torpedo tubes for five torpedoes or twelve mines. There remain some questions over the construction of these vessels and the degree of direct foreign involvement in their manufacture. Hitler ordered Raeder to hold off from construction in 1934, in order not to prompt too early a reaction from the Western powers.

Similarly, Germany's first ocean-going Type I A U-boats, *U–25* and *U–26* built in 1935–36, were directly descended from the Turkish *Gur* (which had previously been the Spanish *E1* built to German design in Cadiz). The Type I A displaced 862 tons surfaced and 983 tons dived and were equipped with six 533mm tubes (four bow; two stern) with fourteen torpedoes or up to twenty-eight mines. The net of covert activity stretched not only to Holland, Spain, Finland and Turkey. Japan was given assistance with submarine construction.

Conclusion

It will be appreciated that, for all its protestations, Weimar Germany had a clear record of attempting to evade the Versailles Treaty's limitations in every substantive way from the day it was signed. It is also clear that, notwithstanding the bravery of some social democrat opponents of rearmament who reported violations to the Allies at great personal risk, most of the German body politic was

in on the conspiracy, though details were left to the military and industrialists. Though it is outside the scope of this article, naval aviation also developed thanks to the Allied powers' laxity, and partly thanks to the loophole which allowed naval anti-aircraft gunners to fire at targets towed by aircraft. Raeder's memoirs go into detail on his unsuccessful battle to retain naval control over naval aviation after the *Luftwaffe* came out of the shadows in 1935. Whether the course of German, and European, history would have been altered by a less humiliating peace remains open to question, though the evidence suggests that any restriction would have invited contempt and an effort at evasion.

Sources

For the actual text of the Versailles Treaty, see *The Treaties of Peace 1919–1923*, Vol 1, Carnegie Endowment for International Peace (New York, 1924). For an assessment of the treaty and German breaches of its naval limitations, see Neil H Petersen, *The Versailles Treaty*, in *Encyclopedia of Arms Control and Disarmament*, Vol II, Richard Dean Burns (ed.), Scribner's (New York, 1993), pp621–37.

For the strength of the German Navy in this period, see *Conway's All the World's Fighting Ships 1922–1946* (London, 1980), pp218–53, though this does contain errors which have been corrected by reference to a key source, Siegfried Breyer, *Die Marine der Weimarer Republik*, Marine-Arsenal Sonderheft, Vol 5 (Friedberg/Dorheim, Germany, 1992). For greater detail on German warships in the period, see Erich Gröner, *German Warships 1815–1945*, Vols I and II, Conway (London, 1990); Hildebrand, Rohr and Steinmetz, *Die Deutschen Kriegsschiffe* (Koehlers/Herford, Germany, 1980).

For details on clandestine naval work within and outside Germany, see William Manchester. *The Arms of Krupp 1587–1968*, Michael Joseph (London, 1969), pp384–408. See also Barton Whaley, *Covert German Rearmament 1919–1939, Deception and Misperception* (Frederick, 1984), and William Shirer, *The Rise and Fall of the Third Reich*, Secker & Warburg (London, 1960).

For the best record of the design process which produced the armoured ship *Deutschland*, see Gerd Sandhofer, *Das Panzerschiff 'A' und die Vorentwürfe von 1920 bis 1928*, Militärgeschichtliche Mitteilungen Vol 1/68, Militärgeschichtlichen Forschungsamt (Germany, 1968), pp35–62.

THE ORIGINS OF THE FRENCH 8,000-TONNE CRUISERS OF 1922

The *Duguay-Trouin* class was the first of the *Marine Nationale*'s interwar cruiser types. **John Jordan** traces the development of the design from the abortive scout cruisers of the *Lamotte-Picquet* class of 1914.

The advent of the dreadnought battleship was to have a particularly disruptive effect on French pre-war naval programmes. Construction in the French shipyards was notoriously slow, and there was in consequence a significant time-lag between the planning process and the completion of a major new type of warship. The first French dreadnoughts of the *Courbet* class were laid down only in 1910–11, and battleship construction then became an urgent priority in the lead-up to the First World War, with eight 'super-dreadnoughts' of the *Bretagne* and the *Normandie* class being laid down by January 1914 and a further four, the *Lyon* class, authorised in 1912.

At the same time it became apparent that there was an important gap in the construction programme. The other major European navies had quickly appreciated the need for a new class of small, fast cruiser to scout in advance of the battle line and to lead the destroyer flotillas. Even the relatively small Italian and Austro-Hungarian navies were constructing their own 27-knot 'scout' cruisers armed with 100mm–120mm guns. The *Marine Nationale*, on the other hand, had only slow, bulky armoured cruisers designed to fight in the pre-dreadnought battle line, together with a handful of elderly protected cruisers completed before the turn of the century.

The first public acknowledgement by the *Marine Nationale* of the need for a more modern type of cruiser was the inclusion of ten *éclaireurs d'escadre* (fleet scouts) in the Naval Programme of March 1912, for completion by 1920. This could hardly be said to constitute an ambitious programme, given that the same law decreed a battle fleet of no fewer than twenty-eight capital ships. There was, moreover, some debate as to the sort of ship required. Initial sketch designs prepared in 1913 were for a 6,000-tonne 'fighting cruiser' similar in conception to the British 'Town' class with 50–100mm belt armour, 10×138.6mm/45 (5.4in) Mod.1910 guns and a speed of 27 knots. This was criticised as too large and too expensive for the scouting role, and, following an extensive review of developments abroad, plans were drawn up for a smaller, faster ship with minimal protection.

The prototype of the new cruisers, named *Lamotte-Picquet*, was to be ordered from the Arsenal de Toulon in 1914, with orders for two further ships to be placed with private shipyards the following year. Designed displacement was 4,500 tonnes, with an armament of eight single 138.6mm/45 Mod.1910 guns, four of which were disposed on the centre-line fore and aft, with the remaining guns in casemates amidships (see drawing). There were also two single 47mm guns and four fixed submerged torpedo tubes of 450mm (17.7in) calibre. A narrow armour belt of 28mm (1.5in) covered only the ship's vitals. A mix of coal- and oil-fired boilers powered four-shaft turbines, providing 40,000shp for a maximum speed of 29 knots. By this time the ships were being referred to as '*Convoyeurs d'escadrilles*' ('Flotilla leaders'), suggesting that their role would be similar to that of the British *Arethusa* class. However, in size, armament and overall configuration they were closer to the latest German light cruisers, which were multi-purpose ships capable of both the scouting and the flotilla role. The principal difference between the *Lamotte-Picquet* and the German ships was the sacrifice of protection for an additional two knots of speed.

The revised design did not find favour in all quarters. In attempting to cover all the latest developments abroad rather than focusing on the specific requirements of the French battle fleet, the designers had all too clearly come up with a compromise design which fell between two stools. The *Lamotte-Picquet* was now too lightly protected to take on other cruisers of comparable size, but was over-gunned for the flotilla leader role and too expensive to be built in the numbers required.

As one might have expected given the tardiness with which the French embarked on the construction of modern light cruisers, there were a number of conservative features in the design. The hull configuration was particularly dated, with its straight stem and casemate guns amidships. Casemates had been abandoned by both the British and the German navies for their light cruisers because they restricted firing arcs and made the guns less responsive in the close-range combat likely in a flotilla

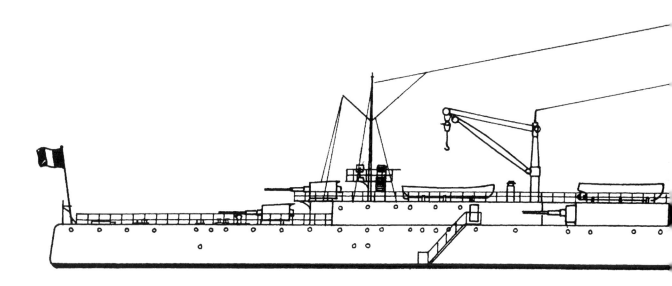

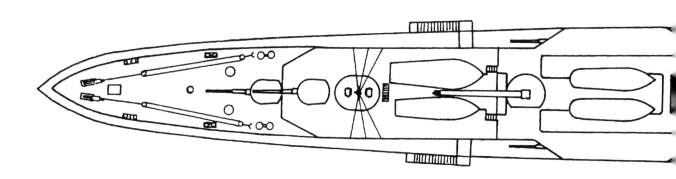

Lamotte-Picquet *1914: profile and plan views.*
Profile and plan views of the Convoyeur d'escadrilles de 4500t, *based on official plans dated Paris, 9 May 1914. Note the traditional hull configuration, with the midships guns in casemates. The funnels are reminiscent of German cruisers of the period. (Drawn by author)*

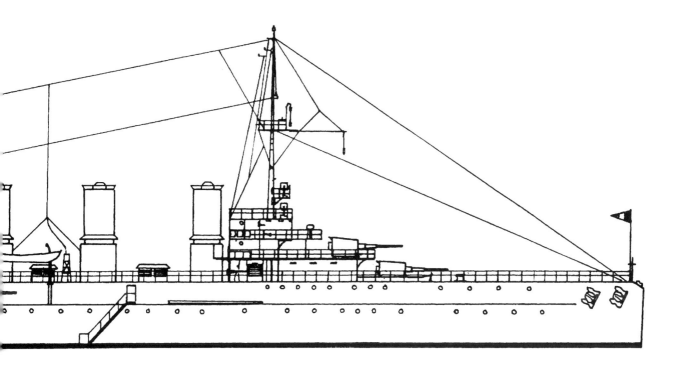

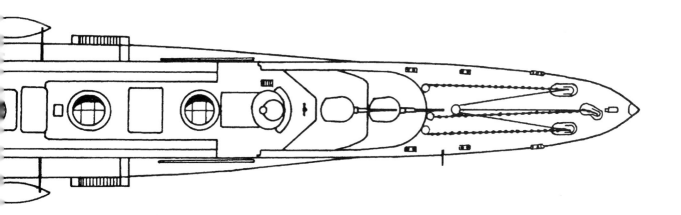

engagement. Once high-side armour was suppressed there was even less justification for their retention in the French design. The *Lamotte-Picquet* also retained a mixed coal- and oil-fuelled 'cruiser' propulsion plant, whereas the latest British scouts of the *Arethusa* class had an uprated 'destroyer' plant fuelled exclusively by oil to give them their designed maximum speed of 30+ knots.

To complicate the issue further, in 1914 the French Naval Staff called for the incorporation of eight *'grands éclaireurs d'escadre'* into the 1912 Programme. Inspired by the British *Queen Elizabeth*s, the first of which had been laid down in 1912, these would have been fast battleships with an armament of eight 12×340mm, a 270–280mm (10.5–11in) main belt and a top speed of 26–28 knots intended to operate on the wing of the battle fleet. It must have been particularly tempting for the *Marine Nationale*, which had no light cruisers of modern design, to opt for the Fisherite concept of using fast battleships or battle-cruisers as the scouting wing of the battlefleet, with close-range tactical scouting performed by large destroyers (a strategy actually implemented during the 1920s with the three-ship *contre-torpilleur* division).

Many younger officers of the *Marine Nationale* would have been particularly receptive to these revolutionary ideas, and in consequence there was little enthusiasm for the *Lamotte-Picquet* design. With the outbreak of war the project was suspended, but the Arsenal de Toulon was charged with continuing its preparatory work on the new cruisers, with a view to beginning construction the following year on a revised design. The Technical Committee met the following July to review the new proposals drawn up by *ingénieur général* Doyère and his design team. The changes to the original design were relatively modest: a slightly larger hull of 5,026 tonnes and an increase in speed of 0.5 knots. The only significant modifications were the addition of four single 65mm

anti-aircraft guns, the suppression of the mainmast to clear arcs for the latter, and a reduction from four to two shafts. The revised design still proved too conservative for the committee, which rejected it by nine votes to two with one abstention.

In the meantime, the naval dockyards had become fully occupied in maintaining a fleet at war, and were unable to cope with current orders; moreover much of the manpower of the dockyards and the private shipyards had been syphoned off to fill the ranks of the French Army. It was therefore decided to abandon the construction of new cruisers until the end of the war, when designs could better be informed by the experience of conflict. Thus the C-in-C of the French Fleet, faced with the need to confront the Austro-Hungarian Navy in the Adriatic, would be compelled to use armoured cruisers in these narrow waters, with the consequent loss of the *Léon Gambetta* to the Austrian submarine *U–5* in 1915.

The light-cruiser project was revived as a matter of urgency in the immediate postwar period. *Projet 171*, a statement of intent placed by the new Navy Minister Georges Leygues before the *Assemblée Nationale* on 13 January 1920, proposed the abandonment of the construction of the battleships of the *Normandie* class, conversion of the battleship *Béarn* into an aircraft carrier, and the institution of a new programme of light craft, including six cruisers and twelve *torpilleurs-éclaireurs*. The last would evolve into the *contre-torpilleurs* of the *Jaguar* class, charged with the dual mission of scouting for the French fleet and countering the destroyer flotillas accompanying the enemy fleet.

The initial proposal for the cruiser, approved by the *Conseil Supérieur de la Marine* in July 1919, was derived from the cruiser designs of 1914–15. The hull was only marginally larger, but power was further increased to 54,000shp for 30 knots, and modifications were made to

LAMOTTE-PICQUET CLASS (1914)

Name	Builder	Laid down	In service	Fate
1914 Programme				
Lamotte-Picquet	Arsenal de Toulon	1915	1918	Cancelled 1915
....		1915	1919	Cancelled 1915
....		1915	1919	Cancelled 1915

Characteristics (as designed)

Displacement	4,500 tonnes normal 6,000 tonnes full load
Length	138.0m pp (453ft)
Beam	13.8m (45ft)
Draught	4.8m (16ft)
Machinery	12 Guyot-du Temple boilers; 4-shaft steam turbines for 40,000shp; speed 29kts
Fuel	coal 300tonnes; oil 500 tonnes; endurance 3,300nm at 16kts, 775nm at 29kts
Armament	8–138.6mm/45 Model 1910 in single mountings; 2 single 47mm saluting guns; 4 single submerged tubes for 450mm torpedoes
Protection (belt)	28mm
Complement	357

FRENCH LIGHT CRUISER PROJECTS 1914–1920

	Lamotte-Picquet 1914 *convoyeur d'escadrilles*	**Modified design July 1915**
Displacement (all tonnes)	4,500	5,026
Length (m)	138 pp	143.8 pp
Beam (m)	13.8	14.25
Draught (m)	4.8	4.9
Propulsion	4 shafts 40,000shp = 29kts 3,300nm at 16kts	2 shafts 44,000shp = 29.5kts 3,800nm at 14kts
Armament	8 × I 138.6mm 2 × I 47mm 4 × I 450mm TT	8 × I 138.6mm 4 × I 65mm AA 4 × I 450mm TT
Armour (mm)	28 belt	(as 1914 design)

	Project 171 Sept 1919 *conducteur d'escadrilles*	**Final design May 1920** *croiseur léger*
Displacement (all tonnes)	5,270	8,000
Length (m)	145 pp	175.3 pp
Beam (m)	14.5	17.2
Draught (m)	5.2	5.6
Propulsion	2 shafts 54,000shp = 30kts	4 shafts 102,000shp = 34kts 4,500nm at 15kts
Armament	4 × II 138.6mm 4 × I 75mm AA 4 × III 550mm TT	4 × II 155mm 4 × I 75mm AA 4 × III 550mm TT
Armour (mm)	30 turrets, CT 20 magazines	

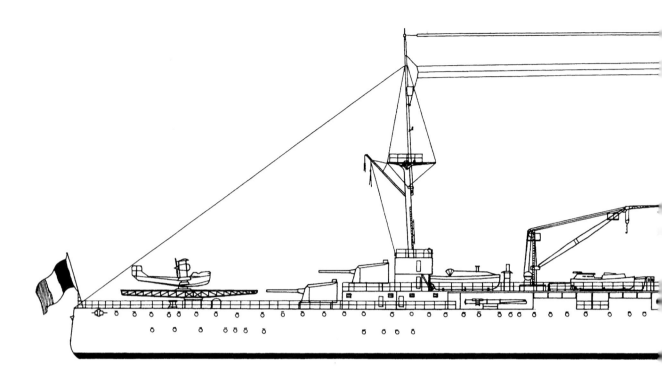

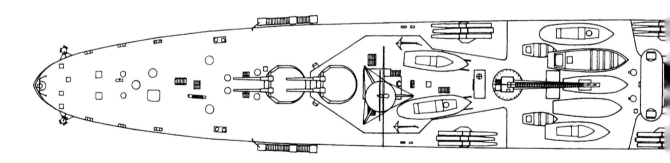

Primauguet *1926: profile and plan views.*
The profile and plan views are based on official plans dated Brest, 26 July 1926. They show Primauguet *as originally completed with the experimental catapult on the quarterdeck. The 4m rangefinders located on the shelter deck between the funnels were found to be unusable when the 75mm AA were fired. The low, slightly raked funnels, the heavy tripod foremast topped by the main fire-control director, and the tall* Duquesne *class. Note the prominent ventilation trunking between and on either side of the twin funnels. (Drawn by author)*

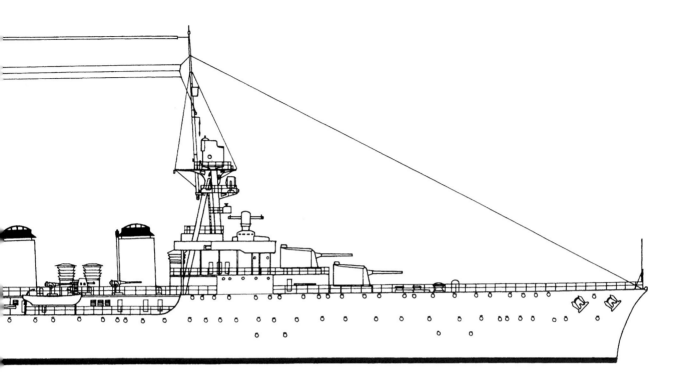

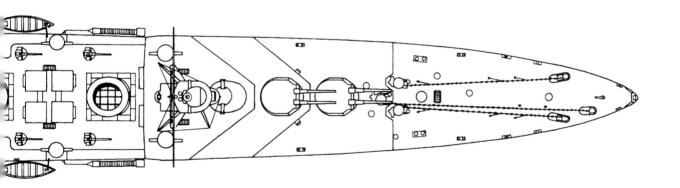

the layout of the armament. The eight 138.6mm guns would be in twin turrets fore and aft, freeing the waist of the ship for four triple banks of tubes for the new 550mm torpedo. The 65mm AA guns of the 1915 proposal were replaced by a 75mm AA gun then under development.

The new cruiser was to fall foul of the change of government in 1920, the project being postponed for further consideration. At the same time technical details of the latest British and American cruisers became available to the *Marine Nationale*. Its deliberations of July 1919 had taken into consideration the Royal Navy's 'D' class and the Italian Navy's *Bixio* class, against either of which the proposed French cruiser could have held its own. However, the British 'E' class and the American *Omaha* class, both of which were laid down in 1918, were larger ships designed for high speeds of 33–34 knots, and the *Marine Nationale* was particularly anxious that the new cruisers should not be outclassed in this respect.

In May 1920 the *Conseil supérieur* estimated that a speed of 34 knots was possible only on a displacement of 7,300 tonnes. However, an armament of 138.6mm guns was deemed inadequate for such a large and expensive ship, particularly as the latest British and American cruisers had 6in (152mm) guns. The main armament was therefore upgunned to 155mm, bringing a further increase in the displacement to 8,000 tonnes and a doubling-up of the 1919 propulsion plant, with 102,000shp and four shafts. Even on this displacement only very light protection could be worked in. The cost of the ship had by now also virtually doubled, from 40m to 70m francs.

Six of the new 8,000-tonne cruisers continued to feature in the future programmes outlined in June 1920 and 1921, but the proposed addition of twelve *torpilleurs* and a further twenty-four submarines to the 1921 proposal would have imposed a serious overload on the naval dockyards and private shipyards, which were still recovering from the disruption of the First World War, and the original programme was subsequently halved. The 1922 Programme authorised by the Senate of the *Assemblée Nationale* on 18 March comprised only three 8,000-tonne cruisers, six *contre-torpilleurs* (the *Jaguar* class), twelve *torpilleurs* and twelve submarines.

Construction

The first hull, that of *Duguay-Trouin*, was laid down in August of the same year at the Arsenal de Brest. *Primauguet* followed her on the slipway one year later, while the second ship, *Lamotte-Picquet*, was laid down in January 1923 at the Arsenal de Lorient. Each of the hulls took approximately three years to complete, but the development of some key items of their equipment proved more problematic, and although the ships were officially accepted into the fleet in 1926–27, they were not fully ready for service until late 1929. In particular there were delays in the delivery of the fire-control system for the main guns; the main fire-control director was installed only in 1928–29, and the late decision to incorporate aviation facilities was responsible for a number of unforeseen modifications.

DUGUAY-TROUIN CLASS

Name	Builder	Laid down	Launched	Completed
1922 Programme				
Duguay-Trouin	Arsenal de Brest	04/08/22	14/08/23	02/11/26
Lamotte-Picquet	Arsenal de Lorient	17/01/23	21/03/24	05/03/27
Primauguet	Arsenal de Brest	16/08/23	21/05/24	01/10/26

Characteristics (as completed)	
Displacement	7,249 tonnes standard
	8,760 tonnes normal
	9,655 tonnes full load
Length	175.3m wl (575ft), 181.0m oa (595ft)
Beam	17.2m (56ft 6in)
Draught	5.2m (17ft)
Machinery	8 Guyot-du Temple small-tube boilers, 18.5kg/cm²; 4-shaft Parsons geared steam turbines for 102,000shp; speed 34kts (designed)
Oil fuel	1,400 tonnes; radius 3,600nm at 14kts, 800nm at 33kts
Armament	8–155mm/50 Model 1920 in twin mountings Model 1921 (1,000 rounds + 30 starshell); 4–75mm/50 Model 1922 HA in single mountings Model 1926 (540 rounds + 120 starshell); 12 tubes for 550mm torpedoes Model 1923D in 4 triple mountings Model 1922T (+12 reloads); rack for fifteen 35kg depth charges
Protection	*magazines:* 20mm
	deck: 10mm / 20mm
	CT: 30mm
	turrets: 30mm
Complement	580

Hull and Superstructures

In contrast to the conservative design of the proposed pre-war scouts, the hull-form of the new ships was in advance of any cruiser type under construction abroad. High free-board allied to a raised forecastle made for a ship with excellent sea-keeping qualities. The fine lines of the forward part of the ship, adopted to secure the desired high speed, were complemented by a clipper bow with gentle sheer and marked flare which kept the forecastle dry even in heavy weather. Even the turning circle, much-criticised in the contemporary *contre-torpilleurs*, was deemed exceptional, averaging 750m with 25° of helm on a length of 175m pp at a speed of 28 knots. The only criticism noted by successive commanding officers was the high centre of gravity, which on a reduced fuel load often resulted in a roll of 14–18° and made the ships less-than-steady gunnery platforms.

The main guns were in twin turrets superimposed fore and aft, with the triple torpedo tubes at upper deck level, in the waist of the ship. The silhouette was kept deliberately low, thereby enhancing the image of a fast ship. A capacious bridge structure was built around the widely spaced feet of a powerful tripod mast designed to secure a firm foundation for the main fire-control director. This was complemented by a heavy pole mainmast aft. An armoured conning tower was incorporated into the bridge structure, topped by a 4m rangefinder.

The boiler rooms were grouped together forward. Despite the doubling of horsepower, a reduction from twelve boilers in the 1914 design to eight in the *Duguay-Trouin*s made possible a reduction to two broad funnels, each incorporating the uptakes for four boilers. The funnels were little higher than the bridge structure in an effort to keep the funnel gases well clear of the director atop the tripod foremast. There was prominent ventilation trunking forward and abaft both funnels, the after air intake doubling as the platform for the after 1.2m searchlight projectors. The four single 75mm AA guns were located abeam the funnels.

Abaft the twin funnels, directly above the engine rooms was a capacious shelter deck atop which the ship's boats were located. These were served by a single long-arm crane with a reach of 11.5m, allowing 3m clearance on either side of the hull.

Protection was minimal, accounting for less than 2 per cent of displacement (166 tonnes). There was 20mm box protection around the magazines. Horizontal protection comprised 20mm plating on the upper deck and 10mm on the main deck; there was also 14mm plating above the steering gear aft. The 155mm gun turrets had 30mm armour (15mm+15mm), and the barbettes (20mm+10mm) and the conning tower (30mm walls and roof) were similarly armoured. This was adequate protection against the lighter 4in and 8.8cm/10.5cm guns of the standard British and German war-built destroyers, but the latest British ships of the 'Modified W' class were armed with the much heavier 4.7in (120mm) gun, and this would become the norm in postwar destroyer construction.

Against the latest cruisers, armed with 6in guns and larger, the light plating of the *Duguay-Trouin* class could provide only splinter protection. However, since none of the early postwar cruisers, including the 10,000-ton 'Treaty Cruisers', was given armour sufficient to protect them against their own kind ('eggshells armed with hammers' was one popular contemporary description), it would be unfair to make this a specific criticism of the French ships. Like other cruisers of their generation, they were designed to outrun ships they could not out-fight. In compensation they were well subdivided, with no fewer than sixteen transverse watertight bulkheads and a double shell worked in abreast the boiler and engine rooms, and the 'stiffening' provided by their light 20/30mm plating at least made for a sturdy, robust hull which was appreciated by successive commanding officers.

Propulsion

The propulsion plant of the new ships comprised eight Indret small-tube boilers of the Guyot-du Temple type and four sets of Parsons single-reduction turbines, powering four shafts. Total machinery weight was 2,497 tonnes, accounting for 28.5 per cent of displacement

The boilers were disposed as two groups of four in two adjacent boiler rooms forward. The uptakes from each of the boiler rooms were led up into one of the two broad funnels. The boilers were exclusively oil-fired and had an operating pressure of 18.5kg/cm^2.

The three engine rooms were directly abaft the boiler rooms. The forward engine room housed the two sets of turbines powering the wing shafts. The centre engine room housed the turbines powering the starboard inner shaft, and the after engine room the turbines for the port inner shaft. The auxiliary machinery was distributed between the two after engine rooms, with the Indret auxiliary boiler in the centre engine room and two of the four 265kW turbo-generators in the after engine room. The other two generators were located well forward, directly beneath the bridge structure, to ensure that electrical power could be maintained in the event of the engine rooms being flooded.

Each set of turbines could be operated independently of the others, and comprised HP and LP cruise turbines operating in series via single-reduction gearing, with the reversing turbine on the LP turbine and a separate cruise turbine. The four propellers were of 3.70m diameter; those fitted in the *Primauguet* and *Lamotte-Picquet* were three-bladed, while those fitted in *Duguay-Trouin* following her sea trials were four-bladed.

Results on trials proved slightly disappointing. The designed figure of 102,000shp was comfortably exceeded, with *Duguay-Trouin* attaining 117,821shp on speed trials conducted on 23 July 1926. However, the maximum speed attained was 33.4 knots, while her two sisters made just over 33 knots. Nevertheless, the cruisers could comfortably maintain speeds in excess of 30 knots in service with only half power. Successive commanding officers praised the flexibility and reliability of the machinery (qualities not always attributable to French marine engineering of the interwar period).

The *Duguay-Trouin* class also proved to be economical

steamers, projections from trials suggesting an endurance of between 4,224nm (*Primauguet*) and 5,472nm (*Duguay-Trouin*) at 15 knots with the maximum usable fuel load of 1,200 tonnes. At a speed of 30 knots just under 1,500nm was projected.

Main Armament

The 155mm calibre adopted for the main armament of the new cruisers was the standard calibre in use with the French Army for its field guns. A primary reason for its adoption was therefore to simplify ammunition supply. The gun itself, which was mounted in twin turrets in the *Duguay-Trouin* class and in single casemate mountings in the converted aircraft carrier *Béarn*, was built with a liner, autofretted A tube, a jacket in two lengths and a breech ring. The traditional Welin screw breech block opened upwards, being balanced about its horizontal axis of rota-

tion. The propellant charge was in halves, and semi-armour-piercing (SAP) and high-explosive (HE) shell were provided. Some of the latter had an internal fuze and weighed 59kg (130lb) instead of the standard weight of 56.5kg (125lb).

The enclosed gunhouses, which were reportedly gastight with forced ventilation, had the guns in separate cradles each with a toothed elevating arc. Training and elevation were electrically powered with hydraulic drive. Maximum elevation was 40°. Remote power control (RPC) was later to be fitted for training.

Shells and charges were hoisted together with the shell in the upper compartment. The lower hoists were of the dredger type with transfer in the working chamber to the upper cage hoists. The shells were moved by tongs into loading trays which traversed into position for loading by spring rammers. The charges were rammed by hand. The complexity of the reloading mechanism effectively reduced the firing cycle to three rounds per minute; this

Primauguet *1926: inboard profile.*
The two boiler rooms, each of which housed four Indret small-tube boilers, were adjacent and were served by prominent ventilation duct. The four sets of Parsons turbines, each of which could be operated independently of the others, were distributed between three engine rooms, and after two being shared with the auxiliary machinery. (Drawn by author)

Key: 1 *75mm starshell magazine*
  2 *155 mm shell rooms*
  3 *155mm magazines*
  4 *75mm magazines*
  5 *operations room*
  6 *wheelhouse*
  7 *conning tower*
  8 *communications room*
  9 *no. 1 boiler room*
  10 *no. 2 boiler room*
  11 *midships W/T office*
  12 *forward engine room (wing shafts)*
  13 *centre engine room (stbd inner shaft)*
  14 *after engine room (port inner shaft)*
  15 *torpedo workshop*
  16 *after W/T office*
  17 *steering gear compartment*
  18 *aviation fuel tank*

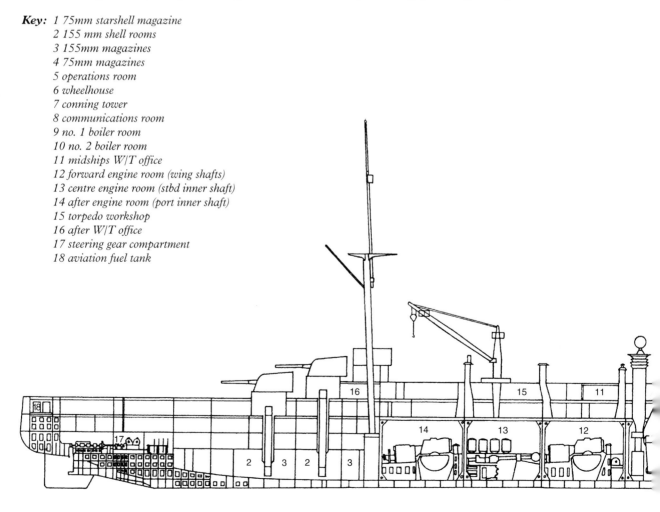

was a disappointment, as the initial contracts stipulated 5–6rpm. Regular breakdowns were also experienced throughout the ships' service lives, a problem never satisfactorily resolved.

Each gun was provided with 125 rounds. In addition 15 starshell and 20 practice rounds were provided for each of the upper turrets ('B' and 'X'), and 60 practice rounds for each of the lower turrets ('A' and 'Y').

Anti-aircraft Weapons

The four single 75mm/50 guns were of the new Model 1922 specially developed following the First World War to provide surface ships with an anti-aircraft capability (they were also installed in the *torpilleurs* and *contre-torpilleurs* of the 1922 Programme). The gun was essentially a modification of the 75mm Model 1902 Schneider, reduced to a length of 50 calibres; only the mounting was different. With a firing cycle of 12rpm, it had a maximum range of 7,500m against aircraft. A total of 540 time-fuzed HE rounds were provided for the four guns, together with 120 starshell and 96 exercise rounds. The 75mm magazines were located immediately forward of the boiler rooms.

Provision was also made for six Hotchkiss twin 8mm machine guns, although the mountings were not fitted until 1928–29. These proved virtually ineffectual against even the aircraft of the day, and were replaced by the Hotchkiss twin 13.2mm weapon during the mid-1930s.

Fire Control

Fire control for the main armament was exercised from the main director control tower (DCT), which was located atop the tripod foremast some 26m above the waterline. It was fitted initially with a 4m coincidence rangefinder for target ranging and a Zeiss 3m stereo model for target observation. Delays in the delivery of the equipment meant that all three ships ran trials without their main directors, which were installed only in 1927–28. A severe fire aboard *Duguay-Trouin* during her refit at Toulon in 1929–30 resulted in damage to the director, which had to be disembarked for repairs; it was replaced only in 1933 during reconstruction at Brest.

A second 4m coincidence rangefinder was installed atop the conning tower, and a further pair were located on the outer edge of the shelter deck between the 75mm guns; they proved to be unusable when the 75mm guns were fired and were removed during the Second World War. As with all French ships of this generation, the 4m base of the main rangefinder proved totally inadequate at the longer ranges projected for future surface engagements, and it was replaced by an 8m stereo model during the late 1930s.

Range clocks for formation firing were installed fore and aft at the base of the foremast and mainmast, respectively. Three 1.2m searchlight projectors were provided for target illumination at night; the forward projector was installed atop a platform directly beneath the foretop, while the after projectors were located side by side atop the after boiler room ventilation housing immediately abaft

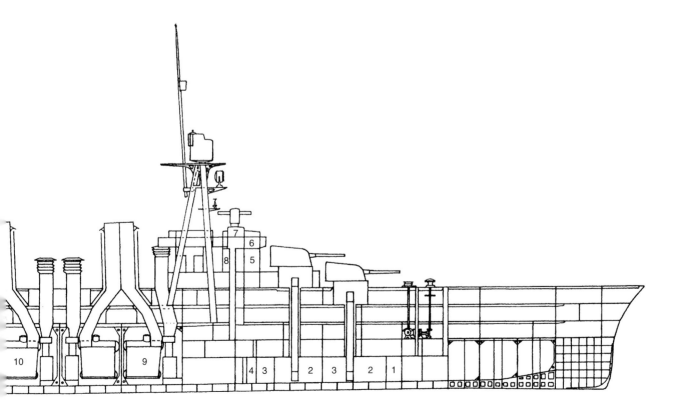

CHARACTERISTICS OF ARTILLERY

	155mm/50 Model 1920	75mm/50 Model 1922
Gun Data		
muzzle velocity (m/sec)	850	850
max. range	26,100m at 40°	14,900m at 45°
ceiling at 80°	n/a	7,500m at 80°
weight of projectile	56.5kg (AP)	5.9kg + 2.2kg BM5 charge
	59kg (HE)	12kg (fixed round)
projectiles	OPf Mod.	OEA Mod.
	OEA Mod.	starshell Mod.
Mounting Data		
weight of turret/mounting (tonnes)	80	1.1
protection	30mm	none
elevation of guns	−5°/+40°	−10°/+90°
max. elevating speed	*c.*6°/sec	
max. training speed	*c.*6.4°/sec	
firing cycle	3–5rpm per gun	10–12rpm

View of Primauguet *at Toulon taken during October 1929, shortly after she joined the Mediterranean Squadron. With her two sisters she formed the 3ᵉ Division Légère, commanded by Rear-Admiral Dubois. The aircraft atop the catapult is the standard FBA 17 spotter floatplane. Note the distinctive white paintwork of the main DCT and the topmasts. (Marius Bar)*

Duguay-Trouin leaving Toulon for Morocco on 13 October 1930, shortly after the dockyard fire which severely damaged the main DCT and led to its temporary removal for repairs. The Minister of War is aboard. Note the FBA 17 spotter in its 'rest' position atop the centre-line pivot abaft the boat crane. (Marius Bar)

the second funnel. Remote power control for training was provided during the mid-1930s.

By comparison with the elaborate arrangements made for control of the main guns, the HA fire-control arrangements were rudimentary and were to be subject to major improvements during the early and mid-1930s.

Underwater Weapons

The heavy torpedo armament of the 8,000-tonne cruisers was intended for use in support of the flotillas. Four triple tubes Model 1922T of the type installed in the contemporary *torpilleurs* and *contre-torpilleurs* were fitted at upper deck level in the waist of the ship, each with a training arc of between 40° and 140°. No fewer than twenty-four torpedoes were carried, twelve of which were housed in the tubes with a further twelve reloads were stowed in lockers on the upper deck, each of which held three torpedoes (see drawing). The warheads were stowed in separate lockers on the deck edge between the tubes. Initially the 550mm torpedo Model 1923D was carried, but this was soon replaced by the 1924D, which had much-improved performance.

As in the Imperial Japanese Navy's heavy cruisers, which were similarly equipped, the location of so many torpedoes and their warheads above the upper deck amidships presented a major fire hazard, especially in combat, although the ships' designers took care to place the warhead lockers on the deck edge so that any explosion would be vented upwards and outwards, thereby minimising damage to the ship's vitals. The arrangement was much criticised by the *Commission permanente d'essais*, and was not repeated on any subsequent French cruiser classes.

The torpedo fire-control position was located in the armoured conning tower, and was served by the 4m rangefinder located atop the latter. Secondary 'rapid-fire' torpedo FC positions similar to those installed in the *contre-torpilleurs* were later fitted in the bridge wings.

550mm Torpedo Model 1923D

Torpedo Data	
length	8.575m
weight	2,210kg
warhead	AG-326: 310kg tolite
propulsion	Brotherhood type fuelled by alcohol
range	14,000m at 35kts
	20,000m at 29kts
deviation	+/– 250m at 14,000m

Mounting Data	
designation	1922T
firing mechanism	compressed air
training arc	40°–140°

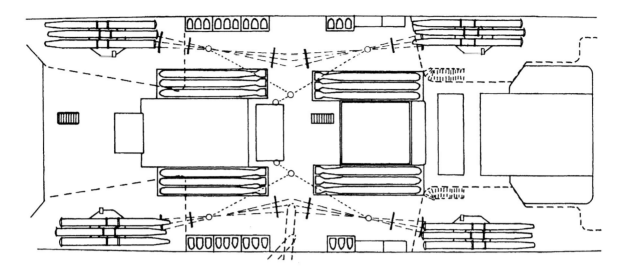

The 8,000-tonne cruisers: torpedo-handling arrangements.
The torpedo-handling arrangements for the 1922 cruisers were unusually elaborate. Reloads were stowed in sets of three in lockers located at upper deck level abeam the midships W/T office and a fully equipped torpedo repair shop. The live warheads for these and the torpedoes in the tubes were stowed separately in deck-edge lockers each holding three warheads located at the outer edges of the upper deck between the triple tubes and protected against splinters by steel bulwarks. A system of overhead cables and pulleys combined with rail-type guides fitted into the upper deck to transfer torpedoes between the lockers and the tubes. (Drawn by author)

Aviation Installations

During construction it was decided to fit a catapult for a spotter floatplane experimentally on *Primauguet*. The catapult, a Penhoët compressed-air model with an overall length of 20.27m, was installed on 1 April 1927, and could launch aircraft with a maximum weight of 1,600kg at 93km/h. It was installed on the ship's axis on the quarterdeck 16.4m from the stern.

Trials were conducted with first a Bresson 35 then an FBA 17, which was to become the standard spotter aircraft for the *Marine Nationale* until the mid-1930s. The trials were regarded as generally successful, and the catapult was installed in the *Primauguet*'s two sisters in March and April 1929 following their completion. The only significant modification to the catapult was a reduction in the height of its cylindrical base from 2.5m to 1.23m in an effort to minimise vibration.

Aircraft stowage and handling arrangements proved more problematical and were subject to a number of improvements. The absence of a hangar meant that the aircraft was exposed to the elements on the open quarterdeck. In 1927 it was decided to fit a 4.5m extension to the boat crane to enable it to lift the floatplane from the water and place it on a pivoting pedestal to be installed atop the shelter deck between the crane and the mainmast. However, the crane still had insufficient reach to place a floatplane on the catapult, and during 1932–34 a collapsible crane 11.5m long was installed on the port side of the quarterdeck specifically to handle the aircraft. From this

time the ships generally deployed with two FBA 17 floatplanes, one of which was carried atop the catapult and the second stowed on the shelter deck. From 1935 these were progressively replaced by the Gourdou-Leseurre GL 832 float monoplane and the Potez 452 seaplane.

The aviation fuel tank, which had a capacity of 2,700 litres, was located directly beneath the stern. Fire-prevention measures included the replacement of used fuel by inert carbon dioxide, and the ability to pump the contents of the tank rapidly into the sea.

The decision to fit the catapult on the quarterdeck effectively displaced the direction-finding equipment it was initially planned to install. It was temporarily relocated atop the aircraft pedestal in *Primauguet*, but this was clearly unsatisfactory and installation was postponed indefinitely for the two remaining two ships. It was finally decided to install the antenna and its associated cabin in the centre of the ventilation trunking between the funnels.

The aircraft arrangements were to be considerably modified in France's first 'Treaty' cruisers, *Duquesne* and *Tourville*, which were otherwise similar to the cruisers of the 1922 Programme in their general arrangements. The catapult was placed atop the shelter deck between the after funnel and the mainmast, the boats and their associated crane being relocated to positions between the funnels (which were more widely spaced). This arrangement provided the FBA 17 floatplanes with more protection from the elements, and was repeated in subsequent classes.

Modifications 1930 to 1940

Significant modifications were made to all three ships during the 1930s as a result of experience with the ships in service. At the same time, newly developed equipment was incorporated where possible to bring them up to date. *Duguay-Trouin*, which was deployed exclusively in home waters and was refitted at Brest 1932–33, served as the prototype for these modifications, which were subsequently extended to her two sisters.

The command spaces were found to be inadequate, particularly as the new cruisers were frequently employed as flagships. The navigation bridge was therefore enlarged to provide an operations/transmissions room, and an admiral's bridge was fitted around the vertical leg of the tripod foremast. In order to accommodate the additional motor launches required by the admiral and his staff, the shelter deck was extended to the ship's sides above the after torpedo tubes to port and to starboard. These sections were removable to facilitate reloading of the tubes when alongside.

The ship's anti-aircraft provision was already deemed insufficient by the early 1930s, and a number of measures were taken to improve it. The 75mm guns were fitted with light duralumin shields for splinter and spray protection, the after ends of the bridge wings were enlarged to accommodate two open HA fire-control directors each with a 3m rangefinder, and a single calculator position was installed. The weight of the new fire-control directors was borne by broad cylindrical supports which rested on the upper deck.

The 8mm machine guns having proved ineffectual, they were replaced by four of a projected six Hotchkiss twin 13.2mm MG Model 1929: one atop the bridge, one atop the after deckhouse abeam the mainmast, two at the outer edges of the boat deck, and two abeam the bridge structure at the level of 'B' gun mounting (these were the last to be installed, due to a shortage of mountings).

During the same refit a new main DCT was installed to replace the one damaged by fire in 1930. The DF antenna and its associated cabin were finally installed between the funnels, and the new collapsible aircraft crane was fitted on the port side of the quarterdeck. The topmasts were lowered, and a steel bulwark was constructed at the after end of the forecastle to port and to starboard.

In 1935 the second phase of the anti-aircraft improvements was undertaken, also at Brest. Remote power control (RPC) for training was fitted to both the 75mm AA guns and to the after searchlight projectors. At the same time the fore topmast, which had been found to obstruct the main DCT on after bearings, was completely removed, and the mainmast top lowered. The catapult was modified to launch the GL 832 and Potez 452 monoplanes, and secondary torpedo FC positions were installed in the bridge wings.

Lamotte-Picquet was taken in hand by Lorient Naval Dockyard in 1933–35, with a view to bringing her up to the same standard as her sister ship. She therefore received all the modifications extended to *Duguay-Trouin* at her 1932–33 and 1935 refits. In addition she was fitted with a new DCT of the type fitted in the 10,000-tonne cruisers.

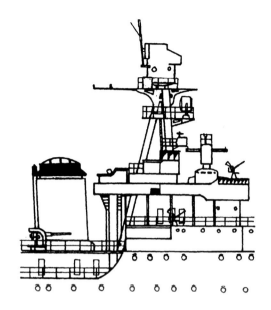

Duguay-Trouin *as modified 1932–35.*
Part view of Duguay-Trouin *following her 1935 refit. The navigation bridge has been extended and enclosed, and an admiral's bridge constructed around the forward leg of the tripod foremast. The after ends of the bridge wings have been extended to accommodate open HA fire-control directors, supported from below by prominent cylindrical supports. The 75mm AA mountings have been fitted with shields, and Hotchkiss twin 13.2mm MG have been installed atop the navigation bridge and abeam the bridge structure. (Drawn by author)*

Primauguet, however, received only the 75mm gun shields (steel, not duralumin) and the collapsible aircraft crane before she deployed to the Far East in 1932 (the navigation bridge was also enlarged), and remained virtually unmodified until 1936 when she returned to metropolitan France. She was subsequently refitted at Lorient in 1936–37, and was brought up to the standard of her two sisters. She received the new HA fire-control arrangements, although the RPC installation was not completed until 1940, and 3m rangefinders were fitted provisionally in the bridge wings pending the development of a new enclosed HA director. At the same time the Hotchkiss 13.2mm twin MG were installed. Like *Lamotte-Picquet* she also received a main DCT 'type croiseurs de 10,000t', but with an 8m stereo RF for ranging, the 3m stereo RF being retained for observation of the target. The original 4m coincidence rangefinders on the shelter deck were replaced by stereo models at the same time. The new rangefinders proved to be much more effective, and similar modifications were extended to *Duguay-Trouin* at Toulon in 1937–38 and to *Lamotte-Picquet* at Saigon in 1939–40.

The new enclosed HA directors, which had a metal roof and glass to the rear, were installed in *Duguay-Trouin* and *Primauguet* only in early 1940, but were not fitted in *Lamotte-Picquet*, which was destined never to return to France. At the same time the 4m base stereo rangefinders

Lamotte-Picquet *leaving Toulon, 14 March 1932. Note the single white band on the second funnel. She was the only ship of her class in service with the Mediterranean Squadron at that time, as* Primauguet *was preparing to depart for a deployment to the Far East and* Duguay-Trouin *was undergoing repairs. (Marius Bar)*

Primauguet *leaves again for the Far East, this time on 4 October 1937. During the 18 months since her return to France she has undergone a considerable transformation. There is now an admiral's bridge around the forward leg of the tripod foremast, and the bridge wings have been extended to support HA fire-control directors port and starboard (3m range-finders have been fitted as a temporary measure). The fore topmast has been suppressed and a new mainmast modelled on that of the 7,600-tonne cruisers of the* La Galissonnière *class fitted. This has resulted in a lower, more streamlined silhouette. The spotter monoplane on the catapult is a Gordon-Leseurre 832, and there is a Potez 452 with wings folded atop the centre-line pivot abaft the boat crane. Note the new 8-metre-base stereo rangefinder in the main DCT. (Marius Bar)*

Duguay-Trouin *as she appeared on 8 July 1938, on the occasion of the review of the Mediterranean Squadron by its C-in-C, Vice-Admiral Abrial. The early model open HA fire-control director can be clearly distinguished at the after end of the bridge wings, as can the forward Hotchkiss twin 13.2mm MG mounting atop the bridge.* Duguay-Trouin *retained her original mainmast until 1940. (Marius Bar)*

originally located on the shelter deck were removed, and installed in place of the 3m RF in the new HA directors. Other modifications to the two home-based ships included the installation of fixed propeller guards above the outer shafts similar to those of the 10,000-tonne cruisers, and the replacement of the original mainmast in *Duguay-Trouin* by a new lightweight model similar to that of the cruisers of the *La Galissonnière* class (see *Warship 1995*), which had been trialled in *Primauguet* since her refit in 1936–37. *Duguay-Trouin* also carried fifteen 35kg depth charges for protection against submarines from this time.

Service Prewar

When first completed all three ships joined the *3ᵉ Division Légère*, which was formed on 19 November 1926 as part of the Atlantic Squadron. In mid-1928 the division was transferred to the Mediterranean, where it remained until 1932. During these years the cruisers saw much active service, taking part in numerous fleet exercises and serving as transports for a number of ministers and other government officials paying official visits to the colonies in North Africa.

By 1932, however, many newer ships had been commissioned and the *3ᵉ Division Légère* was disbanded. *Duguay-Trouin* subsequently began her reconstruction at

Brest, while *Primauguet* embarked on the first of her lengthy deployments to the Far East, returning only in January 1936. *Lamotte-Picquet* was transferred again to the Atlantic Squadron, serving as the flagship of the C-in-C Admiral Drujon until her own extensive refit at Lorient from August 1933 until March 1935. She was succeeded in this role by *Duguay-Trouin*, which in May 1935 became flagship of the newly formed *2ᵉ Division Légère*, in which she was joined by the *Lamotte-Picquet* following her refit.

By 1936 the cruisers were ten years old and approaching obsolescence. *Lamotte-Picquet* was despatched to the Far East, a deployment from which she would never return. *Primauguet* returned to France shortly afterwards, to be extensively refitted at Lorient. In July the *2ᵉ Division Légère* was disbanded, and its sole surviving member, *Duguay-Trouin*, was attached to the *Division d'instruction* (Training Squadron) of the Mediterranean Squadron. Following her refit *Primauguet* joined her sister *Lamotte-Picquet* in the Far East for a long deployment, broken only by a brief interlude with the Middle Eastern division from February to June 1939.

War Service 1939–45

With the approach of war *Duguay-Trouin* was again placed in active service, and was transferred to northwest Africa, flying the flag of Rear-Admiral Moreau commanding the *5ᵉ Escadre*. She would be based at Dakar until January of the following year, when wear and tear on her ageing machinery finally caught up with her and she was despatched to Lorient for a four-month refit. She would subsequently join Force X at Alexandria, under the command of Admiral Godfroy. Together with the battleship *Lorraine,* the 10,000-tonne cruisers *Duquesne, Tourville* and *Suffren* and three 1,500-tonne *torpilleurs* she would be interned following the Armistice until mid-1943, when the ships rejoined the Allied cause. From 1944 to 1945 she served as part of the *3ᵉ Division de croiseurs*, operating for a time with the Mediterranean Flank Force. Following major refurbishment postwar at Toulon she would serve in the Far East from October 1947 to September 1951, when she returned to France to pay off. Placed initially in reserve, she was stricken in March 1952.

The other two ships of the class were less fortunate. *Lamotte-Picquet* continued to serve on the Far East station throughout the early 1940s. On 17 January 1940 she played a major role in a pre-emptive strike against the Siamese Fleet at Koh-Chang, although the Japanese would subsequently impose a peace on the French which compelled them to make a number of concessions. From mid-1941 it became apparent that the ship could not continue in operational service without major boiler repairs, and from March the following year she was laid up along-side. In January 1944 she was placed in 'special reserve' and served as a training ship. She capsized during an attack by US bomber aircraft in January 1945.

Following a major refit at Lorient from October 1939 to March 1940 in which the HA fire-control system was finally installed, *Primauguet* was again dispatched to northwest Africa, being present at the British attack on Dakar during September 1940. She was to remain there for the rest of her career, undergoing an extensive refit at Casablanca in May/June 1942 which included the suppression of her mainmast. As flagship of the *2ᵉ Escadre Légère* (Rear-Admiral Lafond), she was the only cruiser at Casablanca available to oppose the 'Torch' landings of 8 November. Heavily engaged by the American cruisers *Augusta* and *Brooklyn* and attacked by US carrier planes, she was grounded by her commanding officer at the mouth of the harbour. With her bridge wrecked by a bomb which killed her captain she would burn throughout the following day.

Sources

Jean Guiglini and Albert Moreau, *Les croiseurs de 8000t*. Marines (Bourg-en-Bresse 1995).

Official plans of *Primauguet*. Centre d'Archives de l'Armement.

John Campbell, *Naval Weapons of World War Two*. Conway Maritime Press (London 1988).

THE CANADIAN NAVAL AVIATION EXPERIENCE:

The Ships, Aircraft and Operations, 1944–1969

PART 4
HMCS *Bonaventure*: Last of the Breed

In the fourth part of his series, **Thomas G Lynch** looks at the history of the Royal Canadian Navy's last aircraft carrier, HMCS *Bonaventure*.

A decision of the Canadian Cabinet in April 1952 authorised the acquisition and modernisation of an aircraft carrier to replace the *Magnificent*. At the time it appeared that the most suitable ship for this purpose was the modified *Majestic* class light fleet carrier HMS *Powerful* which, after being laid down by Harland and Wolff in November 1943 and launched in February 1946, had been laid-up incomplete at Belfast since May 1946.

During negotiations with the Royal Navy (RN), the Minister of National Defence for Canada, Mr Brooke Claxton, proposed that the United Kingdom should be asked to spend the purchase money (C$21 million) on Canadian cheese! However, the cash-strapped British were forced to decline this somewhat unusual and savoury suggestion. The agreement to buy *Powerful* was finally made on 29 November 1952 back-dated to 12 July, the final price, excluding North American equipment, totalling C$31 million (1952).

The Admiralty in fact handled the contract with Harland and Wolff to complete *Powerful* and, within two weeks of signing, workers in Belfast were back on the job. A team under the Principal Royal Canadian Navy (RCN) Technical Representative was sent to Northern Ireland and during construction worked closely with the firm and Admiralty representatives. Shortly before Christmas 1952, a press release in Ottawa announced that the new carrier's name would be HMCS *Bonaventure*.

Construction Modifications and Improvements

Being of the modified *Majestic* class, the carrier design already had a strengthened flight deck to handle heavier and faster aircraft types. In addition, because of the late date of completion, the RCN was able to take advantage of a series of major British breakthroughs in the technique of operating aircraft. These consisted of three major improvements in design and equipment, namely the angled landing deck, steam catapults and the mirror-landing aid system, all of which had been adopted by the US Navy (USN).

Since the first Sea Vampire jet had landed on the deck of HMS *Ocean* in December 1945, a solution to the problem of how to compensate for the high landing speed of jet aircraft had been sought. In the summer of 1951 a proposal was made to angle the landing area of the deck and trials carried out with an angled painted deck on the flight decks of HMS *Illustrious* and *Triumph*, which proved the feasibility of the scheme. Advantages included the elimination of the crash barrier, a much longer landing area, good deck part forward and the simplification of deck landing. Since then, the angled flight deck had been improved upon, especially by the USN, who extended the fore end of the angled deck out to port thereby increasing the landing distance. The *Bonaventure*'s landing deck was angled at 7.5° from the fore and aft line.

The steam catapult fitted was of the type invented by Cdr(E) C C Mitchell, RNVR, of Brown Brother Ltd, Edinburgh, to provide the answer to the lack of aircraft acceleration when taking-off. The original hydro-pneumatic purchase type of catapult had from early days tended to grow by leaps and bounds in size and weight as increased performance was demanded. With jet aircraft, it reached all practical limits in bulk and complexity, making it impossible to accommodate in a carrier design. The steam catapult gave greatly increased power for launching any jet aircraft at any foreseeable take-off speed and reduced the necessity for a carrier to steam for lengthy periods into the wind in order to fly-off aircraft.

The Mirror Landing Sight, as installed in *Bonaventure*, had evolved in conjunction with a device called 'Audio' which gave audible information on the aircraft's air speed. On the aircraft's final approach, the pilot kept light reflected from a gyrostabilised mirror on the flight deck in

HMCS Bonaventure *being moved out of the fitting-out dock at the RN's Aircraft yard, Sydenham, Belfast, 27 February 1957. (Rudnicki/MARCOM Museum)*

line with a horizontal line with fixed datum lights to left and right of it. To obviate the necessity of looking down at instruments, 'Audio' gave off sound signals from which the pilot could tell whether he was coming in too fast or too slow. It was no longer necessary to cut the engine to land the aircraft on to the deck; the pilot flew straight down at a shallow angle into the arrester wires with engine power on. The system nearly did away with the need for a Landing Signals Officer with his paddles but this function was retained in case of equipment failure.

The *Bonaventure* departed from the traditional Canadian practice of buying British ships with 'as fitted' equipment. The RCN had by this time acquired the McDonnel Douglas F2H3 Banshee jet fighter (to replace the Sea Fury), the Grumman CS2F Tracker (to replace the Avenger) and the Sikorsky S–55 or HO4S–3 'Horse' ASW helicopter. The former two were heavier than anything so far handled by a light fleet carrier in Commonwealth use. To handle these aircraft and utilise their capabilities to the maximum, there had been a marked mixture of British carrier practices, as then current, and US modern equipment, particularly in the areas of radar and communications. Over C$3 million (1953–54) was spent on Canadian innovations to the ship, which included nearly C$2 million in fire-control and radar units, which, although ordered from Canadian firms, were in fact US equipment, sold through 'branch plant' divisions of US companies.

The AA armament was also altered, four twin 3in/50 Mk33 mountings being fitted, while the Bofors 40mm L/70 with GUNAR fire control were specified. However, at the last moment the 40mm L/70s were dropped and 40mm L/60 Mk5C substituted. GUNAR was retained for the 3in/50 mounts in any case.

One Canadian-designed innovation was the aviation fuelling system, designed to mix kerosene and aviation gas in the correct proportion for turbine-driven aircraft, effectively filter out all contaminants, including water, and to optimise both underwing and overwing fuelling. The layout consisted of two sets of fuel blending apparatus and fourteen two-outlet fuelling stations, each complete with fuel filter, water separators, power-operated hose reels and specialised tank-filling nozzles. The blending arrangement was the first to be installed in a major war vessel and was thus a major Canadian industrial achievement. Also, since there were two different kinds of fuel required by Canada's mix of piston-engined and jet aircraft, the aviation fuel capacity of *Bonaventure* was increased over that planned for the *Majestic* class.

The accommodation arrangements were reworked to approach a new Canadian standard, using RCN aluminium furniture, an electric galley and central cafeteria. On the mechanical side, the Admiralty 3-drum main boilers were trunked and fitted with wide-range burners, while the main propulsion machinery was provided with remote controls located in a gastight compartment at the entrance to each main machinery space so that it could be operated safely under NBC (Nuclear, Biological, Chemical) warfare conditions. The electrical generating capacity was increased from the original design to provide 3,200kW DC and 300kW AC. A Lamont forced-circulation auxiliary boiler and Junkers free-piston high-pressure air compressors were also incorporated.

Finally, mention has to be made of her closed-circuit television system, designed from the outset to relay visual information of ships and aircraft in the carrier's vicinity to key points in the ship. Hence in the briefing room, deck operations could be watched by aircrew while, during night briefings, the monitor had its brilliance filtered to preserve night vision.

The starboard mirror deck-landing apparatus aboard HMCS Bonaventure *in 1957 at Halifax, Nova Scotia. (DND/LYNCAN)*

Table 1: *RN CLASS AND SHIP TYPE:* MAJESTIC *CLASS LIGHT FLEET CARRIERS*

Ship Name	HMCS *Bonaventure* (Pennant No. CVL–22)
Dimensions (length (oa) × beam × draft)	720ft × 80ft × 23ft (219.45m × 39.01m × 7.01m) × 112in 6ft (34.3m) at flight deck; 128ft (39m) inc sponsons
Displacement	16,000 tons (standard), 20,000 tons (full load)
Machinery	4 × Admiralty 3-drum type, @ 350 PSI (175 kg/cm^2) 2-shaft, Parsons single-reduction geared steam turbines, 42,000shp 1 × 3-blade propeller (port); 1 × 4-blade propeller (stbd)
Generators	3,200kW DC; 300kW AC
Maximum speed	25.5 knots
Radar: (to 1967)	1 × SPS–12B (warning, air) 1 × SPS–10 (warning, surface) 1 × Sperry Mk2, Mod. 1 High Definition, Warning Surface) 1 × SPS–8A Height Finding
(post-1968)	1 × SPS–501 (warning, air) 1 × SPS–10 (warning, surface) 1 × SPN–8 (carrier-controlled approach radar) 1 × Sperry Mk2 Mod. 3 HDWS 1 × LN 27 (navigation radar) 1 × URN–20A TACAN
Sonar	1 × Type 149 (basic self-defence search)
Armament: Guns	8 × 3in/50 AA (4 × 2) (4 × 3in/50 AA (2 × 2) post-1967) 8 × Twin 40mm l/60 Bofors Mk5C AA (8 × 1) (deleted 1967) 3 × 6pdr (3 × 1) saluting guns
Aircraft 34 (maximum total)	21 CS2F–2 Trackers, 4 CHSS–2 Sea Kings, 1 H04S–3
Crew	1,370 (full complement)

Commissioning and Operations

On 17 January 1957, following traditional religious services, *Bonaventure* was commissioned, Captain H V W Groos becoming her first commanding officer. Trials began on the following day and on 21 January, having completed a series of 'runs' at full power over the Arran measured mile in the Firth of Clyde, the Commodore Superintendent Contract Built Ships, Commodore W P Carne, RN, accepted her on behalf of the Admiralty. In turn, Capt (L) J Deane, RCN, accepted her from the British for the Chief of Naval Technical Services and in turn, Captain Groos signed for the ship, making her the first carrier owned and paid for by the RCN.

Trials continued until the end of January, when the ship shifted to the RN Aircraft Yard, Sydenham, Belfast, where she remained until the end of February, while aircraft-operating equipment was completed and dead-load testing of the steam catapults carried out. On 4 March she shifted to Bangor Bay for heeling trials and then to Plymouth to

load stores and ammunition. Tests of the aviation fuel system were conducted from Portland and on 31 March the ship, her trials complete, moored in Fareham Creek, Portsmouth, ready to begin flying trials. These began on 2 April when, amid foggy patches and merchant shipping, she landed two Sea Hawk fighters, two Trackers, two Gannet ASW aircraft and two Avengers for flying trials. At about noon on 5 April, the first Banshee landed, to be catapulted off that same afternoon.

Flying trials, sonar equipment tests and gunnery exercises in the Channel were completed by 12 April, and it was back to Belfast for final adjustments of the catapults and fuel system, which was completed on 26 May. At-sea refuelling trials followed the next day, and further testing occupied the carrier until 8 June when she returned to Belfast to complete storing and take on a deck cargo that included the experimental hydrofoil craft, *Bras d'Or*, built in the UK for the Defence Research Board of Canada. Finally, on 19 June 1957 she departed for Canada, arriving in Halifax on 26 June in heavy fog.

Completed work-ups, Bonaventure *sets off for Canada, 19 June 1957. The extensive USN-pattern radar suite is quite evident, as are the Mk5C 40mm mounts and sites for the 3in/50 twins. (LYNCAN)*

The carrier remained in Halifax until mid-September, while work on a new Senior Officers' bridge on the flight deck was completed. On 16 September she began a ten-day work-up, followed by her first flying-training evolutions with Trackers and Banshees landing-on. These carrier qualifications went smoothly, since the pilots of the Trackers had, two months previously, qualified on the angled-deck of USS *Wasp*. The Trackers belonged to VS 880 Sqd, while the Banshees belonged to VF 870 Sqd. Drills were interrupted on 2 October, when it was reported that a Banshee, *en route* from Shearwater had crashed, but despite a gruelling search by air and sea, no sign was ever found of the missing jet or pilot.

The H04S–3 ASW helicopters of HS 50 were embarked the following week, and trials with all three aircraft types commenced in waters off Argentia, Newfoundland. Returning to Halifax on 17 October for refuelling, *Bonaventure* was now operational and on the 23rd, with the Senior Canadian Naval Officer Afloat [SCOA(A)], Commodore J V Brock, she sailed for the United Kingdom, accompanied by the destroyer, *Ottawa II. En route*, every possible moment was spent in flying-off and landing evolutions with VS 881 Trackers and VF 870 Banshees, with only one Tracker lost to a badly pitching

deck. The trip was also memorable, with landing and taking-off of a borrowed RCAF S 58 helicopter on a trial helicopter platform fixed over the mortar wells of *Ottawa*. Gaining the quieter waters of the North Channel, the ship flew-off her aircraft and the ship berthed at Sydenham until 3 November.

Flying resumed the following day, with an unusual landing of three tiny Army Auster reconnaissance aircraft in the afternoon, the pilots becoming the first Army personnel to become 'carrier qualified'. Thereafter, *Bonaventure* entered the normal exercise cycle that *Magnificent* had endured during her years with the RCN (see *Warship 1995*). During 11–12 November, she exercised as part of the screening ASW force for a scratch convoy that started in Londonderry. However, persistent bad weather fouled up the air cover capabilities of the carrier and the advantage fell to the attacking submarines. The weather persisted throughout the week, as *Bonaventure* met with the 1st and 3rd CES (Canadian Escort Squadrons) off the English Channel, and was still poor off the Azores, where the ships refuelled at sea from RFA *Wave Prince* on 21 November. From there the ships set off westwards, with the 1st CES detaching to Argentia, and the carrier and 1st CES proceeding to Halifax.

Side-manned, Bonaventure *prepares to enter Halifax Harbour. This elevated bows-on view shows a sample of the ship's Trackers on the centre line, with the rescue/plane guard HO4S–3, 'Pedro', right aft. Three of the four twin 3in/50 mounts show clearly with their barrels elevated. The port mirror deck-landing apparatus sponson is the white platform to the right. The originating light bar is port side, aft, behind the second aerial mast, with a deckhand standing on the catwalk next to it. (LYNCAN)*

Again weather played a large factor in delaying exercises. The start of Exercise Beaverdam was delayed some 24 hours until 6 December 1957. Off the entrance to Halifax, ten Trackers of VS 881 and five H04S–3 helicopters of HS 50 landed on the carrier, while the destroyers *St Laurent, Ottawa, Haida* and *Micmac* took station near the carrier, the whole forming TG 301.0. Low visibility curtailed fly-offs considerably, and close contact with the 'attacking' submarines was never established before the exercise ended the evening of 12 December. The destroyers returned to Halifax that evening, while *Bonaventure* stood off the harbour mouth until the aircraft could be flown off the following morning. Captain Groos handed over command to Captain W M Landymore on 17 December, while the ship commenced lengthy victualling in preparation for a long spring cruise which started on 20 January, with ten Trackers of VS 881, six ASW helicopters from HS 50, and one utility version from HU 21 aboard. With the destroyer escort *Sioux* as plane guard, the ship headed south for the waters off Bermuda.

Speed was built up on 22 January for full-power trials, while the deck was in constant use by pilots eager to gain their landing qualification. For the first time in RCN history, a Canadian carrier conducted flying and refuelling exercises simultaneously, refuelling *Sioux, Nootka, Algonquin* and *Micmac* using both abeam and astern methods. The First Canadian Escort Squadron parted company with *Bonaventure* after refuelling, but rejoined, with Third CES off Puerto Rico, where all ships, including the carrier took on fuel from the USS *Chukawan,* and then anchored for the night in Sir Francis Drake Channel.

For the next three days the Canadian ships and aircraft worked with HM Submarines *Alcide* and *Alliance* on a variety of ASW drills in the general vicinity of the Virgin Islands, followed by another brief spell in Puerto Rico and then more ASW exercises under ASWEX–1–58, which involved three units: a convoy, the USN carrier, USS *Leyte,* and *Bonaventure,* each with their own escort screen. The convoy was opposed by three submarines, one of which was the nuclear-powered *Seawolf.* The excellent water

Bonnie *means business: with her Trackers parked forward and the Banshees stricken below, a lone Tracker is prepared to be 'catted off'. The starboard mirror landing-aid sponson projects to the left, aft of the 'island', while the originating light source shows as four dark balls right aft. (MARCOM Museum)*

Dunking sonar at the trail, H04S–3 '867' speeds off to its next dunking site, off Chebucto Head, Nova Scotia, in October 1957. (DND/LYNCAN)

The McDonnell F2H3 Banshee, shown here overflying Halifax Harbour, was the first (and last) carrier-based jet fighter of the RCN. Bonaventure *is centre-top, under the span of the Angus L MacDonald Bridge. (DND/LYNCAN)*

conditions allowed sonobuoy barrier tactics to be successfully deployed by the Trackers and the four transits of the convoy were judged to have been made without casualties.

Bonaventure called at Mayport, Florida on 15 February, where the helicopters of HS 50 were landed and VF 871 was embarked, after flying down from its Shearwater base in Nova Scotia. Banshee carrier qualifications then began on the 21st, after the carrier, accompanied by *Nootka*, sailed for Charleston, interrupted only when a broken arrester wire forced cancellation of further landings. She then turned back to Mayport where repairs were made after flying the Banshees off, and on the 22nd was again offshore, waiting for the first element of four Banshees to fly back on when she was informed that one had crashed shortly after take-off, killing the pilot.

Another tragedy occurred on 4 March, after the delayed visit to Charleston. A Banshee made a normal deck landing, but suffered a brake failure, which caused it to topple over the port side of the flight deck, and, although the air-sea rescue helicopter was over the scene in seconds, it was too late to save the pilot.

The ship continued on towards Bermuda, where she met up with the RN carrier HMS *Bulwark*, and the two carriers took the opportunity to exercise cross-operating techniques, with *Bonaventure* handling Sea Venoms and Sea Hawks, while *Bulwark* handled Trackers. Banshees made only 'touch-and-go's, since *Bulwark*'s catapults had not been tested to handle an aircraft of this weight. The two carriers were then joined by elements of the Home Fleet exercising in the area and consisting of the cruiser *Ceylon*, the submarine depot ship *Maidstone*, two RFAs, six destroyers, two frigates and two submarines. Exercise Maple Royal I was then undertaken, a co-ordinated programme of ASW and other roles to familiarise both countries' navies with their opposite's techniques and procedures. These manoeuvres ended on 14 March and the combined fleet entered Halifax the same day.

On 18 March commenced Maple Royal II off Chebucto Head, with the Fleet Commander, Cmdre J Brock, RCN in tactical command, while the flag of FOAC, Rear-Admiral H F Pullen was flown from the destroyer, *St Laurent*. The cross-operating exercises with *Bulwark* now paid off, as a Tracker landing at night on *Bonaventure* dipped its port wheel over the deck edge, effectively denying a landing to the two Trackers still airborne. *Bonaventure* had lost her large mobile crane over the side before Maple Royal I, and the crippled Tracker had to be jacked up and moved by a fork-lift, a few feet at a time. The two orphaned Trackers safely landed on *Bulwark*. The exercise ended on 22 March, when the Canadian ships staged a sail-past of their RN counterparts, and the latter departed for the UK, while Canadian units exercised for a further two days in the Grand Banks area.

April 1958 was a bad month for carrier operations. On the Grand Banks from 17–25 April, only six hours were fit to fly in. A convoy protection exercise, New Broom VIII, between Halifax and the Gulf of St Lawrence from 1–5 May, with the carrier keeping two Trackers of VS 881 over the convoy at all times, day and night, the two H04S–3 helicopters during daylight hours, other than for about eight hours when the weather was too thick to

launch in. The ship returned to Halifax on 6 May, arriving at about midnight.

The next day, a week of boiler cleaning, and destoring was carried out, and on 13 May she sailed for Saint John, New Brunswick for refit, with her flight deck looking like a civilian parking lot, 150 cars belonging to the ship's company being carried for transport back to Halifax or for use while standing by the ship. She dry-docked on 15 May, remaining there until 15 August. Trials were conducted between 15–20 August, when the ship returned to Halifax for storing and on 2 September she moved to the new Shearwater Jetty. Flying training commenced on 8 September and continued until 1 October. On 8 October, *Bonaventure*, with VS 881 Trackers and H04S–3s of HS 50 embarked, and escorted by *St Laurent, Ottawa II, Huron* and *Haida*, departed, bound for the Mediterranean.

Hurricane Janice was encountered on the way to Gibraltar, with winds still gusting to 60mph as the ships entered the Straits. They anchored, and were refuelled by tanker before the voyage resumed on 22 October, their course shaped for Malta, with the ships anchored in Grand Harbour on the 24th, awaiting the commencement of Exercise MEDASWEX 26 on 27 October. For this exercise British, Canadian and Italian warships worked together for four days, in some very varied weather that limited flight opportunities, but when aloft, *Bonaventure*'s Trackers and helicopters were highly successful in hunting 'enemy' submarines.

After a brief stop in Malta for the exercise 'wash-up', the Canadian task group made an uneventful night passage through the Straits of Messina to Naples, arriving on 3 November. From there it was to Toulon, and beginning on 8–9 November the Canadian ships met HMS *Sheffield*, flying the flag of Flag Officer Flotillas Mediterranean. Permission to fly fixed-wing aircraft in Italian waters was refused, but ASW exercises with helicopters were carried out successfully. Toulon was reached on 10 November and two days later the combined fleet began Exercise MEDASWEX 27, with *Bonaventure* again experiencing arrester hook failures in her Trackers, then discovering that the arrester gear required a major overhaul, effectively cancelling any further fixed-wing aircraft participation. *Bonaventure* therefore withdrew from the exercise two days early in order to enter Gibraltar to assess the damage. The aircraft were flown off to the RAF Station, North Front, Gibraltar, as the ship went to anchor on 16 November.

It was soon apparent that there would be no landing-on of Trackers until the arrester gear could be repaired at Portsmouth, the next port of call, so the Trackers of VS 881 flew, via Lisbon and Bordeaux, to the USAF Station, Shepherds Grove, in the UK to await the carrier. Meanwhile, the carrier sailed with the task force, although in a much reduced capacity in Exercise Sharp Squall on 24 November, without *Huron* which had suffered a collision with the French destroyer, *Maille-Brézé* during the previous exercise and was then still in dry-dock at Toulon being repaired. *Bonaventure* launched another six Trackers, while the same day off the mouth of the Solent, the destroyer screen was augmented by HMCS *St Croix*.

Repairs effected, the carrier sailed for home on 6

Table 2: *CARRIER-BORNE AIRCRAFT, CANADIAN NAVY, 1945–90*

(**Note:** Grumman Avengers, Wildcats, Barracuda aircraft of HMS *Nabob/Puncher* not listed since these were RN FAA)

Fairey Swordfish

Description	Carrier-based, torpedo-spotter-reconnaissance aircraft, with crew of three for recon; two for torpedo strikes. Metal structure, fabric covered. The Swordfish IV, as used by Canada, had an enclosed cockpit.
Engine	One 690 HP Bristol Pegasus III M3 or 750 HP Pegasus XXX
Performance	Maximum speed 139mph (223.7kph); cruising 104–29mph (167.4–207.6kph). Range 546 miles (878.7km) with normal fuel load and one 1,610lb (730.3kg) torpedo. Maximum recon range without payload and extra fuel 1,030 miles (1,658km). Service ceiling 10,700ft (3,261.4m)
Armament	One Vickers 0.303 MG forward, and one Vickers 'K' gun or one Lewis 0.303 aft. One 18in torpedo or one 1,500lb (640.4kg) mine, or equivalent weight in bombs
Where used	Naval Air Station Dartmouth, 1945–46
Number ordered	22 for Canada

Supermarine Seafire XV

Description	Single-seat, carrier-borne fighter, fighter-bomber, or tactical reconnaissance aircraft. All-metal, stressed-skin construction
Engine	One 1,850hp Rolls-Royce Griffon VI; one four-blade propeller
Performance	Maximum speed 383mph (616.4kph) at 13,500ft (4,115.8m). Cruising 255mph (410.4kph) Range 430 miles (692km) normal, or 640 miles (1,030km) with auxiliary tank. Service ceiling 35,500ft (10,820m)
Armament	Two 20mm cannon and four 0.303 MG
Where used	HMCS *Warrior*
Number ordered	430 produced in total; 18 for Canada

Fairey Firefly FRI

Description	Two-seat, carrier-borne, fighter reconnaissance aircraft. All-metal, stressed-skin construction
Engine	One 1,990hp Griffon XII; three-blade propeller
Performance	Maximum speed 316mph (508.5kph). Range 1,300 miles (2,092km). Service ceiling 28,000ft (8,535m)
Armament	Four fixed 20mm cannon in wings; provision for 8 × 60lb (27.2kg) rockets, or two 1,000lb (453.6kg) bombs under wing
Where used	HMCS *Warrior*
Number ordered	376 produced in total; 18 for Canada

Fairey Firefly IV

Description	As for FRI with following changes: wings clipped; beard radiator replaced by coolant radiators extending from leading edges of centre section; four-blade propeller
Engine	One Rolls-Royce Griffon 74, 2,250hp; four-blade Rotol propeller
Performance	Maximum speed 386mph (622kph). Range 1,300 miles (2,092km). Service ceiling 28,400ft (8,656m)
Armament	Four fixed 20mm cannon in wings; provision for 16 × 60lb (27.2kg) rockets, or two 1,000lb (453.6kg) bombs under wing
Where used	HMCS *Warrior*
Number ordered	160 produced in total; 20 for Canada, postwar

Fairey Firefly V (A/S)

Description	Two-seat, carrier borne, anti-submarine reconnaissance and strike aircraft. All-metal, stressed-skin construction. Improvements over FR IV included: hydraulically powered, wing-folding and locking (over manual), and additional role equipment, such as search/attack radar
Engine	One Rolls-Royce Griffon 74, 2,250hp; four-blade Rotol propeller
Performance	Maximum speed 386mph (622kph). Range 1,300 miles (2,092km). Service ceiling 28,400ft (8,656m)
Armament	Four fixed 20mm cannon in wings; provision for 16 × 60lb (27.2kg) rockets, or two 1,000lb (453.6kg) bombs under wing
Where used	HMCS *Magnificent*
Number ordered	352 produced in total; 22 for Canada

Table 2: CONTINUED

Hawker Sea Fury FB XI

Description	Single-seat, carrier-borne, fighter-bomber. All metal, stressed-skin construction. Power-folding wings (outboard of cannons); radiators in wing leading edge of port wing at the wing root
Engine	One radial Bristol Centaurus 18-cylinder, 2,480hp, 5-blade Rotol propeller
Performance	Maximum speed 460mph (740kph). Range 700 miles (1,126.5km) at 30,000ft (9,144m), or 1,040 miles (1,674km) w/ two 90gal. (409.2l) drop tanks
Armament	Four fixed 20mm Hispano Mk5 cannons in wings, and provision for 12 × 60lb (27.2kg) rockets or two 1,000lb (453.6kg) bombs
Where used	HMCS *Warrior* and *Magnificent*
Number ordered	565 produced in total; 39 for Canada (871 Squadron)

Grumman Avenger AS3 (TBM–3E and 3W2)

Description	Three-seat, carrier-borne or shore-based, anti-submarine strike aircraft. All-metal, stressed-skin construction
Engine	One Wright R–2600–8 Cyclone 14-cylinder, two-row radial, 1,700hp, three-blade Hamilton Hydromatic propeller
Performance	Maximum speed 261mph (420kph). Range 1,130 miles (1,818.5km). Service ceiling 22,600ft (6,888.5m)
Armament	Four depth charges and one homing torpedo; 16 sonobuoys for submarine detection
Where used	HMCS *Magnificent*
Number ordered	311 remanufactured in total; 125 for Canada. Canadian AS3s were modernised (ie, improved electronics) by Fairey Aviation Co of Canada, Dartmouth Jan 1949–Apr 1951. In 1955 four TBM–3Es were converted by Fairey to TBM–3W2 version, by the addition of the AN/APS–20 early-warning radar in a ventral radome, more powerful generator for power, and the blanking-off of the rear portion of the glasshouse canopy to house the radar operator and his scopes. Eighteen 3Es were modified to carry a retractable MAD boom in their tails, with the housing on the starboard side of the fuselage, faired in.

McDonnell Banshee F2H–3

Description	Single-seat, jet fighter. Cantilever low-wing monoplane. Aluminium alloy structure, stressed-skin
Engines	Two Westinghouse J–34–WE 34 turbo-jets, 3,250lb (1,474kg) thrust
Performance	Maximum speed 587mph (944kph) (clean). Range (wing/tip tanks) 2,250 miles (3,621km). Ceiling 52,000ft (15,850m) maximum
Armament	Four M2 20mm cannon in forward fuselage; AIM–7 Sidewinder AA missiles. Westinghouse APQ–41 radar in nose
Where used	HMCS *Bonaventure*
Number ordered	800 produced in total; 39 ex-USN acquired for RCN in 1956

Grumman Tracker CS2F

Description	Carrier-based, anti-submarine search-and-attack aircraft. High-wing monoplane with a crew of four. Assembled in Canada by De Havilland Aircraft Canada
Engines	Two Wright R–1820–82WA radial engines, 1,525hp; to 3-blade VP propellers. Engines built in Canada by Pratt & Whitney
Performance	Maximum speed 287mph (462kph). Range 1,350 miles (2,173km). Service ceiling 22,000ft (6,706m)
Armament	Fuselage bay: two ASW torpedoes. Six underwing hardpoints for rockets, bombs, etc. Total weapons payload 4,810lb (2182kg). One 70 million candlepower Leigh light (starboard wing pod fairing); two sonobuoy stores in rear of each engine nacelle
Where used	HMCS *Bonaventure* (until 1969); shore-based until 1990
Number ordered	775 (S2F–1), 77 (S2F–20 USN; 43 CS2F–1, 57 CSF–2 for Canada. These aircraft were designated Mk I to III by Canada, with Mk III replacing Mk I and featuring updated radar, etc, in 1967. Mk Is were placed in storage and/or converted for pilot training, COD a/c. In 1972–73 these aircraft shifted to a surveillance role, with MAD gear and most ASW systems removed, replaced by camera pods and a SKAD pack (the latter in the fuselage bay). Retired in 1990

Table 2: *CONTINUED*

Sikorsky S–55 (H04S–3)

Description	Twelve-seat utility or ASW helicopter. Two seats, side by side for pilots
Engine	One 700hp Wright R–1300–3 radial engine, one main rotor, three blades, single, two-blade anti-torque tail rotor
Performance	Maximum speed 112mph (180.3kph). Range 360 miles (579.4km). Service ceiling 10,600ft (3,230.9m)
Armament	One Mk43 homing ASW torpedo or two depth bombs on fuselage hard points. One dipping sonar (ASW)
Accommodation	Seven to twelve passenger seats in cabin immediately below main rotor or six stretchers Hydraulic-powered hoist over main sliding door
Where used	HMCS *Magnificent, Bonaventure*/NAS *Shearwater*
Number ordered	61 H04S–3 (USN); 12 H04S–3 ASW/Utility for Canada

Vertol HUP–3 (Retriever)

Description	Medical evacuation and light cargo helicopter
Engine	One Continental R–975–46, 550hp, twin, 3-blade main rotors
Performance	Maximum speed 108mph (174kph). Range 340 miles (547.2km). Service ceiling 10,000ft (3,048m)
Armament	None
Accommodation	Crew of two and four passengers or three stretcher cases. One 400lb (180kg) winch through floor hatch
Where used	HMCS *Magnificent*/NAS *Shearwater*
Number ordered	47 for USN; 3 for Canada

Sikorsky HSS–2 Sea King (S–61)

Description	ASW/utility helicopter. Crew of four. One 600lb (272kg) hoist over main cargo door. Hardened external hook under cabin floor
Engine	Two General Electric T58–GE–8F, 1,250shp, one main rotor (five blades), one anti-torque rotor (five blades)
Performance	Maximum speed 166mph (267kph). Range 471 miles (892km). Service ceiling 14,700ft (4,480m). Maximum lift 8,000lb (3,630kg)
Armament	Two Mk44/46 ASW torpedoes; one 5.56mm MG in 'Gulf' variant (CH–124C)
Where used	HMCS *Bonaventure*, all DDH, 3 AOR
Number ordered	255 for USN; 41 for Canada, made up of 3 Utility, 1 COD (original four delivered from Sikorsky in the US); 37 ASW. As of 1993, 31 still remained in service with the Canadian Navy. ASW variants redesignated CH–124A in 1970; 8 reconfigured for surveillance work in Gulf War (1990) and referred to as 'Gulf' variant or CH–124C; 6 designated CH–124B as of 1991–92 wth HELTASP conversion

December, and off Portland Bill, she altered course to recover her Trackers. Off the Azores, flight training resumed, and that afternoon she refuelled USS *Thomas J Gary*. She arrived back at Shearwater on 15 December, where long leave was granted over the holiday period.

From 15 to 29 January 1959, the carrier was busy in deck-landing qualifications for the Trackers of VS 880, then embarked the helicopters of HS 50 and exercised off Bermuda before returning to Halifax. February was a bad-weather month, with the carrier eventually sent to the waters off Bermuda once again for further landing-on evolutions. On 10 February a landing Tracker engaged two wires, one of which broke, while the other disengaged. Fortunately, the forward deck was clear and, with the pilot standing on the brakes, the aircraft came to a halt just as the nose wheel dropped off the leading edge of the flight deck. The carrier anchored off St David's Head, Bermuda that night to unravel the tangle of wires.

The next flight session took place on 11 February, but the first landing-on Tracker tripped the arresting wire with its nose wheel, which then parted. Clearly the repairs were not good enough and, since there remained insufficient wire to repair the damage, the ship shaped course for Halifax, while *Haida* detached for Bermuda. So ended February, while repairs were made, capped by an uptake explosion when a boiler was being flashed up towards the end of the month.

March was taken up by the preparation for exercise Beaverdam III. However, freezing temperatures and snow flurries made it risky to fly the aircraft off the carrier. The necessary aircraft were flown off and after their taskings flew to Shearwater, returning the next day for the daylight portions of the exercise before returning to Shearwater.

On 25 March *Bonaventure* was bound for Norfolk, Virginia, accompanied by *Algonquin, St Croix, Restigouche, Athabaskan* and *Nootka*, forming Task Group 301.0. After a two-day lay-over, Exercise New Broom IX was undertaken, and during the first portion, a Tracker crashed into the sea while the carrier was recovering aircraft. The plane guard, USS *Rowe* closed the crash site, but none of the crew of four had escaped. After a stay in Norfolk until 6 April, the carrier and escorts shaped course for home, meeting up with *Algonquin* and *Nootka* off New York, arriving in Halifax on the 10th.

The spring cruise of 1959 started on 4 May, with ASW exercises off San Juan and Bermuda held on 26–27, 5–7 June; a visit to New York on 8–13 June; ceremonies surrounding the Royal Visit, 16–18 June; an extended refit period, 19 June–10 September; and a change in command, with Captain J C O'Brien assuming command on 12 September, relieving Captain Landymore. During this cruise the new arrester gear was tested by a hundred Banshee landings between 12–14 September. Further training exercises in local waters were carried out between 17 September and 10 October, with ship back alongside after the 11th preparing for a transatlantic voyage.

The ship departed for the UK on 4 November, arriving five days later and taking part in a 25-ship NATO exercise, Sharp Squall IV, between 11–16 and 19–23 November. She endured a severe storm between 6–7 December, in which monstrous seas swept the flight deck, normally some 39ft above the waterline. Seas battered the window on the starboard side of the compass platform, twisted the port landing mirror, opened all the seams on the starboard mirror sponson, and forced open the forward lift, filling the hangar deck and forward messes until it was forced closed once again. The carrier and her battered escort force finally returned to Halifax on 13 December.

After some examination, it was decided that the ship would have to enter dry-dock for repairs, leaving for Saint John on 10 January 1960 and remaining there until 14 March. Returning to Halifax, a week was spent re-storing the ship and conducting trials. The year 1960 would prove to be as frenzied as 1959, with qualification exercises for VS 880 and HS 50 from mid-March through to 15 April, in which *Bonaventure* clocked her 100,000 miles steamed milestone, while a Tracker of VS 880 completed the five-thousandth arrested landing on the ship.

Operation 'Short Stop' was the next exercise, with *Bonaventure* leaving Halifax on 2 May 1960, and the exercise beginning on the 4th. By the end of the exercise period on 17 May, Trackers of VS 880 had flown 104 sorties in 453 hours and the helicopters of HS 50 had flown 83 sorties in 123.7 hours.

The year 1960 also marked the fiftieth anniversary of the forming of the RCN. On 19 May forty-eight ships conducted a sail-past, with twenty-nine manning and cheering ship for the Chief of the Naval Staff. Fifty naval aircraft roared overhead at the same time, and after passing the reviewing stand, *Bonaventure* catapult-launched a Tracker. Training resumed on 26 May, with training flights and a visit to Philadelphia on 1 June, departing six days later and further ASW training in the Halifax–Bermuda corridor until the ships returned to port on 11 June.

Two further training cruises were made during the period late June–early July. On 17 July she greeted the

Governor-General of Canada, George P Vanier, and his wife off Ingonish Beach, Nova Scotia, acting as their Royal Flagship while they visited Prince Edward Island and Newfoundland. *Bonaventure* returned to Halifax on 22 July, where she fired a salute to the Flag Officer Atlantic Coast, Rear-Admiral Hugh Pullen, who was shortly to retire. The ship had steamed a total of 3,500 miles in that month alone and her annual refit preparations occupied the crew until the end of July, when she entered refit at Saint John Shipbuilding & Drydock Co. until late October.

First operational trials began on 14 November and between then and the 28th, Detachment One of VS 880 and VF 870 qualified for deck landings. Heeling trials were conducted in St Margaret's Bay on the 23rd. More flying exercises ended on the 29th and she berthed in Boston on the 30th. Departure was on 5 December, with *Cayuga* as plane guard/escort, with VF 870 taking part in a ground-support exercise at Camp Gagetown, New Brunswick, between the 6th and 9th. The week 10–16 December was occupied by exercises with Task Force 301, composed of the Canadian ships, *Cape Scott, Haida, Sioux, Micmac, Crescent, Nootka, Inch Arran, Outremont* and *Victoriaville*, before returning to Halifax on the 16th.

Further exercises took place in the waters off Bermuda between 24 January and 10 February. Exercise *Tout Droit* was undertaken between 13 and 14 February, with escorting done by the destroyers *Chaudière, Columbia, Kootenay, Terra Nova* and *Restigouche*. After discharging supernumeries in Norfolk on the 14 February, the ship then undertook six weeks of training in the waters off Bermuda, arriving in Halifax on 28 March. On 5 April, an aircraft demonstration was put on for the Minister of National Defence D L Harkness, before returning to Halifax to prepare for the forthcoming NATO exercise, New Broom X. This exercise plus two local cruises occupied the rest of the month, when the ship was secured for self-maintenance alongside at the Shearwater jetty.

With her aircraft stricken below, *Bonaventure* was at sea once again on 23 May, involved in training exercises that would see her visit Rhode Island, New York, and back to Halifax by 26 June, and having exercised jointly with the USN as Task Force 83.3, which had consisted of the carrier, USS *Essex* and five destroyers.

July was another month of NATO exercises, including Riptide II. During the early stages of this exercise, one of HS 50 H04S–3s crashed ahead of the ship, and the crew was rescued by the USS *Voorhis*. The 'wash-up' was done in Norfolk on the 13th before the ship returned to Halifax. The ship was alongside from the end of July until the third week in September. Command changed in that time, with Captain F C Frewer, RCN, assuming command.

A far-north training exercise was conducted between 22 September and 8 October, in concert with USN warships, with exercises JASWEX 3/61 and Trapline successfully completed. At home again, ten days respite was granted after her 5,200-mile voyage before flight training resumed. VF 870's Banshees were the first to train for pilot requalification. On 14 November the carrier steamed away from the waters of Bermuda towards Charleston, when the nine-thousandth arrested landing was made by a CS2F

Tracker piloted by Lt K Miller, USN. Upon completion of the exercise and return to Halifax, it was found that 2,920 arrested landings had been made in 1961.

The year 1962 largely repeated the cycle of previous years, with *Bonaventure* in Caribbean waters in January through to 16 March, when she returned to Halifax, having exercised on her own with escort and with US Task Group 83.4 between Bermuda and off the Nova Scotia coast. In early April air and sea exercises were begun, and by the 19th the carrier had finished her sea time for the month and also passed the 10,000 mark for arrested landings.

In June the ship resumed training exercises and on the 16th she left harbour with Trackers of VS 880, H04S–3s of HS 50 and one from VX 10, the experimental test and evaluation squadron. A southern cruise was undertaken for flight deck requalification and Exercise JASWEX 1/62 off Bermuda, returning to Halifax on 30 June. Further ASW exercises began on 3 July and ended on the 6th, and the ship paid a port visit to Quebec City from the 7th to 10th. Returning to Halifax, the ship was then due for annual refit, and on 23 July she steamed to Lauzon, Quebec, where she entered the Champlain Dock with a Swedish freighter as company, to begin a refit that lasted until August 1962.

On 17 September 1962 *Bonaventure*, fresh from northern exercises, spearheaded a series of ASW training exercises in the western approaches to Europe. The first week at sea was given over to requalification of pilots from VS 880 with their Trackers. On 24 September, the carrier responded to the SOS of a Flying Tiger Airline Super Constellation aircraft that had been forced to ditch some 300 miles to the north of the carrier. *Bonaventure* acted as Search Area Commander, and flying off Trackers with twenty-man Beaufort rafts in canisters in the aircrafts' torpedo bays. Securing from the search, *Bonaventure* spent the week of 13 to 18 October exercising with NATO partners in Exercise Sharp Squall, where results were most satisfactory, with 59,360 miles being covered by Trackers of VS 880. Ports of call were Portsmouth, where leave was curtailed in light of the Cuban missile crisis, and then back to Halifax.

During the period of November until early December, only the ASW helicopters of HS 50 were aboard the carrier, which conducted local ASW exercises before seasonal leave was granted over the holidays.

The year 1963 started off with a series of MARLANT exercises in waters off Bermuda, including participation in a Joint Maritime Warfare School exercise. The only event of any note was the loss of Tracker 1584 on 8 June, while flying a ASW mission from *Bonaventure*, with the loss of two of its four personnel.

Four H04S–3 'Horses' spotted right aft, while rescue/plane guard 'Pedro' lifts off an errand, sometime in 1966. By this time, the CHSS–2 Sea King was arriving in sufficient numbers that they would replace the 'Horse' by the time Bonaventure *re-emerged from her mid-life refit in 1967. The originating light source bar for the mirror landing aid may be seen to be left. (DND/LYNCAN)*

After her annual refit, she resumed her cycle of re-certification of pilots from VS 880 in September. A strenuous training session in Canadian and north Atlantic waters found the carrier in excellent shape as far as training was concerned, and in November the carrier, with a four helicopter detachment of HS 50 and Trackers of 880, headed south for exercises in more hospitable waters. However, a storm in the third week of the month saw a freak wave break over the flight deck, drenching the Trackers secured there. The aircraft were stricken below singly, where they were decontaminated by washing and flushing with fresh water.

The year 1964 started off with Detachment One of VS 880 and four H04S–3 helicopters aboard the carrier and the usual training cycle was undertaken. These included New Broom in April, JASWEX 1/2/64, Riptide in July and MEDASWEX I exercises in the Mediterranean that spring. *Bonaventure* then began her annual refit in July, while a unique mixed crew ASW operation was begun that same month, when a six-plane detachment of VS 880 departed from Quonset Point Naval Air Station, Rhode Island aboard the USS *Essex*. There would be four such deployments, with the last being in November, designed to keep the air crews certified while *Bonaventure* underwent a fairly lengthy refit.

Same Grind, but a Sole Role

The cycle of carrier operations was constant through 1965, but other changes were happening. The H04S–3 helicopter gave way to the Sikorsky CHSS–2 Sea King, with operational units deploying in 1965. By 1963 the F2H–3 Banshee was retired, reflecting the 1962 decision to configure more closely the Canadian fleet towards its professed role of ASW, coupled with the advancing age of these aircraft. No replacement was purchased, since the viability of carriers was now in doubt, with some declaring that the ICBM and strategic bombers with nuclear weapons would render them obsolete. This effectively left the carrier with no role other than ASW.

Changing Political Climate

In 1963 a new Liberal administration took office in Ottawa, and the effects were nearly immediate. Defence spending was stabilised at C$1.53 billion, a number of new naval programmes were cancelled and the fleet was reduced from its high of sixty-two ships in 1960 to forty-six. Naval jet fighters were also a casualty, with the Banshee being withdrawn from service. The 1964 White Paper on Defence ironically shifted the Navy's role from pure ASW to a more broad set of requirements, a radical turnaround that could not be implemented satisfactorily with the ships then in the fleet.

Coupled with this reversal of policy, was a concept that had had its roots in the three armed forces since 1960: integration of common services such as postal, dental, medical and supply. The Minister of National Defence of the day, Paul Hellyer, expanded this concept to take in integration of the three forces into a homogenised organisation to be known as the Canadian Armed Forces, with members being jacks-of-all-trades. Successive defence budgets pared capital acquisition projects to the bone, while the fleet continued to shrink.

Mid-Life Refit: the Decline and Demise of Carrier Operations

In 1966, *Bonaventure* was clearly ready for her mid-life refit. She entered a sixteen-month refit at Lauzon and returned to Halifax, Nova Scotia, on 29 November 1967, after a C$22 million (originally projected at C$11-million in 1966) refit, ready to resume her role. During the year, the Mk 2A and Mk 2 Trackers had been gradually replaced by Mk 3s. She embarked twelve Trackers and eighteen crews of VS 880, plus 4 CHSS–2 Sea Kings for winter training off Bermuda, but *en route*, seven of the Trackers were rendered unserviceable by severe saltwater damage due to a storm. Upon arrival back in Halifax, these were landed and transferred to Fairey Aviation for extensive inspection.

The year 1968 was as busy as any other, with the customary training and joint exercises, with the ship seeing the usual ports in Puerto Rico, Bermuda, the United States, Ireland, Britain and Denmark. The last NATO exercise of the year was also the largest: Exercise Silver Tower, which saw the ship and her aircraft fully involved with her NATO partners from off the coast of the US, across the north Atlantic, the North Sea and in continental waters off England and northwest Europe. However, the writing was clearly on the wall.

By 1 February 1968 the process of unification was nearing completion, with new organisation, ranks and roles. In May a further review of defence policy was ordered by the new Canadian government. Eleven months later, the new Prime Minister Pierre Trudeau provided a broad outline of current thought and in August 1971, the white paper *Defence in the Seventies* was issued.

In its conclusions, the policy directive promised a significant reorientation of effort within the forces, with ASW further demoted in favour of generalisation. No new equipment was announced to fulfil these nebulous roles; indeed, during fiscal years 1970–73, defence spending was limited to an annual budget of C$1.815 billion. Faced with an ever-decreasing operational financial envelope, the Defense Department was forced to declare *Bonaventure* redundant in 1969, with the last Tracker taking off from her decks on 12 December. On 3 July 1970 she was paid off, effectively ending fixed-wing naval aviation at sea.

Bonaventure was finally sold to William Kennedy of Vancouver on 17 August 1970 for the sum of $851,700. Kennedy resold the ship to Mitsui of Japan for $1.6 million. On 28 October 1970, the carrier departed under tow by the tug *Fuji Maru*, arriving in Kaohsiung, Taiwan, in mid-March 1971 for scrapping. However, the Taiwanese company went bankrupt part way through the break-up, and the carrier was towed to Osaka where her destruction was completed.

However, this would not be the end of true naval

HMCS Bonaventure *in 1966, headed into Halifax, Nova Scotia, just before her mid-life refit. The refit effectively added eleven years of available service to the ship, but within three years she would be sold for scrap. (DND/LYNCAN)*

aviation at sea, but rather a concentration upon a new aspect. Although fixed-wing flying operations at sea ceased with the demise of *Bonaventure*, true naval aviation in its purest form did not. Rather, it took two new directions. The first saw the former assets of the carrier, namely the CP–121 Trackers utilised in the same manner as before but from shore stations, and the second, a concentration of rotary-wing aircraft on the relatively small platforms of destroyers.

Big 'Bird' on a Little Ship

Canada had been toying with the idea of using helicopters aboard RCN ships at the end of the Second World War. In a memorandum from the Senior Officer (Fuel), Operations Division to Naval Defence Headquarters, dated 23 January 1943, it was stated that: 'some of the Canadian frigates under construction should be completed as anti-submarine helicopter carriers'. However,

given the primitive state of development of the helicopter at that time and the urgent need for escort vessels, the suggestion was quickly forgotten amid the press of war.

By the mid-1950s, however, submarine technology was progressing by leaps and bounds. Spurred on by the advances made by the Germans in the closing years of the war, the major naval powers had or were developing conventional submarines that could dive deeper, were quieter, and had greater speed and endurance. The advent of USS *Nautilus*, with its high underwater speed and virtually limitless endurance alarmed countries such as Canada, whose navy's primary role was ASW. Clearly the pendulum had swung away from the surface ASW ship. The ASW helicopter, with its high transit speed, dipping sonar and virtual immunity to submarine attack was seen as the only immediate solution to the growing submarine threat.

True, Canada was operating small helicopters such as the H04S–3 from a light fleet carrier, but this severely limited the helicopter's radius of action. It was thought that the full potential of the ASW helicopter would not be

After her controversial mid-life refit, Bonaventure *returns to Halifax on 29 November 1967. During the refit, two of the twin 3in/50 mounts and sponsons were removed, as well as the mirror landing aids. New radar and TACAN, plus extensive modernisation and modification of the CIC and other facilities made her the most modern light fleet carrier in the Commonwealth at the time. (DND/LYNCAN)*

realised until it was possible to operate them from smaller fleet units such as frigates and destroyers.

The first serious experiments took place in 1956, when a steel platform was fabricated and fitted over the stern of the *Prestonian* class frigate HMCS *Buckingham*, using a H04S–3 'Horse' helicopter, operated by Detachment 3, HU 21 Squadron from Shearwater. Trials were on-going for a period of three months (September–December).

Buckingham, under the command of Lt-Cdr T Conners, conducted the first 'land-on, fly-off' trials in Bedford Basin in early September. These trials then progressed into the approaches of Halifax Harbour. 'Mid-ocean' trials were conducted off Chebucto Head over a three-day period in late October, and were witnessed by the crew of HMCS *Magnificent*. Indeed, *Magnificent*'s CO, Captain A B Fraser-Harris was so intrigued by the idea of landing on such a small platform that he piloted 'NY 226' through three landing sequences! As confidence grew, the ship and helicopter ranged further afield, with several flights in the Bay of Fundy and finally down the US Atlantic coast to Portland, Boston and the Bermudas.

Out of this series of trials some startling conclusions were drawn. Paramount was that the undercarriage of the H04S–3 was not strong enough to take landings on a pitching, rolling flight deck on a small warship. Clearly another helicopter type would be necessary for Phase II testing. This deck was subsequently removed, modified and then installed aboard HMCS *Ottawa* in 1957, with trials being done using a Sikorsky H–34 (S–58) borrowed from the RCAF. Trials with this helicopter were conducted over six weeks and took place on a solo voyage to the UK and back, with the required 'heavy weather' trials conducted off the north coast of Ireland, while in the company of the relatively new HMCS *Bonaventure*.

One of those aboard for these trials was J F Graham, then a young marketing executive with Sikorsky Aircraft. He relates:

With *Ottawa* they [the RCN] were really set up to do trials. They put up a 40 by 40ft steel deck on the back of the ship and put the S–58 on it, tied down. We had to develop the procedures for launching it and getting it back on in rough water. After developing the system, we were quick

With CHSS–2 Sea King ASW helicopters and Trackers of VS 880 aboard, Bonaventure *heads out to sea in April 1968.* *(DND/LYNCAN)*

enough that three sailors on each side would be responsible for tying it down. They had these quick-release straps, fastened to special tie-down points on the helicopter. Releasing it was no problem, of course, but when it landed back on and the deck was moving rapidly, it was another story. As soon as it hit the deck, they'd get their straps on each side and pull them tight. Eventually they could get it all secured in four seconds.

We'd wait for a steady period. We got to know that when the ship came up on a big one [swell] that the ship was going to be steady for a short while and we rigged up lights so that when you felt it coming up on a steady period, you'd switch these deck lights on, the pilot would see these and he'd just drop it on the deck and they'd lash it down. These steady periods were six to eight seconds long and we'd have it on in good time. We could do this when the Trackers, which were alongside on the *Bonaventure*, couldn't fly. Their deck was too rough for them. That proved it could be done.

As well, the RCN was learning other factors in operating

a helicopter in a saltwater environment. When the S–58 was returned to the RCAF it was found to be suffering from such a case of saltwater corrosion that it was stricken from the rolls of operational aircraft.

As things stood after the *Buckingham* and *Ottawa* trials in 1958, the Navy was faced with the developing of three distinct programmes to get a relatively sophisticated helicopter aboard a frigate-sized ship. These were:

1. To design and fit a flight deck, hangar, maintenance facilities and aircrew accommodation in six existing ships and in two unbuilt members of the same type;
2. To procure a helicopter to replace the ageing H04S, with capabilities to match the demands of DDH Staff Requirements;
3. To develop a method of instantly securing the helicopter to the deck upon landing, as well as providing a means of controlled traverse in and out of the fixed hangar. This requirement led to a development contract being awarded to Canadian industry in 1959 (discussed later).

Trackers of 880 Squadron line up before being catapulted off Bonaventure, *2 April 1969, during Operation 'Springboard', off the coast of Puerto Rico. (US Navy/LYNCAN)*

The three programmes came together in HMCS *Assiniboine* in late 1964 when extensive flight-deck and hangar compatibility trials were commenced and the HHRSD system was refined and proved at sea. During this three-year trials period, maintenance support and manning policies were worked out and many changes were made to associated systems. Despite pressures to accelerate key aspects of the system, the Navy firmly resisted, insisting that the safety of the ship, helicopter and personnel was paramount, and that a deliberate, step-by-step procedure was critical. Thus the first operational helicopter/ship system did not go to sea until 1967 (HMCS *Saguenay*).

Accordingly, with the replacement helicopter tentatively identified in early 1961, work on developing the ship's systems could continued. The decision to convert the seven *St Laurent*s was made on 12 September 1961 and the first ship to complete conversion was HMCS *Assiniboine* on 26 June 1963.

As the conversion was nearing completion, the captain and crew eagerly awaited the arrival of the first Sea King. However, what arrived from Halifax, via CN Rail, was a dummy helicopter, carefully constructed from concrete blocks. It had an accurately sized and positioned undercarriage and main probe, plus a centre of gravity that was within 0.5in horizontally and vertically of that of the real

aircraft. Weight could be varied in 1,250lb increments, from 13,000 to 18,000. This would be *Assiniboine*'s 'helicopter' for the next several months.

After work-ups, the ship rejoined the West Coast Fleet, before being transferred to Halifax. In the intervening time, the ship conducted a careful series of straightening and traversing trials, in motions of up to 12° of roll. On the east coast, the ship was used extensively throughout 1964–66 for trials of the prototype haul-down system and in developing helicopter handling techniques.

Meanwhile, while *Assiniboine* was undertaking these trials, the Sea Kings were eagerly awaited at Shearwater by HS 50. However, the first CHSS–2s were actually supplied by the USN, as mentioned later. The USN were interested in the Canadian developments in mating a large ASW helicopter to a destroyer-sized warship, and made sure that one Sea King was provided to VX 10, the RCN's Test Development and Evaluation Squadron. In January 1963 VX 10, under the command of Lt-Cdr Sheldon Rowell, had been directed to assist in the evaluation of the haul-down, rapid securing and deck handling systems installed in HMCS *Assiniboine*, with actual trials starting in November. These were not only to evaluate the equipment, but also to determine whether the theoretical design specification was in fact satisfactory. These trials began with an examination of the flight envelope in the ship's vicinity, the effects of funnel- and hangar-induced turbulence, and possible pilot-orientation techniques relative to the ship.

For the next two years this project continued, hand-in-hand with deliveries of further CHSS–2 aircraft. Flight trials (carried out in conjunction with Fairey) including haul-down and free-deck landings, with and without the Beartrap, were carried out, with satisfactory results. In later stages, the trials investigated the effects upon the helicopter of a sudden release of the tensioned cable and evaluation of haul-down landings and aircraft handling under progressively worsening weather and sea conditions.

By late 1967 numerous changes had been incorporated in both the aircraft and the haul-down and securing system. The final phase was the night/heavy weather trials, flown by Lt-Cdr Gerald Watson as the project pilot, and Lt William Peterson providing the engineering input. These trials were passed with ease, as system maturity had been reached. HS 50 was designated a shore squadron and tasked with providing trained helicopter air detachments to the nine DDH ships. In 1967–68, HS 50 had over 150 aircrew and twenty-five Sea Kings. By 1974 the work load would prove too much for HS 50's administrative staff, and it would be divided into new squadrons: HS 423 and 443, on 31 July.

Helicopter Haul-Down and Rapid Securing Device (HHRSD)

The major danger period during the landing of any helicopter on the flight deck of a small ship had proved to be in the interval between when the helicopter ceases hovering and when it is firmly secured to the flight deck. Hence this was the problem that was presented to Canadian industry in 1959, along with a requirement to provide a means of transferring the helicopter, with its main and tail rotors folded, into the ship's hangar. The specification called for a system that would secure the helicopter within four seconds of the wheels touching the deck, with the deck movement maxima being set at 31° of roll, 9° of pitch and heaving up to 20ft per second in winds of fifty knots.

Fairey Aviation of Canada, Dartmouth, Nova Scotia, took up the challenge and hand-in-hand with the Naval Design Team, set about developing a system. This was known as the Helicopter Haul-Down and Rapid Securing Device, or HHRSD.

One of the stickiest aspects in the development of HHRSD was how to centre the aircraft after it had landed and before being moved into the hangar. A circular rotating framework, using a wire-mesh grid was considered, but the elaborate mechanics to make it work made the idea impracticable.

The Naval Design Team in Ottawa went back to basics. The Director of Aircraft Design and Development, Cdr John Frank, brought in his son's Meccano set, and before long the concept of four powered rails mounted inside a rectangular frame and moving parallel to the sides was

developed. A model was built and presented to Fairey, with instructions to build a prototype and submit a proposal. The result was the Rapid Securing Device, or RSD.

The system adopted consisted of a spring-loaded, retractable probe near the centre of gravity of the helicopter, which is 'trapped' by the jaws of an RSD. The RSD is secured to the ship in the centre of the flight deck. The hold of the RSD (sometimes referred to as the Beartrap for obvious reasons) on the helicopter main probe prevents upwards, forwards and sideways motion. Rotation of the helicopter about the main probe is prevented by another retractable probe located near the tail wheel of the helicopter, which engages a series of slots on the after end of the flight deck and referred to as the Tail Grid.

The RSD was designed to fit under the Sea King and between the main landing gear. This requirement limited the open target area of the RSD to a rectangle measuring 36in × 42in, or an opening of roughly 10.5 sq ft. Thus in order to 'trap' the helicopter successfully, the pilot had to place his main probe within this area, which is totally out of sight in the critical final moments of the recovery operation. Thus aids to the pilot were necessary and three sources were developed:

1. Deck markings, lights and horizon attitude bars were installed to tell the pilot where he was in respect to the flight deck and, more importantly, the RSD, as well as indicating deck motion;
2. A Landing Signals Officer (LSO), who is located on the flight deck in a glass enclosure called the HOWDA, and has a clear view of the RSD and the helicopter's main probe. The LSO talks the pilot down into the RSD and closes the jaws of the RSD on the probe, using the controls on his console;
3. A cable, often incorrectly referred to as the haul-down cable, which passes up through the centre of the RSD and is secured to the helicopter through its main probe. The tension on this cable was controlled by the LSO, with a hydraulic control system below the flight deck maintaining a constant tension on the haul-down cable, with recovery speeds of up to 20ft per second.

Since the hangar door-opening left little clearance, accurate alignment of the helicopter during the traversing of the RSD was necessary. With the helicopter securely held by the RSD, the latter was made so that it could act as a 'mule', pulling the folded helicopter into the hangar. The alignment of the helicopter in relation to the fore and aft centre line of the hangar was solved by engaging the tail probe in a slot that paralleled the RSD's deck track.

With the possibility of the helicopter being secured off-centre in the RSD or the tail probe being outside the slot, a method of straightening the helicopter was necessary. Indeed, this had been handled by allowing the roll of the ship to move the off-centre helicopter to the centre of the Beartrap, plus the swinging of the tail to centre, pivoting about the main probe fixed in the Beartrap in trials to that date. The Technical Project Officer in Naval Headquarters, Lt-Cdr James Atwood, redesigned the tail grid and this resolved some of the difficulties.

However, during calm water trials in Bedford Basin in

1965, the ship was at anchor, with a covering frost. When the straightening of the helicopter was attempted, the combination of 'no traction' and lack of roll prevented the tail swinging – the helicopter simply skidded sideways. This problem was eventually solved by Lt-Cdr Craig Balsom. The solution was the installation of a tail guide winch and cable system. This continuous-loop cable system allowed the deck crew to attach the two ends of the wire to the tail wheel assembly. With the tail probe retracted, the LSO could swing the tail either to port or starboard (while traversing the RSD aft) until the trap bars and probe were centred in the RSD, where they automatically locked. Then the tail was brought back to the centre line, where the pilot lowered the tail probe into the slot and the helicopter traversed into the hangar. Once there, the RSD could be used to secure the helicopter, or after the helicopter was securely lashed down, disengaged and moved out of the way or back on to the flight deck.

A typical landing would have the RSD moved until it centred over the housed haul-down cable. Tension on the cable would be set at zero and the deck crew would then manually haul out about 50ft, flaking it down on the flight deck. The ship would then go to Flying Stations, with its course altered so that any wind would be roughly 30° off the port bow. The helicopter would then be allowed to approach from the stern and would come to a hover 20–25ft above the centre of the flight deck. The pilot would then lower 0.125in messenger wire to the deck, where a crew member grasped it in a pair of grounded tongs, the latter to ensure the discharge of any static electricity. The messenger was then attached to the 0.313in haul-down wire and the two were drawn up through the hollow main probe by the helicopter's messenger winch and then the haul-down wire secured. With the main probe extended, the flight deck was cleared of all personnel other than the LSO.

The LSO then would bring the haul-down winch into operation at minimum tension, recovering the excess of haul-down wire from the deck. When the cable was taut, the LSO then applied 2000lb tension, which the pilot matched by applying lift, and the hover maintained about 8 to 10ft off the deck. The LSO would then judge when the deck was steady, increase tension to 3,000lb and tell the pilot to land. The pilot, in fact, controls the rate of descent and actually flew down, rather than being pulled down.

When the LSO saw the main probe within the RSD, he fired the jaws, which closed around the probe and secured the helicopter to the deck. The tail probe was lowered, engaging the tail grid, the helicopter was straightened and then the blades and tail were folded for the traverse into the hangar.

The Big Bird

The aircraft eventually chosen to replace the venerable H04S–3 'Horse' was the Sikorsky SH–3A Sea King, which was designated CHSS–2 in Canadian use. The Sea King contract was awarded on 20 November 1962, with forty-one eventually being acquired between 1964 and 1968. Equipped with a modern 'dunking sonar' and ASW

torpedoes, Sea King was able to 'dip, sprint, dip' on any submarine, however fast and deep, countering it with lightweight ASW torpedoes.

The CHSS–2 acquisition heralded one of the worst procurement procedures ever conceived in Ottawa. The original order was for eight, four of which were manufactured by Sikorsky in Connecticut and the next four assembled by United Aircraft of Canada at their Longueuil, Quebec, facility. The first so assembled left the plant on 27 August 1964, and by this time the number ordered was twenty, with talk of up to seventy being needed. However, the original price per unit quoted by Sikorsky ballooned because of the government's indecision over just how many would eventually be needed. From 1962 the number was raised by increments, leaving no course open to UA of Canada but to treat each year's requirement as a separate contract. Because these annual orders were so small, UA of Canada were forced to pay premium price for the components from Sikorsky and other subcontractors.

The second order was for twelve; the lowest number ordered in one year was six and the whole process stretched over five years. Indeed, UA of Canada were never informed when the order was complete. They only realised that the programme was at an end when no order was placed in 1968. With this piecemeal acquisition procedure, a Sea King, on average, cost C\$2.1 million (1964) per unit.

Meanwhile, a decision to proceed with the CHSS–2 acquisition in November 1962 saw the first Phase I training classes organised in December 1962 and January 1963. However, because of the US Navy's priority in acquiring Sea King, it was not until August 1963 that the first CHSS–2s arrived at Shearwater. These were the first of four diverted from US Navy requirements and were flown by pilots of HS 50 from Patuxent River to Shearwater for training purposes. US Navy pilots were loaned for familiarisation flights and advanced training of Canadian pilots.

The first of these four was then turned over to VX 10 at Shearwater, this being an experimental group tasked with test development and evaluation of the Sea King. The other three were utilised as training aircraft with HS 50. Gradually, as further Sea Kings were delivered by UA of Canada, the H04S–3 were shifted to HU 21 for utility and search-and-rescue operations before eventually being retired in 1970.

In 1970 the designator of the Sea King was changed from CHSS–2 to CH–124A, the better to reflect the improvements made in the aircraft, and over the past twenty years a steady stream of modernisations and updates has been done to keep the Sea King current.

The 205 Class Conversions: the Other Half of the Equation

One of the critical factors that had contributed to the success of the destroyer/helicopter marriage lay in the characteristics of the ship class. Her built-in reserve of stability meant that she could accommodate the extra top weight of the flight deck, hangar, VDS, and above all, a 10-ton helicopter. Her high free-board meant a helicopter could be operated nearly free of spray, other than in the worst of conditions, and the upper deck arrangement lent itself to the drastic conversion necessary.

The DDH conversion of the 205 class consisted of a fourteen-month refit in which virtually everything aft of the bridge was torched off to the upper deck level. Additionally, one of the two Limbo ASW mortars was removed as a weight-saving measure. The original funnel and uptakes were removed and divided in two, to make room for the forward end of the hangar, to reduce air turbulence in the area and to remove stack gas effluent from the helicopter's approach and hover path. A 78ft × 40ft flight deck was installed and the space immediately below given over to accommodating the helicopter haul-down system. Meanwhile, forward accommodation spaces were reworked as well. One of the gains was a larger and better equipped recreation space forward, plus increased space in all mess decks.

Aft, the stern of the ship had the top angle of transom and deck cut off and a variable-depth sonar well built to accommodate the AN/SQA–501 VDS handling gear, the SQS–504 towed sonar, plus the hoist control hut. In all, the modernisation of *Assiniboine* consumed 2,400,000 man-hours of labour and cost C$24 million to complete. Conversion of the other six of class cost roughly the same.

As well as the above, an active roll-dampening system was devised and installed, albeit at a later date with *Assiniboine*. This system consisted of two non-retractable fins (one on either side of the ship), hydraulically tilted and controlled by a gyro-sensing unit. The fins extended out about four-and-a-half feet from the hull on a spindle and were about nine feet long. They were situated just forward of the boiler room and angle downward at 50° from the horizontal. Range of movement was 15° in elevation and a like amount in depression.

The system was designed to limit rolling motion during extreme weather to about 10°, and was successful in this role. All ships of the *St Laurent* class were retrofitted with these during or shortly after undergoing the 205 DDH Conversion Program, while they were built into the *Annapolis* class.

Status of conversions by April 1964: *Assiniboine* had been completed in June 1963 and was operational; *St Laurent* had been finished in October 1963, and HMCS *Ottawa* and *Saguenay* were due to complete in the fall of 1964. The two purpose-built DDHs, *Nipigon* and *Annapolis*, were to commission in May and September 1964, respectively. Still left to be converted were *Skeena*, *Fraser* and *Margaree*.

Further Applications

With the completion of the conversion of the seven *St Laurent* class and the completion of the two *Annapolis* class by 1966, the concept of carrying relatively heavy ASW helicopters was extended to the new construction DDH–280 class of four ships, only with provision for two CH–124 Sea Kings. About the same time as the conversion of the *St Laurent* class, the same ship/helo interface was applied to the three At-Sea Operational Replenishment (AOR) ships then being built, but with provision for the support and maintenance of up to four Sea Kings.

Nearly thirty years after the first application, the idea of small ship/large helicopter operations in the Canadian Navy continues. The twelve new 'City' class frigates feature an enlarged hangar and improved haul-down system known as RAST, built by Indal Technologies of Canada, and engineered to handle the even-larger EHI-built EH–101 naval variant, to be known as Petrel in Canadian service. However, with the cancellation of the USA programme in 1995, the CH–124 must labour on, ill-equipped for the new ships.

Last Gasp

The last vestige of fixed-wing carrier aircraft, the venerable Tracker, went into gradual decline in importance after 1972, when, stripped of its ASW equipment, it became a pure surveillance aircraft. Finally, in 1989 the decision was made to retire these aircraft, rather than modernise them, and the last disappeared from active service in 1990, leaving only the Sea King at sea.

OPERATION 'DEADLIGHT'

David Miller examines the often farcical story of the Royal Navy's attempts to achieve a mass scuttling of the German Navy's surrendered U-boat fleet toward the end of the Second World War.

Naval histories of the Second World War generally end with a dismissive sentence or two on the subject of Operation 'Deadlight', during which more than one hundred U-boats were scuttled off the Irish coast. The picture left in the reader's mind is of a quick, painless operation conducted with wartime efficiency, with all U-boats delivered to the same point and scuttled according to plan. Unfortunately and interestingly, the reality was quite different.

Background

The war in Europe ended at midnight on 8/9 May 1945 with the German U-boats scattered. Many were in German ports fitting out, undergoing trials or with the training flotilla. Most operational boats were in Norway, Doenitz having ordered them there in the final weeks of the war to create a 'bargaining counter'. Others were on patrol in the Atlantic or around the British coastline, while a small number were in the Far East at U-boat bases at Penang, Singapore and Batavia, or *en route* between Europe and Japan.

The surrender terms included instructions that boats in German ports were to surrender to the Allies, while those in Norway were to await Allied orders. Meanwhile, boats at sea were to surface and broadcast their positions, whereupon they would be given instructions on ports to head for, courses to follow and recognition signals. U-boats in the east Atlantic were directed to the nearest suitable American or Canadian port, while those near the British Isles were ordered either into the nearest port (eg Liverpool or Weymouth), or into Loch Eriboll (at the northwest tip of Scotland) or Loch Ryan (in southwest Scotland).

Almost all U-boats carried out the Allies' instructions, except for those that implemented *Regenbogen* and scuttled themselves in German ports. A small number also made for neutral ports: several went to Spain, two scuttled themselves off the Portuguese coast and two reached Argentina. The U-boats in the Far East were beyond the Allies' reach and were taken over by the Japanese and their crews made prisoners.

It appears that the Allies had given little thought to the postwar fate of the U-boats in the longer term, as the British Chiefs-of-Staff Committee agreed on 15 May

1945 '. . . to ask SHAEF [Supreme Headquarters Allied Expeditionary Force] to order that all U-boats in Norway be sent to the United Kingdom, pending a decision on their ultimate disposal.' This recommendation was passed to the Prime Minister Winston Churchill who endorsed it, subject to the addition of a new sentence, that: 'Ultimate settlement will of course be a matter for the peace talks.'

U-boats in Norway started to sail for the United Kingdom on 30 May, followed by those from German ports in mid-June; most had German crews, although at least one had an all-British crew. Some of these went to Loch Ryan in Scotland, the others to Lisahally in Northern Ireland, but, in addition, the individual boats seem to have moved fairly frequently. *U–1009*, for example, entered Loch Eriboll on 10 May 1945, moved to Lisahally for a formal surrender on 14 May but eventually sailed for scuttling from Loch Ryan.

The fate of the U-boats was one of many problems discussed at the Potsdam Conference, where it was agreed that up to thirty would be distributed to the Allies for experiments and research. In the event, twenty-eight were distributed: Canada – 1; France – 6; Norway – 4; UK – 3; USA – 4; USSR – 10. The Potsdam Conference also established a Tripartite Naval Commission, consisting of two representatives each from the UK, the USA and the USSR, which met in Berlin between 14 August and 6 December 1945; among the decisions reached was one that '. . . all unallocated submarines which are afloat shall be sunk in the open sea in a depth of not less than one hundred metres by 15 February 1946.' The reason for selecting that date is not recorded (possibly because it was six months from the start of the Commission's meetings), but it was to have a significant bearing on the operation, whose implementation was delegated in its entirety to the Royal Navy (RN).

The Plan

Time was now of the essence, as the Royal Navy had already begun its postwar rundown of men and ships, and the Commission had set a tight deadline. The area where the sinkings were to be done was quickly selected and the operation was assigned the codeword 'Deadlight'. The

U-boats at Lisahally. In the foreground are four Type VIICs – from left to right: unidentified; U–278; U–1058; unidentified. U–278 was sunk as part of Operation 'Deadlight' on 31 December 1945, while U–1058 was transferred to the Soviet Union in November 1945 as S–82. In the second row are, from left to right: U–2326; two unidentified Type VIIs; U–826; and U–293. U–2326 was a Type XXIII which spent a short time as British N–35 and was then transferred to France in 1946, where it sank in an accident in December 1946. Both U–293 and U–826 were transferred to Loch Ryan before being sunk in Operation 'Deadlight'. (Ian Henderson)

British then made a late addition to the plan, deciding to take the opportunity to use some of the U-boats as targets for weapons trials and aircrew training, provided that these did not delay the sinking programme. Although the general procedures were the same, the detailed execution of Operation 'Deadlight' was the responsibility first of Naval Officer-in-Charge (NOIC) Loch Ryan and secondly of NOIC Londonderry and, as will be seen, there were minor differences in procedures and terminology at each base. In both cases, however, Captain (Destroyers) 17th Destroyer Flotilla (Captain D17) was in command at sea.

Towing

It was clear from the start that weather and sea conditions in December/January would make it impossible to transfer crews to or from U-boats at sea, a decision which was fully justified by subsequent events. This meant that the U-boats would have to be towed, although it was known from previous RN experience of towing its own submarines that this was a particularly hazardous undertaking. A further complication was that there were insufficient tugs, so warships had to be pressed into service. Towing speeds were 5 knots for 'Hunt' class destroyers, 7 knots for the remainder,

using 7/8in (22mm) towing cables for all except the Type IIDs, which used 3/4in (19mm) cables.

Demolitions

The plan was that the majority of the U-boats would be sunk by demolition charges, which were installed by a team of specialists from HMS *Vernon*, who worked from 15 November to 15 December at Loch Ryan, after which they transferred to Lisahally. In addition, since demolition teams would not be aboard the U-boats to initiate the charges, the *Vernon* team also fitted a firing cable, which was streamed from the U-boat just before it sailed so that it could be picked up by the firing ship at the scuttling position. One of the U-boats on the first flight was blown up in what all agreed was a spectacular explosion, not least because much of the debris fell on the escorting ship standing some distance away; as a result the charge was reduced from Flight 5 onwards. The firing lead was also modified in the light of experience, both to improve its flotation and to make it longer so that the firing vessel did not have to approach the U-boat too closely in rough seas. Demolition charges were not fitted in the U-boats designated as air or submarine targets.

Air targets

It was originally planned that three U-boats in each flight from Loch Ryan would be detailed as air targets, the Fleet Air Arm and the RAF taking a day each in turn, with preference being given to crews with no wartime experience. All U-boats had their numbers painted in large white letters on the side of the conning tower and, in addition, the boats intended as air targets were specially marked with a broad white band painted athwartships on the forecastle to ensure unambiguous recognition in the target area. Unfortunately, it also meant that if a marked boat sank *en route* it could not be replaced by an unmarked boat which survived the voyage to the scuttling area.

These air targets were taken to a special position designated 'Point ZZ' where the tows were slipped, with at least one mile between each boat. Air operations in the target area were strictly controlled by the escort carrier HMS *Nairana*, with no attack starting until the formation leader had established both visual and radio contact with the carrier. *Nairana* also launched its own Barracudas and Fireflies on several occasions.

Torpedo trials

Torpedo trials included eleven single torpedoes fired from one submarine and two salvoes of three from a second. It was also planned to launch two torpedoes from a motor torpedo boat (MTB), although this never happened, probably due to the bad weather.

Locations

As a result of these requirements, there were four designated positions:

Datum position ....XX..56°00′N, 10°05′W
Air target position ....ZZ...55°50′N, 10°05′W
Main scuttling position ..YY ..56°10′N, 10°05′W
Control ship for air attacks.....55°38′N, 08°34′W (area)

Position XX was 180 miles from Loch Ryan and 130 miles from Moville.

The First Phase: Loch Ryan

It was decided to clear Loch Ryan first, where each voyage to the scuttling area was designated a 'flight' and the towing ships were divided by Captain D17 into Group A (six ships) and Group B (seven ships), although numbers varied due to mishaps and operational pressures. Captain D17 (HMS *Onslow*) normally sailed as senior officer Group A and the commanding officer HMS *Onslaught* as senior officer Group B. The U-boats, manned by combined British and German crews, proceeded under their own power from their trots at the head of Loch Ryan to the towing vessels which anchored at the seaward end of Loch Ryan, a distance of six miles. Once the tow was secure, the towing vessel weighed and proceeded slowly, while the U-boat crew released the firing cable over the stern. They then transferred to a launch.

The locations of Operation 'Deadlight'.

XX	Main Datum	56°00′N	10°05′W
YY	Main Scuttling Position	56°10′N	10°05′W
ZZ	Air Target Position	55°50′N	10°05′W
–	Safety Ship (HMS Blencathra)	55°50′N	
–	Air Control (HMS Nairana)	55°50′N	10°05′W (approx.)

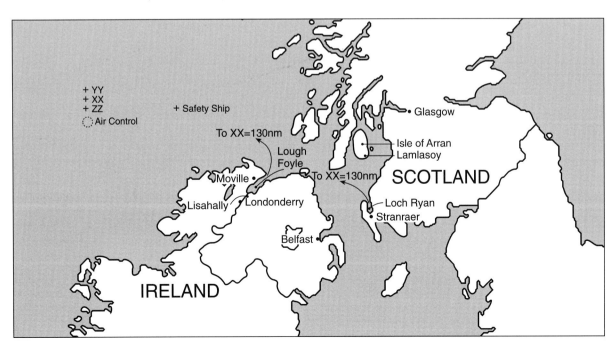

A Short Sunderland flying-boat attacks a Type VII U-boat during Operation 'Deadlight'. The U-boat is unmanned and stationary, offering an ideal target. (Ian Henderson)

Flight 1 (Group A). The first flight of six Type XXIIIs was assembled on 25 November and sailed in two sections of three. The weather was moderate, but even so *U–2328*'s tow parted and the submarine disappeared at about 0600hrs. Of the five that reached Position YY only one could be sunk by demolition charge and the remainder were disposed of by gunfire.

Flight 2 (Group B). The second flight sailed on 26 November in excellent weather and all seven U-boats arrived in Position YY. Unfortunately, it was then discovered that the buffs[1] had become detached from the firing cables, allowing them to sink vertically from the U-boats' sterns, making them irrecoverable. As a result all U-boats had to be sunk by gunfire.

Flight 3 (Group A). The weather deteriorated rapidly and of six starters on 28 November five sank *en route*, leaving only one (*U–328*) to reach Position ZZ. This submarine was attacked first by a Fairey Barracuda from *Nairana*, using a torpedo (which missed), followed by Avengers from the naval air station at Machrihanish, which sank it with bombs at 1308hrs.

Flight 4 (Group B). It was planned to sail Flight 4, consisting of seven U-boats, on 29 November, but *Mendip* experienced severe problems with her towing gear and its intended tow had to return to the submarine trot under its own power. Six U-boats were towed to sea, of which three (including both the intended air targets) sank *en route*, leaving three to arrive at Position YY, where they were sunk by gunfire.

Interlude. At this point both groups of towing ships were diverted into Lamlash Bay on the Isle of Arran, where they were stored and reorganised. In addition, the experience to date was used to make some minor changes to the procedures, particularly with the demolition charges, which, on the only occasion one had been used, had proved too powerful. The weather continued poor, so the ships remained for an extra day at anchor in Lamlash Bay.

Flight 5 (Group A). Returning to Loch Ryan, Group A had some trouble taking on the tows due to repeated dense hailstorms, but eventually sailed on 3 December with seven U-boats. The weather was still bad and it was reported that the wind was Force 8 from the southwest at dawn on 4 December and still Force 7–8 at 0400hrs the next morning. All seven U-boats sank *en route*.

Reducing losses. It was then decided to try to reduce the large number of losses *en route*. The U-boat hulls were in a bad state as they had been lying at an exposed anchorage for many months without any form of hull maintenance and were therefore leaking in numerous places. There seemed to be little point in undertaking a massive work programme for just one voyage, but, on the other hand, the boats had been sailing with bow and stern caps and the upper conning tower hatch open, in order to speed the scuttling process, and it was now decided to leave these closed.

Flight 6 (Group B). Flight 6 sailed on 6 December with six U-boats, of which four were intended as air targets and two as submarine targets. One of the U-boats foundered *en route* and when a second was badly down by the bow it was decided to sink it by gunfire, which, by chance, detonated the charges, causing a spectacular explosion. Two U-boats reached the air target area, where it was learned that the RAF strike had been cancelled due to bad weather, but *Nairana* then generated two Barracudas which launched torpedoes and sank both submarines.

Flight 7 (Group A). Leaving on 7 December, three out of six U-boats reached the scuttling area, of which two were designated for attack by aircraft and one by submarine. The air attacks were carried out by Fairey Firefly aircraft from *Nairana* firing rockets and cannon; the attacks started at 0957hrs and both U-boats had been sunk by 1125hrs. The third U-boat (*U–532*) was sunk by the British submarine *Tantivy* at 1125hrs.

Flight 8 (Group B). It was originally planned that an additional group of three U-boats would be despatched on 8 December to speed up the process and three towing ships were brought across from Londonderry for this purpose. The weather proved to be too bad, however, and the three ships were sent back again. The plan then reverted to the established routine with the Group B ships arriving back at Loch Ryan in the early hours of 9 December; they spent the morning taking on the tows and sailed again at 1400hrs. Owing to various defects among the towing ships only five U-boats could be taken to sea, but the weather was excellent and all five reached the designated area. Submarine *Tantivy* sank both its targets (*U–978* and *U–991*), while three U-boats were dealt with by the RAF, two by rocket-firing Mosquitoes, the third by a mixed group of Liberators, Sunderlands and Warwicks.

Flight 9 (Group A). Group A spent 24 hours in Lamlash Bay and Campbelltown replenishing with fuel, ammunition and stores, returning to Loch Ryan early on 11 December and sailing with five U-boats at 1400hrs. Again all five U-boats reached the target area, which was just as well, as an unusual feature of this flight was that the French, Greek and Norwegian naval attachés accompanied it as observers.

Flight 10 (Group B). Group B returned to Loch Ryan from 24 hours in Lamlash Bay and Campbelltown on 13 December, but weather conditions were too bad for the tows to be connected and the ships anchored until the next day, sailing at 1400hrs with six U-boats. At sea one (*U–1104*) was seen to be down by the bows and, unusually, *Onslow* was able to pick up the firing cable and the charges blew at the first attempt, sinking the U-boat. Three U-boats had been designated as air targets, but one was seen to be foundering on arrival at Point ZZ and was disposed of by gunfire, before air operations started. Two groups of six Mosquitoes attacked one of the remaining targets with rockets, sinking it, following which two Liberators and two Warwicks arrived, but the first aircraft was so accurate that it sank the target immediately, leaving nothing for the other three to do.

Flight 11 (Group A). When Group B unexpectedly spent the night of 13/14 December in Loch Ryan no berths were available for Group B, which was forced to divert into Lamlash Bay and Campbelltown. It then proceeded to Loch Ryan, took seven U-boats under tow and sailed at 1500hrs on 15 December. During the tow, a seaman aboard *Mendip* became very ill, resulting in the ship's being ordered to slip the tow and destroy its U-boat. Attempts to recover the firing cable having failed, the U-boat (*U–1009*) was sunk by gunfire and *Mendip* proceeded into Campbelltown. The remaining six boats reached the scuttling area; three were scheduled to be used as air targets, but the weather was so bad that all were despatched by gunfire.

Flights 12 (Group B) and 13 (Group A). Group B returned from Flight 10 on the morning of 17 December, but, due to bad weather, it was forced to remain at anchor until 20 December, while Group A was, once again, diverted to Lamlash Bay and Campbelltown. The weather on the 20th was, however, comparatively moderate, and it was decided to make a major effort to clear the backlog, with each group taking eight U-boats. Group B was clear of Loch Ryan by 1240hrs with its eight U-boats, but *Rupert* parted its tow just outside the loch and it took some hours and help from another ship to get everything sorted out. Meanwhile, Group A had arrived in Loch Ryan immediately after Group B sailed, and the drills were now so smooth that the last ship of Group A returned to sea, complete with tows, at 1520hrs. Just outside the loch *Rupert* from Group B was now ready to proceed and joined Group A, which now consisted of nine U-boats. Unfortunately, not one of these sixteen boats reached the scuttling area; three foundered and the remainder were sunk by gunfire, well short of Position ZZ.

Flight 14. On completion of Flights 12 and 13, the towing and escorting vessels were despatched to Liverpool, Campbelltown and Greenock to give their crews leave over Christmas, following which all except five ships sailed to Northern Ireland for the second phase of Operation 'Deadlight'. This left three U-boats in Loch Ryan which were towed out to sea on 28 December after a 24-hour delay for bad weather. Two parted their tows *en route* and were sunk by gunfire, leaving *U–1103* to be the last of the Loch Ryan boats to be sunk, also by gunfire, in the designated scuttling area at 1010hrs on 29 December. All ships involved in this final flight then proceeded to Londonderry and Loch Ryan's role was completed.

The Lisahally Operation

The naval facility at Lisahally was built by the US Navy in 1941–42 on the southern bank of the River Foyle approximately two miles downriver from the city of Derry.[2] The dock facilities consisted of a single long wharf some 610m (2,000ft) long, constructed of Oregon pine, which was specially imported from the USA for the purpose. Other facilities included a headquarters complex, a 200-bed hospital, magazine, accommodation and a radio station. It was in full use throughout 1942 and 1943 as an escort base, but the US Navy vacated all except the radio station in July 1944 and handed it over to the Admiralty in September 1944. The jetties provided excellent facilities and were available for Operation 'Deadlight'.

The first group of U-boats arrived on 14 May 1945, having been temporarily held in Loch Eriboll, and consisted of *U–293, U–802, U–826, U–1005, U–1009, U–1058, U–1109* and *U–1305.* Admiral Sir Max Horton flew across to accept their surrender from *Oberleutnant zur See* Klaus Hilgendorf, commanding officer of *U–1009.*

By the end of May there were thirty-four boats at Lisahally with more arriving later. The numbers fluctuated, especially when a party from the Soviet Navy, led by Commodore Morosoff, arrived in November to take over the ten boats allocated to the USSR and sail them to Leningrad.

By the time that 'Deadlight' began there were thirty U-boats moored at Lisahally, and in each case the events started with the U-boats moving downriver under their own power to an anchorage in Loch Foyle off the Irish port of Moville, where they were passed a tow by their designated towing vessel. Each day's sailing was designated a 'lift' ('flight' at Loch Ryan) and consisted of a senior officer's ship, a 'firing ship', which was responsible for sinking the U-boats, and a number of 'towing ships'. Captain D17 in *Onslow* was still responsible at sea, but some additional ships were present.

Lift 1. Five U-boats were towed to sea on the morning of 29 December, of which not one reached the designated scuttling area, as all the tows parted. One (*U–294*) was taken back to Moville by a tug, while the others were sunk by gunfire.

Lift 2. The following day six U-boats set off, including *U–294*, which had been returned to Moville the previous day, but once again not a single U-boat reached the scuttling area. Two tows parted and the boats were sunk by gunfire; but when *U–802* parted its tow from *Pytchley* and could not be found, the remaining three tows were dropped and the U-boats sunk by gunfire so that all ships could look for the missing U-boat. It was never found and was presumed to have foundered.

Lift 3. Seven U-boats left Moville under tow on 31 December, but one tow parted early on, and a tug had to

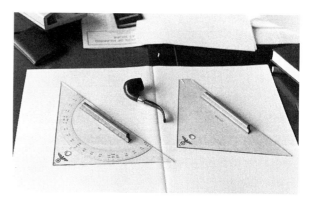

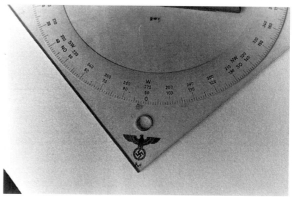

The spoils of war: navigation equipment and a radio set which 'found their way ashore' from the U-boats during their stay at Lisahally. (Ian Henderson)

An aerial view of the dock facility at Lisahally, which was constructed for use by the US Navy. It was handed over to the Royal Navy in 1944, who found it ideal for Operation 'Deadlight'. (Royal Navy Submarine Museum)

moor its own tow before proceeding to recover the drifting U-boat. Thus only five U-boats went to sea, all of which parted their tows and were sunk by gunfire before arriving at Point YY.

Lift 4. No ships sailed on 1 January, which was officially due to bad weather, although celebrations on the first postwar New Year may have influenced the decision. As a result, Lift 4 sailed on 2 January with five U-boats, of which two were designated targets for attack by the submarine *Templar*. In the event, the sea was too rough for the trials and four U-boats were sunk by gunfire and one foundered, all in position 56°06′N, 09°00′W.

Lift 5. *U–2506* had to be towed by two tugs from Lisahally but ran aground before reaching Moville. Thus only three U-boats went to sea on 3 January, of which two quickly parted their tows, but were recovered and returned to Lisahally. Only one U-boat got to sea and when the tow parted it was sunk.

Lift 6. This consisted of five U-boats, which left Moville on 5 January accompanied by the submarine *Templar*. Four of the tows parted and the U-boats were sunk by gunfire, while the fifth was sunk by a torpedo from *Templar*.

Lift 7. Three U-boats were taken to sea on 7 January, the weather having been too severe on the previous day. Two tows parted and the U-boats were sunk by gunfire, while the third foundered, leaving *Templar* with no target. This completed the initially planned 'Deadlight'.

Deadlight (2). Two U-boats were left at Lisahally, *U–975* and *U–3514*, which were not disposed of until February, and, since the team from *Vernon* was no longer available to install demolition charges, it was planned from the start to sink the boats by gunfire or other weapons. Things got off to a bad start for *U–3514*, a Type XXI, when one of the tugs ran aground in the River Foyle on 8 February, following which *U–3514* itself ran aground on 9 February. However, all was eventually resolved and both U-boats were towed to sea late on 9 February. Next day it was decided to cast off *U–975*'s tow and it was sunk by a mixture of gunfire and an attack using the Squid anti-submarine mortar. The other tow, *U–3514* reached Position XX at 0900hrs on 12 February and was sunk by Shark (see below), becoming the last of the 'Deadlight' victims and one of the very few to sink in exactly the correct spot.

Comments

The overall aim of Operation 'Deadlight', to sink the U-boats, was achieved, but faced with the narrative set out above, nobody could claim that it was a smooth and efficient operation. No fewer than fifty-eight (exactly 50 per cent) of the U-boats sank well short of the scuttling area, of which twenty foundered (seventeen from Loch Ryan and three from Lisahally), the worst occasion being Flight 5 when all seven U-boats from Loch Ryan went down early, although this was primarily due to particularly bad weather. Another particularly bad episode occurred on 21/22 December, when eight out of nine U-boats were lost *en route*.

The tugs were obviously best suited to the role, while the warships, and in particular the 'Hunt' class destroyers, were totally unsuitable. Their problems were exacerbated by the strong winds in Loch Ryan and sluicing tides off Moville, both of which made taking into tow a hazardous operation. The U-boat towing cables were the weak link throughout and the reason for so many partings – almost invariably in the middle – was never discovered, since few tows were ever recovered and thus there was no evidence on which to base an explanation. Indeed, some towing cables were so strong that where the U-boat foundered and sank to the bottom the towing vessel remained effectively anchored and unable to proceed until it slipped its tow. Some thought was given to the possibility that the German crews might have sabotaged either the tows or the U-boat hulls, but this was eventually rejected; first, because there was no evidence and, secondly, because it was not clear what purpose could have been achieved.

Blyskawica, one of the Polish destroyers to take part in the Lisahally phase of Operation 'Deadlight'. On 31 December 1945, the destroyer sank U–861, and on 3 January 1946, U–825.

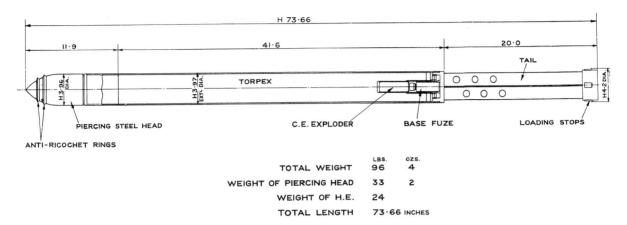

	LBS.	OZS.
TOTAL WEIGHT	96	4
WEIGHT OF PIERCING HEAD	33	2
WEIGHT OF H.E.	24	
TOTAL LENGTH	73·66 INCHES	

The Shark 4in anti-submarine projectile.

The teams from HMS *Vernon* who installed the demolition charges must have been particularly disappointed since, in the final analysis, just two ships were ever scuttled as a result of their efforts.

Seventy-one of all the sinkings were achieved by gunfire, although this proved to be a lengthy and frustrating business – which confirmed experiences in the recent war, and had given rise to the development of the 'Shark' projectile. The only exception was when a shell, by chance, detonated the demolition charges, when the result tended to be sudden and dramatic.

Two major questions arise over this operation. The first is why it was decided to undertake the operation at a time when the weather in the North Atlantic was known to be particularly bad. There are two possible explanations. The first is that it was laid down by the Tripartite Naval Committee in Berlin and nobody ever saw fit to challenge it. Secondly, due to the postconflict rundown of the Royal Navy in both ships and manpower this job just had to be done quickly, while the resources were available. It is clear now that the job would have been better done in the summer months using tugs rather than warships, but everything is always easier with the knowledge conferred by hindsight.

SHARK: Projectile, 4in, Anti-submarine
It was found during the war that when escort vessels armed with 4in guns attacked surfaced U-boats, their SAP (semi-armour piercing) ammunition tended to bounce off the pressure hull; Shark was developed to overcome this. It was an exceptionally large projectile, 73.66in (187cm) in length and 3.97in (101mm) in diameter; it weighed 96lb (43.5kg) and had a muzzle velocity of 500ft/sec (152m/sec). Even the official publication of the day described it as 'heavy and unwieldy'. The projectile had a 33lb (15kg), solid steel, piercing head, with two machined rings designed to ensure that it did not ricochet off the water. It was intended for use at short range and to hit the water just short of the target, where it would continue on its trajectory for a short distance until it hit and then penetrated a submarine's saddle tanks. The delayed action fuse then detonated the charge [24lb (10.9kg) Torpex],

which, with the benefit of the water tamper, penetrated the submarine's pressure hull. Its operation was similar in principle to Barnes Wallis's 'bouncing bombs' used against the Ruhr dams.

In 'Deadlight (2)' Shark was used against *U–3514*, a Type XXI. Six rounds were fired at a range of 2,400ft (732m), of which the fifth and sixth scored hits, exploding on the casing in line with the conning tower. Approximately one minute after the second hit, the U-boat's bow suddenly plunged until the hull was vertical and then disappeared below the surface. This was the last sinking of Operation 'Deadlight' and probably the only successful use of Shark.

Sources
The main sources for this article are the Reports of Proceedings of the Loch Ryan and Lisahally sections of Operation 'Deadlight'. These documents contain the record of each U-boat sunk and may therefore be considered definitive. Several books on Second World War U-boats include details of their fate which differ in detail from these RN lists. It is, however, not surprising that there should be discrepancies, since 1945/46 was a period of great confusion and it is clear that U-boats were moved around and reallocated during it. Even the RN documents quoted include a list of 'U-boats to be sunk' dated 14 November 1945 which differs in detail from the boats which were actually sunk.
In addition to the two Reports of Proceedings other documents consulted include:
Cabinet meetings: PRO/CAB 79/33
General information: PRO/ADM 1/19342
Tripartite Naval Committee: PRO/ADM 228/19
Erich Gröner, *German Warships 1815–1945*. Conway, London, Vol. 2, 1991
Bodo Herzog, *Deutsche U–boote: 1906–66*. Pawlak, 1990

Notes
[1] Buffs, so called from their light brown colour, were floats, which were lashed to the cable to keep it afloat.
[2] Work on this US naval facility started in June 1941 (ie six months before Pearl Harbor) and was carried out by 1,200 US civilian contractors, supervised by 25 officers of the US Navy Civil Engineer Corps, who wore civilian clothes until 9 December 1941.

Table 1: *U-Boats disposed of in Operation 'Deadlight'*

Srl	U-boat Number	Type	Base	Date (Note 1)	Intended Fate (Note 2)	Actual Fate	Location	Remarks
1	*U–143*	II D	Loch Ryan	220315 Dec 45	D	Gunfire	55°58′N 09°35′W	Tow parted
2	*U–145*	II D	Loch Ryan	220350 Dec 45	D	Gunfire	55°47′N	Tow parted
3	*U–149*	II D	Loch Ryan	210335 Dec 45	D	Gunfire	55°40′05″N 08°00′W	Tow parted
4	*U–150*	II D	Loch Ryan	211505 Dec 45	D	Gunfire	56°04′N 09°35′W	Sunk by gunfire; demolition charges blew at 500 fathoms plus
5	*U–155*	IX C	Loch Ryan	211142 Dec 45	D	Gunfire	55°35′N	Tow parted
6	*U–170*	IX C/40	Loch Ryan	301515 Nov 45	D	Gunfire	55°44′N	Towing badly; sinking
7	*U–218*	VII D	Loch Ryan	041208 Dec 45	A	Sank in tow	Inistrahull Light 301° 8.9nm	30 fathoms
8	*U–244*	VII C	Lisahally	300427 Dec 45	D	Gunfire *Piorun*	55°46′N	Tow parted
9	*U–245*	VII C	Loch Ryan	070411 Dec 45	A	Foundered	55°25′N	Tow parted
10	*U–249*	VII C	Loch Ryan	131015 Dec 45	S	Torpedo *Tantivy*	56°10′N 10°04′N	–
11	*U–255*	VII C	Loch Ryan	131030 Dec 45	A	Aircraft	55°50′N 10°05′W	–
12	*U–278*	VII C	Lisahally	312345 Dec 45	D	Gunfire	55°44′N 08°21′W	Tow released as planned but sea too rough for demolition
13	*U–281*	VII C	Loch Ryan	301404 Nov 45	A	Foundered	55°32′50″N 07°38′10″W	–
14	*U–291*	VII C	Loch Ryan	210835 Dec 45	D	Gunfire	55°50′30″N 09°08′W	Tow parted
15	*U–293*	VII C	Loch Ryan	131100 Dec 45	A	Gunfire	55°50′W 10°05′W	Damaged by aircraft: sunk by gunfire
16	*U–294*	VII C	Lisahally	311015 Dec 45	D	Gunfire	55°44′N	Released and sunk so that all could search for *U–802*. (See also *U–883*, *U–1165*, *U–802*)

Table 1: *CONTINUED*

Srl	U-boat Number	Type	Base	Date (Note 1)	Intended Fate (Note 2)	Actual Fate	Location	Remarks
17	*U–295*	VII C	Loch Ryan	171030 Dec 45	S	Gunfire	56°14′W	Too rough for *Tantivy*
18	*U–298*	VII C	Loch Ryan	291654 Nov 45	A	Gunfire	55°35′N	Crewman had acute appendicitis; Slipped tow
19	*U–299*	VII C	Loch Ryan	041949 Dec 45	D	Foundered	55°38′40″N 07°54′W	Tow parted: U-boat disappeared in 40 fathoms
20	*U–312*	VII C	Loch Ryan	291654 Nov 45	A	Foundered	55°35′N 07°54′W	Sank in tow
21	*U–313*	VII C	Loch Ryan	211520 Dec 45	D	Foundered	55°40′N	55 fathoms
22	*U–318*	VII C	Loch Ryan	210710 Dec 45	D	Gunfire	55°47′N 08°30′W	Sunk after tow parted
23	*U–328*	VII C	Loch Ryan	301300 Nov 45	A	Aircraft	55°50′N	Sunk by Avengers (bombs)
24	*U–363*	VII C	Lisahally	312345 Dec 45	D	Gunfire	55°45′N 08°18′W	Tow released as planned but sea too rough for demolition
25	*U–368*	VII C	Loch Ryan	171030 Dec 45	S	Gunfire	56°14′N	Too rough for *Tantivy*
26	*U–427*	VII C	Loch Ryan	301105 Nov 45	A	Foundered	55°31′40″N	Sinking assisted by gunfire
27	*U–427*	VII C	Loch Ryan	211505 Dec 45	D	Gunfire	56°04′N 09°35′W	500 fathoms
28	*U–481*	VII C	Loch Ryan	301008 Nov 45	D	Gunfire	56°11′N 10°00′W	Tow parted. Sunk by gunfire
29	*U–483*	VII C	Loch Ryan	161200 Dec 45	D	Gunfire	56°10′N 10°05′W	
30	*U–485*	VII C	Loch Ryan	080900 Dec 45	D	Torpedo *Tantivy*	56°10′N 10°05′W	
31	*U–516*	IX C	Lisahally	031036 Jan 46	S	Foundered	56°06′N 09°00′W	Apparently in correct place
32	*U–532*	IX C	Loch Ryan	091121 Dec 45	S	Torpedo *Tantivy*	56°08′N 10°07′W	Using CCR pistol
33	*U–539*	IX C/40	Loch Ryan	041845 Dec 45	D	Foundered	55°38′30″N	Sank in tow in 42 fathoms

Table 1: *CONTINUED*

Srl	U-boat Number	Type	Base	Date (Note 1)	Intended Fate (Note 2)	Actual Fate	Location	Remarks
34	*U–541*	IX C/40	Lisahally	052355 Jan 46	D	Gunfire *Onslaught*	55°38′N 07°35′30″W	Tow parted
35	*U–637*	VII C	Loch Ryan	211402 Dec 45	D	Foundered	55°35′N 07°46′W	38 fathoms
36	*U–668*	VII C	Lisahally	010645 Jan 46	D	Gunfire *Onslaught*	56°03′N 09°24′W	Tow parted: sunk short of YY
37	*U–680*	VII C	Loch Ryan	282015 Dec 45	D	Gunfire	55°24′N 06°29′W	Tow parted
38	*U–716*	VII C	Loch Ryan	111215 Dec 45	A	Aircraft	55°50′N 10°05′W	–
39	*U–720*	VII C	Loch Ryan	211505 Dec 45	D	Gunfire	56°04′N 09°35′W	Over 500 fathoms
40	*U–739*	VII C	Loch Ryan	161200 Dec 45	A	Aircraft	55°50′N 10°05′W	–
41	*U–760*	VII C	Loch Ryan	131000 Dec 45	A	Aircraft	55°50′N 10°05′W	–
42	*U–764*	VII C	Lisahally	031030 Jan 46	S	Gunfire *Piorun*	56°06′N 09°00′W	Due for torpedo trials but sea too rough
43	*U–773*	VII C	Loch Ryan	080900 Dec 45	S	Torpedo *Tantivy*	56°10′N 10°05′W	–
44	*U–775*	VII C	Loch Ryan	082035 Dec 45	A	Gunfire	55°40′N 05°30′01″W	48 fathoms
45	*U–776*	VII C	Loch Ryan	031855 Dec 45	D	Foundered	55°08′04″N 05°30′01″W	48 fathoms
46	*U–778*	VII C	Loch Ryan	041228 Dec 45	D	Sank in tow	Inistrahull light 308° 11.2 miles	34 fathoms
47	*U–779*	VII C	Loch Ryan	171036 Dec 45	A	Gunfire	55°50′N 10°05′W	Air attack cancelled
48	*U–802*	IX	Lisahally	31 (am) Dec 45	D	Foundered	55°30′N 08°25′N (estimate)	Tow parted and U-boat could not be found
49	*U–806*	IX C/40	Loch Ryan	211601 Dec 45	D	Gunfire	55°44′N 08°18′W	Boat waterlogged: tow slipped, sunk by gunfire
50	*U–825*	VII C	Lisahally	031640 Jan 46	D	Gunfire *Blyskawica*	55°31′N 07°30′W	a. Tow parted and sunk short of YY b. Only U-boat in Lift 5 to get to sea to be sunk

Table 1: *CONTINUED*

Srl	U-boat Number	Type	Base	Date (Note 1)	Intended Fate (Note 2)	Actual Fate	Location	Remarks
51	*U–826*	VII C	Loch Ryan	010900 Dec 45	D	Gunfire	56°10′N 10°05′W	–
52	*U–861*	IX D$_2$	Lisahally	311445 Dec 45	D	Gunfire *Blyskawica*	55°25′N 07°15′W	Tug *Freedom* engine broke down: U-boat sunk by gunfire
53	*U–868*	IX C	Loch Ryan	300005 Nov 45	A	Foundered	55°48′30″N 08°33′W	Sank in steep dive in 70 fathoms
54	*U–874*	IX D$_2$	Lisahally	310759 Dec 45	D	Gunfire *Offa*	55°47′N 09°27′W	Tow parted
55	*U–875*	IX D$_2$	Lisahally	310047 Dec 45	D	Gunfire *Offa*	55°41′N 08°28′W	Tow parted
56	*U–883*	IX D/42	Lisahally	311015 Dec 45	D	Gunfire	55°44′N 08°40′W	Released and sunk so that tow ships could search for *U–802* (see also *U–294, U–1165, U–802*)
57	*U–901*	VII C	Lisahally	06 Jan 45	D	Gunfire *Onslaught*	55°50′N 08°30′W	In planned location
58	*U–907*	VII C	Loch Ryan	072235 Dec 45	D	Foundered	55°17′N 05°59′W	Dived to bottom in 77 fathoms
59	*U–928*	VII C	Loch Ryan	161200 Dec 45	A	Aircraft	55°50′N 10°05′W	–
60	*U–930*	VII C	Lisahally	292325 Dec 45	D	Gunfire *Onslow*	55°22′N 07°35′W	Tow parted
61	*U–956*	VII C	Loch Ryan	171033 Dec 45	A	Gunfire	55°50′N 10°05′W	Air attack cancelled
62	*U–968*	VII C	Loch Ryan	280300 Nov 45	D	Foundered	55°24′N 06°22′45″W	Sank in 80 fathoms
63	*U–975*	VII C	Lisahally	101610 Feb 45	G	Squid	55°42′N 09°01′W	'Deadlight(2)'
64	*U–978*	VII C	Loch Ryan	111215 Dec 45	S	Torpedo *Tantivy*	55°50′N 10°05′W	–
65	*U–991*	VII C	Loch Ryan	111215 Dec 45	S	Torpedo *Tantivy*	56°10′N 10°05′W	–
66	*U–992*	VII C	Loch Ryan	161200 Dec 45	D	Gunfire	56°10′N 10°05′W	–
67	*U–994*	VII C	Loch Ryan	050703 Dec 45	D	Foundered	55°50′N 08°30′W	Sank in tow in 52 fathoms

Table 1: *CONTINUED*

Srl	U-boat Number	Type	Base	Date (Note 1)	Intended Fate (Note 2)	Actual Fate	Location	Remarks
68	*U–997*	VII C	Loch Ryan	111215 Dec 45	A	Aircraft	55°50′N 10°05′W	–
69	*U–1002*	VII C	Loch Ryan	131045 Dec 45	S	Torpedo *Tantivy*	56°10′N 10°05′W	–
70	*U–1004*	VII C	Loch Ryan	010900 Dec 45	D	Gunfire *Tantivy*	56°10′N 10°05′W	–
71	*U–1005*	VII C	Loch Ryan	050015 Dec 45	A	Foundered	55°33′N 08°27′W	Sank in tow in 48 fathoms
72	*U–1009*	VII C	Loch Ryan	160928 Dec 45	A	Gunfire *Tantivy*	55°31′05″N 10°05′W	Sunk early due to sick sailor aboard towing ship
73	*U–1010*	VII C	Lisahally	071900 Jan 46	G	Gunfire *Garland*	55°37′09″N 07°49′05″W	Tow parted
74	*U–1019*	VII C	Loch Ryan	071633 Dec 45	A	Gunfire	55°27′N 07°56′W	U-boat losing buoyancy
75	*U–1022*	VII C	Loch Ryan	292350 Dec 45	D	Gunfire *Piorun*	55°40′N 08°15′W	Tow parted
76	*U–1023*	VII C	Loch Ryan	080020 Jan 46	G	Foundered	55°49′N 08°24′W	Used briefly for tests by RN as N83
77	*U–1052*	VII C	Loch Ryan	090900 Dec 45	A	Aircraft	55°50′N 10°05′W	816 San aircraft using RP
78	*U–1061*	VII F	Loch Ryan	010900 Dec 45	D	Gunfire	56°10′N 10°05′W	–
79	*U–1102*	VII C	Loch Ryan	211505 Dec 45	D	Gunfire	56°04′N 09°35′W	Over 500 fathoms
80	*U–1103*	VII C	Loch Ryan	301010 Dec 45	D	Gunfire	56°03′N 10°05′W	–
81	*U–1104*	VII C	Loch Ryan	151625 Dec 45	A	Demolition	55°35′N 10°05′W	Sank early as in sinking condition
82	*U–1109*	VII C	Lisahally	061100 Jan 46	S	Torpedo *Templar*	55°49′N 08°31′W	–
83	*U–1110*	VII C	Loch Ryan	211608 Jan 46	D	Gunfire	55°45′N 08°19′W	Tow parted three times. Third time, sunk by gunfire
84	*U–1163*	VII C	Loch Ryan	111216 Dec 45	A	Aircraft	55°50′N 10°05′W	–

Table 1: *CONTINUED*

Srl	U-boat Number	Type	Base	Date (Note 1)	Intended Fate (Note 2)	Actual Fate	Location	Remarks
85	*U–1165*	VII C	Lisahally	311015 Dec 45	D	Gunfire	55°44′N 08°40′W	Released and sunk so that all could search for *U–802* (see also *U–294, U–883, U–802*)
86	*U–1194*	VII C	Loch Ryan	220400 Jan 46	D	Gunfire	55°59′N 09°55′W	Tow parted
87	*U–1198*	VII C	Loch Ryan	171030 Dec 45	S	Gunfire	56°14′N 10°37′05″W	Too rough for *Tantivy*
88	*U–1203*	VII C	Loch Ryan	080900 Dec 45	A	Aircraft	55°50′N 10°05′W	–
89	*U–1230*	IX C40	Loch Ryan	171040 Dec 45	A	Gunfire	55°50′N 10°05′W	Air attack cancelled
90	*U–1233*	IX C40	Loch Ryan	290933 Dec 45	D	Gunfire	55°51′N 08°54′W	–
91	*U–1271*	VII C	Loch Ryan	080904 Dec 45	A	Foundered	55°28′50″N 07°20′40″W	Tow parted
92	*U–1272*	VII C	Loch Ryan	080900 Dec 45	A	Aircraft	55°50′N 10°05′W	Sank in tow in 30 fathoms
93	*U–1301*	VII C	Loch Ryan	161200 Dec 45	D	Gunfire	56°10′N 10°05′W	– –
94	*U–1307*	VII C	Loch Ryan	090900 Dec 45	A	Aircraft 816 Sqn	55°50′N 10°05′W	Rockets
95	*U–2321*	XXIII	Loch Ryan	270900 Nov 45	D	Gunfire	56°10′N 10°05′W	–
96	*U–2322*	XXIII	Loch Ryan	270900 Nov 45	D	Gunfire	56°10′N 10°05′W	–
97	*U–2324*	XXIII	Loch Ryan	270900 Nov 45	D	Gunfire	56°10′N 10°05′W	–
98	*U–2325*	XXIII	Loch Ryan	280900 Nov 45	D	Gunfire	56°10′N 10°05′W	–
99	*U–2328*	XXIII	Loch Ryan	270600 Nov 45	D	Foundered	56°12′N 09°48′W	Tow parted. Searched for but could not find
100	*U–2329*	XXIII	Loch Ryan	280900 Nov 45	D	Gunfire	56°10′N 10°05′W	–
101	*U–2334*	XXIII	Loch Ryan	280900 Nov 45	D	Gunfire	56°10′N 10°05′W	–
102	*U–2335*	XXIII	Loch Ryan	280900 Nov 45	D	Gunfire	56°10′N 10°05′W	–

Table 1: *CONTINUED*

Srl	U-boat Number	Type	Base	Date (Note 1)	Intended Fate (Note 2)	Actual Fate	Location	Remarks
103	*U–2336*	XXIII	Lisahally	031036 Jan 46	D	Gunfire	56°06′N 09°00′W	Apparently in correct place
104	*U–2337*	XXIII	Loch Ryan	280900 Nov 45	D	Gunfire	56°10′N 10°05′W	–
105	*U–2341*	XXIII	Lisahally	312345 Dec 45	D	Gunfire	55°44′N 08°19′W	Tow released as planned but sea too rough for demolition
106	*U–2345*	XXIII	Loch Ryan	270900 Nov 45	D	Demolition	56°10′N 10°05′W	–
107	*U–2350*	XXIII	Loch Ryan	280900 Nov 45	D	Gunfire	56°10′N 10°05′W	–
108	*U–2351*	XXIII	Lisahally	031036 Jan 46	D	Gunfire	56°06′N 09°00′W	a. Bombed in Kiel but taken to NI for D/L b. Apparently sunk in right place
109	*U–2354*	XXIII	Loch Ryan	220901 Dec 45	D	Gunfire	56°00′N 10°05′W	–
110	*U–2356*	XXIII	Lisahally	06 Jan 46	D	Gunfire *Onslaught*	55°50′N 08°20′W	In planned location
111	*U–2361*	XXIII	Loch Ryan	270900 Nov 45	D	Gunfire	56°10′N 10°05′W	–
112	*U–2363*	XXIII	Loch Ryan	280900 Nov 45	D	Gunfire	56°10′N 10°05′W	–
113	*U–2502*	XXI	Lisahally	031030 Jan 46	S	Gunfire *Piorun*	56°06′N 09°00′N	Due for torpedo trials but sea too rough
114	*U–2506*	XXI	Lisahally	051810 Jan 46	D	Gunfire *Onslaught*	55°37′N 07°30′W	Tow parted
115	*U–2511*	XXI	Lisahally	071940 Jan 46	G	Gunfire *Sole Bay*	55°33′08″N 07°38′07″W	Tow parted
116	*U–3514*	XXIII	Lisahally	111104 Feb 46	G	Shark *Loch Arkaig*	56°00′N 10°05′W	'Deadlight(2)'

Notes:

1. Date/time group shows day first (eg 02 . . .), then actual time (eg 2158) then month and year. Thus, 301008 Nov 45 is 1008hrs on 30 November 1945.
2. Intended sinking method: A = aircraft, D = demolition, G = gunfire, S = submarine

Table 2: *OPERATION 'DEADLIGHT' SINKINGS*

Flight/ Lift	Sunk *en route*			Sunk in area						Totals
	Gunfire	Foundered	Demolition	Gunfire	Demolition	Aircraft	Squid	Shark	Torpedo	
Loch Ryan										
1		1		4						6
2				7						7
3	2	3				1				6
4	2	1		3						6
5		7								7
6	1	1				2			2	6
7	1	2				2			1	6
8						3			2	5
9						3			2	5
10			1	3		2				6
11	1			6						7
12	3			4						7
13	6	2		1						9
14	2			1						3
Totals	18	17	1	29	1	13			7	86
Lisahally										
1	3									3
2	5	1								6
3	4			1						5
4	2	1		2						5
5	1									1
6	2			2					1	5
7	2	1								3
Deadlight (2)								1		2
Totals	20	3		5				1	1	30
Grand Totals	38	20	1	34	1	13		1	8	116

Table 3: *Surface Ships Involved in Operation 'Deadlight'*

Phase	Type	Class	Ships	Remarks
Loch Ryan	Destroyer	'O' class	*Onslow, Orwell*	Senior officers' ships
		'Hunt' class (Type 1)	*Blencathra, Mendip, Pytchley, Quantock, Southdown*	*Blencathra* served as safety ship
		'Hunt' class (Type 2)	*Krakowiak* (Polish), *Zetland*	
	Frigates	'Bay' class	*Cawsand Bay*	
		'Captain' class (ex-US Navy DEs)	*Cosby, Cubitt, Rupert*	
		'Loch' class	*Loch Shin*	
	Sloop	*Shoreham* class	*Fowey*	
	Tugs		*Bustler, Emulous, Enforcer, Enchanter, Freedom, Masterful, Obedient, Prosperous, Saucy*	
	Aircraft carrier	*Vindex* class escort carrier	*Nairana*	Controlled air operations
Lisahally	Destroyers	*Grom* class	*Blyskawica* (Polish)	
		'G' class	*Garland* (Polish)	
		'N' class	*Piorun* (Polish)	
		'O' class	*Onslow, Onslaught, Offa*	
		'Z' class	*Zealous*	
		'Hunt' class (Type 1)	*Blencathra, Mendip, Pytchley, Quantock*	
		'Hunt' class (Type 2)	*Krakowiak* (Polish), *Zetland*	
	Frigates	'Bay' class	*Cawsand Bay, Sole Bay*	
		'Captain' class (ex-US Navy DEs)	*Cubitt, Cosby*	
		'Loch' class	*Loch Shin*	
		Shoreham class	*Fowey*	
	Tugs		*Enchanter, Freedom, Saucy*	
	Aircraft carrier	*Vindex* class escort carrier	*Nairana*	Air control ship
'Deadlight(2)'	Frigate	'Loch' class	*Loch Arkaig, Loch Shin*	
	Tug		*Prosperous*	

GERMAN TA TORPEDO BOATS AT WAR

Pierre Hervieux details the operations of the torpedo boats taken over by the *Kriegsmarine* from defeated navies – and the Italian navy, its erstwhile ally.

TA is the German abbreviation of *Torpedoboote Auslandisch* – ex-enemy torpedo boat, and this study covers the Italian *Ariete* and *Animoso* torpedo boat classes which were captured by the Germans and used by the *Kriegsmarine* during the Second World War.

The Royal Italian Navy laid down sixteen *Ariete* class torpedo boats between January 1942 and March 1943. Only the name-class ship was completed before the Italian armistice of 8 September 1943 and the country surrendered to the Allies. The fifteen other units were captured by the Germans in the shipyards of northern Italy, fourteen of them being commissioned. In addition, four *Animoso* class torpedo boats were also captured by the Germans, three of them being commissioned, out of sixteen which were laid down by the Royal Italian Navy between April 1941 and January 1942.

It would be too time-consuming to mention all the many missions effected by the 10th Flotilla's torpedo boats in the Ligurian and the Tyrrhenian seas; a few of them will be covered as well as the land-shelling operations in which they were involved. The first two units ready for action were *TA24* (ex-*Arturo*) and *TA23* (ex-*Impavido*) which were, respectively, commissioned on 4 October and 17 October 1943, under the command of *Kapitänleutnant* Albrand and *Kapitänleutnant* Reinhardt. Their first mission took place on the night of 22/23 December when, with the minelayer *Niedersachsen*, they carried out the mining operation '*Attacke*', off the northern extremity of Corsica. On 31 December this minefield was responsible for the loss of two British ships, the minesweeping sloop *Clacton* (1941, 656 tons) and the landing ship *LST411* (1942, 1,625 tons) which were on passage from Maddalena to Bastia. The latter was abandoned on 1 January 1944 owing to heavy weather.

From the night of 27/28 January 1944 to the night of 17/18 March 1945, *TA23*, *TA24*, *TA25*, *TA26*, *TA27*, *TA28*, *TA29* and *TA30* accomplished 91 minelaying missions, 79 reconnaissance missions, 13 coastal shelling missions, 5 escort missions, 3 intruding missions and 2 meteorological missions.

In addition to these eight boats, *TA31* and *TA32* must also be mentioned; the former accomplished two reconnaissance missions and the latter twelve of them, plus five minelaying and one coastal shelling mission. For instance,

on the night of 16/17 February 1944 the minelaying operation '*Kobra*' took place with *TA23*, *TA26* and *TA28* which dropped 100 mines and 125 explosive floats between the south of Civitavecchia and La Spezia. It was the third operation for the newly formed 10th Torpedo Boat Flotilla, under the command of the Flotilla Leader Wirich von Gartzen (*Korvettenkapitän*) from 31 January 1944. On the way back, in the early morning hours, they were attacked by enemy fighter-bombers and also they saw a violent air attack on the harbour of San Stefano. They spent seventeen hours at sea and the operation was successful, despite several shortcomings. *TA28* had sailed for only eight hours before that mission, five for her sea trials and three for her transfer from Genoa to La Spezia. *TA26* had never carried mines before and *TA23*'s captain, having been wounded a few days before, had been replaced by an *Oberleutnant zur See*. On the night of 18/19 February, in operation '*Hecke*', *TA24*, *TA27* and *TA28* had to drop a minefield south of the Tiber estuary. They left La Spezia at about 1500hrs and sailed south at 24 knots. After a good hour that speed had to be reduced to 21 knots because *TA24* was having trouble with her ventilation system. A little later the torpedo boats were flown over by nine enemy fighters which did not attack but had perhaps noted their position; the torpedo boats were not yet equipped with any radar. At 2140hrs they passed by the island of Gianutri and were sailing to Civitavecchia; at 2219hrs a great quantity of flares burst over the torpedo boats and it was suddenly like bright daylight; then followed medium-calibre shells, probably from British destroyers. The German torpedo boats were in a bad situation; because of the mines they were overloaded and could use only one of their two banks of torpedo tubes, but they succeeded in reaching 30 knots and zig-zagged. With the help of a smoke screen, they escaped with great luck as *TA28* was hit only once by a shell, which did not explode. Because of the troubles in her boiler room, *TA24* had to reduce her speed temporarily to 17 knots and, consequently, the other torpedo boats too. Around midnight, three or four enemy MTBs attacked, near the island of Giglio, but the torpedoes were outmanoeuvred. In a few minutes the three torpedo boats fired 854 shots of all calibres, and two of the MTBs were left on fire. After again a total of seventeen hours at sea the torpedo boats were

The German torpedo boat TA23 (ex-Italian Impavido*) which was the second unit to be commissioned, on 17 October 1943, shortly after the TA24. (Author's collection)*

The TA24 (ex-Italian Arturo*) probably in Genoa harbour. In the foreground the artillery ferry AFP (ex-MFP) 503. (Author's collection)*

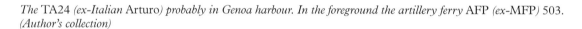

safely back in La Spezia, with their mission accomplished, with only one seriously and four slightly wounded men aboard *TA28*. That mission was a warning for what would happen in the future, and the day bringing radar equipment much anticipated.

The missions of coastal shelling are particularly interesting, because they were much more dangerous for the torpedo boats who had to fire by night, almost without any air support and in the face of total Allied air and naval superiority. They could be relatively quickly located by their firing position and could not stay for long in one location. The first such action took place on the night of 1/2 March 1944, when *TA24* and *TA28* shelled the harbour of Bastia in Corsica (Operation '*Nuss-Knacker*'). A German plane helped them in dropping flares and the salvoes were then fired at a quick rate, starting at 0101hrs. They fired 170 shots of 100mm and four torpedoes, with visible success, stopping the firing at 0113hrs. It must be recalled that the two torpedo boats were carrying a total of only four 100mm guns. Enemy coastal batteries hit back without any result, and one torpedo attack by enemy MTBs was repulsed. At 0735hrs *TA24* and *TA28* arrived safely in La Spezia without having been attacked on the way back.

On 22 April, at 2030hrs, *TA23*, *TA26* and *TA29* sailed from Porto Ferraio in Elba for another shelling of Bastia harbour, coinciding with an air attack from the Luftwaffe and taking the opportunity of the flares to adjust their gunfire. At 0040hrs, 23 April, the shelling began and lasted for 10 minutes, during which 172 shots of 100mm were fired by three boats' eight guns, together with five torpedoes. Fires were observed as the torpedo boats were sailing north for Capraia and then north again to La Spezia, which was reached at 0630hrs. On 24 April, at 2000hrs, *TA23*, *TA26* and *TA29* sailed south again to lay a minefield a few miles south of Capraia. At 0118hrs, 25 April, the first mines were laid and, 12 minutes later, the operation was over. At 0145hrs, as the boats were sailing back home at 21 knots, *TA23* was shaken by a strong explosion in 43°02N/09°45E. It was a mine from a field laid on the night of 10/11 April 1944 by the co-belligerent Italian torpedo boat *Sirio* and *TA23* had hit it after the torpedo boats had entered the minefield at 0138hrs. She was so heavily damaged that she had to be towed slowly by *TA26*, with *TA29* sailing behind them. They left the minefield at 0402hrs and were very lucky in not hitting another mine.

Later on there was an attack by the three American MTBs *PT202*, *PT213* and *PT218* which launched six torpedoes, then several air attacks by fighter-bombers, all without any success. But at 0632hrs it was impossible to keep going; *TA23*'s freeboard was 30cm above the sea, and 300 tons of water had poured into the ship. So, at 0645hrs, *TA24* launched a torpedo (450mm) at her but the effect not being decisive, she used a second torpedo and that time an ammunition magazine was hit, all the survivors having been previously rescued by *TA26* and *TA29*. On 31 May, in an engagement on the Ligurian coast, between *TA29*, *TA30* and the American MTBs

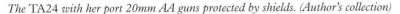

The TA24 *with her port 20mm AA guns protected by shields. (Author's collection)*

The TA23 *sinking, on 25 April 1944, after hitting a mine. Other sources claim that the photograph was taken during the shelling of Bastia which took place between 0040hrs and 0050hrs on 23 April. It was then pitch dark! In addition it will be noted that the third 100mm gun is facing rearwards. (Author's collection)*

The TA25 *(ex-Italian* Ardito*) in the roadstead of La Spezia in 1944, before leaving the Ligurian base for a minelaying mission. (Author's collection)*

The TA29 *(ex-Italian* Eridano*) in Genoa harbour with an anti-torpedo barrage in the foreground. (Author's collection)*

PT304, *PT306* and *PT307*, both sides sustained light damage.

On 9 June, at 1200hrs, during an American air raid on the harbour of Porto Ferraio (Elba), *TA27* was hit by two bombs in the stern. Shortly after, a third bomb hit amidships and ready-to-use ammunition exploded. The crew was rescued by *TA30*, which shot down one of the attackers, and the heavily damaged torpedo boat capsized during the following night.

During the minelaying operation 'Nadel', on the night of 14/15 June, *TA26* and *TA30* were attacked by the American MTBs *PT552*, *PT558* and *PT559*. Despite a strong defensive fire, *TA26* was hit by two torpedoes from one of the two latter PTs and *TA30* was hit by a third from *PT552*. They both sank with heavy loss of life; *TA26* lost 90 men out of 170 and *TA30* 20 men out of 140. The two torpedo boats had laid their mines between 0140hrs and 0157hrs and were on the way back when they were attacked at 0414hrs, approaching La Spezia, in position 44°04N/09°32E.

On the night of 17/18 June, *TA24* and *TA29*, while laying the mine barrage 'Stein', were involved in an engagement with the American MTB *PT207*, the British *MTB633*, *MTB655*, *MGB658* and *MGB663*, east of Elba. On 18 June, at about 0100hrs, the two torpedo boats were located by *MTB655* which launched torpedoes, but they missed and exploded on the coast. *TA29* noticed the action and tried to ram one of the British boats (*MGB658*); the torpedo boat touched just behind her stern, pushing the MGB alongside her hull. Both boats

were firing at each other with all their guns. The MGB was hit, three men were killed and five were seriously wounded. Among the latter was the captain, Lieutenant Bates; there were also casualties aboard the torpedo boat. The MGB was not heavily damaged, but the antenna fell upon the commanding bridge and blocked the steering wheel, putting her out of control. *MTB655* was also hit and had men killed and wounded. Such an action was very dangerous for the two German boats, for they still had mines on board. After the encounter was brought to an end, they were laid, the last mine being dropped at 0134hrs. Despite another attack by MGBs, *TA24* and *TA29* reached La Spezia at around 0600hrs.

On the night of 20/21 June, *TA25* and *TA29* carried out the minelaying operation 'Messer'. The minefield was laid between Leghorn and Gorgona, the first mine being dropped at 0027 and the last at 0051hrs. On the way back they were attacked by three American PT-boats and one of them succeeded in hitting *TA25* amidships with one torpedo. The torpedo boat sank in 43°49N/10°12E and 137 members of her crew were rescued: 85 by the Arno's pilot boat and fishermen and 52 by *TA29* which was back in La Spezia at 0615hrs. As stated earlier, most of the minelaying missions and reconnaissance sorties are not covered, but it must be mentioned that, between 6 and 26 July, *TA24*, *TA28* and *TA29* put to sea practically every night, mainly on reconnaissance sorties, but also on mining and coastal-shelling operations, having several engagements with Allied MGBs, MTBs and PTs.

On 25 July, at 2354hrs, *TA24*, *TA28* and *TA29* left La

Table 1: *Ships probably sunk by* TA *Boat Mines in the Ligurian and Tyrrhenian Seas*

31/12/43	Minesweeping sloop *Clacton* (1941, 656 tons)	off Bastia
1/1/44	*LST411* (1942, 1,625 tons)	off Bastia
17/6/44	*LCF15* (1942, 470 tons)	near Elba (invasion of the island)
27/6/44	*MTB640* (1942, 102 tons)	south of Leghorn
12/7/44	*ML443* (1941, 75 tons)	off Leghorn
29/8/44	Italian steamer *Lucrino*	off Sardinia
1/9/44	*MMS117* (1942, 165 tons)	near Civitavecchia
12/10/44	*MMS170* (1942, 165 tons)	off Gorgona Island
18/11/44	US MTB *PT311* (1943, 46 tons)	west of Cape Corse, 43°N/9°E approx
31/1/45	Italian goelette *Mafalda*	west of Civitavecchia
15/3/45	Italian goelette *Nasello*	near Monte Argentario
25/6/45	*MMS168* (1942, 165 tons)	off Genoa
17/7/45	Naval tug *Athlete* (1943, 570 tons)	off Leghorn

Notes:

Unless otherwise stated, all the ships were British.
There were also naval and merchant vessels sunk off Toulon, Marseilles and Port de Bouc, but they are not included since those places were covered by the *Admiral der Französischen Südküste* and TA boats were not responsible for the losses.

Spezia for operation 'Panther', a coastal-shelling mission, between the south of Marina di Pisa and the Arno estuary, along the front line. They were going to support the German troops and their intervention had an undeniable impact on morale, since they were helped from the sea by the *Kriegsmarine*. The torpedo boats sailed south at 21 knots and, after the alarm for action-stations was given at 0152hrs, at 0202hrs the Flotilla leader *TA29* opened fire with five star shells, at a distance of 5,000m from the coast, followed by the torpedo boats' six 100mm guns firing inland at a distance of between 5,000 and 8,000m. At 0209hrs the gunfire was stopped after 252 shells had been spent, and the three torpedo boats sailed back for La Spezia. On the way, at 0252hrs, three enemy MTBs were located at a distance of 3,000/3,500m and, after the torpedo boats fired star shells, the MTBs turned away. At 0430hrs *TA24*, *TA28* and *TA29* were back in La Spezia. On 26 July, at 0045hrs, *TA24*, *TA28* and *TA29* sailed again for a coastal-shelling mission in the same area, between Marina di Pisa and the Arno estuary. The Allies were probably not expecting them on the next night. At 0232hrs, *TA29* once again opened fire, first with a few star shells, followed at 0235hrs by all the torpedo boats' main 100mm guns. Many flames and explosions were observed on land, probably an ammunition depot was hit. At 0245hrs the shelling ended and the torpedo boats were safely back in La Spezia at 0431hrs. In all, 340 shells of 100mm were fired on that second sortie and the torpedo boats were thanked and congratulated by the German Army Headquarters for their spectacular intervention.

Another, and the last, coastal shelling took place on the night of 30/31 August, when *TA24*, *TA29*, *TA31* and *TA32* left Genoa to pound the same area, the Arno estuary. *TA31* was the former prewar Italian destroyer *Dardo*, which had been commissioned on 25 April 1944 in the *Kriegsmarine*. She developed trouble with her rudder and had to give up the operation, returning to La Spezia to be repaired. *TA32* was a recent newcomer to the 10th Flotilla, having been commissioned on 21 July 1944. She was the

ex-Italian *Premuda*, which was the ex-Yugoslav *Dubrovnik*, captured by the Italian Navy on 17 April 1941. The four torpedo boats had left Genoa around midnight and the three who kept on were attacked at 0139hrs by enemy planes which dropped six or eight bombs, helped by clear moonlight, but all missed. At 0213hrs a solitary plane attacked again, but faced with all the torpedo boats' guns firing at it, it did not insist. At 0410hrs the shelling began with *TA24* firing star shells, and then the torpedo boats fired together with their explosive shells of 105mm (*TA32*) and 100mm for eight minutes. *TA29* reported shells falling off her starboard side, at a distance of about 100m. The total used was 39 star shells and 206 explosive shells. On the way back, enemy planes kept contact but, despite flares being dropped and a remarkable luminosity, no air attack took place and *TA24*, *TA29* and *TA32* were safely back in La Spezia at 0514hrs.

It was obvious to the Allies that, despite heavy losses suffered in June, with *TA25*, *TA26*, *TA27* and *TA30* sunk, the few units left were more active than ever before, and they had to do something to destroy them which, even after the landings in southern France two weeks earlier, eluded the hundreds of Allied ships who were sandwiching them between Provence and Italy.

On 1 September, *TA24*, *TA29*, *TA31* and *TA32* sailed from La Spezia to Genoa, joining *TA28* which was already in the northern Italian harbour, and where *TA33* [ex-Italian *Corsaro* (II), ex-*Squadrista*] was being completed and being rearmed with three 105mm, one 88mm, four 37mm AA, twenty-eight 20mm AA (5x4, 4x2) guns and six torpedo 533mm (2x3) tubes. But, on 4 September, between 1250hrs and 1400hrs, 140 American heavy bombers attacked the harbour installations of Genoa and dropped between 600 and 800 heavy bombs amounting to 438 tons. Among the ships sunk or damaged were *TA28*, which was hit by three bombs and capsized in dock, and *TA33* which also received three direct hits and was damaged beyond repair. *TA33* was going to be commissioned by the end of September. *TA29* was damaged but was

The destroyer TA32 *(ex-Italian* Premuda*) and ex-Yugoslav* Dubrovnik*) was commissioned in the* Kriegsmarine *as a torpedo boat because of the smaller calibre of her new guns (105mm). (Author's collection)*

The TA30 (ex-Italian Dragone*) between April and June 1944. (Author's collection)*

back to operations on 1 October. Amid the bad news there was at least something positive for the 'Mohawks', as they were nicknamed by their crews, they were now at last equipped with radar.

During a reconnaissance mission on the night of 1/2 October, *TA24*, *TA29* and *TA32* had an inconclusive engagement with a big destroyer, probably French, in the western part of the Gulf of Genoa, close to the coast and between San Remo and Imperia. *TA32* made a torpedo attack on her, but was outmanoeuvred by the opponent which straddled *TA32* with her gunfire. The German torpedo boats fired with their guns and *TA24* and *TA29* also launched their torpedoes, but with no result. It seemed that the 'unknown' destroyer (or light cruiser) was hit twice by *TA24*'s fire. The German torpedo boats were back in Genoa at 0315hrs.

In the meantime in the Adriatic, TA boats were also being completed in January 1944. The first was *TA37* (ex-*Gladio*) which was commissioned on 8 January, and was followed a week later by *TA36* (ex-*Stella Polare*). On 12 February *TA37* and *TA38* (ex-*Spada*), which was commissioned the same day, took an escorting part in the first mining operation, '*Muskete*'.

On 29 February the German cargo ship *Kapitän Diedrichsen* [ex-Italian *Sebastiano Venier* (II), 1943, 6,406 tons] sailed from Pola to Piraeus, escorted by *TA36*, *TA37*, two submarine-chasers and three motor minesweepers. West of Isto the convoy was attacked by the French destroyers *Le Malin* and *Le Terrible*. The cargo ship was put on fire by 138mm shells from the latter and one submarine-chaser (*UJ201*) was damaged by a torpedo from the former. The cargo ship's survivors were rescued by *TA36* and the other submarine-chaser, while the R-boats stood by the burning ship. *TA37* was heavily damaged by two gunfire salvoes, particularly by a shell hit in the engine room. Her speed was reduced to 10 knots, but 10 miles south of Pola, unable to manoeuvre, she had to be towed into the harbour. On 1 March, at 1145hrs, *Kapitän Diedrichsen* sank.

On 18 March, *TA36* set out from Trieste for a mining operation in the company of the old *TA21* (ex-Italian *Insidioso*), one minelayer and one submarine-chaser. At 2015hrs, 15 miles south-southwest of Fiume, she ran on an old Italian mine barrage and sank ten minutes later at 45°07N/14°21E, the survivors being rescued by the submarine-chaser *UJ205*.

On 25 June, at 1420hrs, *TA38* and *TA39* sailed from Trieste to support, with their flak, the old *TA22* (ex-Italian *G. Missori*) which had been attacked by ten fighter-bombers and severely damaged while running trials. At 1523hrs *TA22* started to be towed back to Trieste, where she was paid off and scuttled later, on 2 May 1945. Like their sisters in the Ligurian Sea, the Adriatic TA boats took part in many operations. To avoid repetition, these are those accomplished between 12 February and 13 August 1944: Escort missions: *TA36*/1, *TA37*/8, *TA38*/4, *TA40*/3; minelaying missions: *TA36*/1, *TA37*/9, *TA38*/11, *TA39*/10, *TA40*/4.

Two other minelaying missions were accomplished by unidentified TA boats, together with the minelayer *Kiebitz* on 26 and 28 August.

In September a very daring action took place which shows up the fighting spirit of the *Kriegsmarine*. It was decided to send three torpedo boats to Greece, to protect the transfer of the last German ships in the Aegean from Piraeus to Salonika and, on the same occasion, to lay minefields, particularly off Piraeus. The sacrificed units were *TA37*, *TA38* and *TA39* which, under the command of *Kapitänleutnant* Lange on the last, sailed from Trieste on 20 September, at 0230hrs, for Pola, where they arrived at 0620hrs. The operation was appropriately and romantically named '*Odysseus*'. On the same day they set out at 1830hrs and at 1920hrs were joined by the S-boats *S30* and *S36*, which later returned to Pola, while the torpedo boats were sailing on at 24 knots. Off Vis *TA37* developed troubles with her machinery and rudder and was left behind. At 0200hrs she was out of sight. *TA38* and *TA39* were not seen by enemy planes and safely reached the Kotor estuary at 0630hrs. There was, of course, no direct air support to be expected from the Luftwaffe, only a few reconnaissance sorties, but no fighters and, as *TA37* was sailing down south, off the islands of Pelagosa and Lastovo, she was under air attack between 0545hrs and 0620hrs five times and luckily escaped unhurt, reaching Kotor safely at 0730hrs. After *TA37* was repaired, the three torpedo boats sailed on 22 September at 2040hrs. On the next morning, they reached the Strait of Otranto, where there was a short and indecisive engagement with the escort destroyers HMS *Belvoir* and HMS *Whaddon*, between 0550hrs and 0620hrs. At 0730hrs the torpedo boats dropped anchor in the Corfu Channel, protected by the island. Their crews had a deserved rest and, on 24 September, at 0200hrs, they sailed for the Gulf of Patras, the Corinth Canal and Piraeus where they safely arrived at 2037hrs. Operation '*Odysseus*' was a daring achievement and a total success, but it must be admitted that the enemy air force was much hampered by bad weather.

Of the 9th Flotilla, made up of old TA boats, there was only one left, *TA18* (ex-Italian *Solferino*) and she was joined by the three torpedo boats who provided a much-needed reinforcement. *TA18* had been commissioned on 25 July 1944, and the four boats were divided into two *rotten*, *TA38* with *TA39* and *TA37* with *TA18*. It is interesting to know how many operations they achieved during their short career in the Aegean between the end of September and the middle of October and here are some details about them.

On 28 September, at 2150hrs, *TA18*, *TA37*, *TA38* and *TA39* sailed from Piraeus for Salonika, in the company of the freighters *Zeus* and *Lola*, with 2,000 *Kriegsmarine* staff on board. The convoy sailed at 12 knots and, on 29 September around midday, there was a submarine alert off the Kassandra peninsula, without any result. *TA38* and *TA39* increased speed, as they were going to participate in a minelaying mission, and reached Salonika well before the convoy. At 1802hrs the convoy was passing the net barrage near Kara Burnu and at 1842hrs dropped anchor in the Salonika roadstead. The planned minelaying operation was nevertheless cancelled and it was on 30 September, at 2005hrs, that *TA38* and *TA39* sailed for the mining operation '*Tulpe*'. The minefield had to be laid northeast of Skyros. Around 0330 minelaying started, and

The TA38 *(ex-Italian* Spada*) during her transfer from the Adriatic to the Aegean, between 20 and 24 September 1944. (Author's collection)*

then the two torpedo boats sailed back home safely, being berthed at the oil-pier of Perama near Piraeus at 0954hrs on 1 October.

On 2 October, at 0200hrs, *TA38* and *TA39* sailed for another minelaying mission, each of them carrying twenty-four EMP mines. The mines were dropped from 0321hrs to 0346hrs, between Idra and Georgios. At 0559hrs both torpedo boats were berthed at the mine-pier and, on the same day, 2 October, at 1759hrs, they sailed again from Piraeus for another mining operation. At 1945hrs, east of Georgios they sailed east, reaching the south of Tinos at 2140hrs. By midnight they were in position 37°33N/25°40E. They then sailed southeast and, five miles off Ikaria, at 0040hrs, 3 October, they sailed south-southeast in the direction of Amorgos. They reached a point five miles northeast of the island's eastern tip at 0206hrs and the boats then parted, *TA38* starting her minelaying at 0234hrs from that island point in an easterly direction, while *TA39* was doing the same to a point ten miles west of Levita, dropping her first mine at 0243hrs. They respectively ended their minelaying at 0256hrs and 0253hrs. At 0308hrs both boats sailed back to Piraeus, where they safely arrived at 0935hrs and 0946hrs. *TA39* developed troubles with her boiler system, having only one ton of water left, and needed a 36-hour repair.

On 4 October, at 1849hrs, *TA38* and *TA39* sailed to escort *Zeus*, which was met south of Cape Sunion at 2300hrs. Then the three ships sailed through the Mandri Channel. Off Caraliani, the torpedo boats parted from *Zeus*, at 0150hrs, 5 October, and sailed back to Piraeus at 21 knots. Early in the afternoon of the same day they accomplished the last minelaying mission, '*Schwedenweg*', between Keos and Hagios Georgios. As they were sailing back to Piraeus, near Keos, at 2055hrs, one motor boat was in sight. After having identified her as being enemy, the leader boat, *TA38*, gave the order to sink her. *TA39* put the motor boat ablaze with her anti-aircraft light guns and she exploded, the crew of eleven being rescued by *TA39*. They were British, and the boat was *HDML1227* who had misidentified the German torpedo boats as being two British destroyers.

On 6 October, at 1351hrs, an air attack began on the harbour of Piraeus, and *TA38* shot down one of the low-level attacking aircraft with her 37mm and 20mm AA guns. There were two more attacks, at 1402hrs and 1437hrs, but the aircraft did not approach *TA38* again and she escaped any damage. At 1745hrs *TA38* and *TA39* left to sail through the Euboea Channel to meet and escort two freighters. Off the Caraliani mine-barrage, on 7 October at 0038hrs, the merchant ships *Lautern* and *Lolo* were sighted by *TA39* and then escorted to Piraeus, where the four ships arrived safely at 0610hrs.

On the night of 6/7 October, southwest of Kassandra-Huk, *TA37* was escorting the minelayer *Zeus* which had 1,125 men on board, together with the submarine-chaser

Table 2: Ships probably sunk by *TA* Boat Mines in the Adriatic

12/9/44	*MGB657* (1942, 90 tons) damaged beyond repair	off Rimini
16/9/44	*ML258* (1941, 75 tons)	east of Rimini
10/10/44	*MGB663* (1942, 90 tons)	off Maestra Point, near Rimini
12/10/44	Destroyer *Loyal* (1941, 1,950 tons) damaged beyond repair	off the northeast of Italy
14/12/44	Escort destroyer *Aldenham* (1941, 1,087 tons)	30 miles north of Zadar
21/3/45	*MTB655* (1943, 102 tons)	Quarnero Gulf
23/3/45	*MTB705* (1943, 102 tons)	Maknare Channel
1/4/45	Yugoslav armed boat *MB-11* (*Crvena Zvijezda*)	near Quarnero Gulf
10/4/45	*MTB710* (1943, 102 tons)	west of Zara, off Sarurego Island
17/4/45	*MTB697* (1943, 102 tons)	off Krk Island
28/4/45	*BYMS2053* (1942, 207 tons)	20 miles northeast of Ravenna
5/5/45	Armed trawler *Coriolanus* (1940, 545 tons)	off western coast of Istria
5/5/45	*ML558* (1942, 75 tons)	off western coast of Istria

Notes:

Unless otherwise stated, all the ships were British.
Among the above losses, *MGB663*, destroyer *Loyal* and escort destroyer *Aldenham* are known to have been victims of S-boat mines. For the remaining units, it is not known whether TA, R or S-boats were responsible. Some small patrol boats (14 lost during the war) and small transports, used by the Yugoslav partisans, were also sunk or captured by TA torpedo boats or their mines. On 24/7/44, *MTB372* (1943, 37 tons) was sunk off Cape Loviste, in the northern Adriatic, by gunfire from an unidentified German surface ship, perhaps *TA40*.

Table 3: Ships probably sunk by *TA* Boat Mines in Greek waters

14/10/44	*MFV117* (1943, 50 tons)	near Pasha, northern Aegean
15/10/44	Greek minesweeper *Kassos* (1942, 207 tons, ex-*BYMS2074*)	off Piraeus
15/10/44	Greek minesweeper *Kos* (1943, 215 tons, ex-*BYMS2191*)	off Piraeus
15/10/44	Water-boat *Petronella* (ex-Dutch tanker, 1927, 2,770 tons)	off Piraeus
15/10/44	*ML870* (1944, 75 tons)	off Piraeus
25/10/44	*BYMS2077* (1942, 207 tons)	Gulf of Corinth
25/10/44	*LCT377* (1941, 350 tons)	Gulf of Patras
5/11/44	*LCT339* (1941, 350 tons)	between Patras and Taranto
29/11/44	*MMS101* (1942, 165 tons)	near Salonika
30/11/44	South African armed whaler *Bever* (1930, 252 tons)	off Piraeus
1/12/44	Ferry *Empire Dace* (716 tons)	harbour entrance of Missolonghi
5/12/44	*LCT328* (1941, 350 tons)	Gulf of Patras
12/1/45	Fleet minesweeper *Regulus* (1943, 1,010 tons)	Corfu Channel
4/2/45	*MMS68* (1941, 165 tons)	7 miles northwest of Zakynthos (Zante)
24/2/45	*LST178* (1942, 1,625 tons)	on passage to Corfu, grounded, total wreck

Notes:

Most, if not all, by mines from TA38 and TA39
On 5/10/44, *HDML1227* (1942, 46 tons), near Keos, was sunk by gunfire from *TA39*. On 22/6/45, the US cargo ship *Pierre Gibault* (1943, 7,176 tons) hit a mine off Rhodes at 36°08N/29°30E. She was beached, refloated and towed to Piraeus, being considered damaged beyond repair and scrapped. Was it a detached and floating mine from one of the two minefields laid, on 3/10/44, by *TA38* and *TA39* off Amorgos?

The TA39 *(ex-Italian* Daga*) on the Dalmatian coast in 1944. (Author's collection)*

UJ2101 and the harbour patrol boat *GK32*, when they were attacked by the destroyers HMS *Termagant* and *Tuscan*. The three escorts were sunk by the destroyers through a hail of 120mm shells, *TA37* losing two officers and 96 ratings and sinking in 40°36N/22°46E but, thanks to their sacrifice, *Zeus* escaped. On 7 October, *TA38* and *TA39* sailed respectively at 1745hrs and 1800hrs, to escort to Piraeus, the troop transport *Anna* through the Euboea Channel. At 2140hrs they met and escorted her, reducing their speed to 7 knots, *Anna*'s maximum speed. Near Hagios Georgios, at 2320hrs, an enemy MTB was sighted by *TA38* and at 2333hrs two more, the torpedo boat firing at them with her 20mm AA guns. Both torpedo boats and the *Anna*, nevertheless, safely reached Piraeus despite their low speed.

On 8 October *TA38* and *TA39* were ordered to escort from Piraeus the merchant vessels *Laudon* and *Engers* together with two R-boats, off Cape Sunion, through the Mandri Channel and up the Euboea Channel. At 0002hrs, 9 October, the torpedo boats sailed back to Piraeus at 21 knots, just after they had detected enemy MTBs, which were again localised at 0112hrs, action stations being sounded. At 0127hrs, two more enemy MTBs were standing at 5,000m ahead on the port side, but evidently had not sighted the torpedo boats and were laying stopped. Soon after, near Makrouisi, *TA38* went aground and asked *TA39* to take her in tow.

The two MTBs were still stopped and it was a dangerous operation because of them. But the TA boats were unnoticed and, after *TA39* came back to the scene at 12 knots, she towed her sistership after she was put afloat again. Both torpedo boats sailed for Cavaliani and reached it after a towing journey which lasted until 0541hrs. Then *TA39* sailed again for Piraeus at 24 knots and *TA38*, towed by tug 157, sailed for Chalkis. At 0722hrs two reconnaissance aircraft approached from the port side and *TA38* opened fire with all her available AA guns, and one was shot down. The other aircraft called for fighter-bombers and, at 0839hrs they attacked *TA38* in three waves. Six bombs exploded nearby, then at 0849hrs the second air attack damaged the ship. The aircraft were from the carrier HMS *Stalker*'s 809 Squadron. The drinking water compartment was holed and salt water poured in; the after-ship ammunition room and oil reserve were also damaged. At 0900hrs the third attack by three aircraft took place. One of them was hit by AA gunfire and crashed on land. At 0926hrs there was a fourth air attack, but *TA38* succeeded in reaching the harbour of Chalkis at 1235hrs. Here another air raid took place, but the attack remained beyond the AA gunfire barrage. At 1902hrs, 10 October, *TA38* sailed to be repaired in Volos, escorted by a GA boat. They reached the roadstead at 0500hrs, 11 October, and were in the harbour at 0742hrs.

In the meantime *TA39*, on the morning of 9 October, loaded 28 mines on board in Skaramanga for her last minelaying mission. She sailed at 2004hrs and laid her mines in the Strait of Phleves, between 2104hrs and 2131hrs, after the evacuation of Piraeus. *TA39* then escorted the steamers *Anna* and *Lola* with two R-boats and three GA-boats. At 0045, 10 October, *TA39* parted with the latter steamer and stayed with *Anna*. At 0110hrs

one small German boat was sighted ahead. She was the light S-boat *LS10*, which was sunk in Volos the next day by air attack. Through the Chalkis Channel, at 0644hrs, the harbour of Chalkis was reached, *TA38* being already there and transferring oil and water to *TA39*. The latter then sailed to Syra, where the motor ship *Kalidon* was waiting with the island's small garrison of ninety men on board. *TA39* took fifty of them with her. These men had to accomplish demolitions in Chalkis harbour before the arrival of the Allies, so the motor ship sailed away on her own. Then, in sailing to Chalkis in the morning, *TA39* outsailed *Kalidon* in the Euboea Channel, her urgent mission preventing her from escorting the motor ship, which was sighted by fighter-bombers, attacked and sunk, with heavy loss of life. After Chalkis *TA39* safely reached Volos. *TA38* was berthed there, damaged, with no boilers working and no more water; the ammunition room could still be used, but probably not for long, and the rudder was completely unreliable; partisan forces coming from Larissa were approaching the harbour. The crew determined to 'welcome' them and, from 0520hrs, 12 October, until 1820hrs, the two 100mm guns fired on their positions to the last shell. On the next day, at 1255hrs, twelve high-altitude bombers attacked the harbour of Volos, causing stored ammunition to explode. At 1800hrs, *Leutnant zur See* Scheller assembled his crew, thanked them for their courageous behaviour, and was brought aboard *TA39* by a motor boat. At 1930hrs *TA38* was towed to the entrance of the harbour and scuttled as a block-ship with depth charges.

On 14 October *TA39* left the harbour, with *TA38*'s crew on board, and had to meet the minelayer *Zeus* at sea to escort her to Salonika. The meeting took place at 0157hrs, 15 October, and both ships reached the harbour at 0528hrs. On the same day, at 2050hrs, the indefatigable *TA39* sailed again south to Volos, with R-boats 185 and 195, to pick up German soldiers. At 0135hrs, 16 October, 45 miles south of Salonika, *TA39* hit a mine and sank at 0146hrs, with no casualties, in a depth of 46m. Her crew was rescued by an R-boat, while the other one kept on to Volos to embark the soldiers. That was the end of the trio which had haunted the Adriatic and the Aegean Seas, from Trieste to Salonika, through the Otranto Strait and the Corinth Canal. But there was still a surviving TA boat at sea, the old *TA18*, but she did not survive for long. On 19 October, at 2250hrs, off Skiathos, she was attacked and heavily damaged by 120mm gunfire from HMS *Termagant* and *Tuscan* and was driven ashore, being destroyed by their gunfire at 2340hrs, most of the crew being shot by Greek partisans.

The war was over in the Aegean. Piraeus had been evacuated by German forces on 12 October, Salonika on 31 October, but sister ships were keeping on fighting in the Adriatic and in the Ligurian Sea. In the former theatre two new TA boats had recently been commissioned: *TA41* (ex-Italian *Lancia*) and *TA45* (ex-Italian *Spica*).

Between 9 and 11 October operation 'Dacapo' took place, when *TA40* sailed from Pola, with the submarine-chasers *UJ202*, *UJ208* and eight S-boats. Their target was the island of Melada, in the approximate position 44°N/15°E, where there was an enemy radio station which

The TA41 *(ex-Italian* Lancia*) with another torpedo boat behind, both being covered with some camouflage. (Author's collection)*

had to be destroyed. The mission was accomplished with success, and the island's lighthouse was also destroyed by gunfire. One of the S-boats was damaged by 40mm gunfire and had to be towed back. As they were starting back, masts were seen over the horizon. They belonged to the hospital ship *Gradisca*, which was coming from Alexandria with wounded German soldiers released by the British. *TA40* went to meet her, and circled the ship, but she had to leave her and rejoin the other warships. Nevertheless, the return to Trieste was happier after that encounter. Soon after, *TA40* was attacked by fighter-bombers but with no result. On the way back home the two submarine-chasers were attacked by British MTBs and MGBs. *TA40*, which was following, damaged two of them with gunfire, and was herself damaged by many hits from an MGB which fired at very short distance.

On the night of 12/13 October, the steamer *Prometheus* was escorted by *TA40*, two submarine-chasers and the escort vessel *G234* from Pola to Trieste, and an attack by enemy MTBs was repulsed. On the night of 2/3 November, *TA40* and *TA45* escorted the minelayer *Kiebitz* during the minelaying operation '*Lama 3*' in the northern Adriatic. On leaving Trieste, the three ships were attacked by nine fighter-bombers and shot down three of them. The mines were later on successfully laid. In the first days of November too, the steamer *Goffredo Mamelli*, escorted by three R-boats, was sailing from Trieste to Pola. Off Pirano, after she hit a mine, *TA40* and *TA45* came to her rescue and succeeded in bringing her to the Bay of Stringnano, and later *TA40* towed her to Trieste. On the

night of 11/12 November, *TA40*, *TA45* and the minelayer *Fasana* (ex-Italian) carried out the mining operation '*Emma 1*'.

On 23 November, *TA40* and *TA45* escorted the *Fasana* and one MFP on another minelaying mission. On the morning of 24 November they were back in Pola. On 25 November another mission took place, '*Emma 3*', but *Fasana*, without her rudder working, had to be towed to Pola by *TA45*. On 7 December, off the island of Pag, *TA40* hit an underwater rock and sustained some damage. On her way back she was attacked by British MTBs, which launched torpedoes at her, but they missed.

On 10 December 1944 and 10, 12 and 19 January 1945, four minelaying operations were covered by TA torpedo boats, *Fasana*, R-boats and MFPs off Pola and San Sego. On 17 February, *TA41*, in the shipyard of San Rocco in Trieste, was hit and seriously damaged by a bomb during an air raid, *TA44* (ex-Italian destroyer *Antonio Pigafetta*, being sunk. The remaining TA boats, *TA40*, *TA42* and *TA45*, kept on with coastal shelling, reconnaissance and escort missions. Motor sailing vessels, motor boats and sailing vessels belonging to the Yugoslav partisans were sunk by them.

On 20 February, in the harbour of Trieste, *TA40* was hit by a bomb during an air raid, and stayed out of service for three weeks, while the old *TA48* (ex-Yugoslav *T3*) was sunk. On the same day *TA46*, which was in Fiume in the Quarnero shipyard, was bombed and heavily damaged by an air attack, as was also *TA47*, which was on the slip and not yet launched. *TA46* had been commissioned a few

Table 4: *TA TORPEDO-BOAT ACTIVITY IN THE LIGURIAN AND TYRRHENIAN SEAS: 22 DECEMBER 1943 AND 18 MARCH 1945*

The 10th Torpedo-Boat Flotilla was created on 31 January 1944 and was under the command of *Korvettenkapitän* von Gartzen from then to 31 October 1944, *Korvettenkapitän* Burkart from the latter date to the end of March 1945 and *Kapitänleutnant* Kopka to the end of the war.

Minelaying missions: 98

TA23: 11	*TA24*: 18	*TA25*: 3	*TA26*: 8	*TA27*: 12
TA28: 12	*TA29*: 22	*TA30*: 7	*TA32*: 5	

Reconnaissance missions: 93

TA23: 3	*TA24*: 25	*TA25*: 1	*TA26*: 6	*TA27*: 3
TA28: 8	*TA29*: 26	*TA30*: 7	*TA31*: 2	*TA32*: 12

Land-shelling missions: 14

TA23: 1	*TA24*: 4	*TA26*: 1	*TA28*: 3	*TA29*: 4
TA32: 1				

Escort missions: 5

TA24: 3	*TA29*: 2

Intruding missions: 3

TA23: 1	*TA24*: 1	*TA26*: 1

Meteorological missions: 2

TA28: 1	*TA29*: 1

Total: 215

Notes:
TA23 and *TA24* belonged to the *3. Geleit-Flottille* before being incorporated in the *10. Torpedobootsflottille* on 16 February 1944, when they joined *TA27* and *TA28*, being joined later by *TA29*, *TA30*, *TA31* and *TA32*; but *TA25* and *TA26* also belonged first to the *3. Geleit-Flottille* and then to the *13. Sicherungs-Flottille*, to which they belonged at the time they were sunk.

Table 5: *LIGURIAN/TYRRHENIAN SEA TORPEDO BOATS*

German Designation	Ex-Italian name	Launched	Commissioned
TA24	*Arturo*	27/3/43	4/10/43
TA23★	*Impavido*	24/2/43	17/10/43
TA26★	*Intrepido*	8/9/43	18/12/43
TA27	*Auriga*	15/4/43	29/12/43
TA25★	*Ardito*	14/3/43	16/1/44
TA28	*Rigel*	22/5/43	23/1/44
TA29	*Eridano*	12/7/43	6/3/44
TA30	*Dragone*	14/8/43	15/4/44

Notes:
★ *Animoso* class, otherwise *Ariete* class. TA numbers given to the ex-*Ardito* and ex-*Intrepido* have been unintentionally reversed in previously published information. For the specifications of the *Animoso* and the *Ariete* class see Conway's *All the World's Fighting Ships, 1922–1946*.

Table 6: *ADRIATIC/AEGEAN SEA TORPEDO BOATS*

German Designation	Ex-Italian name	Launched	Commissioned
TA37	Gladio	15/6/43	8/1/44
TA36	Stella Polare	11/7/43	15/1/44
TA38	Spada	1/7/43	12/2/44
TA39	Daga	15/7/43	27/3/44
TA40	Pugnale	1/8/43	7/7/44
TA45	Spica	30/1/44	8/9/44
TA41	Lancia	7/5/44	21/10/44
TA42	Alabarda	7/5/44	27/11/44
TA46	Fionda	1944	Feb 1945
TA47	Balestra	not launched	not commissioned

Notes:
All *Ariete* class.

days before, under the command of *Oberleutnant zur See* Scheller, ex-*TA38*'s *Leutnant zur See.*

In the Ligurian Sea there were still three TA boats in action at that time: *TA24*, *TA29* and *TA32*. *TA31* had been paid off, after technical troubles, on 20 October 1944 and, five days later, was heavily damaged during an air raid over Genoa. On 4 February 1945, a coastal shelling operation had been planned with the three torpedo boats, but was cancelled because *TA32* developed engine troubles and was able to reach a maximum speed of only 25 knots. She was repaired and made ready for the next operation, which took place on the night of 17/18 March. *TA24*, *TA29* and *TA32*, all loaded with mines, sailed from Genoa and the beginning of the operation was without any problems. The two small torpedo boats dropped their 56 mines, south of Gorgona, while *TA32* sailed south and, around 0030hrs, 18 March, laid her 72 mines north of Cape Corse. After joining up, all three sailed back to Genoa, *TA24* leading, with *TA29* in the middle and *TA32* trailing a little further behind. At 0059hrs shore radar in Leghorn detected them, as they were about 20 miles north of Cape Corse. There were four Allied destroyers carrying out a concertina patrol in accordance with Flank Force instructions, in the order from west to east: French *Basque*, French *Tempête*, HMS *Meteor* and HMS *Lookout*. An enemy report was made via Leghorn W T which reached those concerned, except *Meteor*, at between 0140hrs and 0145hrs. Subsequent enemy reports based on shore radar gave his position at 0119hrs, 0129hrs, 0141hrs, 0215hrs, 0235 and 0305hrs, about which time HMS *Lookout* made contact. Before that she turned to 060°, 28 knots, at 0140hrs, passed out her position, course and speed on the Ligurian Operational Wave, which was not received by any ship. But she also called HMS *Meteor* on TBS, giving her course and speed. This was the first intimation *Meteor* had that something was afoot, and she altered at once to 060° and increased to full speed. Meantime, *Tempête* (Captain Morazzani, Senior Officer) had ordered *Meteor* (Captain Pankhurst) and *Lookout* (Captain Hetherington) to intercept, and himself turned to 050° at 24 knots ordering *Basque* (Captain Jourdan) to join him. At 0230hrs the

second enemy report based on shore radar was received, and indicated that the enemy's course was southwesterly. *Tempête* therefore altered course to 130° and told *Basque* to follow, in order to cover a convoy which was approaching the swept channel north of Cape Corse. When the third enemy report showed the enemy's course to be northerly, *Tempête* led round to a course of 040°, increasing gradually to 26 knots, her speed limit with fuel available. *Lookout* made radar contact with the enemy at 0301hrs and plotted them as steering 350° at 15 knots, later amended to 20 knots. Gunfire was opened at 0310hrs under radar control at 4,500m and the ship turned to a similar course 2 minutes later, when torpedoes were fired. Gun hits (120mm) were obtained on the leading and the second German torpedo boat (*TA24* and *TA29*) and the latter dropped out of the line while her consorts made off. *Lookout* concentrated on the damaged *TA29* from a reduced distance of 1,800–2,700m, and left her a blazing wreck, which sank at about 0420hrs, in position 43°36N/08°58E. *Meteor* saw a star shell fired by *Lookout* but was not aware that she was engaging the enemy until 0328hrs, when course was altered to 160° in support. At 0352hrs *Meteor* gained one radar contact bearing 130° at 7 miles distance and plot gave *TA24*'s course and speed as 006°, 30 knots. She came closer and opened gunfire under radar control at 7,300m turning to port. Hits were immediately obtained and torpedoes were fired a few minutes later, one of them hitting *TA24*, which sank in position 43°49N/09°27E at 0405. *Meteor* rescued 119 German survivors including the Flotilla Commander (*Korvettenkapitän* Burkart) who were taken to Golfe Juan. About 125 German survivors were picked up by coastal forces and one LC(I) and taken to Leghorn.

Since this was the most important last surface action of the Second World War, it is appropriate to give more details of it: an approach from ahead at high speed was used by *Lookout* and *Meteor*. This gave the German ships little time to co-ordinate their fire and movement, and even the British destroyers were surprised by the rapidly closing rate. The German TA boats, being committed to an escape to the north, were at a disadvantage. They had to maintain their course and speed, whereas the attackers were able to alter course at will after fire was opened. This served to throw the TA boats out of line both in gunnery and torpedo fire and was probably the major cause of the British destroyers' avoidance of damage. It must be pointed out that it took *Lookout* a long time to sink *TA29* with her 120mm shells, circling round and hitting her again and again, but without the desired result. For some time, though on fire, *TA29* fought back well. Her fire was quite accurate and she obtained a large number of near misses, but scored no hits with her main armament. A burst of 20mm fire hit the smoke-floats on *Lookout*'s quarterdeck and started a fire, but this was quickly extinguished by jettisoning the smokefloats. *TA29* was hit upwards of forty times before she sank, on fire from end to end.

By the middle of March *TA40*, *TA42* and *TA45* were still operational in the northern Adriatic. On 18 March, *TA40* and *TA42* sailed for Venice, where they anchored in the *Arsenal Marittima*. Three days later, at 1510hrs, fighter-bombers made a surprise attack, flying unexpectedly over the land. *TA42* was heavily hit and sank with casualties. *TA40* was left intact and there were no casualties. As the Yugoslav partisans were threatening Fiume, it was decided to remind them that the *Kriegsmarine* still existed. An operation of coastal shelling, near Senj, was mounted for the night of 12/13 April. At 0001hrs, on the 13th, *TA40* and *TA45* sailed south from Fiume for the coastal area of Senj. *TA40* was the leader and *TA45* was following her on the port side. Aboard *TA40* British radio messages were intercepted and made it clear that British MGBs and MTBs were at sea in the area. At 0230hrs, as they were in the Morlacca Channel, the two torpedo boats were attacked by two British MTBs which soon launched torpedoes at them. They were *MTB670* and *MTB697*; the former's two torpedoes were avoided by *TA40*, thanks to a violent evasive action, but two minutes later *MTB697*'s first torpedo hit *TA45* between the forward 100mm gun and the bridge, followed by the second which hit at the height of the engines. The amidship part of the torpedo boat immediately sank, the bows stayed afloat and the stern sank with the propellers still revolving. Nevertheless, the majority of the engine room's complement escaped by climbing out, but more than half the ship's complement was lost. *TA40* made a smoke screen

and escaped a second attack from the MTBs. In the grey of the morning she passed Pola, sailed between Brioni and the coast, and finally reached Trieste safely. Unfortunately for the British, four days later, the big *MTB697* (1943, 102 tons) was lost after having struck a mine off Krk, in an area which was supposed to have been cleared by the partisans, the boat breaking in half and most of her crew being killed. She was the last British MTB lost operationally during the Second World War.

The advancing Allied forces were by now threatening the harbours of northern Italy, and in the Adriatic as well as in the Ligurian Sea the problems were the same for the *Kriegsmarine*. Before Genoa was abandoned many warships and merchant ships were sunk in the harbour and blown up in the yards by German troops. *TA31* and *TA32* were both scuttled on 24 April, together with *TA28* which had been salvaged and was under repair, after having capsized on 4 September 1944. *TA41* was scuttled, on 1 May, in Trieste, together with *TA43* (ex-Yugoslav *Beograd*), the old *TA22* and *TA35* being scuttled there two days later, as well as *TA46* and *TA47* in Fiume on 3 May, and *TA40* in Monfalcone on the next day. The torpedo boats' slaughter was over.

Korvettenkapitän Wirich von Gartzen, 10th Torpedo-Boat Flotilla's leader, told the author that, when a crew member was killed or wounded he could not be replaced for they were too short of personnel. To fight exhaustion, the crews consumed a lot of coffee during the many night sorties. Those measures show to what extent the struggle was unequal for the *Kriegsmarine* in the face of a greater strength. The 18 March 1945 battle illustrated particularly the discrepancy existing between the two sides: *Lookout* and *Meteor* armed with twelve 120mm guns against *TA24* and *TA29* armed with four 100mm guns, the *TA32*, with her four 105mm guns, having taken virtually no part in the fight.

Regarding the 29 February 1944 action in the Adriatic, the fate of the German submarine-chaser *UJ201* (ex-Italian *Egeria*) is subject to conflicting versions: according to Italian information, the wreck was found in Moufalcone harbour, probably scuttled by the Germans on 24 April 1945. According to the French, the *UJ20*, was sunk with all hands by the *Le Malin*'s torpedo.

HMS *TIRADE* AND THE SINKING OF *UC–55*

An incident from the Great War

M W Williams throws new light on an obscure destroyer *v.* submarine action in 1917,
illustrating the 'texture' of the war at sea.

A number of naval events and actions from the Great War will always be remembered and often related. But there are many more minor episodes that have now been all but forgotten, recollected only by the dwindling few participants who lived through those epic days.

Some of these obscure incidents at sea could in the grand scheme of things be regarded as routine affairs by even those taking part. But such 'trivial' incidents constituted the very day-to-day fabric of conducting a vigorous and successful war at sea, with the continual and unrelenting exercise of imposing control, protecting one's lines of communication, and refusing one's enemies free passage through blockade. This was the real heart of the Allied success at sea in the First World War, not just the occasional battlecruiser clash or rare set-piece battle.

It is with an investigation of this small ship 'routine' that this article deals, involving as it does a single destroyer, and the individuals who served on board her. Sometimes it is only from such participants that personal accounts emerge. But these uncelebrated events are ones which not only shaped the lives of those who took part in them, but the outcome of the war itself.

One such individual was Sublieutenant Arthur G D Bagot, fresh from a week's torpedo training course at HMS *Vernon*. Newly appointed to the destroyer HMS *Tirade*, then nearing completion at Scotts' yard at Greenock on the Clyde, he arrived on board on Sunday, 26 June 1917, just before her commissioning two days later.

He was to go on to relate an encounter which overtook this new destroyer on the afternoon of 29 September 1917, when she clashed with the German minelaying submarine *UC–55*, just to the east of the Shetland Islands in a short, sharp, small-ship action, never, as far as I can tell, investigated or related previously.

Before describing this event I shall review the career of the *Tirade* up to that epic point. By doing so I shall demonstrate the demanding nature of her employment during those intensely challenging days.

This particular destroyer, a member of the eleven-strong Admiralty Modified 'R' class, was launched on 21 April 1917, where she was fitted out over the next two months. This much-needed destroyer displaced 1,173 tons under a deep loading, while her structure was 276ft in overall length and 26ft 8in on the beam, and had a maximum 11ft 9in draught. For her offensive capabilities she was well provided for, with three 4in guns, one 2pdr Pom-pom, four 21in torpedo tubes in two twin mountings, along with an unspecified load of depth charges aft. However, her outfit may be estimated at around thirty depth charges, perhaps up to a maximum of forty. In July 1917 the average weekly output was only 140 but this would rise to 500 by October and 800 in December.

At this time there was no effective means of detecting, locating or hunting a submerged vessel. That was until the introduction of the first early acoustic listening devices, ASDIC, in 1918, derived from experiments and trials at the HMS *Tarlair* establishment at Hawkcraig in Fife. Along with the later provision of depth-charge throwers, capable of deploying an effective pattern out to 100 yards from the ship, 'straddling a craft' constituted the first actual means of anti-submarine warfare. However, for a destroyer in 1917 the most effective anti-submarine measure could still be said to be the most primitive and archaic: ramming.

The *Tirade* and her sisters in this subclass differed from the general 51-unit 'R' class in one major respect, in that they had their No. 1 and No. 2 boiler rooms transposed, back-to-back. This gave them a rather fat, combined forward funnel tight abaft the foremast, and a thinner one aft, instead of the original 'R' class three-funnel layout for the design's installation of three Yarrow boilers. These pressure vessels were oil-fired, drawing on a maximum bunkerage of some 300 tons and providing steam to drive the pair of Brown Curtiss all-geared turbines and twin screws, to give the ability to achieve a speed of 36 knots.

Her commanding officer was Lieutenant-Commander Henry Dawson Crawford Stanistreet, DSO, RN, while her First Lieutenant was A W Hore, RN, who, along with Engineer Lieutenant C B Hockin and Sublieutenant Bagot, were to be the principal officers for her ninety-five

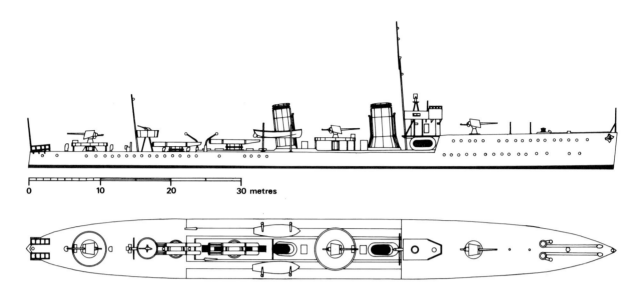

HMS Tirade, *her general features and lines, markedly different from the preceding standard 'R' class, with the combined fore funnel, allowing the bridge and forecastle gun to be located further aft.*

(eighty-two in peacetime) crew. Formed mostly from hostilities-only personnel, with a core of regular Navy men to strengthen their number, her complement would also have involved a Surgeon Probationer and a midshipman, but their identities are unknown.

Upon commissioning, the ship was destined to join the 15th Destroyer Flotilla of the Grand Fleet. But before this she was to work-up in the first half of July, presumably in the secure Firth of Clyde and the Irish Sea, before undertaking what were to be regular convoy-protection duties.

Organised Atlantic convoys had just been inaugurated from Hampton Roads that June, and from Sydney (Cape Breton), New York, Gibraltar, and belatedly in home waters in the weeks that followed. This was to be a successful effort that finally checked the unrestricted German submarine campaign, which had recommenced on 1 February 1917.

The general area in which the *Tirade* was initially to operate in encompassed Patrol Areas I, covering the Outer Hebrides, XVII the Inner Hebrides approaches to the Clyde, along with XVIII and XIX, to the northwest of Ireland, from the twenty-one patrol areas around the British Isles which had been instigated in December 1914.

As originally planned, a typical 'slow' convoy contained ships capable of between 8 and 12.5 knots, and a 'fast' one for those between 12.5 and 16 knots. Vessels capable of speeds above this did not as a rule sail in convoy, but instead trusted their superior speed and possibly a deck-mounted armament to avoid and deter the enemy.

The organisation of the convoy system had occurred just in time for the Allies. On one day, 11 April 1917, no fewer than eleven British merchantmen and eight fishing vessels were sunk by submarines. While in that same month one out of every four merchant ships setting out from the British Isles never returned. Convoys effectively halted this potentially fatal haemorrhage just in time.

In the waters where *Tirade* was to operate, outward-bound convoys were tenaciously accompanied by destroyers and sloops 300 to 400 miles out into the Atlantic, through the most hazardous waters, where the merchantmen were freely dispersed and allowed to steam on unattended. The escort then went to another predetermined rendezvous, where it met a laden homeward-bound convoy and escorted it through the submarine danger zone. However such meetings in the broad Atlantic were often subject to difficulties and delays, with wireless communication of limited range between the formations, inexact navigational positions due to bad weather, and halts caused through machinery faults. All combined to throw off schedules, and retard plans to the extent where there was always the risk of running out of fuel.

During her work-up period through early July, a defect with the steering gear and another in a 4in gun mounting arose, but these were deemed quite acceptable. There were never enough destroyers now with the introduction of convoys, with their demands on escorts from the limited resources of the Grand Fleet. A ship with such 'minor' problems was now regarded as an indispensable unit, one which had to be actively employed.

With her problems unresolved, on 21 July she left the Clyde for her first active deployment, based at Buncrana in Lough Swilly, Donegal, to embark upon her escort duties off the northwest coast of Ireland, covering the vital approaches to the Firth of Clyde (Glasgow) and the Irish Sea (Liverpool). On this station the usual routine was to spend about five days on patrol or escort and thirty hours in harbour to correct any defects, as well as rest her physically exhausted crew.

Typically *Tirade* and her escorts in the flotilla screened their charges in the waters extending out from the Western Isles lying at 7°W, the Outer Hebrides, out to 17°W, well into the Atlantic, past the exposed Rockall pinnacle, around 300 miles from even the remote and distant St Kilda, embracing the known most active submarine areas in its extent. Each convoy consisted of between twenty and thirty vessels, which a mixed screen of eight to ten light craft, comprising destroyers, old torpedo boats or sloops, was required to protect. On track in these infested waters a zig-zag course was maintained to confuse and throw off any shadowing U-boat.

During one of her early August sailings, an inward-bound ship in convoy was torpedoed and sank in just three minutes; the *Tirade* along with the destroyer *Rapid* (repeat 'M' class) was dispatched to hunt the suspected area for the submarine responsible. After an hour and a half of fruitless search, during which all they saw was wreckage and a horse swimming in the sea, which was mercifully dispatched, they were recalled by the convoy commodore.

It was while they were steaming back to rejoin the convoy, that the gunner on board the *Tirade*, T Cockburn, spotted what appeared to be the conning tower of a surfaced submarine six miles away, trailing the convoy. The sighting must have been mutual because the U-boat promptly began to dive, with the plume of her vented ballast tanks being clearly visible to those on board. The two destroyers in company quickly closed, allowing the *Tirade* to release two depth charges over the estimated spot. But nothing appeared to confirm a definite kill or even the possibility of damage. The futile hunt was then abandoned and the destroyers rejoined the convoy's depleted screen.

Depth charges were to prove to be second only to mines in terms of kills against U-boats. Of the 178 German submarines sunk in the Great War, it is thought that 44

succumbed to mines while 38 were dispatched by depth charges. A depth charge was merely a steel canister containing 300lb of TNT or amatol, detonated by means of a hydrostatic device at a preset depth. The devices were kept in racks at the stern, and could be released from the bridge by means of an arrangement like a pump handle.

The effective killing range of a depth charge was, however, quite limited. It was necessary to explode within just 14 feet of a submarine to inflict a mortal breach of the pressure hull. Up to 28 feet away the explosion might effectively disable a submarine, forcing it to the surface, while out to 60 feet the overall effects could cause considerable concussion damage. Although first used on 6 July 1916 by the motorboat *Salmon* to dispatch *UC–7* off Lowestoft, by the middle of 1917 it was still a relatively new weapon, and procedures and techniques in its effective employment were still being perfected.

However, at a conference held on 6 May 1917, a number of U-boat officers met. Here the recent experiences of *U–49* were noted, with her commander Lieutenant Spiess relating in some detail his encounter with depth charges. To him this development was a new and potent piece introduced to the chessboard of war under the sea. It harried and chased the U-boat in its own element, submarine missiles for submarine boats.

On another convoy in August there was one more brief encounter with the enemy. Three destroyers, including the *Tirade*, were escorting three empty oilers westwards at about 8 knots when one was torpedoed at dawn. Although damaged and listing she managed to return to Buncrana, with one destroyer covering her limping passage, unmo-

HMS Tirade, *seen from her starboard bow, moored off Harwich in 1919. (NMM. N2576)*

lested by any follow-up U-boat attack. The submarine commander though was obviously determined to concentrate upon the undamaged oilers that night. The reduced group continued slowly west; their passage, however, was to be contested when, just before midnight, a torpedo (possible one of a spread) just missed the *Tirade* astern, and also one of the oilers. Evidently the persistent enemy submarine (which now retired) had been tracking them all day, awaiting its moment to strike again that night, which was moonlit. But no counterattack could be launched due to the impossibility of accurately interpreting the situation which had arisen.

After a strenuous month of escort work, the continuing defect with her steering gear required *Tirade* to sail back to Stephens' yard on the Clyde for repairs; these lasted for twelve days, taking her into September.

From her refit she now headed for Scapa Flow and service within the 15th Flotilla again, but this time in northern waters, stopping over *en route* at Oban. Arriving at Scapa she tied up alongside her depot ship *Sandhurst* (the ex-dummy, decoy battlecruiser *Inflexible*, built upon the hull of the former *Manipur*), before commencing an intensive period of gunnery and torpedo exercises to fill in the gaps from her initial work-up. It was recorded that here she managed to loose off a number of practice torpedoes for the first time during these trials, and lost several of them.

She was soon detached for deployment to Lerwick in the Shetland Islands, to undertake escort duties from this vital supply point across the contested North Sea to neutral Norway; an interval which can only be regarded as strenuous in these inhospitable waters; given its closer proximity to enemy bases and the vital nature of this trade route, all contributed to her greatly increased possibility of encountering the enemy on the surface and below.

It is interesting to note here the inauguration of a system of 'protected sailings' in the autumn of 1916 for this Scandinavian route, predating the introduction of the 'official' universal convoy system of mid-1917. Admiralty reservations and concerns about the convoy system in general appear to have been waived for this zone, in the light of the serious disruption then being experienced along the 180-mile route between the Norwegian coast and the Shetlands. Indeed, by April 1917 further 'protective' measures were instigated, running all merchantmen, with their close escort screens through certain guarded routes, distantly covered by cruiser squadrons. These were procedures well in advance of practices seen in every other theatre.

The *Tirade*'s crew were soon to discover that the typical tramp steamers plying their trade in these disputed waters averaged only some 7 to 8 knots in perfectly calm weather. These were conditions not usually associated with the upper North Sea, where strong winds and high seas could be regarded as the norm, reducing the progress of a homeward bound convoy to a crawling 4 knots. Furthermore, Bagot noted that the vessels did not darken ship sufficiently and could not obey manoeuvring orders well, while the escorts found it difficult to keep station at 'slow both', a trying ordeal for agile and deft destroyers.

There were two principal commodities being transported along this route. One was timber and the second

iron ore from northern Sweden, entrained across land, then shipped out of Narvik, then 700 miles south to Bergen. Both of these were indispensable raw materials for Britain's war effort. This was so obvious a vital commodity route that Germany had to contest it.

Lerwick acted as a vital junction for this shipping, and sailings to Scandinavia set out from the port in the late afternoon, with a close escort of two or three destroyers, accompanied by armed trawlers. Upon reaching the Norwegian coast the next day, the convoy dispersed in the safe waters off Bergen, while the destroyers picked up an already assembled westbound convoy at dusk for the return run. From Lerwick further protected sailings were organised down the east coast of Scotland and England to the final destinations.

The average protection for a convoy at this time was customarily two destroyers and four elderly torpedo-boat or trawler escorts, effectively just an anti-submarine screen. It was recognised at the time that this vital supply line was vulnerable, and it was confidently expected on board the *Tirade* that these lightly defended sailings would one day be disputed, by either agile light-cruiser or modern torpedo-boat units of the German High Seas Fleet.

This was indeed to occur later in the year with the coming of this regions' long winter nights. At what passed for dawn on 16 October 1917, the German light cruisers *Brummer* and *Bremse* (both modern 5,856-ton, four 5.9in and two 3.45in, 25kt units) descended upon such an empty, eastbound convoy. In this onslaught upon the 12-vessel convoy, screened by the destroyers *Mary Rose* and *Strongbow* and accompanied by three armed trawlers, no fewer than ten merchantmen, along with the two destroyers were sunk.

A subsequent German sweep by four large torpedo boats attacked another eastbound convoy two months later on 12 December, about twenty-five miles off the Norwegian coast. In this all six merchantmen along with one destroyer and four trawlers were sunk, with the other destroyer being heavily damaged.

With German bases just fifteen hours away at a comfortable cruising speed of 20 knots, a well-equipped, skilful raiding force could, under cover of a winter's night, easily manage the distance between its base and this route, search, locate, strike, overwhelm and retire, before reinforcements or support from the distant cruiser squadrons could arrive upon the scene. Clearly this trade was dangerous to both merchantmen and screen. The unpredictably rough weather, with mines both laid and cast adrift, and the ever-present threat posed by submarines, resulted in a demanding environment in which *Tirade* and her kind had to operate.

As the *Tirade* was to discover, a round trip to Norway and back could take something like thirty-six hours. This was usually followed by a break of twenty-four hours in harbour to refuel and rest before the next departure, in a near continuous chain of sailings.

On station in this remote northern base, the crew's recreation ashore was limited, but at least it was deemed better than at Scapa Flow. In Lerwick they could enjoy the distractions of regular dances at the town hall and other places ashore. One destroyer's company once staged a 'small mutiny' after an undisclosed incident, when they were not allowed to attend a dance.

We now come to *Tirade*'s moment of glory, which was to take place on an unusually fine, clear and calm North Sea day, 29 September 1917. Here, along with the *Mameluke* (completed in 1915) under Lieutenant Commander E C Bradley, RN, she was escorting a solitary, but valuable, fully loaded steamer from Norway. This small, three-strong group was almost home, with the Shetlands in sight, when fate intervened.

A submarine had been sighted earlier that day at 6.30am, by the minesweeping trawler *Moravia* with Lieutenant Arthur Sanderson, DSC, RNR, on board, four miles east of Mousa, in the southern approaches to Lerwick harbour. This sighting was rapidly confirmed by her companion, *Laurel II*, under Skipper W Brown, at 6.35am.

Captain (D) in the destroyer depot ship *Leander* at Lerwick, Commander Tindal, RN, ordered the old destroyers *Sylvia*, under Lieutenant Peter Shaw with his first officer temporary Lieutenant William Taylor, and *Arab* to investigate. Once steam had been raised they left at 8am.

At 12.25pm further details were received when the submarine rose again. *Laurel II* reported seeing her still in a locality four miles east of Mousa, but shortly after she headed in a westerly direction inshore. The submarine was on the surface for a full five minutes before submerging; the *Moravia* also closed upon the scene and commenced to follow the enemy's possible track northwards. Several fishing boats in the vicinity, however, had seen nothing.

As noted earlier, a signal informing *Tirade*'s convoy about these developments had been received, and its arrival at Lerwick would have to be delayed while a safe approach was swept in case the submarine had already laid mines. In leading positions of the minesweeping trawlers then based there were Lieutenant Sandison, his usual command being the trawler *Collena*, and Lieutenant T W Cander, RNR, in the trawler *Ambitious*.

This was not the first nor the last occasion that German minelayers visited the Shetlands. On the basis of an Admiralty chart, five principal areas seem to have been involved. The important approaches to Lerwick and around Bressay obviously being the most active with a total of 108 mines detected, 28 located off Whalsay, 3 off Unst, 12 off Yell Sound, and finally 58 off Papa Stour.

Shortly after 2pm, the three ships of the convoy slowly cruised off the eastern Shetlands, awaiting permission to enter Lerwick. Midshipman Bagot, officer of the watch on the *Tirade*'s bridge, roused by a call from Leading Signalman James Brown, sighted some seven miles off a surfaced submarine giving off a great amount of smoke. As long as it remained apparently 'basking' on the surface, the U-boat was in a potentially favourable position for those on board the destroyer, that is between them and the shore. Once she submerged, which was thought to be the enemy's obvious move, tracking and attacking her would be a different proposition. One unnamed witness ashore later stated that this action was to take place approximately 1,600 metres south of Kirkabister Ness lighthouse on Bressay. But most accounts indicate that it actually took place around 7,000 metres southeast of the promontory of Bard Ness.

The *Moravia* had also again sighted the submarine at this time, as she was four miles east off Bard Head. The

The veteran destroyer HMS Sylvia. *This photograph, taken off the vessel's port beam view in 1898, provides an excellent view of her squat and basic features. (NMM. N2136)*

enemy was bearing south-southwest from her, on the surface three miles off, with its conning tower and hull evidently well out of the water, a prominent object on the surface, apparently stationary. This information was immediately broadcast to the old, moored, command light cruiser *Brilliant* in Lerwick, as the *Moravia* turned, manned her 6pdr gun and headed directly towards the submarine, with her ensign and challenge flags flying, as well as her 'green flag', denoting a submarine on the starboard bow. She also observed the *Sylvia* to the south and the *Tirade* and *Mameluke* to the east. A potentially effective net to trap the submarine was already in place.

But even before the first shot was fired, the U-boat was fatally crippled. At about 2pm she had been preparing to lay mines, when at a depth of 20 metres she abruptly and inexplicably lost her trim and began to dive bow first. Strenuous efforts were made to get her back on to an even keel by rushing the crew aft, and when the boat had reached a depth of 50 metres the descent was checked by blowing out her ballast tanks. This enabled her again to rise to an even 20 metres, when her motors were slowed down, and the tanks vented to prevent her breaking the surface, violently 'porpoising'.

But as soon as the vents were opened to stabilise her 20m trim, the boat again began to sink by the head and could not be stopped until the control room was at a depth of 90 metres, with her bows having reached a crushing depth of 105 to 100 metres (although a chart of this scene indicates a depth of 95 metres) and stern rising above this into safer waters. This excessive pressure forward caused the hull plating to deform, with seams and joints giving way, allowing a rush of water to enter, which almost immediately caused a plume of chlorine to be emitted from the batteries, with these cells also catching fire, probably because of a short circuit. Poisonous fumes now seeped through the boat.

By desperately blowing her tanks, the U-boat did, however, halt her catastrophic plunge, and first slowly, then rapidly she rose unchecked to the surface. Once there she was for the moment in no condition to submerge, as her conning tower hatch was opened, to allow the chlorine and smoke from below to escape. But with her diesels

A schematic plan of the action, which commenced at dawn on 29 September 1917 with Moravia's *sighting of* UC–55 *off Mousa. After lingering in this area for about six hours, the submarine finally headed northwards in the early afternoon towards the approaches to Lerwick, pursued by a number of British light craft. The chase concluded some 7,000 metres southwest of Bard Head at 2.29pm, after the U-boat's mysterious diving accident half an hour earlier, and subsequent encounter with the aroused pack of light craft. The only relatively accurate ship track's outlined here belong to the* Tirade *and to the perceived final movements of* UC–55 *seen from the British vessel. The remainder portray the general scene, and clearly indicate the dire position the crippled German submarine found herself in at the end.*

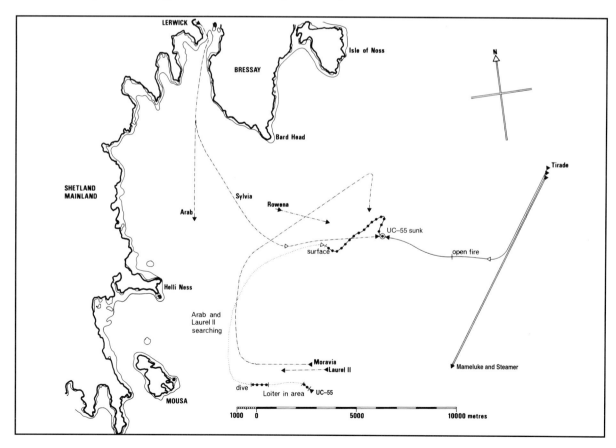

eventually connected up she proceeded slowly ahead, then full ahead, while compressing air to restore the depleted reserves in her air bottles was undertaken, as she took on some ballast, settling back in the water, with her casing almost awash. She had been so engaged for only ten minutes, when the *Moravia* was sighted, which immediately altered course towards her. Shortly afterwards several other light warships were observed, one of them the *Tirade*, her Nemesis.

As the *Tirade* closed, the *Mameluke* remained with the group's valuable charge, since who could tell whether this was the only submarine in these waters? Further to this, she did not open fire because the *Tirade* had fouled her range, while she headed southwest, away from the sighting to a safe area inshore off Helli Ness as the *Tirade* steamed direct towards the submarine at full speed, just as the U-boat began to get under way.

The *Tirade*'s crew offered a searchlight challenge during her rapid approach in case the submarine was friendly. No satisfactory response was to be forthcoming. Indeed, the submarine was apparently taking no notice of the events unfolding, apart from actually moving.

Gunfire was opened by the forecastle piece at about 3 to 4 miles, around 2.15pm, with Lieutenant Hore directing and PO Thomas Kelly as Gunlayer. Their first shell fell short. They held their fire until a range of 3,400 yards was ordered by Hore, but the second also fell short, though the third 4in round dispatched managed to hit the base of the enemy's conning tower. *Tirade* now effectively left her in a distressed state unable to dive, with her fate to all intents and purposes inevitably sealed.

Unknown to the British involved at that time, the now beleaguered enemy craft was the *UC–55* under Lieutenant Ruehle von Lilienstern, from the Elbe-based flotilla attached to the High Seas Fleet, which had its extensive area of operations designated as the waters north of Flamborough Head, encompassing the Shetlands.

She had left Hamburg on 16 September for Brunsbüttel, thence to Heligoland, before setting out for the Shetlands on the 25th, arriving off her fated destination, Lerwick, on the 29th to lay her mines in the approaches to this important port.

The *UC–55* was a 480-ton (surfaced), 511-ton (submerged), 172ft-long, minelaying submarine of the *UC–16* class (UC II type) primarily outfitted for this role with six near vertical 100cm (39.4in) mine tubes holding 18 UC 200-type mines. These buoy-shaped containers, roughly 3ft in diameter and 5.5ft tall, contained between 250 and 350lb of guncotton, trinitrotoluene (TNT) or amatol, in about half the interior, the rest acting as an air chamber for the necessary buoyancy. This charge was detonated by five or more soft leaden 'horns', set to fracture a glass tube inside at a 50lb blow, bridge a circuit and detonate.

This system of mine stowage in sealed tubes did, however, have one drawback: once the mines were loaded into their tubes no adjustment to their settings could be carried out, so the devices had to be preset before loading, virtually committing the commander to a pre-arranged specific objective, depth and field deployment.

The UC II type of craft was double-hulled, with improved range and sea-keeping abilities over the early UC I types. Underwater endurance was calculated at being 54nm at 4 knots, while a maximum endurance of some 8,750nm could be expected through economical surface speeds.

Apart from her mine load, she had a very potent defensive capability with her three 50cm (19.7in) torpedo tubes, with the two external ones at the bow, which could not be reloaded, and one rechargeable tube aft, and a total of seven torpedoes on board. But in a surface action her most important weapon would have been her single, effective 3.45in (8.8cm) deck gun mounted on the fore casing, with its 250 shells allowance.

One has only to refer to the epic fight put up by a sister craft the *UC–71*, under Reinhold Salzwedel, one of the renowned Zeebrugge flotilla, against the Q-ship *Dunraven* (ex-*Boverton*), of 3,117grt, armed with one 4in, at least four 12pdrs, one 2.5pdr, four 'large' depth charges aft, and two torpedo tubes, under the command of one of Britain's ablest anti-submarine experts Gordon Campbell. The cautious U-boat, suspecting a Q-ship ambush, not only succeeded in getting out of a well-prepared entrapment, but fought back in what was admittedly a one-sided gunnery duel, and eventually sank her powerful adversary in a memorable action on 8 August 1917. This does show that a typical minelayer's single 8.8cm deck gun was a potentially very effective piece, not only in commerce war but also against naval vessels, even if they were auxiliary conversions. But for the beleaguered crew of the *UC–55* the odds were gradually stacking against her. They never returned fire.

The *Tirade*'s fourth shot just missed, but her fifth round also registered a hit on the *UC–55*'s aft casing below the waterline – excellent shooting on this distant, low-lying target. Lieutenant Commander Broadley in the *Mameluke* observed these early hits and ascertained that they were undoubtedly from 4in shells. As the *Tirade* rapidly closed she displaced a further twelve shells, some of which might also have struck home but were lost in the confused and intense minutes which followed.

Owing to the conditions prevailing on board the wallowing and battered *UC–55*, it is now impossible to arrive at a definite conclusion as to the final cause of her sinking. But surviving accounts tell of a dramatic picture of hardened submariners confronted by impossible odds. Von Lilienstern ordered the vents to be opened and explosive charges to be fixed to all the vital parts of the submarine, ready for firing.

This was the moment the *Tirade* increased speed to attempt a combined ramming and depth-charge attack on the seemingly lame and impotent submarine.

From the *Tirade*'s rather exposed and unprotected open bridge atop the charthouse, the *Sylvia* was then observed rapidly approaching from the west, firing as she closed.

The *Sylvia* was one of the numerous light craft which had found vital, if routine and wearing, employment throughout the Great War on coastal patrol work. She was typical of the type, being a Doxford-built '30 knotter' destroyer dating from 1887, possessing the then archaic Victorian appearance of a turtle-backed forecastle, cutdown open bridge and three stumpy funnels. For armament she had one 12pdr and five 6pdrs, with two

A stern perspective of UC–78, *another UC II-type minelaying submarine, a close sister of* UC–55, *of which no image exists. However, a very good visual note of the* UC–55's *overall appearance was penned by Lieutenant Peter Shaw from the* Sylvia. *He wrote that the finish of the U-boat was 'overall light French grey' and that its appearance 'new', suggesting that it had not been weathered or worn. Shaw could detect no heraldic device, emblem, or number on the sides of the conning tower. The forward edge of the conning tower was pointed, not curved, and it rose vertically from the deck, which was generally flat, except for the forward rise for the mine tubes, and a 'well' for the single 3.45in deck gun. No radio masts were visible, just the stumps of two retracted periscopes, and a prominent jumping wire, running from bow, tower, to aft. (NMM. N2576)*

18in torpedo tubes, and by 1917 an unspecified depth-charge outfit aft. Overall she was relatively small, weighing 400 tons under deep load and measuring 215ft overall, 21ft in the beam, with a draught of 9ft 7in. The captain Lieutenant Peter Shaw had 62 men under him.

Although it is stated in the official account of this encounter, that the *Sylvia*'s three 12pdr rounds all missed, witnesses on board her (gunner George H Bartlett, CPO W H Walker, Leading Signalman Ernest Bell and Gunlayer III Jude Ellis) agreed that the first was just short, the second at 2,600 yards appeared to hit, along with the third round at 2,500 yards and Lieutenant Shaw stated quite categorically that all personnel on deck during the action could testify to this sequence of events. But this was never accepted. For reasons never made clear, the *Tirade* was to be singled out for official recognition for the kill, with the *Sylvia*'s part deemed only a minor contribution to the result.

From the bridge of the *Tirade*, the *Rowena* and the *Moravia* were now also seen approaching, evidently

aroused by the sound of the now one-sided gunnery duel and the chance of actually coming face to face with their elusive enemy. They had patiently stalked the enemy for eight hours, and this was their just reward.

The *Rowena* never entered effective range, but the *Moravia* did open fire at 4,000 yards, the first round was observed short; the sights were lifted 400 yards and although the fall of the second shot was not observed it was thought that a hit had been obtained. In fact they did not strike the submarine. Upon altering course to get out of the line of fire from the *Tirade*, the *Moravia* fired another shot, the results of which were also not seen on board.

However, two light shells burst close to the *Tirade* during this phase, one close under the port bow throwing up a column of water over the forecastle gun and bridge. These were later attributed to the eager trawler, but at the time were thought to have been fired by the *UC–55*.

As the ring closed, the accumulated damage to *UC–55* finally crippled her, as helmsman Able Seaman Unruh suddenly found the controls jammed, while, according to

HMS Sylvia *under way in 1907. This view offers a good impression of how the* Sylvia *might have appeared to the crew of* UC–55 *in her final approach. (NMM. N2137)*

Engine Room PO Sommer, water suddenly entered his compartment from the POs' mess aft, the stern was holed and she was sinking by the stern, the effects of *Tirade*'s fifth shot. The mass of water already below now cascaded aft through the boat, swiftly increasing the stern-down attitude. Von Lilienstern ordered abandon ship as the vent valves were opened. He remained on board, staying with his command to the end and leaving his second in command, Sublieutenant Sauer, to organise the crew for their evacuation under fire.

As the *Sylvia*, still capable of a respectable 25 knots when pushed, for which her Artificer Engineer James Pearson was later commended, and the more distant 30kt-plus *Tirade* raced each other for the honour of the kill, the beleaguered enemy suddenly sank stern first, when the *Tirade* was, according to Stanistreet, just 200 yards away with her strengthened cutting bows. But before the *Tirade* arrived upon the scene, the *Sylvia*, turning sharply to port with PO Archibald Hawkey applying starboard helm to avoid ramming the submarine with her unstrengthened bow, passed over the site, which witnesses variously state was 60, 30 or 20 feet away from the spot where *UC–55* had just sunk. *Sylvia* reportedly dropped her port depth charge some 15 yards from the submarine's port bow and her starboard charge just 8 yards from its starboard bow, effectively straddling the submarine which all agree was already lost.

Closed submarine, but we did not ram her as she was sinking, and men jumping into the water. Dropped two Type 'D' depth charges alongside submarine, which was blown up by the two explosions. *Lieutenant Shaw.*

From Bagot's account it would appear that the *Tirade* very nearly ran over these men in her own run-in to drop two of her depth charges, since she was just about 300 yards away when the *Sylvia* attacked, indicating how close he thought that they were to each other in their determined lunge at the fast disappearing submarine. But observers on board the torpedo boat claimed that this distance might have been as much as 1,000 yards, as the *Sylvia*'s brace of charges exploded and before the *Tirade* finally closed to deliver the *coup de grace.*

The ill-fated craft broke up underwater at 2.29pm, with her ruptured hull releasing a massive air bubble and quantities of fuel oil, a buoyant mine from her load was also seen to break the disturbed, oil-covered surface among the debris. An underwater explosion preceded the vessel's break-up, but whether this was the effect of one of the depth charges, perhaps setting off a primed mine or even a torpedo warhead, or the last act of a defiant and courageous von Lilienstern in detonating his demolition explosives, will never be known.

Now arises one telling point in the conduct of the aroused pack of the Royal Navy ships which had descended upon the crippled *UC–55*. In my initial research it appeared that the submarine was indeed sinking stern first by the time of the final lunge over the site of her by *Tirade* and *Sylvia*, and that through their combined depth charge onslaught the *UC–55* broke apart underwater, allowing the majority of her crew to escape.

But it now seems unmistakable that the *UC–55*'s crew, led by Sublieutenant Sauer, had actually abandoned or were obviously in the process of evacuating their fated craft before this. With men in the water and visible on deck, it is obvious that their dire position must have been clear to all those on board *Tirade* and *Sylvia*, who were only a matter of yards away.

It must also have been apparent to all on board the closing ships that any hostile action from the submarine towards its end was highly improbable, coupled with the fact that any advance in her final minutes must have been minimal, as her movement ceased with her flooded engine room. Therefore those who had abandoned ship must have been relatively close to their craft at the end. There were men in the water all around the sinking *UC–55*, as well as those struggling to escape through her hatches as she sank, in full view of numerous British witnesses.

One can only imagine the massive concussive effects of the depth charges, methodically and deliberately unleashed in two separate runs, culminating in the final explosive end of the *UC–55*. Indeed, the survival of nineteen men who managed to escape was miraculous, and certainly not due to any restraint by the British that day.

After the sinking the victors descended upon the scene with lifebelts, lines, and buoys thrown to the struggling survivors, with the *Sylvia* saving ten men, *Rowena* six, and *Moravia* one, while the *Tirade*'s whaler was also lowered to rescue her former opponents. In this she managed to pick up two men from the freezing northern waters.

The pair of Germans on board the *Tirade*, both engine room ratings, Christian Hausen and Alfred Damm [?], were initially placed in the shelter of the after bandstand to be revived. They were soon taken below to recover in the warmth of the messdeck, where they were well treated, clothed and given rum. Bagot mentions that some useful information was freely obtained from them without duress. Although if, as Stanistreet related in his official report, no-one on board could speak fluent German, communication was probably difficult.

However, it was noted that they had been expecting to be left in the water to die or at best shot outright once on board, which was not surprising after the onslaught they

A size comparison between some of the participants, with the Tirade *(top) a good representative of a war-built destroyer and the* UC–55 *(centre) of the small, German minelaying type. Admiralty trawlers (bottom), based at Lerwick, are harder to identify, but it is conceivable that they were made up from the three standard purpose-built designs mass produced in the war –* Mersey *(655 tons full load),* Castle *(547 tons) and* Strath *(429 tons) classes, all capable of between 10 and 11 knots and armed with one 12pdr gun – or they might just have been some of the 1,400 requisitioned commercial trawlers taken over during the war.*

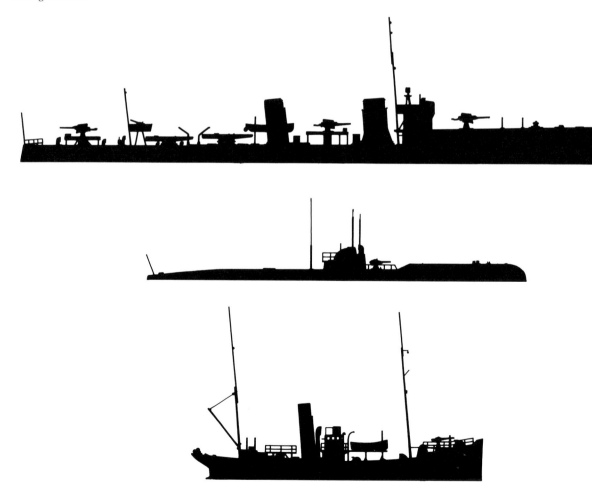

had just survived. They were instead very grateful for the fashion in which they had been saved and humanely treated by their fellow sailors, who held no animosity towards them once defeated.

The following day, after the harbour approaches had been cleared of the *UC–55*'s possible minefield, they and the rest of the survivors were landed at Lerwick. Seventeen of the survivors were placed on board the *Leander*. Here they were further cross-questioned by the Lieutenant Sandison and Captain Sullivan. Two with slight injuries were put on board the Hospital Ship *Berbice*.

Shortly after the event, the *Tirade* took all the prisoners, who had evidently by then recovered from their traumatic experience, and proceeded with them to Aberdeen before handing them over to a military guard. During the passage, Bagot (in his broken German, perhaps) had a chance to talk with the three captive German officers, '. . . and learnt a little more about them and the state of Germany. The Germans were under the impression that they are winning the war'. Unmistakably the morale of the Germans was high even after their awful experience.

The commanding officers of the *Tirade, Sylvia* and *Moravia*, along with PO Thomas Kelly (ON 233985) were all subsequently mentioned in dispatches for their parts in the destruction of the *UC–55*.

The following month, almost to the day of her principal naval encounter, the *Tirade* claimed her only other distinction, a dubious one this time, when on 21 October she was involved in a collision with a companion destroyer the *Marmion* (Lieutenant Herbert Lyon), during another Lerwick to Bergen convoy. Although no serious damage was inflicted on the *Tirade*, the *Marmion*, despite an attempt to tow, foundered later that day, but thankfully without loss of life. The *Tirade*'s specially strengthened stem was indeed a potent weapon.

The remainder of the *Tirade*'s war was to be relatively uneventful after her very active first four months in commission. She was to go through the winter of 1917 up to November 1918 in the unrecorded duties so vital to the successful conclusion of the war for the Allies: convoying, escorting, and succouring merchantmen in the northern waters. Eventually she was placed on the disposal list shortly after the Armistice, finally being sold for scrap in November 1921. The *Sylvia*, like her entire generation of now worn-out sisters, had already gone, being broken up in 1919.

One final chapter in the *Tirade v. UC–55* encounter was to be enacted after the war, when a ruling by the Prize Court sitting in London, under its president Sir Henry Duke made orders for the payment of a bounty of £145 to Lieutenant-Commander Stanistreet, in February 1920. The other individual who would have shared in this, Lieutenant Peter Shaw, had died before this award.

Sources

The prime source used was the private wartime journal of Midshipman Arthur G D Bagot. Born on 5 November 1895, he initially served on board the ill-fated battlecruiser *Queen Mary* as a RNR midshipman, subsequently entering RN service. Just before Jutland, on 23 March 1916, Bagot was posted to the sloop *Pentstemon* for service in the Mediterranean, then to the *Tirade* in home waters. He served in the Royal Navy between the wars and saw service during the Second World War, primarily in Ceylon. After this he undertook various tasks, such as participating in the Palk Strait oil transhipment scheme in 1945–46 and acting as an observer in the Greek elections of 1946. He finished off his long and distinguished service as a Commander of LST craft during the Korean War.

Other sources

Shetland Islands Council, Library Department and the Shetland Archives: for information concerning the approximate location of the action, some individuals involved and the parts they played and the Prize Court details. Derived primarily from the *Shetland News*, 26 February 1920.

All the World's Warships 1860/1905 and *1905/1921*, Conway Maritime Press: for the general specifications and particulars of the vessels involved.

Lowell Thomas, *Raiders of the Deep*, Windmill Press, 1934: reveals the activities of German U-boats.

Captain Taprell Dorling (*Taffrail*), *Endless Story,* Hodder & Stoughton, 1931: an informative work detailing the active service of destroyers in the First World War.

Captain Taprell Dorling, *Swept Channels*, Hodder & Stoughton, 1935: covers British mine countermeasures and sweeping in considerable detail.

Keble Chatterton, *Fighting the U-boats*, Hurst & Blackett, 1942: a narrative setting out the tactical, technical and means of deception employed by the Royal Navy in the First World War.

Public Record Office, ADM 137/1374, Folios 153 to 183: the official case files on the sinking of *UC–55*.

THE TRAGIC LOSS OF HMS *CURACOA*

When the liner RMS *Queen Mary* sank the elderly anti-aircraft cruiser HMS *Curacoa* in 1942 the details were heavily censored. **Peter Kelly** examines the tragic event.

Built at Pembroke Dockyard and completed in February 1918, HMS *Curacoa* was one of five *Ceres* class cruisers built under the Emergency War Programme of the First World War. The *Ceres* class were a subclass of the 'C' class cruisers that contributed much in both world wars. On completion *Curacoa* became the flagship of Rear-Admiral Sir Reginald Tyrwhitt, commander of the famous Harwich Force. Following the demise of the Grand Fleet in 1919, and the subsequent reorganisation in the spring of that year, the Harwich Force became a detachment of the reconstituted Atlantic Fleet. Within a few days *Curacoa* sailed for the Baltic as flagship of the First Light Cruiser Squadron. A week or so later she struck a mine. Fortunately there were no casualties. In an announcement on 22 May 1919, the *Times* reported her damage as 'slight', though tugs were required to tow her to Chatham for repairs. Between the wars *Curacoa* served with Light Cruiser Squadrons in the Atlantic and Mediterranean Fleets, before going into reserve in 1932. She commissioned from reserve in 1938, when the Munich crisis brought the world to the brink of war.

By the time the Second World War appeared on the horizon the 'C' and 'D' class cruisers were old ships, long since outclassed and rendered obsolete by the bigger, more powerful German and Italian cruisers. Under a programme designed to meet the growing menace of air attack at sea, the Admiralty decided to convert these old vessels to anti-aircraft cruisers. *Curacoa* was the last of the old 'C' class cruisers converted before the outbreak of war

in 1939, though others of the class followed in the early years of the war. In one attack, during the evacuation of Norway in late April 1940, *Curacoa* suffered extensive damage at the hands of German dive-bombers, forcing a return to England for repair. Thirty of her ship's company died in the attack, while a large number received severe wounds. On completion of her refit she joined the newly formed Western Approaches Command,[1] as a destroyer flotilla leader. She provided anti-aircraft protection to North Atlantic convoys in the Western Approaches and British coastal waters on the final leg of their Atlantic crossing. The destroyers provided anti-submarine protection against the deadly U-boats. It was while in this role that *Curacoa* (Captain John W Boutwood, RN) was lost in a tragic collision on 2 October 1942, with the converted troopship RMS *Queen Mary*, off Northern Ireland near the appropriately named Bloody Foreland. Subsequent documentation gives the position as Latitude 55° 50' North and Longitude 8° 38' West.

With an increasing demand for travel throughout the 1920s, and good figures projected for the early 1930s, the future looked bright for the trans-Atlantic passenger trade. The Cunard Company began looking at designs for fast passenger ships as replacements for its ageing liners *Mauretania*, *Berengaria* and *Aquitania*. The company envisaged two fast luxury liners,[2] each of over 1,000 feet in length and capable of producing a maximum speed in excess of 27.5 knots, to maintain the current schedule then operated by the three smaller ships. The first of the

HMS Curacoa. *(CPL)*

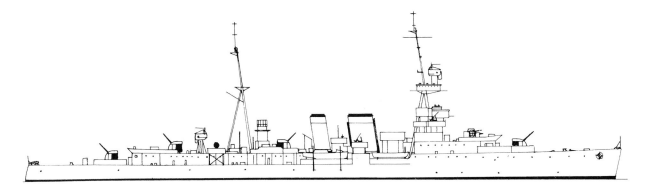

two new liners was laid down in December 1930 at John Brown's shipyard on the banks of Scotland's famous River Clyde. She became known simply as 'Job No. 534'. Just five months short of the proposed launch date in February 1932, the Great Depression brought construction to a halt. 'Job No. 534' received no subsidy from the British government. Unlike the pre-First World War liners *Mauretania* and *Lusitania*, it was envisaged 'Job No. 534' would not be requisitioned for use in a future war. The unfinished liner lay on the stocks for more than two years. Following a concerted campaign by Mr David Kirkwood, Labour MP for Dumbarton Burghs, the British government reluctantly agreed to offer Cunard a loan to complete the project. In a clever move designed to rid itself of a financial burden, the government stipulated as a condition of the loan, that Cunard should merge with the declining White Star Line company, which it had been financially 'propping up' from the public purse for some time. Cunard readily agreed to the government's conditions, and the Cunard White Star Line came into being. In early April 1934 workmen began cleaning some 130 tons of accumulated rust and dirt from 'Job No. 534'. In May John Brown's yard received formal notice to recommence construction.

As the new ship neared completion there was much speculation about what she would be called, but it remained a secret until Her Majesty Queen Mary announced the name when she launched the new liner on Wednesday 26 September 1934. RMS *Queen Mary* completed her first trans-Atlantic crossing two years later, in June 1936, under Captain Sir Edgar Britten. In August 1938 she wrested the Blue Riband from her French rival *Normandie*, for the fastest round-trip crossing of the Atlantic. She made her last pre-Second World War departure from Southampton on 30 August 1939, arriving in New York on 4 September, following the declaration of war. The liner was immediately laid up at her old berth alongside Pier 90. Beside her at the next pier lay *Normandie*. After a 'hushed up' dash across the Atlantic from her builders' yard, the near-completed *Queen Elizabeth* joined *Queen Mary* on 7 March 1940 when she berthed on the opposite side of Pier 90.

The visage of the three largest luxury liners in the world, laid up side by side, was short-lived. *Queen Mary* sailed for Sydney, Australia, on 21 March, for conversion to a troopship. After the United States entered the Second World War, the *Queen Mary* began ferrying large contingents of American troops across the Atlantic to the United Kingdom. On 2 October 1942 she was approaching the north coast of Ireland bound for Gourock in the River Clyde. On board were some 10,000 to 11,000 American soldiers, and a crew of 908 hands, including naval ratings who manned her wartime armament. With six destroyers, *Curacoa* was ordered to rendezvous with the *Queen Mary*

HM Troop Transport Queen Mary *anchored in Gage Roads in the Fremantle Outer Harbour in 1940. The Royal Australian Navy oiler HMAS* Kurumba *is alongside. (Royal Australian Air Force/CPL)*

(Captain Charles G Illingworth, Master) in a position near Longitude 12° West, at approximately 0700hrs on 2 October 1942, for escort to Gourock. This was the fourth occasion on which *Curacoa* had escorted the liner. In August Captain Boutwood had called on the master of the *Queen Mary*, to discuss details of the escorting operation because on previous occasions she had been under a different master. Captain Illingworth indicated he proposed to use 'Zig-zag Pattern No. 8' on his return crossing.

Friday 2 October 1942 dawned fine and clear, with a moderate breeze of about force 4, and a heavy westerly swell. When *Curacoa* reached the rendezvous position there was no sign of the *Queen Mary*, and when she had not been sighted an hour later, Captain Boutwood ordered the destroyers to reverse their course. He likewise reversed his course in *Curacoa*, but only for a short time to take note of the cruiser's behaviour in the prevailing conditions, before continuing westwards to meet the liner. From his meeting with Captain Illingworth in August, Captain Boutwood expected the *Queen Mary* would be steering her course according to 'Zig-zag Pattern No. 8', which was well known to both men. The *Queen Mary* was eventually sighted steering the expected zig-zag pattern, travelling at high speed towards the rendezvous. Captain Boutwood again reversed his course and increased speed from 13 to 18.5 knots, positioning the cruiser ahead of the liner's mean line of advance.

In conforming to 'Zig-zag No. 8' a vessel must steam on her mean course for four minutes, then effect a turn of 25° to starboard. The new course, or 'starboard leg', of the zig-zag is pursued for eight minutes, when the vessel turns 50° to port. The 'port leg' of the zig-zag is then pursued for eight minutes, when a turn of 25° is made to starboard, which returns the vessel to her mean course. The details of 'Zig-zag No. 8' were posted on a blackboard in the wheelhouse on board *Queen Mary*, conveniently positioned for easy reference by the helmsman. In addition a 'zig-zag clock' was also fitted in the wheelhouse, which would sound an alarm when it was time for a course alteration. When the alarm rang the helmsman would push a button above his head, which would sound an electric buzzer on the bridge to attract the attention of the Officer of the Watch. The helmsman would then report the course alteration he was about to make to the Officer of the Watch, and if correct, the officer would tell him to 'Carry on'. The necessary alteration was then made. In this manoeuvre, which takes just less than forty minutes to complete, a vessel is calculated to advance on her mean course 93 per cent of the total distance run.

About 1000hrs *Queen Mary* was observed to be rapidly gaining on *Curacoa*, so the cruiser's speed was increased first to 23 knots, and a short while later to 25 knots. To afford *Queen Mary* the maximum anti-aircraft protection, Captain Boutwood intended to steer a straight course along the liner's mean line of advance. In doing so, he would remain within range of the liner for the longest possible time, thus affording her the greatest anti-aircraft protection. In an exchange of signals at 1130hrs *Queen Mary* confirmed her course and speed made good, were 108° at 26.5 knots.[3] Part of this information was later shown to be incorrect, due to a fault which caused the

gyrocompass to register 2° high. In a signal to *Queen Mary* at 1220hrs. *Curacoa* indicated: 'I am doing my best speed, 25 knots, on course 108° . . .' A simple calculation showed if *Curacoa* continued steering a straight line at her best speed, the bigger ship would overtake her at the rate of approximately 1.5 knots per hour. During the latter part of the forenoon Captain Boutwood noticed the *Queen Mary*'s mean line of advance was taking her progressively to the northwards of *Curacoa*'s line of advance. He went below for lunch at 1230hrs, and returned to the bridge at 1300hrs. On his return, the vessels were nearing an area of greater risk from enemy air attack. Captain Boutwood observed *Curacoa* was outside the southerly limit of *Queen Mary*'s zig-zag, so he altered course to 105°, and a few minutes later to 100°, to adjust his course closer to the *Queen Mary*'s mean line of advance. He steered 100° until he judged the liner would cross his wake on the next starboard leg of her zig-zag, then returned to his original course of 108°.

The Senior First Officer, Mr Robinson, was Officer of the Watch on board *Queen Mary* from midday until 1600hrs. His junior was Mr Hewitt, the Senior Third Officer. During the first hour and a half of the watch, Mr Robinson noticed the *Queen Mary* gradually gaining on *Curacoa*, as expected. For eight minutes prior to 1330hrs the *Queen Mary* steered 131° on the starboard leg of her zig-zag. At 1332hrs it was time to alter course 50° to port, the liner being then off the cruiser's starboard quarter. Mr Robinson commenced the turn, altering course towards 081°. He interrupted the swing after some 25° to 30°, judging he would pass too close to *Curacoa* as he crossed her wake. He ordered the helm steadied on approximately 101° or 102°. As the ship steadied Mr Wright, the Junior First Officer, came on the bridge to relieve Mr Robinson for lunch, while Mr Heighway, the Junior Third Officer, relieved Mr Hewitt. Mr Heighway immediately went to the starboard wing of the bridge, where he took a sight of the sun and retired to the starboard chartroom to work out the ship's longitude. In handing over, Mr Robinson informed his relief of the interruption to the zig-zag and gave his reason. Soon after Mr Robinson left the bridge, Mr Wright ordered the helm to port to regain the course correct on 081°. When still some 5° short of his course he also judged the liner would pass too close to the cruiser, so he ordered the helm put 5° to starboard, and a short time later ordered hard-a-starboard. On hearing these helm orders, Captain Illingworth came onto the port wing of the bridge and enquired what was happening. When Mr Wright informed him a 'close quarters' situation had developed, he said: 'Carry on with the zig-zag. These chaps are used to escorting; they will keep out of your way and won't interfere with you.' The *Queen Mary* was then put on her course of 081° and passed close under the stern of the cruiser, to a position about a mile off *Curacoa*'s port quarter.

On board *Curacoa* Captain Boutwood saw the *Queen Mary* cross his wake on the starboard leg of her zig-zag and take up a position off his starboard quarter, about a mile distant. A little later she again crossed his wake from starboard to port, finally resuming her mean line of advance on a course approximately parallel to his own. As

HMS Curacoa *in peacetime. (CPL)*

the liner overhauled the cruiser along her port side, Captain Boutwood took bearings of her at frequent intervals until her stem was abeam of the cruiser's bridge.

Mr Heighway came onto the bridge again at 1400hrs, at which time the *Queen Mary* turned on to her mean course. He judged the cruiser to be about a mile distant, and five to six points on the liner's starboard bow. A moment later Mr Robinson and Mr Hewitt returned to the bridge from their lunch, where they were informed of what the captain had said about the cruiser keeping out of their way. Mr Hewitt went to the extreme starboard wing of the bridge, where he studied those on the bridge of the cruiser through a telescope, in a bid to recognise any of the ship's officers. He had met a number of *Curacoa*'s officers on a previous occasion. He studied the people on the cruiser's bridge for approximately two minutes. When Mr Robinson relieved Mr Wright as Officer of the Watch, the cruiser appeared to be steering almost parallel with the liner, in a position about four points on the starboard bow and two cables distant. At 1404hrs, the *Queen Mary* began altering course to starboard for the starboard leg of her zig-zag.

From the bridge of *Curacoa*, the *Queen Mary* was observed to be 'falling off' to starboard. Captain Boutwood at first thought the liner could be yawing to starboard as a result of the natural action of a ship in a following sea. When the *Queen Mary* continued her swing to starboard, it became apparent the liner was acting under helm. Captain Boutwood realised a dangerous situation was rapidly developing, and ordered: 'Starboard 15°' through the voice-pipe to his helmsman in the steering flat three decks below. Immediately following this order Captain Boutwood checked his compass, where he discovered *Curacoa* had yawed 7° to port of her course. He

saw the *Queen Mary* still swinging to starboard, and noticed the cruiser had not responded to his helm order of a few seconds previously. He stepped immediately to the gyrocompass, thus indicating he had taken personal control of the ship.

When Mr Robinson relieved Mr Wright on board *Queen Mary*, he checked his course and found it to be 131° by the gyrocompass repeater located on the starboard wing of the bridge. He judged *Curacoa*'s course to be about 110° at that time, and noticed the two vessels were converging at an angle of about two points. He responded by giving the order 'Port a little' through the voice-pipe on the wing of the bridge, then watched the helmsman through the wheelhouse door as he put the helm over one and a half turns. He noticed the time by the wheelhouse clock was a few seconds after 1410hrs. A minute later Mr Robinson saw the vessels were converging rapidly and gave the order: 'Hard-a-port!' through the voice-pipe. On hearing this, Mr Heighway went into the wheelhouse and checked the helmsman had put the wheel hard-a-port. In less than a minute the *Queen Mary*, still making about 28.5 knots through the water, struck the *Curacoa* on her port side near the forward end of her after superstructure, between the second funnel and 'X' gun position. As the liner's momentum carried her forwards her stem sliced through the cruiser, cutting off her after end and pushing the forward section onto her beam-ends. The after end sank almost immediately, but the fore part of *Curacoa* righted itself, then followed the stern section to the bottom a few minutes later. The force of the impact reduced *Queen Mary*'s speed to about 14 knots. In those few terrible minutes 329 officers and men lost their lives, from a total of 430 on board.

Troops and members of the crew who saw the collision from the deck of the *Queen Mary* were at first numbed with shock, but recovered quickly and sprang to the life-jackets. They began throwing them overboard among the survivors. Being in waters where German U-boats were likely to be encountered, the *Queen Mary* was unable to stop to rescue survivors. To have done so would have risked the lives of a far greater number among her passengers and crew. She immediately notified the destroyers some seven miles or more to the east, who turned back to rescue men and bodies from the oily water. Captain Boutwood, one other officer, and ninety-nine ratings were hauled aboard the destroyers. On board the *Queen Mary*, water rushed in through the damaged stern. The forward collision bulkhead was hurriedly shored up with timber kept available for just such an emergency as this. Her reduced speed slowed the inward rush of water, which in turn applied less pressure against her collision bulkhead. The collision bulkhead held, and the liner remained watertight behind it. She arrived safely at Gourock, where she discharged her cargo of American troops.

The holes in *Queen Mary*'s damaged bow were plugged using a cement mixture. These temporary repairs allowed her to complete the return crossing to the United States at an average speed of 24 knots. She arrived at Boston for dry-docking and a full assessment of the damage. Her bow was crumpled to the height of *Curacoa*'s weather deck. This section had been forced back and 'folded away' towards her port side, applying a partially effective form of 'crimp' seal across the damaged section. The cement mixture applied in Scotland rendered the crumpled bow almost watertight, though it remained somewhat unsightly. At Boston a new stem section awaited her, which had been hurriedly constructed from templates rushed across from her builders on the Clyde. American repair facilities were working at 'near capacity' during the war, which resulted in a quick turn-around time for the *Queen Mary*. She sailed again from New York on 8 December 1942 to begin what is known as her 'Long Voyage', trooping around the world, before returning to New York once again in June 1943.

For reasons I have been unable to discover, the tragic circumstances surrounding the loss of HMS *Curacoa* were kept quiet until after the war. Perhaps it was thought such news may have damaged the national morale, something similar to the reasons why the bombing of Darwin, Australia, in 1942 received so little recognition at the time. Whatever the reason, the Admiralty took umbrage at the loss of their anti-aircraft cruiser. No doubt the loss of the lives of so many officers and men also weighed heavily

Queen Mary *in dry dock at Southampton for a refit in 1947. A new stem is being fitted in place of the temporary repairs carried out after the collision with HMS* Curacoa. *(CPL)*

upon the collective naval mind of the Admiralty officials. They issued a writ on 22 September 1943 in the High Court of Justice, Admiralty Division, against Cunard White Star. The Treasury Solicitor acted on behalf of the Admiralty, and Cunard White Star engaged the services of Hill Dickinson & Company to represent their interests in the legal case.

Following the issue of the writ, little appears to have happened until 24 January 1945, when the Treasury Solicitor filed a document of 'Preliminary Acts and Pleadings' stating the Admiralty's version of the facts. In response, Hill Dickinson & Company filed a similar document on 26 February 1945 outlining the Defendants' version of events. There followed a 'Statement of Claim' by the Admiralty, in which they claimed judgement against Cunard White Star for eight points of negligence, including failure to comply with the Regulations for Preventing Collisions at Sea. This claim was submitted on 2 March 1945 by the Treasury Solicitor. A counterclaim was submitted by Hill Dickinson & Company a month later on 4 April 1945, listing thirteen points of negligence against the Admiralty. This document could be said to have 'hotted up' the debate somewhat. It certainly brought a quick reaction from the Admiralty! A reply was filed three days later indicating the Admiralty would 'join issue upon the Defence' in this matter.

Since the loss of *Curacoa* in 1942, witnesses had become scattered around the world, while pursuing the normal course of their careers. A number were recalled from overseas to appear before the court to give evidence.

The case was heard before Mr Justice Pilcher. On behalf of the Admiralty, Captain Boutwood gave his evidence in June 1945. He was the only material witness called by the Admiralty to give evidence. Also in June 1945, Messrs Robinson, Wright and Hewitt gave evidence on behalf of Cunard White Star, Mr Wright having been brought back from the United States especially for this purpose, though much of his testimony was later disregarded because he was considered 'a thoroughly unsatisfactory witness'. Following the June sitting, Mr Justice Pilcher adjourned the case until November 1945, when evidence was taken from Mr Heighway, an Australian who was returned to the United Kingdom to testify. Two of *Queen Mary*'s quartermasters, Messrs Lockhart and Leyden, also gave evidence at that time. The hearing was again adjourned until December 1946.

In the meantime, to the casual observer the case appeared to lay idle, but behind the scenes there was still plenty of activity. Throughout the hearings, argument flowed back and forth concerning the speed of one vessel or the other in an attempt to mathematically prove their exact positions before the point of collision. Much of it centred on possible differences of half a knot or less in the reported speed through the water of either vessel due to the vagaries of weather and current. Combined nautical and legal talents on either side devoted months to argument and experiment, and wrestled with physics and mathematics to prove half a knot or less one way or the other. In his final summing up, Mr Justice Pilcher disregarded such argument saying it is '. . . impossible to be

Queen Mary seen in the 1960s, after she had returned to operation as an ocean liner. (CPL)

dogmatic within half a knot or so upon the actual speed . . .' of either vessel through the water. In October 1946 Mr Justice Pilcher, in company with the Elder Brethren[4] from Trinity House, accepted an invitation from the defendants to attend a number of experiments conducted with models of *Curacoa* and *Queen Mary* in the experimental tank at the National Physical Laboratory at Teddington. These experiments were conducted by Commodore Sir James Bissett, Commodore of the Cunard White Star Line and former master of the *Queen Mary*. They showed the interaction between the two ships just before the moment of collision, and determined an approximate angle of collision, but left the timing of the *Queen Mary*'s zig-zag and the speed through the water of either vessel, still open to interpretation. At one point, turning-circle experiments were conducted with a sister ship of *Curacoa*, which showed the cruiser would turn through four points in less than 70 seconds when 15° of rudder was applied in a calm sea. These experiments failed to show the effect when 15° of rudder was applied in sea and weather conditions similar to the day of the disaster. The results ultimately proved of little value.

Captain Illingworth gave his evidence before the court when the hearing resumed in December 1946. He was questioned about the nature of his orders from the naval authorities in the United States prior to his departure from New York. Captain Illingworth said he received type-written sailing orders for the crossing, but these had since been destroyed in accordance with usual wartime practice. He could recall no specific instructions, except that he was to zig-zag on the passage across the Atlantic. He confirmed he had told Captain Boutwood in August 1942 that he proposed to use Zig-zag Pattern No. 8 on his return trip. Further technical and expert advice was called by both sides before the hearing concluded, leaving Mr Justice Pilcher to consider his judgement. The High Court of Justice, Admiralty Division, reconvened at the Royal Courts of Justice on 21 January 1947 to hear Mr Justice Pilcher hand down his judgement. He was assisted by Captain W E Crumplin and Captain G C H Noakes, RD, Trinity Masters. Appearing as Counsel for the Admiralty were Messrs K S Carpmael, KC, O Bateson, KC, and M Rena, KC, instructed by the Treasury Solicitor of Storey's Gate. Cunard White Star was represented by Messrs R F Hayward, KC, W Porges and H E G Browning from Hill Dickinson & Company of Bury Court. In his judgement Mr Justice Pilcher found the evidence given by witnesses from the *Queen Mary* to be substantially accurate, while rejecting much of Captain Boutwood's evidence. He found the *Queen Mary* free from blame and attributed blame to the negligence of those on board *Curacoa*. The Admiralty appealed this decision, which resulted in the Court of Appeal attributing one third of the blame to Cunard White Star, and two thirds to the Royal Navy. Cunard White Star appealed to the House of Lords, but the decision was upheld.

Today, the *Queen Mary* dozes peacefully in her twilight years at Long Beach, California. Occasionally we are confronted with oddments of footage on her long and successful life. Perhaps it might be a television documentary, or a travelogue extolling her virtues as an hotel and convention centre. In some of these programmes we are treated to the story of 'The Ghost of the *Queen Mary*', which supposedly resides 'deep in the bowels of the ship, right up forward, near the stem'. One must ask: 'Is there really a ghost?' Alternatively, we might ask: 'Could there perhaps be 329 ghosts in the for'ard part of the ship – the spirits of a wartime tragedy?'

Notes

[1] Then under Admiral Sir Percy Noble, but later to become famous under Admiral Sir Max Horton.
[2] The second ship eventually became the *Queen Elizabeth*.
[3] Her actual speed through the water being about 28.5 knots.
[4] Nautical Assessors in the High Court, Admiralty Division.

Sources

David F Hutchings, *RMS* Queen Mary, *Fifty Years of Splendour*. Kingfisher Railway Productions, Southampton, 1986.

Peter Kemp (ed.), *The Oxford Companion to Ships and the Sea*. Oxford University Press, Oxford, 1976.

Alan Raven and John Roberts, *British Cruisers of World War Two*. Naval Institute Press, Annapolis.

'EIGHT SIX-INCH GUNS IN PAIRS'

THE *LEANDER* AND *SYDNEY* CLASS CRUISERS

The *Leander* class vessels and their improved successors epitomised the Royal Navy's ideas on light cruisers before Japanese and American developments forced a steep rise in size and cost. **Keith McBride** looks at these hard-worked ships.

The Washington Treaty of 1921 was intended to reduce the burden of naval armaments, but, to the surprise of everyone except some members of the United States Navy, it gave birth to a new and very expensive type of warship: the so-called 'Treaty Cruiser' or 'Tinclad'[1], which was built up to the Treaty limits of 10,000 tons ('without fuel or reserve feed water' – a huge weight) and 8in guns. As Italy's Chief Constructor, General da Fea, observed, those limits could include anything from a very small battleship to an ultrafast, virtually unprotected vessel. With memories of the fate of the slow British armoured cruisers at Jutland, most navies went for the latter idea, and found the costs to be enormous: £2,000,000 per ship in Britain, or £200 a ton, roughly twice the 1914 price, and horrifying to governments in the postwar slump.

There were two exceptions to this: in Japan, where the 2,890-ton *Yubari* was built, purely as an experiment, and in France. The latter had built no new cruisers between 1904 and 1918, although two classes had been authorised up to 1914. After long study and much controversy, the *Duguay-Trouin* class emerged in 1924–25. In many ways, they were smaller versions of the 'Tinclads'. They were 7,249 tons by the new Washington 'Standard' measurement, with high speed, virtually no armour and a battery of eight 6.1in guns in twin turrets. The calibre was a new one for *Le Royale*, already extensively used by the French Army and adopted in preference to designing an up-to-date model of the traditional 164.7mm cruiser gun.

The class made a great impression abroad, especially after the *Duguay-Trouin* passed the battleship *Marlborough* in a gale. Some thinking on 6in gun cruisers was done in the Admiralty during 1924, but with no immediate effect. The lesson drawn from the First World War was that the opponent with the heavier guns would almost certainly win. Not until 1926–27 were cruisers below the full treaty limit considered, and then the initial move was to the *York*, with six 8in guns instead of eight. She was followed the next year by the *Exeter*, but the type found little favour. The four Japanese ships with six 8in guns had been designed before the Washington Treaty, as a counter to the *Hawkins* class.

Experience on exercises with the *Hawkins* showed that they were far too conspicuous for night shadowing and other fleet duties, and this led to pressure for a smaller type, to replace the numerous 'C's and 'D's when they eventually wore out. The need for as many 'Eyes' as possible on the trade routes also required smaller and more numerous cruisers.

The first thoughts of 1924–25 were of a ship of about 8,500 tons – the size of the *York*, with 100,000 shp like the *Duguay-Trouin* – a speed of 34.5 knots and eight 6in guns in four twin turrets. The power would come from eight boilers, which would make the most economic use of the space available, and fuel capacity would be 1,800 tons. Protection would be less than in the 10,000-ton ships: at most the magazines and the Transmitting Station (USN 'Main Battery Plot') could be protected; the propelling machinery would have to take its chance, as in foreign designs. Radius of action was estimated at 7,000 miles at 12 knots, plus another 1,000 miles if an additional 400 tons of oil were carried in above-water 'Peace Tanks'. This would give the same radius as the 10,000-ton *Kent*s: the peace tanks would have to be emptied before the ship arrived in a combat area. Cost, including machinery, armament, ammunition and stores, was estimated at £1,600,000, against £2,000,000 for a *Kent*.

For the next three years, which included the abortive Geneva Conference of 1927, discussion and thinking on smaller cruisers continued: the *York* and *Exeter* were authorised, and apparently rejected before completion as not meeting the Admiralty's requirements. Finally, towards the end of 1928, a Staff Requirement for a 6in cruiser was issued, and one ship was proposed for the 1929–30 Estimates, together with the heavily armoured 8in ships *Surrey* and *Northumberland*.

Sir William Berry, the DNC, and his staff prepared Designs 1 to 5 for light cruisers to meet it. The basis for all was a 6,000-ton (Standard) vessel with lines for about 31 knots. Design 1 carried five shielded ('Weather Mounting') 6in guns on the centre line, Design 2, six 5.5in, Design 3, eight 6in in turrets, Design 4, six turreted 6in and Design 5, six 6in in twin turrets and two singles. Design 5's turrets were apparently carried forward and her singles in shields aft, to permit the use of triple shafts, as in the German 'K' class. This allowed the use of three *Kent* turbine sets.

A total of 60,000shp were provided, which, it was hoped, would give 31.25 knots at 6,000 tons and 29.75 at deep load with 2,000 tons oil, or 30 with 1,600 tons. If three shafts were used, they would be best for subdivision of the after part of the ship and were accordingly shown on the drawing for Design 1. If, however, turrets were placed aft, four shafts would be needed, as magazines, shell rooms and handing rooms would require all the hold space at the centre line. Relative efficiency of propellers was considered equal for the two arrangements.

The usual spaces beneath the machinery and below the lower deck fore and aft would hold about 1,600 tons of oil. To increase this to 2,000 tons, some of the spaces on the lower deck aft usually occupied by provision and store rooms would have to be taken for oil, leading to some congestion on the lower deck forward.

At 16 knots, starting from deep load and using all oil except 10 per cent residue, endurance at sea was expected to be 6,000 'knots' for 1,600 tons and 7,000 for 2,000 tons, these figures being based on *Berwick*'s recent trials.

In one respect, the new design benefited from a 'virtuous circle'. Due to her high speed and consequent length, her hull had to be robust amidships. This required the normal hull plating to be one inch on the side and deck in wake of the machinery spaces. Plating in these areas was available for both strength and protection. This thickness of one inch could be looked on as the least that had to be provided in this part of the ship.

This weight was included in that of 'hull', leaving only thicknesses in excess of one inch to be considered when making up the complete weight of protection. The protection weight was the only one available to counterbalance differences in other items if all the designs were to be brought to the same standard displacement.

In making up the legends and to compare the five designs, it was assumed in the first place that they would all have the same magazine/shell room and machinery space protection, and the same protection in other areas.

Magazines and shell rooms were required to be immune from 6in shell and to withstand destroyer gunfire. As against 6in, the sides were to be immune above 10,000 yards and the crown immune at all ranges. This could be met by: 3in sides and 2in crowns, both of non-cemented armour plating. The machinery spaces were to be protected as in *York*: 3in side, deck over, 1.5 in, both of high tensile (HT) steel, as in *Omaha*, while the deck was better than in *Danae* and *Emerald*.

In beam fighting, the side would be proof against 6in shell above 16,500 yards, and the deck against 6in shell below 13,000 yards and against 4.7in shell at all ranges.

With armament as above and with the same scale of magazine and machinery protection in all cases, the standard displacement became:

Designs 1 and 2	6,000 tons
Design 3	6,400 tons
Designs 4 and 5	6,200 tons

Since the designs were built to the same lines, Design 3 would have been some nine inches deeper in draught than Design 1 and her speed at standard displacement would be reduced by slightly more than one knot.

Designs 3, 4 and 5 could only be brought to a standard displacement of 6,000 tons by reducing the amount of protection provided. Such protection could only weigh 245 tons in Design 3, 340 tons in Design 4 and 360 tons in Design 5. The weight required to protect magazines and shell rooms with 3in side and 2in crown armour and to provide for the other items except machinery protection was 375 tons in Design 3, 340 tons in Design 4 and 360 tons in Design 5.

Thus in Design 3 not only was it impossible to provide anything above the minimum thickness of one inch at the machinery, but the protection of the magazines and shell rooms had to be reduced in order to make up the 130 tons still required to balance the displacement. On this basis the permissible protection became side 2in, crown 1.25in. In Designs 4 and 5 there was a small margin of weight after the magazines had been provided for, but this was only sufficient to add 0.25in to Design 4 and 0.5in to Design 5, to the side only abreast the machinery. The latest British 6in gun pierced armour much better than previous models, and it had to be assumed that foreign navies had made, or soon would make, similar progress.

'Cost of building:
Approximate price of each design, including hull, armour, gun mountings, torpedo tubes, guns and ammunition including reserves:
Design 1: £1,150,000, Design 2: £1,150,000, Design 3: £1,390,000, Design 4: £1,280,000, Design 5: £1,250,000. These prices are for the ships shown on the Legend form, where the full prot to the mags and mach spaces is included.

W J Berry DNC
23 January 1929'

At a meeting of 30 January 1929 chaired by the First Sea Lord, it was decided that there was no point in carrying 5.5in guns, and that Design 3, with eight 6in guns in four twin turrets, was preferable to Design 1 with five singles. Displacement was to be 6,500 tons, which would permit a much better ship than 6,000. As usual, the Engineer-in-Chief said that the space provided for machinery was inadequate. The 60,000shp called for, and needed, was the same as for the *York*, which had much more space, and it was agreed that a little more space could be provided. There was a long discussion as to whether the speed of 30 knots at deep load was enough or not, but no more could be obtained. The design promised rapid acceleration, which was often more valuable than

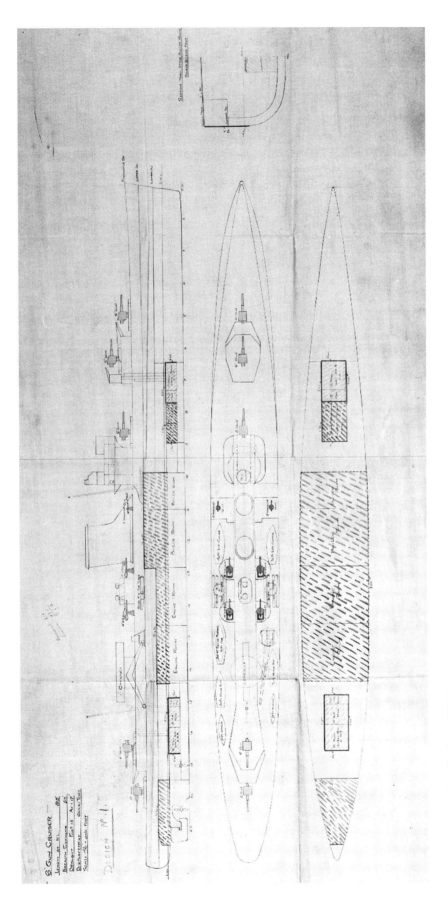

Design 1: plan and profile views. (PRO)

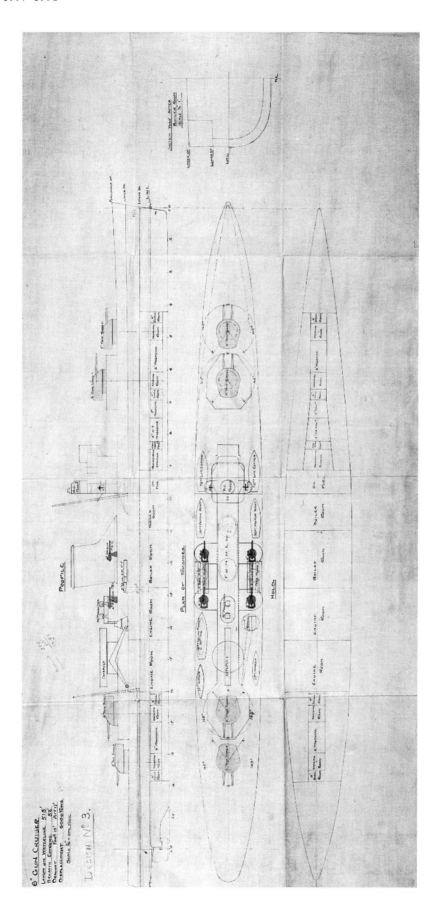

Design 3: plan and profile views. (PRO)

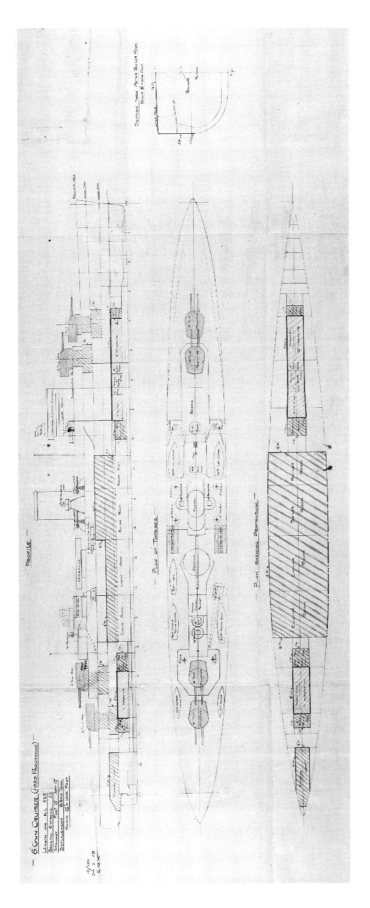

1929 Programme design: plan and profile views. (PRO)

outright speed. With 1,800 tons of oil, 6,500 'knots' at 16 speed were expected, and would be acceptable.

The 6in guns were to be given sufficient elevation to reach 18,000 yards, with a director and control system forward, and a less elaborate arrangement aft. The problem with anti-aircraft fire was that a full High Angle Control System was bulky and heavy: if carried, it would only leave enough weight for a few AA shells. Anything short of a full system would be of little use: if the mountings could take the strain, it might be worth giving the 6in guns 50° or 60° elevation. Otherwise, reliance would have to be placed on the four 4in and two quadruple 0.5in machine guns[2]. It was hoped to fit more of these, to cover the stern sectors, if weight allowed. The quintuple torpedo mount was not showing promise, so quad mounts were accepted, using the J-type destroyer torpedo, which had a single speed setting: 11,000 yards at 35 knots. It did not need enriched air. The Assistant Chief of Naval Staff praised the way the DNC and his staff had provided more than the protection asked for, but he was worried by the unprotected ammunition trunks, which might enable one shell to disable two turrets. The meeting agreed that armoured trunks were essential, even at the cost of 100 tons.

The turrets themselves were discussed at another meeting, on 29 February 1929. Four designs were considered, and the one adopted was a modification of one produced in anticipation of the abortive Geneva Conference of 1927. The modification consisted of a break in the cordite hoists. This was adopted as being lighter, easier to produce, though theoretically less safe. It would require nineteen ammunition handlers per turret. ASDIC (Sonar) was to be fitted, with a streamlined retractable dome and control positions immediately above it and on the lower bridge. This was hampered by the flat keel being only 18 inches wide at the ASDIC position, 60 feet from the bow. Eight boats and a raft were provided and the ship was to be anchored by three stockless 90cwt, one 12cwt and one 5cwt Admiralty anchors. The bower cables were to be 2.125in studded chain, the sheet one 6.5in FSWR, with a short length of spare 2.125in. The electrical power was to come from four 225kw turbogenerators, in two widely separated pairs, with a 14kw low-power generator on the shafts of all four.

In late April, the DNC asked the Admiralty Experimental works to run model tests on the new design. Two models – 'FG', a cruiser type and 'FH' a destroyer type based on the *Miranda* of 1913–14 – were tried at speeds of from 10 to 34 knots. 'FG' proved superior except at 33.5 knots or more, and was adopted. These tests came rather late in the design process, presumably Sir William Berry and his staff were fairly confident of their work already.

For planning purposes, the original idea was to have three Treaty cruisers, to keep up with the Americans, in the 1929–30 Naval Estimates. As a further Naval Limitation Conference was under consideration, the Board of Admiralty decided in March 1929, to propose one Treaty cruiser and two of the new type for 1929–30. Two and one were also considered at one stage. In the event, the coming of the Ramsay MacDonald Labour government and the 1929 Stock Exchange crash led to a cut to one *Leander*, half a destroyer flotilla and four submarines instead of six. The Royal Australian Navy (RAN) was interested in the design and there was at one time a possibility of one or more of the class being built at Cockatoo Island, Sydney, like the older *Brisbane* and *Adelaide* had been.

As design work proceeded, the *Leander* grew. Many were worried by all the boiler rooms being together – in contrast to the 'E's – and during the summer of 1929 the arrangement of two boiler and two engine rooms was changed to three and three. The third engine room was actually a gearing room. This change meant that the machinery spaces had to be lengthened by nineteen feet and the ship by twelve feet, fifty tons had to be added to raise power to 72,000shp and fittings as a flagship weighed another twenty. It was felt that the extra subdivision might make all the difference if the ship were badly damaged. Turrets were given extra elevation for anti-aircraft defence, which also increased their surface range.

Leander herself was laid down at Chatham Dockyard on 8 September 1930, and completed in January 1933. Opinion was generally favourable, though some complained that she was much larger than the German 'K' class, and others objected to all the boiler rooms being in one block. The *Leander* was the first single-funnelled Royal Navy cruiser for many years. The writer has an idea that at one time it was intended to have three funnels, giving a 'County'-like silhouette and perhaps confusing the enemy. One fault was noted on trials: a lot of spray came inboard just aft of the break of the forecastle, which had to be extended aft to avoid damaging the boats. Three more ships followed in 1930–31, and one in 1931–2. The names were all those of previous big ships.

The Apollo *class*

For that year and 1932–33, the last three of the class were given divided machinery, as a further precaution against flooding, and became a separate class. All were transferred to the Royal Australian Navy after a brief period of Royal Navy service.

In service, the *Leander*s were well thought of, *Leander*'s first captain reporting that 'she makes a seamanlike and workmanlike impression; the ship sits well on the water when trimmed two feet by the stern.' The next cruisers were the smaller *Arethusa*s, virtually the 'minimum practical cruiser' by Royal Navy ideas. Thereafter the *Mogami* revolutionised the situation, bringing forth the *Brooklyn* and then the *Southampton*. The *Leander*'s upright funnel was followed in the *Arethusa*s and *Apollo*s, reverting to raked ones in the *Birmingham*s and most later ships.

During the Second World War, like most RN cruisers, the *Leander*s covered vast distances, achieved much, but at the price of heavy losses. At the outset, *Ajax* and *Achilles* gained prestige at the Battle of the River Plate, scoring eighteen hits on the *Admiral Graf Spee*, causing heavy casualties and worrying the Germans considerably, but not inflicting vital damage.[3] The *Graf Spee*'s captain, thinking he had met one cruiser and a convoy, had closed

Leander *on the Thames in 1935. (NMM. N31788)*

in to around 8,000 yards range, losing the advantage of his heavier guns.

Ajax received two 11in hits, one bringing down her main-topmast, while the other penetrated about forty feet, jamming one turret and disabling another. Seven men were killed and ten wounded. A 'short' on *Achilles* sprayed up splinters, which killed four men and wounded three in her director. Control was shifted to the two-man after director, but the two men there were so shaken by blasts from the after turrets that the wounded men in the damaged forward director had to resume the task. *Ajax's* 'Seafox' seaplane was flown off despite gun blast and did some good spotting, also reporting a *Graf Spee* torpedo. One hoist failed in *Ajax* but was soon repaired. The battle was inconclusive, but the fact that ordinary cruisers had engaged one of the dreaded pocket battleships in daylight and good weather, and fought her to a draw, was a great relief to the Allies.

One night in January 1940, *Neptune* closed a merchantman to look her over, and went away satisfied. The merchantman was a British Q-ship, whose captain reported that he could have disabled the cruiser with two torpedoes and swept her upper deck. This situation had occurred in the First World War, and was to recur.

On Italy's entry into the war, *Orion*, *Neptune* and *Sydney* (with *Liverpool*) were with the Mediterranean Fleet and soon saw action, being present at the action off Calabria (Punta Stilo) on 9 July 1940, when the Italians had sixteen cruisers with their two battleships. However, the British had an equaliser: the *Warspite*, 'acting as a battlecruiser'. Ten days later, the *Sydney*, commanded by the redoubtable John Collins, engaged two roughly equivalent *Bande Nere* class cruisers in the Aegean.

In the ensuing combat, the *Bartolomeo Colleoni* was disabled and eventually sunk by torpedoes, while the *Giovanni delle Bande Nere* received two 6in hits, but escaped. *Sydney* received one hit through a funnel. This lop-sided victory was due to several factors. Captain Collins had disregarded his orders, thus enabling his ship to be at hand when the Italians attacked some nearby British destroyers. Visibility favoured the Australian ship, Collins coolly waited until the range was down to 19,000 yards before opening fire, to get a good fire-control 'solution', and his eight 6in guns scored more hits than the Italians' sixteen. Italian fire tended to be 'good but not good enough', due to their ammunition being made to excessive tolerances, and the *Bande Nere*s had only 0.8in (20mm) armour[4], so that any of the few hits scored could

Ajax *returning to Chatham Dockyard in February 1940 for repairs to damage sustained during the Battle of the River Plate. (NMM. N31282)*

cause serious damage. The Italian commander's tactics were affected by the danger from the destroyers' guns.

The action and the photographs of the *Colleoni* in her last moments, with her bow blown off, fire round her bridge and fore funnel, and a big hole on the main deck aft, gave a boost to British morale, and suggested that the Italian Navy was a joke – an opinion not shared by those who actually met it. Incidentally, when bombarding Rhodes, *Sydney* rigged a dummy trunk to her fore funnel, to simulate a *Bande Nere*.

Later, the *Ajax*, repaired and fitted with radar, joined the Mediterranean Fleet. In October, she, too, met the Italians, with rather different results. On the night of 11/12 October, the Fleet was covering Malta convoy with a cruiser screen including the *Ajax* spread to the north. The German Naval liaison staff had been urging their allies to use their many torpedo craft in night attacks on the British. On this occasion, four destroyers and three torpedo boats were sent to attack.

In the resulting combat, two torpedo boats, the *Airone* and *Ariel*, were sunk, and the destroyer *Artigliere* damaged. She was taken in tow by a consort, but had to be cast off when the *York* and others gave chase after daylight. *Ajax* knew she had been in a fight: she received seven hits,

having fourteen men killed and twenty-three wounded – more casualties than those inflicted by the *Admiral Graf Spee*. Fortunately, the Italian torpedo work was not up to the standard of their gunnery: fourteen torpedoes were sighted. It was fortunate that the attack had fallen on the only Mediterranean Fleet cruiser with radar.

British cruisers had shown that they could cope with enemy ones, but air attack was a different proposition. The Italian high-level bombing was ineffective, though very good of its kind, but their torpedo aircraft damaged several British ships, and, when they appeared, the German dive-bombers were devastating. They first showed their mettle on 10 January 1941, when the *Southampton* was sunk and the *Illustrious* put out of action. The *Leander*s, however, did not meet them until the Battle of Crete. In the meantime, there was one more episode of the semi-immunity from air attack which had lasted since the start of the Mediterranean war.

Orion, Ajax and *Perth* (replacing *Sydney*) took part in the Battle of Cape Matapan on 28 March 1941. During the preliminary feints and manoeuvres, both sides' cruisers tried to lure the enemy onto their own battleships. After the battle turned into a pursuit, they and *Gloucester* were sent ahead to regain contact. Destroyers had also been sent ahead to attack, while the battlefleet followed up, hoping to engage before daylight, by which time the Italians would be within range of Ju.87s.

The cruisers saw the gunflashes of the dusk attack by naval Swordfish, and the *Orion* made radar contact with the *Pola* which they had disabled. Reports of this enabled the battlefleet to close her. *Ajax* apparently detected the ill-fated Italian rescue force which was also closing her, but someone was using the wrong radio channel and this information did not get through. It might have made a lot of difference, but the British pursuers and the Italian rescuers reached the *Pola* simultaneously, and the former destroyed the latter. The cruisers received only minor damage, but things were to change very soon. The immediate predecessor of the *Leander*s, the *York*, had been disabled by another new weapon, the explosive motorboat, in Suda Bay only two days before, and never sailed again.

In late May, there was excellent information that the Axis were planning an airborne invasion of Crete, with seaborne follow-up. The RAF was unable to provide air cover, and the Mediterranean Fleet's carrier had only a few aircraft, so any naval effort to prevent seaborne landings meant a straight fight between aircraft, especially dive-bombers, and naval anti-aircraft guns. The fleet was in great strength, with four battleships, a carrier, a dozen cruisers and some thirty destroyers. Most ships had 4in heavy AA guns, and the 5.25in and 4.5in dual-purpose guns which were regarded as highly effective. For close-range defence there were pompoms, quadruple 0.5in guns, captured Italian 20mm Bredas and a miscellany of light machine-guns. With the cruisers' 6in guns used at high elevation, plus early warning radar, the Fleet seemed well defended.

The Admiralty knew better. Their Scientific Adviser had warned them before the war that the service AA Fire-Control System was fundamentally unsound. Light, 'Close-Range' weapons had to rely on hand aiming: development of a proper control system had been abandoned in 1929 as unnecessary.

When the attack began on 20 May, the Luftwaffe concentrated on ground support, which their airborne troops urgently needed against a ferocious defence. The next day, the *Juno* was sunk by a fluky high-level attack, the *Ajax* near-missed and the real battle began. At 2130hrs Rear-Admiral Glennie's Force D, including *Orion* and *Ajax*, met a German invasion convoy eighteen miles north of Canea. The main escort, the Italian torpedo boat *Lupo*, made a brave defence, but was driven off heavily damaged – she had eighteen killed and forty wounded out of a crew of 120. The British thought that they had obliterated her, while she thought she had torpedoed *Ajax*. *Ajax*'s searchlights picked up what looked like a millionaire's yacht and she was able to fire in a broadside at a half-mile range. The action went on for two and a half hours and ten craft were sunk. Germans in a caique fired small arms at the ship which had rammed them and was pushing the caique sideways. The British thought that they had killed some 4,000 Germans – actually there were only some 2,300 in the convoy, most of whom reached the shore. *Lupo*'s survival was probably due to several of the eighteen 6in shells that hit her passing right through without

exploding. This can easily happen at close ranges, if the shells do not hit something heavy.

The following day it was *Perth*'s turn. As part of Force C she was searching for another convoy of caiques north of Heraklion under heavy air attack. Single ships were sunk at 0830hrs and 0909hrs. Much of Force C's gunfire had to be directed at aircraft. The expected convoy was sighted at 1010hrs, but was screened with smoke by the torpedo boat *Sagittario*, and Admiral King decided that he could not follow up in the face of the air attack and a rapidly reducing ammunition supply. Force C retired to the west, joining up with the battleships of Force A1 at 1321hrs. *Perth* had suffered a damaging near miss and *Carlisle* had lost her captain.

A further series of mishaps led to the loss of *Greyhound*, *Gloucester* and *Fiji*. Survivors were machine-gunned in the water – the Germans had heard of the disaster to the Canea convoy. Very few German aircraft were shot down. They only lost nine Ju.87s in the whole operation – the bad decision of 1929 was now being paid for. Though their troops had been badly mauled, the Germans exploited their one success – seizing the airfield at Maleme – and on the 27 May the decision was taken to evacuate.

The first priority was the 4,000 troops at Heraklion, towards the east end of Crete's northern coast, who had completely beaten their attackers, captured 500 and chased the survivors into the hills. Force B, comprising most of the former Force D, *Orion*, *Ajax*, *Dido* and six destroyers, commanded by Rear-Admiral Rawlings, sailed at dawn on 28 May to lift the troops. Late that day, the Force was attacked, *Ajax* and the destroyer *Imperial* being near-missed. *Ajax* reported damage too severe to continue, which Admiral Cunningham later considered over-cautious. The troops were quickly embarked between 2330hrs and 0300hrs, cruisers taking 1,250 each and destroyers 250. The ships sailed at 0320hrs. They had to pass very close to the airfield at Scarpanto, but air cover from Cyprus had been arranged. Then things started to go badly wrong.

At 0345hrs *Imperial*'s rudder head broke from the after-effects of her near miss. *Hotspur* took off her crew and passengers and sank her, following Force B with 900 men aboard. She would have little hope by herself after dawn, so her captain planned to turn west along the south coast of Crete once through Kaso Strait. Just before dawn, she sighted ships ahead: the Admiral had slowed down to wait for her, losing 90 minutes and throwing out the fighter cover arrangements. Attacks began at 0600hrs before *Hotspur* was back in formation and continued till mid-afternoon. At first, enemy aircraft could be seen in the circuit over Scarpanto.

Within a few minutes *Hereward* was crippled and had to be left behind – she beached herself on the Cretan coast. German aircraft began machine-gunning survivors, but were thwarted by an Italian seaplane which circled over them. Near misses slowed the force first to 25 knots, then 21. *Orion* and *Dido* were both hit on forward turrets, Captain Back of *Orion* was mortally wounded by strafing. The ships hit back and the troops joined in with machine-guns and small arms, but few aircraft were shot down. The fighters shot down or scared off a few more, but never sighted the ships. Nevertheless, by 1030hrs, the force was almost out of range of the Ju.87s which were the most dangerous enemy. At 1045hrs, a force of eleven arrived, to make a last effort against the victims who were slipping from their grasp. The leading Ju.87 pressed its attack too low, and crashed just ahead of the *Orion*, however, its big bomb penetrated her bridge and exploded between decks. A great ball of smoke burst out of the ship. Heavy flooding took place, the ship listed, steering gear and communications were disrupted, contaminated fuel slowed her to 14 knots and for a time she headed back towards Scarpanto. The slaughter on the crowded messdecks was fearful: it is thought that 260 were killed and 280 wounded. Captain Back was heard to call out 'It's all right, boys, that one's over' before dying.

That was the climax. *Orion* was brought back onto her course for Alexandria, cloud cover increased, and, without the Ju.87s, later attacks were less intense. They continued, however, until Force B was within 100 miles of Alexandria. It arrived at 2000hrs, having saved, at fearful cost, 80 per cent of the Heraklion garrison. After the war, the garrison commander reflected that those left behind in the *Hereward* were in some ways the luckiest: few of the 3,200 men landed at Alexandria survived the years of bitter fighting that followed. *Orion* reached Alexandria with ten tons of oil and two rounds of 6in ammunition. She required a major refit; Admiral Cunningham visited her to deliver a pep-talk, which was not well received.

The rest of the garrison's evacuation was from Sfakia on the south coast of Crete. Air cover could be provided, and the only setback was the sinking of the *Calcutta* within 60 miles of Alexandria by an enterprising pair of Ju.88s. After the battle, the only Mediterranean Fleet ships immediately available were two battleships, one cruiser and seventeen destroyers.

A comparative naval lull followed, during which the *Perth* engaged a French *contre-torpilleur* off Syria, and major operations resumed in November, being closely linked to the attack and defence of the Italian convoy traffic, on which the Axis forces in Libya depended. At first, the attack was led by the small *Aurora* and *Penelope*, but later the *Ajax* and *Neptune* were sent to Malta to reinforce them. In mid-month, after covering a run by the fast transport *Breconshire* to Malta and a scuffle with the Italian Fleet, who were covering a convoy of their own, a group of Malta-based ships was hastily refuelled and sailed to intercept the Italian convoy just before it reached Tripoli. Captain R C 'Rory' O'Connor of *Neptune* was in command.

At 0039hrs of 19 December, twenty miles from Tripoli, *Neptune*'s paravanes exploded a mine. She went 'full astern' and hit another aft, wrecking her propellers. Little water came in, but she was in a desperate position. *Aurora* hauled out of line, hit another mine and received even worse damage. One of the destroyers got a hawser aboard *Neptune*, but was ordered to cast off and help *Aurora*, who was escorted towards Malta while the rest of the force waited for *Neptune* to drift clear of the minefield. About 0230hrs, she hit a third mine and began settling. *Kandahar*, the senior destroyer, entered the field to help her, but was herself mined and disabled.

Orion lies damaged, with one turret removed, at Simonstown in July 1941. (NMM. N31904)

With daylight approaching, Captain Nicholl of *Penelope* realised that he had to get out of aircraft range – quickly. He signalled 'God be with you; I clearly cannot help you', and retired at 25 knots. *Neptune* remained afloat until about 0400hrs, when she struck a fourth mine and capsized. The survivors were not found for a long time and one by one they succumbed to the sea and the cold. Rory O'Connor died on 23 December. A few hours later, the sole survivor, Leading Seaman J Walters, was picked up by an Italian torpedo boat. The Axis were apparently unaware of what had happened; *Kandahar* remained afloat and unmolested apart from being circled by a bemused Ju.88. If anyone from *Neptune* tried to reach her, none succeeded. Malta sailed the only available destroyer, *Jaguar*, commanded by Lt-Cdr L R K Tyrwhitt, son of the great 'Commodore T', with orders to search for the disabled ships but to be well clear by daylight of 20 May. A radar-equipped Wellington found *Kandahar* and guided the destroyer. The weather prevented her from going alongside, but 178 survivors swam across, well after daylight, and were carried to Malta. The Irish Republic was neutral, although a lot of its citizens were not, and Rory O'Connor's death was ascribed in their press to a 'boating accident', which no doubt amused his shade greatly.

The minefield had been laid by the Italians in August, using German mines, to prevent any repetition of the April bombardment of Tripoli by the Mediterranean Fleet battleships. Unintentionally, it had ended the short but brilliant offensive by Malta-based surface craft. In contrast to 1914–18, *Neptune* was the only British cruiser sunk by mines during the Second World War. At almost the same moment as she sank, the two remaining Mediterranean Fleet battleships were crippled by Italian '*Maiale*' operators in Alexandria harbour, a brilliant success after many disappointments.

A month earlier, one of the Australian 'Modified *Leander*s' had been lost, without any survivors. After leaving the Mediterranean, *Sydney* had carried out anti-raider and escort duties in the Indian Ocean. The defences of Singapore were being built up and on 11 November, *Sydney* left Fremantle escorting a troopship to Sunda Strait, where a Singapore-based escort took over. She then turned back, advising that she would arrive at Fremantle in the afternoon of 19 November. She later amended this to the morning of 20 November. This was the last heard of her by the Allies.

The German disguised raider (auxiliary cruiser) *Kormoran* had been operating, with little success, in the Indian Ocean for some months, and planned to lay mines in Shark Bay at the northwest tip of Australia. On the late afternoon of 19 November, she was steering northeast, some 100 miles off the outlying coastal islands. According to her account, *Kormoran* sighted what was at first thought to be a sailing vessel to the north. On recognising it to be a cruiser, she turned west and southwest to evade. However, the *Sydney* followed, overtaking from the starboard quarter at 25 knots.

By 1725hrs she had closed to about 1,500 yards on a parallel course. *Kormoran* sent slow and misleading answers to signals, hoping that the cruiser would go away, but finally the *Sydney* sent an unintelligible signal – actu-

ally 'make your secret identity signal'. *Kormoran*, who was at action stations, ran up her colours, unmasked her guns, and opened fire. Several 5.9in shells began hitting within seconds, machine-gun fire cut down men on *Sydney*'s deck, and a torpedo hit abreast her forward turrets. After a few vital seconds, *Sydney*'s after turrets began firing, and scored four hits. One went into *Kormoran*'s engine-room, wrecked it and started a fatal fire. The cruiser was briefly hidden by smoke, and next appeared on *Kormoran*'s port side, slowly curving away to the southwards. She fired four torpedoes and machine-gun bullets without effect. *Kormoran* replied with two of her own, which also missed just before she came to a halt, and went on firing for some forty minutes, by which time *Sydney* was over 10,000 yards away, burning from bridge to mainmast, and limping to the southeast at about five knots.

Kormoran was abandoned over the next few hours, having lost some twenty killed and sixty drowned. Some of her crew said they saw *Sydney* blow up about 2200hrs. Over the next few days, *Kormoran*'s survivors either reached the coast or were picked up by passing ships. Nothing was found of *Sydney* except some small wreckage until a Carley float, with the remains of a body on it, was picked up near Christmas Island nearly three months later. Many attempts have been made to solve the mystery of her fate and that of her crew, but most of the doubts remain. R J Montgomery, the orphan of one of her officers, was able to find that some sort of cover-up took place, but not what lay behind it.

From the naval point of view, the puzzle is, why did a presumably competent captain approach so closely to a merchantman which might have been, and in this one-in-a-thousand case, actually was, a disguised raider, without taking precautions? From the human angle, *Sydney* was the only Allied cruiser lost with all hands, as *Neptune* was the only one with a single survivor. *Sydney* absorbed some fifty 5.9in shells and a torpedo, which was more than enough to sink her. At close range, the *Kormoran*'s old 5.9in guns were as effective as more modern ones, and it is likely that most of *Sydney*'s senior officers were killed early on, crippling attempts at fire fighting and other damage control[5].

Soon afterwards, Japan entered the war, and the Royal Australian Navy found itself in a desperate home-defence campaign. *Perth* and *Hobart* served in the ABDA force which tried to stop the southward advance of the Japanese through what were then the Netherlands East Indies. The Japanese carrier and battleship forces remained in support, while their many amphibious landings were covered by numerous cruisers and destroyers, plus their shore-based aircraft. Fortunately, the latter had used all their torpedoes against the *Prince of Wales* and *Repulse*; their high-level bombing, like the Italians', produced few results, though good of its kind.

On 15 February, *Hobart* was part of a fifteen-ship force which tried to thwart the enemy landings at Palembang, Sumatra. The Dutch commander, Rear-Admiral Doorman, led his force between Billiton and Bangka before dawn, hoping to reach the northern entrance of Bangka Strait and sweep south between it and Sumatra, destroying the Japanese landing force. He was sighted by

HMAS Hobart *in 1940. (NMM. N32229)*

aircraft, and his opponent, Vice-Admiral Ozawa, sent in waves of aircraft from shore bases and the small carrier *Ryujo*, while assembling his own heavy cruisers and a destroyer flotilla to meet Doorman. Skilful evasive action foiled the aircraft, but delayed the allied force. Doorman was not prepared to commit his ships to the narrow Bangka Strait under air attack, and turned back, losing the Palembang oilfields.

Under the threat of multiple landings, the ABDA force was unable to assemble or use its full strength. Soon only Java remained, and a massive landing – ninety-seven transports – was in the offing. On 25/26 February, *Exeter, Perth* and three destroyers were transferred from Tandjong Priok in the west to Surabaya in east Java, to join Doorman's force, which now amounted to five cruisers and nine destroyers, of four navies, two languages and three different systems of tactics and signals. *Hobart* had to drop out, as no tanker was available to refuel her.

'After the fastest and most dangerous car ride of our lives', Captain Bell of *Exeter* and Captain Waller of *Perth* reached a conference at which Admiral Doorman explained his plans, and the force sailed the same evening to search along the shore for the eastern half of the Japanese invasion force, forty-one transports covered by four cruis-

ers and fourteen destroyers. Nothing was sighted that night and the search continued until early afternoon, when the force was about to re-enter the outer harbour. It had been shadowed by aircraft and attacked by a few of them.

At 1427hrs, news was received of the troop convoy and a force of two cruisers and six destroyers some 60 miles off shore and the ABDA force headed northwest to engage them. The five cruisers were in single column, in the order *De Ruyter* (Flag – 5.9in), *Exeter* (8in), *Houston* (8in), *Perth* (6in) and *Java* (5.9in). Just after 1600hrs, a Japanese destroyer flotilla was sighted and engaged, then a second. It was realised that other enemy ships would probably be nearby, and that the situation was desperate. Within a few minutes, two heavy cruisers came over the horizon, and the battle developed on parallel courses to the westward. None of the Allied ships had a seaplane available; the Japanese did, and their crews did admirable reporting work.

Perth was mostly outranged, but was able to damage a destroyer as it closed to attack. For a time the ABDA force held its own, but its rudimentary signals and liaison system could not cope with a crisis. This came at 1708hrs, when a *Haguro* 8in shell plunged into *Exeter*'s boiler room, slowing her to a crawl and sending up clouds of steam, just

HMS Amphion *served for a brief spell in the Royal Navy before her transfer in 1939 to the Royal Australian Navy.*
(NMM. N20758)

as a second Japanese destroyer attack was developing. *Exeter* turned away to port, *Houston* conformed, thinking the British ship had been torpedoed, and Doorman found four of his five cruisers apparently running away. Captain Waller rose to the occasion, engaging Japanese destroyers working round to the west and laying a smoke screen.

Despite its many problems, the allied force managed to reform, in the order *De Ruyter, Perth, Houston* and *Java,* plus six destroyers. *Exeter* limped back to Surabaya, escorted by one destroyer, two others had been sunk. For some time the opponents engaged in and out of smoke screens, but eventually the Japanese retired towards their convoy.

Just after dark, the reduced ABDA force again sighted and engaged the Japanese; *Perth*'s fire appeared accurate but she soon spotted the flash of torpedo fire and turned away, followed by the rest of the force.

The accuracy of Japanese torpedo fire was about to be shown, and the Allies' best chance had been lost; the enemy had been lying stopped while recovering aircraft, and only the torpedo salvo – from *Jintzu* – saved the situation. For the next four hours, Doorman sought the enemy, and all the destroyers on both sides dropped out. Guided by his seaplanes, Admiral Takagi, the Japanese commander, placed his ships between the ABDA force and the invasion convoy. The last round began at 2300hrs, when *Nachi* and *Haguro*, steaming south, reversed course to engage the four Allied cruisers. After a few minutes firing, Doorman began a turn away in succession. At

2336hrs, *Java*, the last in column, was torpedoed near the stern, burst into flames and fell out. Doorman began another turn to starboard, and *De Ruyter* also burst into flames. Captain Waller decided that there was nothing more to be done, and broke off the action, heading for Tandjong Priok with *Houston*.

The two ships arrived at 1330hrs on 28 February, and hastily refuelled, intending to sail for Tjilatjap on the south coast via Sunda Strait, as a Japanese landing near the strait was expected that night. *Perth* was undamaged, *Houston* had been hit twice, but both ships were short of ammunition. The RAN ship embarked a fire engine and a number of pilgrim rafts. They sailed at 1930hrs, steaming along the shore at 25 knots in bright moonlight. Captain Waller told his officers that he expected orders to make for Australia or Ceylon.

Between 2240hrs and 2255hrs, the destroyer *Fubuki*, patrolling east of the Japanese invasion fleet, sighted the two cruisers approaching and reported them, though uncertain of their identity. At 2306hrs, *Perth* sighted a Japanese ship on her port bow, reported 'One hostile' and opened fire. The Japanese transports had anchored along the shore of Bantam Bay, and were landing troops. Their close covering force; *Mogami, Mikuma, Natori* and a flotilla of destroyers, came to the rescue, but almost too late. *Perth* sent her last report: 'Many hostile'.

Perth and *Houston* were between the Japanese cruisers and their convoy, engaging both, while the heavy cruisers fired 8in shells and the destroyers made attack after attack. There were more targets than the Allies had gun mountings. In the mêlée, two Japanese transports were sunk and two more beached, while a minesweeper was torpedoed, by whom, no-one knows. *Mikuma* and five destroyers were hit. For half an hour, *Perth* suffered little, receiving a minor shell hit at 2326hrs and then two others. Captain Waller kept speed at 25 knots, which baffled the Japanese fire control, and at midnight *Perth* was still largely intact.

However, the Gunnery Officer reported that almost all ammunition had been expended, and Captain Waller increased to full speed and headed for Prinsen Island, possibly intending to beach the ship. Within a few minutes a torpedo hit *Perth* on the starboard side abreast the fore funnel. Part of the deck glowed red hot and caved in, two shafts stopped, and then a third. As the various guns fired their last rounds, Japanese shells hit in numbers. Then a second torpedo hit, and Waller ordered 'Abandon ship'; 'Prepare to abandon ship, Sir?', 'No, abandon ship'.

Perth began to list to starboard, as a third and then a fourth torpedo hit. Despite the damage, many men got up from below and into the water. She began to settle by the stern. Captain Waller was last seen with his arms resting on the front of her bridge. The tip of her bow vanished beneath the waters of Sunda Strait at 0025hrs of 1 March, just as *Houston* was abandoning ship. The strong currents carried many survivors, Australian, American and Japanese, out into the Indian Ocean; 335 out of 686 men from *Perth* and 368 out of 1,064 men from *Houston* survived the battle; 100 from *Perth* and 76 from *Houston* died in captivity.

This was the last surface combat of the *Leander*s and *Sydney*s for a very long time; many of the later battles in the Far East and Pacific were 'over the horizon' ones involving carrier aircraft, and none of the class were engaged in the fierce night actions of the Guadalcanal Campaign. Similarly, in the Mediterranean and Atlantic wars, none of them engaged enemy cruisers after the end of 1941. As the opportunity occurred, the ships were fitted with improved radar and extra anti-aircraft armament, to deal with what was clearly the greatest threat. In several cases, 'X' turret was removed to compensate for the extra weight.

After the North Africa landings had transformed the Mediterranean war, *Ajax* was sent to Bone as part of 'Force Q' to operate against the Axis convoy routes; however, she still retained her propensity for getting damaged. Only two days after arrival, a bomb went down her funnel during an air raid, and she was 'out' for a long time again. As the war proceeded, cruisers in the Mediterranean were increasingly employed on anti-aircraft and bombardment duties.

All this time, *Leander* had pursued an uneventful career. In July 1943, she was attached to a US Navy task force in

HMAS Perth *in 1941. (NMM. N32237)*

the Solomons as a replacement for the *Helena*, sunk by Japanese destroyers on July 6/7. Only a week later, *Honolulu*, *St Louis* and *Leander*, with five destroyers ahead and five astern, met a Japanese force of *Jintzu* and five destroyers off Kolombangara, about half-way along the Solomons 'Slot'.

It was a bright, clear night, and the two forces met starboard bow to starboard bow. Both launched torpedoes and opened heavy gunfire. The two US cruisers pumped out a vast amount of ammunition; nine 15-gun broadsides a minute, *Leander* contributing twenty 8-gun broadsides; *Jintzu* was riddled and set ablaze. Remembering the previous week's action, Admiral Ainsworth turned away after a few minutes, to avoid torpedoes, but *Leander* was hit on her port side abreast the funnel as she came round onto an easterly course.

She dropped out of formation with a heavy list; all engines stopped. Two destroyers were left with her, and the rest of the force pursued the Japanese. *Leander*'s damage control was excellent, she was moving within a few minutes and soon had part of her armament working again. In the meantime, the Japanese destroyers reloaded their tubes and came back to deliver a Parthian shaft which blew off the bows of *Honolulu* and *St Louis* and fatally damaged *Gwin*. *Leander*'s repairs lasted the rest of the war. In July 1943, *Hobart* was torpedoed and damaged by a Japanese submarine.

During the rest of the war the surviving ships of the class bombarded, escorted and repelled air attacks. Most were

sold within a few years afterwards. *Ajax* was hit by a waterspout, which sounded spectacular, but did little damage.

They had shown a capacity for giving and receiving punishment; despite their boiler rooms being so close together, they were difficult to disable. Being fairly small, they were eminently suitable for warfare in narrow seas, their only big weakness being in anti-aircraft defence. They seem to have shown far more resistance than the earlier Italian '*Condottieri*' classes; the later ones were very different, bigger and far more robust. No doubt bigger and better-armed ships would have been preferable, but bearing in mind the parlous state of the British economy when they were conceived, the planners and designers had done remarkably well with the resources available to them, and their crews had made fine use of them, in situations undreamed of in 1929.

Notes

[1] This term was originally used for the thinly armoured gunboats used on American rivers in the Civil War.

[2] These were Vickers guns, and proved almost useless. The Italian Air Force and the Japanese Army Air Force used them in aircraft, with poor results.

[3] *Exeter*'s two 8in hits worried them even more: one almost pierced *Admiral Graf Spee*'s armoured deck.

[4] They were known as *Cartone Volante*, roughly 'Flying Shoeboxes'.

[5] This happened to the *Southampton* in January 1941.

WARSHIP NOTES

This section comprises a number of short articles and notes, generally highlighting little-known aspects of warship history.

VISBY, THE SWEDISH NAVY'S STEALTH CORVETTE

Antony Preston follows the progress of the Swedish Navy's new 'invisible' vessel.

The keel laying of the new corvette *Visby* at Karlskrona on 17 December last year was a major milestone in the Royal Swedish Navy's YS 2000 programme. Over ten years ago the Defence Material Command (FMV) initiated a series of design studies to meet the needs of future surface warfare. Following trials with the technology demonstrator *Smyge*, the choice settled on a new multi-role corvette, designated YS 2000.

The new corvette was intended to be a flexible multi-mission design, with top performance at both low and high speeds and the ability to undertake mine countermeasures (MCM), anti-submarine warfare (ASW), mine-laying, surveillance and surface combat missions. The hull would also have a low radar cross-section (RCS) and low acoustic and magnetic signatures.

The hull is built of a composite sandwich consisting of a PVC core with carbon fibre and vinyl laminate to give maximum strength and rigidity, low weight, good resistance to shock and low radar and magnetic signatures. Hull modules are built of flat panels manufactured by vacuum injection. The ship will have a truncated pyramidal superstructure, using flat fibre-reinforced plastic (FRP)

sandwich panels. Weapons and sensors are hidden behind hatches below a 'shelter deck', and equipment located above decks has been designed to reduce its RCS. This applies particularly to the retractable main surveillance radar, which is designed for low probability of intercept (LPI), and the new Bofors 57mm L/70 Mk3 mounting, in which the gun barrel retracts into the cupola when not firing. External surfaces of the hull are clad in frequency-selective surfaces (FSS) and radar-absorbent material (RAM).

Infra-red (IR) signatures are controlled by a combination of measures. The FRP hull provides good thermal insulation, and engine and air-conditioning exhaust vents are designed to reduce heat emissions. An external sprinkler system is fitted to cool the hull, and special low-IR paint is used. Acoustic signatures are controlled by the use of waterjets, locating noisy equipment above the waterline under acoustic hoods, double-resilient mountings for machinery and an optional underwater/above-water engine exhaust. The FRP hull has a minimal magnetic signature, but in addition key systems are located as high as possible. A degaussing system is fitted, and the electrical systems are designed to eliminate conductive loops.

Underwater electric potential (UEP) effect is minimised by the choice of a non-magnetic hull material and the choice of KaMeWa waterjets. Pressure signature is also low because of the lightweight hull structure and the fine hullform.

A combined diesel or gas turbine (CODOG) arrangement was chosen. Four AlliedSignal TF50A gas turbines developing 16,000kW will provide medium and high speed, driving two

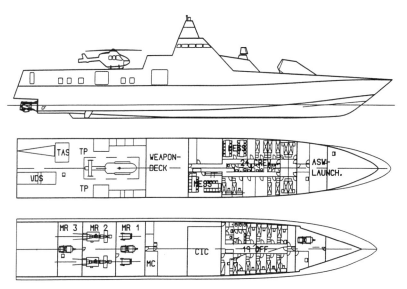

Visby, *the Swedish Navy's new stealth corvette.*

carbon fibre shafts. Two MTU diesels developing a total of 2,600kW will drive the ship at cruising and low speed. The propulsors are KaMeWa 125 SII waterjets.

The *Visby* is the first of four Series I ships, all to be configured for MCM and ASW. For MCM missions the ships will have remotely operated vehicles (ROVs). One of these, designated ROV-S, will carry a high-frequency sonar and TV camera for detection and classification of mines. The others, designated ROV-Es, will be expendable robots for final identification and destruction. For ASW missions the ships will have a hull-mounted medium-frequency sonar and a variable-depth towed sonar array. Weapons include 400mm lightweight torpedoes and grenade-launchers.

Unusually, the FMV contract with Karlskronavarvet is for the hulls only. Procurement decisions on a number of systems have not yet been made, and detailed design work on some is still in progress. FMV's design team emphasises that the main parameters of weight and dimensions for all specified systems are known, avoiding potential problems in installation. The *Visby* will be delivered in the spring of 2000 and two years of intensive trials will follow.

Series II will be optimised for surface warfare, with RBS 15 Mk2 anti-ship missiles, but will in other respects be identical to Series I. No date has been announced for the Series II order, but work is unlikely to start until the last of the *Visby* class is in the water, around 2004–2005, with the ships entering service in 2007–2008.

'THE SHIP OF HAPPIEST MEMORY'

Mary Berg, great-granddaughter of Charles Jones, who served on the Victorian battleship HMS Marlborough, *looks at life on her ancestor's vessel.*

Lord Charles Beresford described HMS *Marlborough* as 'The Ship of Happiest Memory'.[1] It was also the favourite ship of a boy who joined the navy at the age of thirteen and retired

from the sea some twenty-seven years later. That boy was Charles Jones who first served on the frigate *Melampus* and, incidentally, was a member of the guard of honour when Queen Victoria laid the foundation stone of Netley hospital. After that, he would be a lifelong royalist!

HMS *Marlborough* was the flagship of the Mediterranean fleet when Charles Beresford was appointed naval cadet in 1861. Charles Jones had joined the ship three years earlier and was a foretopman. According to Beresford:

Charles Jones, aged 20.

The *Marlborough* was a wooden line of battleship, three-decker launched in 1835, 4,000 tons in old measure, 6,390 displacement in new measure, fitted with a single screw horizontal Maudslay engine. The length of her gun deck was 245 feet 6 inches, her extreme beam was 61 feet, her maximum draught was 26 feet. Her complement was 950, and she always carried 100 or more supernumeraries. She was pierced for 131 guns and she carried 121 guns. She was one of the first ships to be fitted with lower rigging. In the *Marlborough* the old 24in hemp cable was used for laying out anchor at drill. It was the same class of cable which was used in Nelson's time; it was superseded by the chain cable.

Beresford also describes in great detail the procedures and tasks which ensured the smooth operation of the ship. The forecastlemen were the most experienced and they manned the foreyard. The foretopmen came next working the foretopsail, foretopgallant and foreroyal yards and so on. The task of the maintopmen is self explanatory and the mizentopmen worked the mizen sails. The gunners were followed by the afterguard, the Royal Marines and the idlers. The idlers were the artificers and called idlers because they did not have to turn out until 4am. An interesting note is that there were several negroes in the company and Beresford commented that 'it was often the case that the captain of the hold and the copper were coloured men.'

Gunnery was generally not given high priority at this time as it was considered that anyone could fire a gun, but in the *Marlborough* they were proud of their gunnery and used to practice, for example by firing at the cliff at Malta harbour. Most of the guns were the same type as those used in Nelson's time and the *Marlborough* was fitted with a cupola for heating round-shot, which were carried red-hot to the gun in an iron bucket. Beresford knew 'of no other ship which was thus equipped.'

Another source of great pride in the *Marlborough* was the sail drill and it was claimed that the crew was the fastest in the fleet. Once in the Bay of Naples, the masts were stripped of sails and all sails were hoisted in 9 minutes 30 seconds against a previous best in the fleet of 13 minutes set by HMS *Prince Regent*. Jones was one of the two equal fastest men of the foretopgallant yard and these two were said to be always 'six to ten ratlines ahead of the other yard men.' Sailors were barefoot and one day Jones lost a toe 'cut clean off by the fid of the foretopgallant mast.' Beresford reported that 'Jones continued his work as though nothing had

Lord Beresford as a naval cadet.

HMS *Marlborough.*

happened, until the drill was ended, when he hopped to the sick bay.' He was as quick as ever after the accident and from then on the sailors called him Ninepin Jack.

Beresford left the *Marlborough* in 1863 to his 'great grief'. It is a measure of his attachment that he remained in touch with a number of the sailors ensuring in some cases that they and their families were looked after in later years. When three of Jones' sons went to sea as boys in the 1890s, Beresford took an interest in their progress and, when he published his memoirs, he sent Jones a copy inscribed 'To my friend Charles Jones'.

Jones also left some modest memoirs in the form of newspaper interviews in the Bath local papers. By that time he was ferryman across the Avon between Warleigh and Claverton, a post he held for forty-three years until he was 82, when he retired because of his wife's ill health. Jones recalled that, as a result of their days together in the *Marlborough*, Beresford asked for him to be released from *Excellent* in September 1875 to join the *Serapis* which was to take the then Prince of Wales to India with Beresford as his ADC for the visit. During the long voyage, Jones was presented to the Prince and was able to recount how he had

climbed to the top of *Marlborough*'s mast and floated the Prince of Wales standard and that of the Princess of Wales on their wedding day in 1863, an act for which he received a commendation at the time.

Although life in the navy in the 19th century was hard, there was clearly room for some humanity and for companionship among men whose lives depended on the communal effort. Beresford had a distinguished career in both the Royal Navy and in politics. He became an admiral in 1906.

[1] *Memoirs of Lord Charles Beresford*, Lord Charles Beresford, Methuen, 1914.

THE GERMAN HIGH SEAS FLEET'S SURRENDER

These photos, submitted by R D Layman, are among 96 aerial views of units of the German High Seas Fleet steaming into the Firth of Forth to surrender on 21 November 1918. They were taken by Lieutenant Wilfred S Adams, RAF, from a Sopwith 1½ Strutter piloted by Melvin H Rattray, RAF, who was promoted to captain the next day (at this time the Royal Air Force employed army ranks). They have been copied from Rattray's photo album and are published by kind permission of his grandson, Josh G Rattray of Owensborough, Kentucky.

Above: *Battlecruiser* Moltke.   Below: *Battlecruiser* Von der Tann.

Admiral Sir David Beatty, commander of the Grand Fleet, and his flag captain, Ernie Chatfield, on the bridge of HMS Queen Elizabeth *during the surrender. The third officer is identified only as Commander G Blake.*
(Photographer unknown)

Battlecruisers of Scouting Group I at anchor in the Firth of Forth after the surrender.

Below: *Unidentified destroyers.*

Battlecruiser Von der Tann.

Unidentified destroyers.

Light cruiser Nürnberg.

HMS *PHEASANT* – THE DESTROYER WHICH VANISHED

Readers may have seen items in the press about the rediscovery of this First World War destroyer, the only one of sixty-seven destroyers lost whose fate remained in doubt. Keith McBride discusses her mysterious disappearance in March 1917.

HMS *Pheasant*, the seventh of her name to serve in the Royal Navy, was one of the 107 'M' class destroyers built or acquired between 1913 and 1917. They were designed in 1912 for the 1913–14 Naval Programme, a repeat batch was ordered for 1914–15 just as the First World War broke out, and they were adopted as the standard destroyer design from August 1914 to July 1915, when they were succeeded in the shipyards by the 'R' class, which were very similar but had more economical geared turbines, giving a wider cruising range. They soon used up all available 'M' names, and moved on into 'N', 'O' and 'P'. An article on the class was included in *Warship 1991*.

They gave excellent wartime service and played a vital role in screening the Grand Fleet, hunting submarines, laying mines and escorting convoys. At the Battle of Jutland in 1916, forty-one of the seventy-eight British destroyers present were 'M's and they inflicted about as much loss as the rest of the British fleet put together. They also carried out many difficult rescues. By the end of the war, however, they were showing signs of their hard service and all were scrapped by about 1930.

They were of about 1,025 tons 'Legend', 270 to 275 feet long overall, with three 4in, one or two 2pdr pom-poms, four torpedo tubes, usually three funnels and a maximum speed of about 34 knots. The seventh *Pheasant* was one of a batch of twenty ordered in May 1915. She was built at Fairfield's and launched on 23 October, 1916. She was commissioned on 10 November, 1916 and went to the 15th Destroyer Flotilla,

part of the Grand Fleet at Scapa Flow. Her captain was Lt-Cdr H W D Griffith, who was considered a good officer. In late February or early March 1917, she took her turn on the 'Hoy Patrol'.

The entrance to the Flow normally used by the Fleet was the southern one, Hoxa Sound, which was heavily guarded and patrolled. Hoy Sound, the western 'side' entrance, was more lightly protected. At night, drifters and trawlers patrolled outside it. By day a destroyer, assigned for a week at a time, patrolled outside, lying at anchor in the Flow at night. The *Pheasant* was ordered to send a weather report at 0530hrs on 1 March 1917, as Commodore Hawksley, Commodore (F), planned to hold gunnery practice for his destroyers. The signal station at Stromness saw her leave the Sound at that time. There was a long northerly or westerly swell.

About 0610hrs, men aboard two trawlers anchored inshore heard an explosion, and from one they saw black smoke to the northwest. One of the witnesses said that the explosion was two miles away; the other, five. The Second Hand (Mate) of this trawler, the *Grouse*, got under way. He steamed out 1.5 or 2 miles, searched for fifteen minutes, found nothing, and returned to his anchorage (he didn't wake the Skipper: 'that's the way we do things in trawlers'). An hour later, the 5th Fleet Sweeping Flotilla of trawlers came out of Hoy Sound and began a routine sweep for mines; they soon found oil, wreckage and the body of Midshipman Cotter of the *Pheasant* in two lifebelts. Another body sank out of reach. A coat was found, belonging to another *Pheasant* officer, thought to be Acting Lieutenant Henry W E Hearn the First Lieutenant; one sleeve of this was inside out, suggesting that he had struggled out of it in the water. Attempts to revive Midshipman Cotter failed; one witness said he was just alive in the water but died as he was being taken aboard. His watch had stopped at 0610/11hrs and had water behind the glass. His face was blackened but he looked very peaceful. His body was buried in Lyness Naval Cemetery.

The enquiry found that the ship was mined, probably by a drifting

mine which had broken loose from the Whiten Bank field[1]. It is thought that the mine could have set off a magazine, but that an accidental explosion was unlikely. It also said that it was a pity the *Grouse* had not tried harder. The Enquiry Files in the Public Record Office are ADM 137/3218 & ADM 137/3716.

Very little is known about the *Pheasant*; probably because she was lost so soon after commissioning – there does not even seem to be a photo of her. The *Simoom*, an 'R', very similar to an 'M', was torpedoed on 23 January; her forward magazine exploded, destroying her as far back as her bridge, killing the captain and many others, but the rest of her remained afloat until she was sunk as impossible to tow home. The suggestion has been made that two ships were mined more or less simultaneously, which was possible if a lot of mines broke adrift at the same time. Finally, the *Pheasant* may have been sunk by a U-boat, which was itself lost soon afterwards. One 'possible' is known, *UC–43*, a minelayer – which sailed on 25 February and was sunk by HM Submarine *G–13* off Muckle Flugga, the north point of the Shetlands, on 10 March.

Two other British destroyers were lost with all hands in the First World War. The *Racoon* was wrecked in a snowstorm outside Lough Swilly, Ireland, on 9 January 1918; radio distress signals were received from her but rescue was impossible. Her wreck was found by fishermen during 1996. On 12 January, 1918, the *Opal* and *Narbrough* were wrecked off the Orkneys, also in a snowstorm. One man survived from the *Opal* and radio distress messages were received from her, but again the weather made rescue impossible.

The search for the *Pheasant* began in 1994; the Army Sub-Aqua Club were seeking a dive target in the Orkneys for 1995, and the writer, who had enquired about their 1991 Jutland dives, suggested her, as she was known to have been lost in that area but had never been located. A preliminary visit in 1995 showed that base facilities were available for a diving team, and that fishermen had been snagging their nets in the 'area of probability' for years. It was decided to postpone Phase II, involving deeper diving, until the spring of 1996, when 'mixed-gas' diving training had been completed and better weather could be hoped for.

The 1996 expedition arrived at the Ness Battery by Hoy Sound in May 1996 and deep dives began on the 13th Diving conditions were extremely difficult; tide tables were useless, due to the rapid and unpredictable flow of water, and the depth, around 80 metres, meant that multigas or 'technical' diving techniques had to be used, with several pauses on descent and ascent. Each dive was planned for 77 minutes by a pair of divers, of which only 14 minutes could be spent on the bottom. The search involved skilled diving, hard work and considerable danger. A towed sonar made three contacts close to the position fixed by the trawler *Kildonan Castle* on the day of the destroyer's loss. The wreck of the *Pheasant* was found by the second pair of divers down, who landed on deck close to the ship's torpedo tubes. Damage extended as far aft as the engine room.

The deck had separated from the hull, which lay on its side. The ship was badly broken up as far aft as the engine room. Several 4in shells, probably from a ready-use rack, were found, also an electrical distribution box, thought to have come from the back of the bridge. Much thin plating was thought to have come from the ship's three funnels. One of her three boilers was intact, probably cold at the time of her loss; two boilers would permit up to 24–25 knots. She lay at a mean depth of 82 metres, heading roughly east and west, in Latitude 58°52.07′ North, Longitude 03°27.41′ West, 1.5–2nm southwest of Hoy and about seven nm – round a headland – from the entrance to Hoy Sound; this agrees fairly well with the 40 minutes between her leaving the sound and the explosion being heard.

Videos of the wreck were hampered by the fact that only divers' torches were available, and no positive identification could be made, although, the *Pheasant* was the only destroyer lost immediately west of the Orkneys. All the sixty-seven British destroyers lost in the First World War are now accounted for, and this deep and

tricky dive was executed safely. Since this expedition, another team have found the ship's bow and her foremost 4in gun. The Army dive team are drawing up a detailed report, but the mystery surrounding the *Pheasant* is now at last largely dispelled.

ANDREW GORDON'S JUTLAND
David K Brown adds a supplementary note to Antony Preston's review of The Rules of the Game *by Andrew Gordon (John Murray, 1996) which appeared in* Warship *1996, p188.*

I feel bound to add a personal note on this fascinating book. The review seems to me to show the Battle of Jutland as a special example of the general rule that, in all services in all nations, peacetime leaders rarely succeed in war, Andrew Cunningham being a rare exception. Gordon is clearly right in his central theme of lack of initiative, even at quite high level. There are far too many well-documented stories from Jutland of captains failing to open fire or even to report an enemy sighting, seeing this as the admiral's job.

The one area in which I would disagree is in the ability of Beatty. There are two types of rebel against a conventional hierarchy: those who want more initiative and those who are too idle to live up to primary standards. In my view, Beatty's signalling failures in earlier battles, his failure to meet Evan-Thomas before the battle, further signalling failures and his neglect of keeping Jellicoe informed suggest that his rebellion was from incompetence and this is supported by his postwar attempts to alter the record. I hasten to add that I am not pro-Jellicoe, although he did at least reach bare competence.

I am also concerned by the difference between Gordon's account and that of Layman (*see Naval Books of the Year*) on the attitudes of Jellicoe, Beatty and others to naval aviation. It is possible that they were conventional and formal in their main business, the clash of battle lines, while acting in

more progressive style on the more peripheral subject of aviation. There are many subplots in this story.

NEWS FROM VARIOUS WARSHIP MUSEUMS AND OTHER NAVAL ESTABLISHMENTS

ROYAL NAVAL MUSEUM, PORTSMOUTH
In September 1997 building work began on the Royal Naval Museum's £10-million, five-year development plan to create new and exciting displays, exhibitions and a state-of-the-art research centre. The scheme, made possible by a grant of £2.8 million from the National Heritage Lottery Fund, will also see the creation of vastly improved collection storage facilities. A key feature of the plan is an exhibition of HMS *Victory*, Nelson's flagship at the Battle of Trafalgar, which includes the 'Trafalgar Experience' – the sights, sounds and smells of the battle – the 'Gundeck' – an interactive exploration of life on board – and a new and dramatic presentation of Wyllie's panoramic painting of the battle.

OPEN MUSEUM
As part of the National Maritime Museum's commitment to providing wider public access to its collections and a broader understanding of their significance, it is running a programme of course and lectures under the title 'Open Museum'. The events, organised in association with Goldsmiths College, University of London, will run from October 1997 through to June 1998, and will explore diverse topics from aspects of the sea and shipping to time, astronomy, and navigation, local history and the arts.

The programme offers something for people of all ages, whether learning for pleasure or academic study. A number of one-day 'Hidden Collections' seminars will be held for enthusiasts to go behind the scenes to view some of the museum's reserve collections, including ship models and plans, ceramics, oil paintings, prints and drawings, historic photographs, scientific and navigational material, or to see conservators at work.

Open Museum speakers are drawn from the National Maritime Museum, other major national museums, universities and colleges, and from specialist societies and institutions. All are experts in their chosen fields.

Further information can be obtained from National Maritime Museum, Romney Road, Greenwich, London, SE10 9NF, Tel: 0181 312 6747, Internet: http://www. nmm.ac.uk

MARINEMUSEUM, DEN HELDER, THE NETHERLANDS

From 1997 this national naval museum consists of a new central building with a large video/lecture room. The museum's old monumental building has been completely restored, providing further space for a number of special temporary exhibitions as well as its permanent collection.

Attractions include the triple-hull submarine *Tonijn* (1966) (*pictured below*) of the *Dolfijn* class. This type of submarine formed the heart of the Royal Netherlands Navy submarine fleet between 1960 and 1991. Also open to inspection is the minesweeper *Abraham Crijnssen* (1936), which became famous for the spectacular way it escaped the Japanese invasion force in 1942. It was camouflaged with branches and foliage and thus was able to sail to Australia. Restoration is being carried out to a landing craft and various guns. In the future a large boathouse will be open to the public.

Situated nearby is the Dockyard museum, where there are two

restoration projects: the hydrograph *Snellius* (1952) and the old gunboat (steam warship 4th class) *Bonaire* (1880).

'FORTRESS GUERNSEY' SYMPOSIUM

Under the banner 'Fortress Guernsey' the Bailiwick of Guernsey proposes to hold an International Symposium between 5 and 10 June 1998. The main theme of the event, 'Outposts of the Realm', will address the role of the islands of Guernsey, Alderney and Sark in the maritime defence of Britain from the 13th century to the Second World War. This is the first such event to be held in the Channel Islands and the presentation and discussions will be of a general nature covering the whole historical perspective under review, taking in many of the surviving sites in the islands. For the main part, the symposium will take place on Guernsey. A one-day visit to the island of Alderney will also be included. A leaflet can be obtained by writing to Fortress Guernsey International Symposium, c/o Guernsey Tourist Board, PO Box 23, St Peter Port, Guernsey, Channel Islands, GY1 3AN, Tel: 01481 726611, Fax: 01481 721246.

USS *CONSTITUTION*

The 200-year-old frigate USS *Constitution* went to sea in July 1997, her first voyage under sail for 116 years. She is manned by a crew of Naval Academy midshipmen, active and reserve US Navy personnel and Navy civilians. The history of taking

famous ships to sea is not a happy one, witness the loss of the *Foudroyant* in the 1880s, but the US Navy has promised that this veteran of the War of 1812 will always be under close escort from a pair of frigates and will be connected by a towline.　　AP

'HUMAN TORPEDOES'

A report in the *Times* on 20 August 1997 noting the restoration of a 'human torpedo' or Chariot Mk II raised some eyebrows when it suggested that this was a unique example. The report also talked about the Chariot as a 'missile', suggesting it was 'fired' by a submarine at its target, whereas it was what is known today as a swimmer-delivery vehicle. An example of the original Italian Navy '*Maiale*' ('pig'), from which the Chariot Mk I was copied, can be seen in the Arsenal Museum at La Spezia. The restored Chariot Mk II is in display at the Teesside Training and Enterprise Council near Middlesbrough.　　AP

HMS *CAVALIER*

The last classic fleet destroyer to serve in the Royal Navy, HMS *Cavalier*, seems to have come to the end of the road. She has been offered for sale by the South Tyneside Council and may be bought by a Malaysian theme-park operator. Despite the dedication of the HMS *Cavalier* Trust the last twenty years seem to have been a chapter of disasters as the destroyer was moved from one location to another, an 'economic refugee'.　　AP

NAVAL BOOKS OF THE YEAR

This section is divided into full-length reviews, short descriptive notices, a list of books announced, and naval videos.

R D Layman, Naval Aviation in the First World War. *Chatham Publishing, London, 1966.*
224 pages, 39 illustrations.
ISBN 1 86176 007 8. £22.50

This is one of the first wave of books from Chatham Publishing and it is a good start. The author, well known as one of the foremost naval aviation historians, describes his book as 'philosophical', omitting technical detail. He maintains that the contribution of aviation to naval operations in the First World War has been underrated and, in the case of Britain, there is a specific cause. As a matter of policy, it was decided that all aviation history should be considered as part of the RAF's official history and, as a result, there is little mention of the air in the naval history. Though the RAF history devotes space to maritime operations, the authors were not inclined to credit the Admiralty for their success.

In particular, the author debunks the myth of the battleship admiral who believed that the big gun would settle everything, dismissing aviation as an unimportant distraction. On the contrary, most admirals were enthusiastic supporters of aviation, sometimes to a fault, in expecting too much from these flimsy and unreliable flying machines.

Consideration is given to the use of naval aircraft in combat, in tactical and strategic attack, in reconnaissance and particularly in anti-submarine operations. It seems fairly clear that the Royal Naval Air Service (RNAS) was the leader in strategic bombing, although their attacks were mainly shore-based until the first real aircraft carrier, HMS *Argus*, was commissioned just before the Armistice. One may see the attack on the airship bases at Friedrichshafen on 21 November 1914 and on Cuxhaven the following month in this light. The big bombers which were just becoming operational at the end of the war were ordered by the RNAS, while on the other side the airship raids on England were initiated by the German Navy. The use of aircraft by German raiders is covered, as are operations such as those in the Dardanelles and the destruction of the *Königsberg*.

The book covers aviation in all navies, although the Royal Navy had by far the biggest force. At the end of its existence RNAS it operated some 3,000 heavier-than-air craft, 111 airships and about 200 balloons with 55,000 men. The US Navy was about two-thirds that size, France and Germany about half, while Russia and Italy had substantial forces too.

The illustrations are well chosen from a wide range of nations and most were new to this reviewer.

David K Brown, RCNC

James F Tent, E-boat Alert.
Airlife, Shrewsbury, 1996,
303 pages, 52 illustrations.
ISBN 1 85310 792 1. £19.95

This book tells the story of E-boat operations against the allied invasion of Normandy from the sinking of US tank landing ships (LSTs) in Lyme Bay in April 1944 to the virtual destruction of the Channel E-boat force by Bomber Command on 14 June. The book opens with a dramatic account of the attack on an invasion rehearsal in Lyme Bay, mainly in the words of survivors. The Royal Navy escort was inadequate and was not kept in touch with the threat, while the US LSTs were not made aware of any threat at all.

There follows an account of the history of fast torpedo boats, German ones in particular. Much attention is given to the few and not very successful German boats of the First World War while the much more effective British CMBs are dismissed briefly. However, by the outbreak of the Second World War the Germans had a small number of very effective craft. Their operations in the early part of the war are outlined before the book switches to a short but well-organised history of Bomber Command and of 617 Squadron in particular.

Turning to the invasion itself, there are a number of tables showing that, in the early days, the small number of E-boats caused serious damage to the allied fleets. The raids on Le Havre put an end to this; the daylight attack was led by 22 Lancasters of 617 Squadron, each carrying a Barnes Wallis 12,000lb 'Tallboy' bomb and followed by other Lancasters with smaller but more numerous bombs, 1,200 tons in all. This was followed by a night raid. As a result the Germans lost three small destroyers with two more out of action and 13 E-boats sunk or permanently out of action, together with numerous minesweepers and other smaller ships.

The success of the E-boat was largely due to its successful and powerful Daimler-Benz diesels and the author has some interesting views on these. Production was demanding in skilled labour, scarce materials and specialised machine tools; at best, output was only ten units a month. Life between overhauls was only 400 hours. By 1944 the armament of the E-boat and its electronics were inadequate, and the author suggests they should have been backed up by smaller, cheaper and more numerous craft.

The general style of the E-boat may be seen as the forerunner of most current fast attack craft (FACs) and they were, in general, very good sea boats. Peter Scott (in *The Battle of the Narrow Seas*) makes an interesting comparison with the 'D'-type Fairmiles which went out to receive two surrendered E-boats at the war's end. The Germans had crossed the North Sea at an easy 32 knots but had to slow to 20 knots, which was the best the 'D's could do in a moderate sea – the E-boats were much drier. On the other hand, the Fairmiles rolled much less and hence were better gun platforms with heavier armament.

This is an interesting book which uses sources little known in the UK, and many of the photographs are unfamiliar and useful; but there are a number of annoying errors, mainly trivial. One in particular I must object to: an LST designed by Rowland Baker would not sink if the vehicle deck were flooded.

David K Brown, RCNC

John Parker, SBS: The Inside Story of the Special Boat Service. *Headline, 1997. £16.99*

This is a gripping account of some of the adventures, over the last fifty or so years, of men who preferred looking for and engaging the enemy in small parties, rather than in a battleship or an army.

The adventures, often told in the men's own words, are the best part of the book. The 'inside story' is complicated and often difficult to follow:

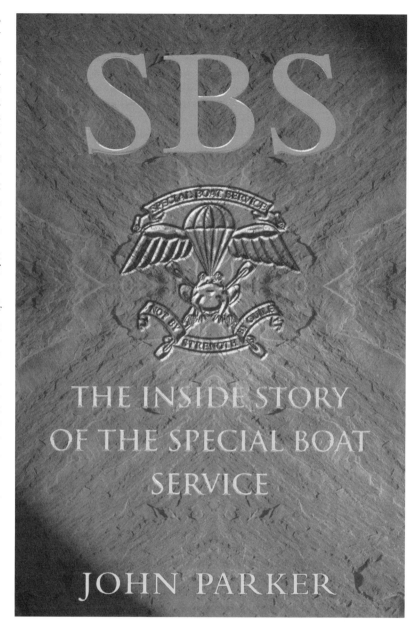

decisions and events were frequently muddled, there was jealousy from members of the regular forces, and incomprehension, reluctance and incompetence from many authorities.

The SBS was founded in 1941 by soldiers chiefly engaged in sabotage against the enemy in the Mediterranean. A naval organisation called Combined Operations Pilotage Parties (COPP) was founded in 1942 by a navigator, Lieutenant-Commander Nigel Willmott, RN, who had realised that since Hitler now commanded most of the coast of Europe, Britain would soon have to land armies on

beaches and had not studied how to do this: existing charts and air photographs were not nearly enough. Actual reconnaissance under the direction of trained hydrographers or navigators, swimming into the beaches at night, would be needed. Willmott's ideas were at first turned down: but Operation 'Torch', the North African landings in November 1942, proved how right Willmott was – not, incidentally, as stated on p89 of Parker's book, the Dieppe landings, which were hardly an invasion. Lack of preparations recommended for the North African landings nearly caused a major disaster, only avoided because there was no serious opposition.

I must here declare an interest: I was a member of COPP 7, which was trained in cold home waters and then became the first COPP party to operate in warm waters off Burma and Sumatra. Parker devotes a whole and very fair chapter to COPP. He might, I think, have said a bit more about our training. For the swimmer at night off enemy shores to rendezvous with his canoe, and for the canoe to find its submarine or other carrier, required endless practice and some luck. We learned that the dangers of the job were far more from the weather than from the enemy. The remarkable and successful reconnaissances of the Normandy beaches proved that.

What we did during the war was taken over by the SBS. Parker writes that COPP techniques still held good fifty years later 'and were demonstrated with the first British task force landings in the Falklands, for which the SBS opened the door'.

The grim dramas of SBS involvement in the Falklands are well told, as is the extraordinary story, told 'with benefit of previously unpublished detail', of terrorists threatening to blow up the *QE2* (in mid-Atlantic) if \$350,000 in cash was not paid by the following day. The threat was taken seriously and involved a four-man SBS parachute drop close to the QE2. The drop was made successfully (only just), no bombs were ever found, and the money was never picked up. A strange story.

And then there was Saddam Hussein and the Gulf War, various terrorist attacks, and the IRA. SBS units have been continuously busy; we can be proud of them, and admire this excellent book.

Ruari McLean

Robert Dumas and Jean Moulin, Les Escorteurs d'Escadre. *Marines Edition, 1997. 280 pages, 300 illustrations. ISBN 2 909675 29 7. 395 F*

Jean Moulin was the author of *L'Escorteur Maille-Brézé,* written to commemorate that vessel's preservation as a museum ship at Nantes.

Robert Dumas is well known to readers of *Warship* for his work on the early French dreadnoughts, and has written a number of monographs on the later French battleships for the same publisher. They have now produced a book celebrating the eighteen 'Fleet Escorts' of the T47, T53 and T56 classes built after the war.

The first section deals with the genesis of the design, and contains some interesting insights into French thinking of the period. The T47 was essentially an attempt to replicate the US *Gearing* class, but using French methods of construction (hence the raised forecastle and the revised layout of the main armament) and home-grown weapons and electronics. The result was a 'fighting carrier escort' with a useful dual-purpose armament, but with relatively little attention given to anti-submarine warfare (short homing torpedoes were subsequently added at the design stage). Handsome though they were, the ships were conceptually obsolescent by the time they were completed, and major rebuilding was necessary during the 1960s to equip them for modern warfare.

The technical section which follows is packed with information, and is illustrated with detailed drawings accompanied by an outstanding series of close-up photographs of the various items of equipment described in the text. There is full coverage both of the weapons systems originally fitted and of the modifications made at refits. The publisher is to be congratulated on the clarity of the presentation of this section; the tables are excellent, and the photos are used to best effect.

The second half of the book, in the *Marines* tradition, is dedicated to a detailed service history of each of the eighteen ships of the series. The histories are accompanied by photographs and line drawings showing the ships' appearance at the various stages of their careers.

This is a first-class book, and I hope it will be but the first of a series on other classes of ship built for the postwar *Marine Nationale.*

John Jordan

David Lyon, The First Destroyers. *Chatham Publishing, 1996. 128 pages, 197 photographs and drawings. ISBN 1 86176 005 1. £30*

I must declare an interest. As a former colleague of the author I spent many hours discussing the subject of torpedo boats and destroyers, which helps to explain his kind comments in the Acknowledgements. That said, this handsome book enshrines David Lyon's unique grasp of his subject, resulting from assiduous research in private shipbuilders' records and the collection of Admiralty technical material, Ships' Covers, 'as fitted' drawings, specifications etc, held in the National Maritime Museum.

Nothing has been spared to give the reader satisfaction: a section on terminology, pre-history, a detailed design history from the first '26-knotters' to the last '30-knotters' delivered as late as 1909, details on each builder, clear photographs and the first comprehensive view of technical drawings. The icing on the cake is a set of detailed cut-away drawings of the first 'torpedo boat destroyer' or TBD, HMS *Havock,* and a modeller's drawing of HMS *Velox,* all drawn by John Roberts.

The TBD epitomised the enormous advantages to the Royal Navy of the partnership between industry and the Admiralty. The torpedo gunboats (TGBs) had apparently proved unsatisfactory as a counter to the French torpedo boats (TBs) in fair weather. Under the energetic leadership of the Controller, Capt J A Fisher, RN, and equally enthusiastic prompting from the specialist builders, the Admiralty turned to Thornycroft and Yarrow to build two prototypes each (*Daring* and *Decoy* from the former, *Havock* and *Hornet* from the latter). The early ships had considerable drawbacks, but the Admiralty was sufficiently impressed to throw open the competition for later programmes to the greatest number of shipyards. They were all fragile and never capable of making their designed speeds, but they were a great improvement over the TBs. More important, they proved so successful as a counter to the French TB threat that all the leading navies started to build TBDs.

ShipShape

The First Destroyers

David Lyon

the Royal Navy's Coastal Forces in the Second World War. Although it does not claim to be a technical history, the author has shown how design and production interacted with operational experience. Many of the events have been described in greater detail elsewhere, but the author sheds light on the prewar efforts to reintroduce small, high-speed torpedo craft to the Royal Navy. He also describes the very early wartime efforts of the Malta-based motor torpedo boats (MTBs) and the evolution of the Motor Gun Boat (MGB) to meet changing tactical needs. Not all the photographs are new, but they are well captioned. Some are from private collections, and one in particular stands out: a view of Ostend after the disastrous explosion on 14 February 1945. After *MTB255* blew up, the fire destroyed virtually all the MTBs of the Canadian 29th Flotilla.

Antony Preston

Denis Griffiths, Steam at Sea. *Conway Maritime Press, London, 1997. 252 pages, 315 illustrations. ISBN 0 85177 66 3. £30*

Good books on the history of marine engineering are rare and this fine work by a experienced writer who is, himself, a marine engineer is welcome indeed. Dr Griffiths covers both merchant ships and warships in separate chapters of his book. The treatment is broadly chronological but subdivided into engines – paddle, screw, compound, triple-expansion and turbine – boilers in two chapters, and auxiliaries. Nuclear steam plants are included. The coverage of auxiliary machinery and of details such as tube fastenings is particularly interesting. The importance of apparently minor features such as piston rings and the corrugated furnace is well brought out. I loved the account of a trial of hydraulic steering in *Achilles* in 1869. The motor was powered by sea pressure and discharged into the bilges from which the sea was pumped out. It was not repeated! The gradual shift from coal to oil is described.

One chapter is devoted to the

As the author shows, TBD design was at the leading edge of contemporary shipbuilding and engineering capability, but the prototypes created a sound basis for development. Turbines eventually replaced triple-expansion engines, and not even the unrelated loss of the prototypes *Viper* and *Cobra* could delay the introduction of the Parsons turbine at the end of the '30-knotter' programmes.

This book is a handsome tribute to the designers, builders and operators of the first TBDs, and is a model of how a technical history should be written. The standard of production, moreover, matches the treatment of what is undoubtedly the definitive history of these innovative warships.

Antony Preston

David Jefferson, Coastal Forces at War. *Patrick Stephens Ltd, 1996. 208 pages, 106 photographs. ISBN 1 85260 499 9. £17.99*

This is a small but very useful book, which gives a very good overview of

engineer at sea, with discipline as a major problem. Naval engineers had no direct authority and had to bring their men before a seaman officer for discipline. Merchant-navy engineers had an even rougher time and might get involved in fisticuffs. Particularly in the merchant navy, pay was quite good and there were plenty of young men willing to take up the challenge. Gradually, engineers attained professional authority, helped by the formation of the Institute of Marine Engineers.

The book is aimed at the general reader but the author uses his skill as a teacher in putting over quite difficult points of engineering in a clear and simple fashion. I like his description of the parallel-motion linkages in some early engines and also his account of the difference between impulse and reaction turbines.

The numerous illustrations are an outstanding feature of the book; many are reproductions of contemporary line drawings and are clearly reproduced and are directly relevant to the text. The author makes clear his view that British shipowners' reluctance to shift from steam to diesel in the 1930s was an important factor in the decline of British merchant shipping.

I would put a slightly different emphasis on the Admiralty's encouragement of innovation in marine engineering particularly concerning the screw propeller and, later, the Parsons steam turbine. The battleship *Victoria* had a very early turbine in 1885 driving a dynamo for lighting and *Turbinia*'s appearance at the 1897 review was no surprise to the Admiralty since both the E-in-C and DNC had been out on earlier trials. Sennett's work on boiler safety around 1888, which led to warship boilers being considerably lighter than those of merchant ships with, in all probability, greater safety, was another example of Admiralty initiative. It is also of interest that, though there was prejudice against engineer officers at lower level, there does not seem to be any instance of the Board failing to take the professional advice of their outstanding Engineers-in-Chief. This book should be on every engineer's shelf.

David K Brown, RCNC

David K Brown, Warrior to Dreadnought, Warship Development 1860–1905. *Chatham Publishing, 1997. 224 pages, many photographs, drawings and diagrams. ISBN 1 86176 0221. £35*

This is a truly magnificent effort, both in content and presentation, a long overdue tribute to the people who designed and built the Royal Navy's ships from the mid-Victorian era of the ironclad battleship, through to the Edwardian heyday, before the Anglo-German arms race got into its stride. Although not all the photographs are unknown (it would be virtually impossible at this late stage to find new collections) they are well reproduced and the format permits many to be large. A large number of 'as fitted' drawings are also reproduced.

The author has the authority, as former Deputy chief Naval Architect of the Royal Corps of Naval Constructors and a prime mover in alerting RCNC colleagues to the importance of design history, to demolish the myths about the Victorian Navy and to give it the credit it deserves. Inevitably the book devotes a lot of space to the evolution of the battleship, David Brown deals with cruisers, torpedo boats, destroyers and lesser craft. He also puts them into the correct political and economic contexts, showing how foreign designs effected British plans.

As a former constructor, his insights into the procurement process are fascinating. One of the many points he makes is the way in which the Childers 'reforms' virtually neutered the staff function of the Admiralty Board. This gave the design team great freedom, but it resulted in a number of design features which pandered to the passing whims of admirals and their political masters. In this context, the achievements of Sir William White and his team can be seen to be even more impressive than previously thought.

Although the book deals with the Royal Navy rather than its competitors, as the world leader in technology and tactical skill, its influence was paramount. Its faults stemmed primarily from the lack of relevant

war-experience, not from an antipathy to new ideas.

Antony Preston

René Greger, Battleships of the World. *Greenhill Books. 258 pages, 192 photographs, about 100 drawings. ISBN 1 85367 275 0. £29.95*

In a single book, not very large, the author attempts to describe all the world's battleships of this century, a topic which would normally run over several thick volumes. By and large, he has been successful and this is a useful survey for those who do not wish to delve too deep.

The book opens with an excellent introduction outlining the development of the battleship from the mid-nineteenth century. There are plenty of tables comparing the strengths of the navies. Each of the major powers is considered in turn, starting with Germany. This begins with eleven pages on the background to German battleships up to the end of the Second World War. The individual classes of battleships and battlecruisers are described with one page per class containing an excellent plan and elevation and one or two photos as well as the text. The photos are very good throughout but the aerial pictures of the First World War German ships are outstanding. I would disagree strongly with the author's practice of adding together the thickness of all decks and calling the sum 'deck' armour. This is not the way a shell sees it. The German section continues with seven pages of build up to the Second World War and describes the later ships in similar style: a total of thirty-one pages.

Other major powers are treated in similar style – the Royal Navy gets fifty-five pages, the US Navy forty. Finally, there are eleven pages on the battleships of minor powers.

The book was originally published in German and has been admirably translated by Geoffrey Brooks. This leads to a different viewpoint from that of many British writers which is often welcome. Sometimes it goes too far: it is incorrect to say (p100) that *Marlborough* returned from Jutland under tow, she arrived alongside under her own power. Similarly, it is incorrect in saying that *Seydlitz* reached the German coast under her own power but she then rested on the bottom until pumped out. 'Best' is word to avoid and after examination of the wreck few would apply it to *Bismarck*, a repeat *Baden* with bigger engines. (p59) Though the naval limitation treaties are outlined, it is not brought out that the Axis powers grossly broke the limits which they had agreed to.

Overall, the book is a useful summary of the world's battleship building with many excellent and little-known illustrations.

David K Brown, RCNC

Raimondo Luraghi, A History of the Confederate Navy. *Chatham Publishing, London, 1996, 535 pages, 21 illustrations, 14 maps. ISBN 1 86176 021 3. £30.00*

The hero of this detailed account is undoubtedly Stephen R Mallory, the Confederate Secretary of the Navy, who had a vision of winning command of the sea by using advanced technology such as armoured ships and powerful breech-loading guns. Much of the book describes the problems of implementing this vision in a Confederacy with inadequate supplies of iron, little industry, poor communications and lacking in industrial management skills.

Imaginative design and improvisation overcame some of these problems and led to the construction of a number of powerful ironclads of which several had to be destroyed before completion to prevent their capture by advancing Union forces. The Confederacy carried out the first successful attack by a submarine and built some ingenious torpedo boats, but all this came against a background of chaos. Iron was scarce so armour was rolled from railway lines and there were cases in which a railway line ripped up for its iron was found to be an essential logistic link. There were other cases in which essential items were thrown off trains by local 'war lords' to make way for less important goods.

The numerous actions are clearly

described, helped by excellent maps which emphasise the importance of the few railways then operating. The illustrations are poorly reproduced and most are well known. This book was originally published in Italian and has been translated. This may account for a lack of clarity in some of the more technical passages, some of which are almost incomprehensible, for instance, the variation of the specific gravity of iron with its carbon content.

The American Civil War was only the second to involve novel technologies in naval warfare such as armour and breech-loading guns and is an interesting case study of the influence of technology. This book, written from the Confederate viewpoint, is an important addition to the literature.

David K Brown, RCNC

Bernard Ireland and Tony Gibbons, Jane's Battleships of the 20th Century. *HarperCollins, 1996. 192 pages, many drawings and photographs. ISBN 0 00 479997 7. £25*

Covering capital ships from 1900 to the 'final curtain' for the USS *Iowa* and USS *Missouri* in the Gulf War six years ago, the book deals with navies in alphabetical order. Each section contains spreads covering aspects such as the Washington Treaty, hunting the *Bismarck*, etc. The text is competent but adds little that is new. The same can be said for most of the photographs, and one senses a temptation to 'pad' with a number of barely relevant views of cruisers and aircraft carriers, and even a destroyer and an

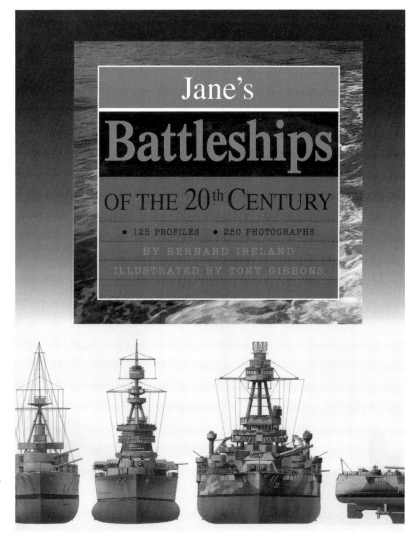

F–117 'stealth' fighter. It is stretching credibility to include the Russian *Kirov/Admiral Ushakov* class ships. They were always rated by the Russian Navy as nuclear missile cruisers, and only as 'battlecruisers' by Western doom-mongers. One solecism caught my eye: there was no such person as 'Admiral Sir "Jackie" Fisher'. Refer to the great reformer by his nickname, his rank or his title as you wish, but an amalgam is simply sloppy.

The artwork appeared in an earlier book by Tony Gibbons, published by Salamander in 1983. Although decorative, it is disappointig, lacking the degree of accuracy in detail demanded by modellers or devotees of ship equipment. A great deal of effort has gone into providing 'realistic' rust streaks and shading to suggest flare and hull-shape, but this reviewer found it unconvincing, when compared with line-drawings done by such masters of their craft as R A Burt and John Roberts. The verdict must be that £25 ($30 in the United States and $42 in luckless Canada) is a stiff price to pay for some standard information and re-used artwork.

Antony Preston

Robert Jackson, Suez: The Forgotten Invasion. *Airlife, Shrewsbury, 1996, 153 pages, 30 photographs, 5 maps. ISBN 1 85310 7743. £12.95 (paperback)*

Though there have been many books on the politics of the Suez operation 'Musketeer', there has been little on the military aspects. This excellent little book gives a clear outline of the successes and failures of that operation. Political manoeuvring meant that there was no chance of surprise, but on the other hand, there was no pre-emptive strike on the Anglo-French force.

Substantial numbers of French and British aircraft were used to destroy the generally more modern Egyptian aircraft on the ground. Bombing attacks on runways were ineffective but allied fighter-bombers were very successful. Landings were spearheaded by a parachute drop and followed by helicopter landings. Despite the capacity of the small

helicopters available (three men), the landings were successful and an omen for the future.

The landing area was cleared quickly and the main force with tanks cleared the towns of Port Said and Port Fuad and began to press down the canal before being stopped by the ceasefire. We learnt that the use of force in limited operations was to be a feature of modern life, one which could not be solved by nuclear weapons. Amphibious and airborne operations regained importance. The brief quarrel with the USA was soon cured – at least in military matters.

The photographs are clear and well reproduced, showing the difficulty in hitting airfield runways. The maps are excellent.

David K Brown, RCNC

W Laird Clowes, The Royal Navy: A History from the Earliest Times to 1900, Vol 1. *Chatham Publishing, London, 1996. 722 pages, 100 illustrations. ISBN 1 86176 010 8. £18*

Laird Clowes's history was originally published in seven volumes between 1897 and 1903 and is now appearing in a paperback facsimile edition. He was assisted in this work by a distinguished group of co-authors: Mahan, Markham, Wilson and Theodore Roosevelt. Much of the original introduction was devoted to deploring the paucity and quality of overall naval history in the United Kingdom. That his work is worth reprinting and reading a hundred years later shows how little has changed and how little it is recognised that Britain's prosperity was based on seapower.

Volume I takes the story from near-legendary early times to the Spanish Armada in a comprehensive and readable style. Clearly, there are many specific topics which have been overtaken by later research and by the recovery of vessels such as the Bremen cog *Vasa* and the *Mary Rose*. However, there is no alternative currently available which follows the complete sweep of history. References are comprehensive so that serious students may decide whether a passage remains acceptable while the less

serious can enjoy the story, which is basically sound.

The great war with Spain is covered at length with the preliminaries, the raid on Cadiz and the planning of the Armada and its fate. The story is largely told by lengthy quotations from contemporary writers, Spanish as well as English. Voyages of exploration are described by Sir Clements Markham. The illustrations are mainly well known and have reproduced fairly well.

David K Brown, RCNC

A S Pavlov, Warships of the USSR and Russia 1945–1995. *Chatham Publishing, London, 1997. 350 pages, 300 photographs, 100 plans. ISBN 1 86176 039 6. £35*

The author is a naval architect who for many years kept his private records of Soviet and, later, Russian ship designs. Helped by his friends, he published the first edition of this book himself, even stitching the pages together. This much expanded English language version is edited by Dr Norman Friedman whose involvement goes far to give confidence in the overall accuracy of the material presented. The editor also supplies an informative introduction to the background of Soviet building programmes, including a very useful list of Central Design Bureaux.

The style of the book is straightforward: the usual parameters are presented in tabular form with photographs, and, in the case of the more important classes, plans as well. The numerous photographs are well selected, generally of good quality and most have not been seen before. There is usually a brief note on the background to the design and how it evolved. Designs which were not built are not covered explicitly but there may be a brief mention when such designs form a missing link to later construction.

Though the broad picture of the Soviet Navy is well known, there are many less familiar categories in this book. The very powerful river gunboats are little known and most interesting. There were a large number of hydrofoils and hovercraft, though few went into series production and the prototype WIGs are well covered. This book is strongly recommended to anyone interested in the history of this once-great navy. It is sad that most of the ships described are corroding away.

I am delighted that the author has named the designer for most classes!

David K Brown, RCNC

William Mowll, Building a Working Model Warship. *Chatham Publishing, London, 1997. 200 pages, 175 photographs, 75 drawings. ISBN 0 86176 019 . £24*

Many engineers enjoy making models, a sufficient excuse to review this fascinating book. The author describes in detail the task of building an 8-feet-long working model of HMS *Warrior* (1860). He begins with a brief history of the ship and her significance. The next chapter deals with the workshop, tools and materials, showing how modern procedures can be used to portray historic craftsmanship.

Making the various parts, hull, decks, boats, sails and flags etc, are described in detail in the following chapters. Each section clearly describes the work carried out and there are numerous photographs showing details of the work. If you have a few years to spare, it would be easy to follow the author's example. Understandably, the steam engine and boiler which drives the model are not replicas of *Warrior*'s Penn trunk engine. The funnels seem to be the height used in service and not the short version tried unsuccessfully on completion and reproduced on the ship itself.

The model was floated before the machinery went in to determine the weight and position of the ballast needed: four bricks and three buckets of water brought her to the designed waterline with a displacement of 145 pounds. The watertightness of the stern gland was also proved.

The book is easy and enjoyable to read. There are a few dubious touches in describing the real ship. The author attributes a major role in the design

to John Scott Russell, something which the Admiralty formally denied. He also says that she spent most of her time at sea under sail alone; Admiral Warsop gives the correct figures as 22 per cent sail alone, 36 per cent steam only and 42 per cent both. Perhaps this book will lead to a fleet of models!

David K Brown, RCNC

John S de Winser, Short Sea: Long War. *World Ship Society, PO Box 706, Gravesend, DA12 5UB, 1997. 160 pages, 132 illustrations. ISBN 0 905 617 86 X. £21 (£12 to Society Members) PLUS £1.50 P&P*

This excellent little book tells the Second World War story of 119 coastal ferries of the United Kingdom, France, Belgium and Holland. The book opens with a seven-page chronology of the war as it affected these ships. It continues with individual histories of the ships, grouped by the routes which they plied before the war, eg 'North Sea Passenger Ships'. Their wartime service took many far afield. Twenty-three supported the Mediterranean landings and other operations in that sea, they crossed the Atlantic, went to North Russia and to the Far East.

The author has identified no less than forty different wartime roles such as minelayers, balloon carriers, convoy escort etc, though the majority ended as some form of landing ship. Many of the foreign-owned ships served in the Royal Navy, usually, but not always under anglicised versions of their original name – eg *Köningin Emma* became *Queen Emma*. The smaller number of ships which served in the German Navy are also covered.

The photos are well reproduced and many have not been seen before. I particularly like the unusual pictures of convoy rescue vessels such as *Accrington* and *Melrose Abbey*. The few lower-quality pictures are action scenes, well justified by excitement. Modern navigators will probably be surprised at the number of collisions in those days when radar was in its

infancy and satellites undreamt of. My only complaint is that there should have been brief particulars of the ships whose careers are so well described. It is a worthy sequel to the author's *The D-Day Ships.*

David K Brown RCNC

I Sturton, (ed) All The World's Battleships, 1906 to the present. *Conway Maritime Press, London, 1997. 192 pages, over 500 photographs and drawings. ISBN 0 85177 691 4. £15*

The core of this book is formed by the text and tabular particulars from the battleship sections of Conway's *All the World's Fighting Ships 1906–21* and *1922–46*. The text has been corrected and amplified in places. In general, the source books had a single drawing of the ship as completed and new drawings have been added to represent major changes in appearance; for example, the *Queen Elizabeth* class now has three such drawings. Similarly, the number of photographs has been considerably increased.

The original authors were carefully chosen for their knowledge of their topics and Sturton, who is well known for his own books on battleships, has done a fine job of editing. The book provides details and illustrations of the ships of two world wars, backed by intelligent commentary.

The most important aspect of the book is its price. At only £15 it is remarkable value for money and if you do not already possess the 'Fighting Ship' volumes and want a record of the battleship, this book is highly recommended.

David K Brown, RCNC

NAVAL BOOKS ANNOUNCED

Norman Franks, Dark Sky, Deep Water. *Grub Street, 1997. £17.99*
First-hand reflections on the anti-U-boat campaign in European waters in the Second World War.

Norman Friedman, Seapower and Space. *Chatham Publishing, 1997. £25*

The impact of space capabilities on naval operations since the 1960s.

Eric Grove (ed), Great Battles of the Royal Navy. *Avebury, 1997. £14.99*

Illustrated accounts of twenty-five naval actions.

R Jackson, The Royal Navy in World War 2. *Airlife, 1997. £19.95*

Philip Kaplan, Wolfpack. *Aurum Press, 1997. £19.99*

The story of the U-boat crews.

Paul Kemp, U-Boat Destroyed. *Arms & Armour Press, 1997. £25*

Comprehensive summary of German submarine losses in both world wars.

Charles Owen, Plain Yarns from the Fleet. *Sutton Publishing, 1997. £18.99*

A view of the Royal Navy from 1900 to 1945.

Jürgen Rohwer, Allied Submarine Attacks of World War Two: European Theatre of Operations 1939–1945. *Greenhill Books, 1997. £20*

John and Noreen Steele, They Were Never Told: The Tragedy of HMS *Dasher. Argyll Publishing, 1997. £14.99*

Julian Thompson, The Imperial War Museum Book of the War at Sea. *Sidgwick & Jackson, 1997. £15.99*

The Second World War at sea as recorded by sailors of all ranks, in diaries, letters and interviews.

Professor William N Still, Jr (ed), The Confederate Navy: The Ships, Men and Organization, 1861–65. *Conway Maritime Press, 1997. £40*

The only complete guide to every aspect of the short-lived Confederate States Navy.

INTERNET

In August 1997 British computer games company On-line launched its unique 3D Internet naval simulation game, *Iron Wolves*. The game allows players worldwide to enter an exciting, ever-evolving, real-time sea war, fighting against each other in either a U-boat, a corvette, a destroyer, or a heavy submarine – all of which are authentically armed and equipped – taking on the drones, or doing both. The virtual ocean has attracted attention from naval and computer enthusiasts alike as far afield as the West Indies, Australia, South Korea and the United States, with players battling it out twenty-four hours a day. Players are charged £6.00 per fortnight for unlimited play, and there are no extra charges during this period. Anyone interested can get a feel of *Iron Wolves* by signing up for a free trial game, playing as a 'non-attacking' tanker.

Iron Wolves is compatible with Windows 95, and Windows NT 4.0. It can be played over the Internet with a keyboard or a mouse, has 256-colour or 16-bit graphics and uses Direct X for its authentic, digitised sound effects. Additional information and screen shots are on the World Wide Web at http://www.on-line.co.uk/iw.

THE NAVAL YEAR IN REVIEW

Antony Preston looks at current naval developments around the world, noting new construction and developing trends.

West European Navies

Albania: The Albanian Navy has virtually ceased to exist as a result of the collapse of government authority. At least one of the surviving Russian-built PO–2-type patrol craft sank in the Adriatic when intercepted by Italian warships trying to stem the flow of refugees. Ironically, things had been looking better last year, when three ex-US Navy Mk III patrol craft and two new SeaArk 15-tonne craft were acquired. The last of the Soviet Project 613 'Whiskey'-type diesel-electric submarines (SSKs), the *Qemel*, was taken out of service at the end of 1995.

Denmark: The Royal Danish Navy is taking part in joint discussions with its neighbours Norway and Sweden to seek a common-hull replacement for its *Tumleren* and *Narhvalen* class submarines (*see Sweden*).

Finland: The Finnish Navy has ordered the first of a new group of improved *Rauma* class fast attack craft (FACs). Although it has observer-status in the Swedish 'Viking' submarine project, talk of buying submarines appears to have come to nothing, but this may change. Four of the six *Kuha*-type minesweepers are being modernised by the Tyovenne shipyard. This includes fitting a Reson SeaBat mine-avoidance sonar and lengthening the hull.

France: In July last year the French Ministry of Defence confirmed severe cuts to the strength of the *Marine*

Nationale. This meant the paying-off of the carrier *Clemenceau*, while her sister *Foch* will go into reserve as soon as the new nuclear-powered carrier (CVN) *Charles de Gaulle* becomes operational in 1999. In theory the *Foch* will be recommissioned when the *Charles de Gaulle* goes into dockyard hands for a major refit, but the CVN does not get her first *Rafale*-M squadron until 2004. In effect the French Navy will be reduced to a single carrier.

The fourth and final unit of the *Rubis* class nuclear attack submarines (SSNs) completed an upgrading, which makes them equal to their half-sisters of the *Améthyste* class. The *Agosta* class diesel-electric submarines (SSKs) will not be replaced when they pay off after the turn of the century. The nuclear strategic missile submarine (SSBN) *Le Triomphant* fired an M45 missile successfully (following a failed launch), and began her first operational deployment earlier this year. *Le Téméraire* will start her first patrol next year.

Although the surface fleet will be smaller, the *Georges Leygues* class destroyers are having their air-defence capability improved. The second *La Fayette* class frigate, the *Surcouf*, has been commissioned, and the *Courbet* is at sea on extended trials. The fifth unit, fitting out at Lorient in July this year, was to have been named *Guépratte*, will now be called *Aconit*, taking the name of the large frigate which is to be paid off early and commemorating the Free French 'Flower' class corvette. The sixth *La Fayette* will not be built.

Three redundant Tripartite mine-hunters were bought from the Belgian Navy late last year, increasing the French total to thirteen units. The new names are *Cephée* (ex-*Fuchsia*), *Verseau* (ex-*Iris*) and *Capricorne* (ex-*Dianthus*), and the ships sailed for Brest this summer.

French amphibious forces have survived the cuts, and two more *Foudre* class amphibious dock transports (LPDs) have been approved, one to replace the 33-year-old helicopter carrier/training ship *Jeanne d'Arc*. The first should be laid down in 2001 and the second in 2003, but French naval building plans are notorious for being derailed.

Germany: The German Navy changed its name from the *Bundesmarine* to *Deutschemarine* in January last year to reflect the unified nation. Tight constraints on defence spending mean that several programmes have moved to the right, but replacement of obsolescent tonnage is now very urgent. The first Type 212 SSK will be laid down in September next year, and the four will be delivered in 2003–2006, but the current total of twelve Type 206A boats will fall to four by 2005. Negotiations have just been completed with Indonesia to sell five unmodernised Type 206 boats.

Funding for three Type 124 *Sachsen* class frigates was approved late last year, with an option for a fourth, the *Thüringen*. They will replace the three *Lütjens* class US-built destroyers, but there seems little chance of the option being exercised for the fourth ship. The *Mecklenburg-*

Vorpommern, last of four Type 123 *Brandenburg* class, was delivered in December 1996.

Although design work on the Type 130 corvette continues, the project may fall victim to budget cuts. They are intended to replace ageing FACs, and up to fifteen are planned. The Type 148 FACs are down to sixteen units, and six more are earmarked for sale to Chile this year or next.

The modernisation of the mine-countermeasures force continues, with the eleventh and the twelfth Type 332 *Frankenthal* class minehunters to be delivered next year. Tenders are expected to be solicited this summer for the MJ-2000 programme, which will upgrade systems in the *Frankenthal* class, and the slightly older Type 343 *Hameln* class. The much older Types 331, 351 and 394 will start to be paid off from 2000.

Only one of the four Type 702 combat support ships (AOEs), the *Sachsenwald*, has been funded. She will be delivered in 2001, and a second may be funded later. This is a blow to the German Navy's hopes of extending its reach when taking part in peacekeeping operations; at present German task groups have an endurance of twenty-one days, and the Type 704 ships are intended to increase this to forty-five.

Greece: The Hellenic Navy has just bought the former Dutch frigate *Kortenaer*, bringing its total to six. The new MEKO 200 frigate HS *Psara* was delivered in the spring, and the last of four, HS *Salamis*, will follow in December.

Italy: The Italian Navy will pay off the hybrid helicopter-carrying missile cruiser *Vittorio Veneto* in the near future, and will replace her with a *Nuova Unità Maggiore* (new major unit). The decision may have been influenced by a grounding during recent operations off Albania, but the fleet flagship is in any case approaching her thirtieth year of service, and is expensive to maintain. Models and drawings of the replacement show a support carrier resemble the Spanish *Principe de Asturias* or a large amphibious ship, displacing about 20,000 tonnes. First funding was provided in the 1996 budget, but the ship is unlikely to be delivered before 2004.

A number of Italian warships, including some of the amphibious ships, have been operating off Albania this year, rescuing foreigners caught up in the fighting and trying to keep out illegal immigrants. This is the biggest deployment of Italian warships

The new MILAS standoff anti-submarine missile, launched from the deck of the Italian frigate Carabiniere. *(Matra BAe Dynamics)*

in over half a century, and justifies the money spent on the three amphibious dock transports (LPDs) of the *San Giorgio* class.

Netherlands: The Royal Netherlands Navy has suffered severely from budget cuts, but continues to operate modern and powerful ships. The first two air defence/command frigates (LCFs), *de Zeven Provincien* and *Tromp* were ordered in 1995, and two more, the *de Ruyter* and *Evertsen*, lacking the command facilities, were ordered in October last year. When they join the fleet from 2001 onwards the old air defence destroyers, the existing *Tromp* and *de Ruyter*, will be paid off. The additional funds have been secured by reducing the scale of the modernisation planned for the frigates *Jacob van Heemskerck* and *Witte de With*. In theory, the *Kortenaer* class anti-submarine frigates are now down to four ships, but the apparent collapse of the United Arab Emirates' plans to buy up to six LCFs may result in only one being handed over to the UAE.

The plans to overhaul the mine-countermeasures force have not yet matured. Apart from phasing out the last two of the *Dokkum* class coastal minesweepers last December, three of the *Alkmaar* class Tripartite mine-hunters will be converted to control ships for *Troika* drones, four will be upgraded, seven will be refitted but not upgraded and the fifteenth will be converted to a hydrographic survey ship. The new LPD *Amsterdam* was launched earlier this year and will be delivered by December.

Norway: The Royal Norwegian Navy has reversed an earlier decision to rely solely on FACs, and is procuring a new class of up to six frigates, to replace the *Oslo* class. No decision has yet been taken on the critical options: construction in a Norwegian shipyard to a foreign design, construction in a foreign shipyard, purchase of an existing design off-the-shelf, or a one-off design tailored to specific Norwegian requirements. A few details are settled, notably the adoption of a new long-range successor to the *Penguin* anti-ship missile, a *Kongsberg* command system, and a medium

helicopter. The first frigate is to be in service by 2005.

To replace ageing FACs the Naval Materiel Administration has ordered the *Skjold*, first of a planned total of seven 260-ton, 52-knot surface-effect FACs. She is to be delivered in July next year by Kvaerner Mandal, and will undergo a series of trials before the production order is placed. The technology has been developed from the SES minehunters of the *Oksøy* class, and the common-hull *Alta* class minesweepers, the last of which, KNN *Glomma*, was delivered this year.

Like Denmark, Norway has been invited to join the Swedish 'Viking' project, to build a common-hull submarine (*see Sweden*).

Spain: The Spanish Navy caused a major upset last year, when plans to build its F-100 frigate with the Signaal APAR phased-array radar and other common components of the German Type 124 and Dutch LCF designs were dropped. Instead the F-100 will be designed around the Lockheed (formerly RCA) *Aegis* weapon-direction system, using the AN/SPY-1D radar and the *Standard* SM-2 air defence missile, as well as the RIM-7PTC Evolved *Sea Sparrow* Missile (ESSM). The ships were ordered last year from Bazán's Ferrol shipyard and are to be in service by 2005.

The minehunter *Segura* was launched in June this year at Cartagena, and will enter service in May next year. Her sisters *Sella*, *Tambre* and *Turia* will be in service by September 2000. Although widely credited as a modified *Sandown* design, the *Segura* bears only a superficial resemblance to the Royal Navy design; the internal layout and even the make-up of the composite hull are different.

The 12,500-tonne amphibious dock transport *Galicia* (L-51) was launched in June this year and will be in service next. Outline approval to build a sister was agreed in the Council of Ministers in May this year, using funds released by the sale of nine AV-8S *Matador* (*Harrier I*) STOVL aircraft to Thailand.

Sweden: The Royal Swedish Navy's submarine force will fall to nine SSKs by 1999, by which time the last *Sjöcbjörnen* class and of the three

Nåcken class will be out of service. The *Uppland*, second of three *Gotland* class, was launched in February last year, followed by the *Halland* seven months later. Both will be delivered in September or October this year. In future submarine construction will be concentrated at the Karlskronavarvet yard, although Kockums' design facility will remain at Malmö.

The working group set up to discuss the feasibility of a tripartite SSK programme for Sweden, Norway and Denmark reached agreement in May this year on ways to harmonise conflicting staff requirements. It seems that a modular approach will be adopted, permitting each navy to make specific equipment changes without following the expensive route of trying to accommodate all requirements within one design. The May meeting agreed to continue work on the 'Viking' project, to provide a basis for a decision on the building specification. If that hurdle is crossed, construction could start in 2002.

On 17 December 1996 the keel of the *Visby* was laid at Karlskronavarvet, the first of a class of four YS 2000-type corvettes, and the order for Nos 3 and 4 was confirmed.

HSwMS *Styrsö*, first of a new class of four YSB type GRP minehunters, was commissioned in September last year, while the second, the *Sparö*, was launched in August.

Turkey: After a year of backstairs lobbying and a very public 'difference of opinion' between Washington and Ankara, Congress indicated in July this year that it had dropped its objections to supplying three missile-armed frigates to the Turkish Navy. The ships, the USS *Antrim* (FFG-20), *Flatley* (FFG-25) and *Clifton Sprague* (FFG-16), will be renamed TCG *Gaziantep* (F-490), *Giresun* (F-491) and *Gemlik* (F-492). When these ships are delivered later this year it is almost certain that the last ex-USN destroyers will be paid off. TCG *Sahilreis*, the third of four enlarged MEKO 200-type frigates, will be commissioned towards the end of next year, bringing the total of modern escorts to fifteen, excluding the new acquisitions.

The SSK force is also being modernised. The completion of the *Sakarya* last December brings the total of

The Spanish Navy's new F-100 type frigate. (Lockheed Martin)

modern boats to eight, with two more to be delivered in 1998–99. The five 'Guppy'-type boats are likely to be paid off, although the more modern ex-*Tang* class may be retained for training purposes.

United Kingdom: Although short of funds the UK Royal Navy has managed its budget better than some other navies, notably in securing funds for significant new construction. The most important event this year has been 'Ocean Wave', a lengthy deployment to the Far East which lasted seven months.

HMS *Vigilant*, the third *Vanguard* class Trident SSBN was commissioned in November last year, shortly after the paying-off of HMS *Repulse*, last of the Polaris SSBNs. The fourth, HMS *Vengeance*, is well advanced at GEC Marine's Barrow-in-Furness

yard (formerly VSEL), and will start her first patrol in 1999. Three *Astute* class SSNs were approved in March this year, at a total cost of nearly £2 billion. It is now admitted that these SSNs will be a major advance over the *Trafalgar* class, a confirmation that the designation 'Batch 2 *Trafalgar* Class' (B2TC) was largely a fiction. They will, however, have the same armament and sensors as their predecessors: *Spearfish* torpedoes, UGM-84C *Sub-Harpoon* anti-ship missiles, BGM-109 Tomahawk land-attack missiles, the 2076 integrated sonar suite and a variant of the SMCS command system.

The four redundant *Upholder* class SSKs are still laid up at Barrow Shipyard awaiting a buyer, with Canada and South Africa considered to be the hottest favourites.

The delays in starting the 'Horizon'

tri-national frigate programme bear heavily on the RN's *Birmingham* and *Manchester* class (Type 42) destroyers. The oldest of these will be twenty-eight years old if the first 'Horizon' is delivered in 2004 as planned. In a 'worst-case scenario', if 'Horizon' has to be cancelled, the RN must either go it alone or look to the US Navy for help.

HMS *Sutherland* (F-81) joined the Fleet this July, the thirteenth 'Duke' class (Type 23) frigate, and the last three will be delivered in 2000–2001. The minehunter *Penzance* (M-106) was launched in March this year at Woolston, and her sister *Pembroke* (M-107) will follow in December. The amphibious assault helicopter carrier (LPH) *Ocean* is fitting out at Barrow for delivery next summer. With the order for two new assault ships (LPDs) approved in March this

The new Royal Navy assault ships Albion *and* Bulwark. *(RINA)*

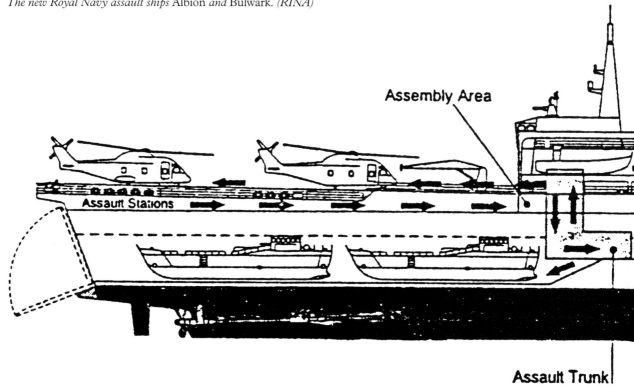

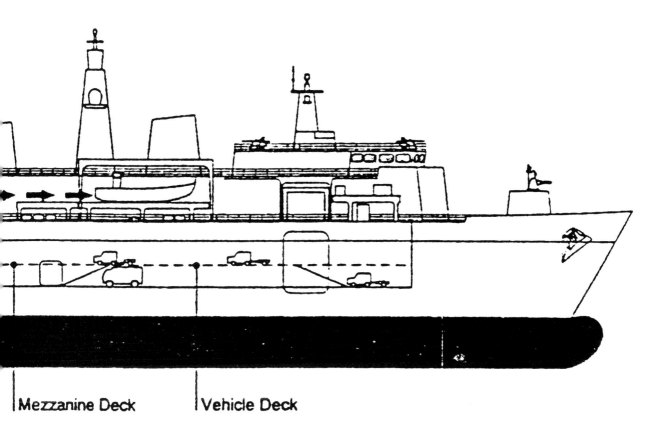

| Mezzanine Deck | Vehicle Deck |

Above: *The new ocean survey vessel HMS* Scott. *(BAe SEMA)*

Left: *The assault helicopter carrier* Ocean *arrives at Barrow-in-Furness. (GEC Marine/VSEL)*

year, first steel will be cut for the *Albion* and *Bulwark* in November. The ships will be ready in 2002 and 2003, respectively.

The first of two new chartered commercial vehicle transports, the 23,986grt *Sea Crusader* (A-96), arrived from Japan in November last year. With the new amphibious warfare ships already mentioned, the new acquisitions guarantee the renewal of the Royal Navy's amphibious capability, which had been targeted for abolition in the 1981 'Way Ahead' review and was thereafter constantly under threat. Unfortunately, the modernisation and 'stretching' of the logistic landing ship (L5L) RFA *Sir Bedivere* has run into trouble, largely because of 'emergent work', and the ship will be late and over-budget when she is returned to service in September this year.

The new large ocean survey vessel, the 13,300-ton HMS *Scott*, was delivered earlier this year, and a contract was placed with GEC Marine to build the 30,000-ton oilers *Wave Knight* and *Wave Ruler*. RFA *Resource* returned from Split in Croatia, where she has

been stationed for five years as a support ship for British Army units operating in the former Yugoslavia. She has since been sold.

The US and Russian Navies

United States: With the 'drawdown' in strength virtually over, the US Navy is smaller but better equipped than it was in the days of the artificially inflated '600-ship Navy' of the Reagan era. Arms limitation agreements have reduced the SSBN force to eighteen *Ohio* (SSBN-726) class Trident SSBNs. The oldest four will be converted to other duties, and from 2000 the force will be uniformly armed with the D5 Trident II missile system. The *Los Angeles* (SSN-688) class has been cut to fifty-six units, and will fall to forty-five in three years. The 9,000-ton *Seawolf* (SSN-21) was commissioned in May this year, and work will start on the 7,700-ton New Attack Submarine (NAS) next year. Only sixteen of the older SSNs are left, including two ex-SSBNs converted to carry special forces (SEALs).

The carrier programme continues, with the eighth *Nimitz* class, the *Harry S Truman* (CVN-75), to be delivered next summer. The *Ronald Reagan* (CVN-76) is to be laid down next year; *CVN-77* has been approved; and design work continues on the CVX concept. The conventionally powered USS *Independence* will be decommissioned at the end of this year, leaving only three CVs in service.

Only four of the large nuclear-powered cruisers remain in service, and two are in reserve. The core of the cruiser force now comprises the twenty-seven *Ticonderoga* (CG-47) class *Aegis* cruisers.

Rebuilding of the destroyer force continues apace, with three more *Arleigh Burke* (DDG-51) *Aegis* ships delivered this year, making a total of twenty delivered since 1991. The design has already been upgraded to Flight IIA standard, with a double hangar and flight deck. To date forty-one have been approved, through to Fiscal Year 2001. The run-down of the frigate force was halted when the USN found itself critically short of ships for general patrol duties, but

The Aegis *destroyer USS* Ross *(DDG-71). (Litton Industries/Ingalls Shipbuilding)*

only forty-two *Oliver Hazard Perry* (FFG-7) class are left.

Amphibious forces have a high priority, with the large assault ship *Bataan* (LHD-5) delivered in September this year, and two more under construction. The last two small assault helicopter carriers (LPHs) are to be decommissioned next year; but after lengthy delays the first of the *San Antonio* (LPD-17) class dock transports was ordered in December last year. These ships will be more flexible than previous LPDs, with extensive command facilities and Evolved *Sea Sparrow* missiles for self-defence.

The last of twelve *Whidbey Island* (LSD-41) and *Harper's Ferry* (LSD-49) class dock-anding ships, the *Pearl Harbor* (LSD-52) will be delivered next spring. Only sixteen of the original fleet of LSDs and LPDs are left, and three *Newport* (LST-1179) class tank-landing ships.

Mine countermeasures seem to have slipped down the list of priorities once more. Although the minehunter *Cardinal* (MHC-60) was delivered in July this year, and the last two of a class of twelve are to be delivered next year, four of the larger *Avenger* (MCM-1) class have been given to the Reserves.

Russia: The American problems are nothing compared with those of the former Soviet Navy, which is still struggling to maintain a credible level of competence. Several exercises have been held with NATO participation, but pay for officers and ratings (and even more critical) for shipyard workers is in arrears. This leads to demoralisation and corruption. In effect, the main effective force is now the Northern Fleet; the Baltic Fleet is mainly for training, the Black Sea Fleet has been carved up with Ukraine, and the Pacific Fleet has all but collapsed.

The SSBN force is still active, not least because it is one of Russia's few remaining status symbols of a major military power. One new SSBN, the 17,000-ton Project 955 *Borey* ('Arctic Wind') class *Yuri Dolgoruky*, was laid down in November last year. The eleventh Project 949A *Antey* 'Oscar II' cruise missile submarine (SSGN), the *Tomsk* (K-512), joined the fleet in January this year. The twelfth, *K-530*,

will be completed next year. Only two of a planned total of seven Project 885 *Severodvinsk* class are under construction, and new advanced nuclear-powered designs will be deferred until money is available to pay the arrears to the shipyards. To support marketing efforts one SSK of the Project 1450 *Amur* type will be laid down this year. An AIP plant will be fitted as a 'hull-plug' if required by a customer.

No new surface warships have been laid down since 1991, and official statements suggest that none will be

started before 2005. In the meantime the large force of minor vessels, ranging from corvettes down to patrol craft, is suffering all the problems of block obsolescence.

Middle Eastern Navies

Bahrain: Bahrain's capability on paper has more than doubled, with the transfer of the former US Navy missile frigate *Jack Williams* (FFG-24). She was renamed *Sabha*.

RNOV Al Mua'zzar *is the second of two 83-metre corvettes built for Oman. (Vesper Thorneycroft)*

Israel: Israel's most important acquisition, the SSK *Dolphin*, has been running trials since November last year, and will be commissioned next spring. Her sister *Leviathan* was launched in May this year, and the third boat will be launched at Emden next January. Five-sixths of the cost is being met by Germany as military aid, with *Sub-Harpoon* missiles and NT-37F torpedoes supplied by the US. The 20-year-old *Gal* class, built at Barrow to an IKL 540 design, will serve until the end of the century.

The FAC force has been reduced to thirteen units, and some of the oldest, the five *Reshef* class, may be sold. The three *Eilat* class 86.4-metre corvettes have been running since 1994–95, but fitting of the *Elbit* combat system did not start until late last year. It is reported to have suffered software problems during development.

Kuwait: The first three of eight P-37BRL-type patrol craft ordered by Kuwait have been launched by CMN at Cherbourg this year. After a hard-fought battle the British Aerospace ship-launched *Sea Skua* was recently selected as the armament. The ships will be delivered between November this year and the summer of 1999.

Oman: Oman's new missile corvette *Qahir al Amwaj* (Q-31) left for Muscat in June last year, followed by her sister *Al Mua'zzar* (Q-32) in April this year. The offshore patrol vessel SNOV *Al Najah* (B-3) left Cherbourg for the Gulf in June last year. She and her two sisters have been rearmed with 76mm L/62 *Super Rapid* guns at the Wudam shipyard.

Qatar: Two of the Qatari Emiri Navy's new 56-metre FACs, QENS *Barzan* (Q-04) and *Huwar* (Q-05) sailed from Vesper Thornycroft's Woolston shipyard in July this year. Their sisters *Al Udeid* (Q-06) and *Al Debeel* (Q-07) will follow at the end of the year.

Saudi Arabia: Saudi Arabia finally confirmed an order for three air-defence frigates in May this year. The older *Madina* class have started a cycle of overhauls at Toulon, along with the two French-built replenishment ships of the *Boraida* class. The third *Sandown*-type minehunter *Al Kharj* completed vibration trials, and left for Saudi Arabia in the summer. The builders hope to receive the funds for the second batch of three.

Yemen: To meet short-term needs caused by a disagreement with Eritrea over the ownership of the Hanish

Al Kharj is the third minehunter for the Royal Saudi Navy. (Vesper Thorneycroft)

Islands in the Red Sea last year, the Republic of Yemen ordered a number of small inshore patrol craft from neighbouring states. The French CMN yard also supplied four 15.5-metre *Baklan* class. Although credited with two Russian- and Chinese-built Project 1241 '*Tarantul* I' corvettes, three 'Hounan' type FACs and four Project 1400M 'Zhuk'-type patrol craft, very few of these are believed to be fully operational.

Africa

Algeria: Algeria's navy is badly affected by the political turmoil in the country. The Russian-built SSK *El Hadj Slimane* completed a refit at St Petersburg in March last year, two years after her sister *Rais Hadj Mubarek*.

Egypt: On 13 July this year the Egyptian Navy commissioned the frigates *Mubarak* (F-911) and *Taba* (F-916) at Ras el Tin naval base. They are the former USS *Copeland* (FFG-25) and USS *Gallery* (FFG-26), and a third unit, the USS *Duncan* (FFG-10), may be handed over later this year.

The last of four Chinese-built '*Romeo*' type SSKs, No. 855, completed a major modernisation in January this year, with a German sonar, American fire control, *Sub-Harpoon* missiles and NT-37F torpedoes. No decision has been made on new SSKs, but bids from HDW in Germany and from Russia have been received.

The Egyptian predilection for very old ships is hard to explain. The former RN destroyer *El Fateh* (ex-HMS *Zenith*) and the frigate *Tariq* (ex-HMS *Whimbrel*) are past their half century. With eight modern escorts in service (albeit built in three different countries) the time has come to rationalise by scrapping these veterans.

Morocco: The Royal Navy of Morocco has recently received its fourth offshore patrol vessel, the *Rais Maaninou* (321), from the French builders Leroux & Lotz. The fifth, *Rais al Mounastiri* (322) will be delivered in December. The new support ship *Dakhla* was delivered at the beginning of August.

The Morrocan support ship Dakhla *was built at Lorient and delivered in August. (Leroux & Lotz)*

South Africa: The South African Navy (SAN) celebrated its anniversary in April this year, but it is in the middle of a major crisis. The submarine force is becoming more and more expensive to maintain as the French-built *Daphné* class approach their third decade of service. The strike craft (FACs) are not suited to the new peacekeeping and surveillance missions of the SAN, and a smaller number of corvettes would be more effective. But the

The fast attack craft SAS Adam Kok *(formerly* Frederic Creswell*) has been modernised. (Antony Preston)*

defence budget is under pressure, and the SAN is struggling to make a case for new programmes.

In March this year the former 'Minister' class FACs were renamed the 'Warrior' class: *Shaka, Adam Kok, Sekhukhuni, Isaac Dyobha, Rene Sethren, Galeshewe, Job Masego* and *Makhanda*. In fact the *Sekhukhuni* has been stripped, and is unlikely to be recommissioned, and only six of the class will receive the full modernisation.

The wrangle over funds led to the cancellation of the original plan to order four corvettes from EN Bazán in Spain in 1995. Since then GEC Marine has produced a very attractive countertrade package, but the lack of a decision has encouraged both the French and the Germans to renew their efforts. The British offer is particularly appealing because it would include the four *Upholder* class SSKs on a lease or at very favourable terms.

The Asia-Pacific Region

Australia: The Royal Australian Navy (RAN) modernisation plans are well advanced. HMAS *Collins*, first of six new SSKs, was commissioned in July last year, and HMAS *Farncomb* was delivered in July this year. Unfortunately, software problems with the American Rockwell Collins command system have delayed full operational capability for at least two years. Only two of the original six *Oberons* remain in service; HMAS *Otama* will be paid off next year and HMAS *Onslow* in 1999.

HMS *Anzac* (F-150) has been running extensive first-of-class trials since May last year, and contracts have been placed to fit the missing RGM-84C *Harpoon* missiles and the second 8-cell *Sea Sparrow* VL system. The *Arunta* (F-151) was launched in June last year and will be delivered in March 1998. Plans to upgrade the six *Adelaide* class frigates are well advanced.

The timetable for building up to twelve offshore patrol combatants (OPCs) still depends on the Malaysian NGPV decision (see below). Hull lay-up work is well advanced on the third of the *Huon* coastal minehunters, the *Norman* (M-84), and the *Huon* (M-82) is set for delivery in 1999. Conversion of the ex-USN tank-landing ships HMAS *Kanimbla* (L-51) and HMAS *Manoora* (L-52) to the new assault ship (LPA) role is in hand at the Forgacs yard in Newcastle, NSW.

HMAS Kanimbla, *a former US Navy* Newport (LST-1179) *class tank-landing ship, under conversion to a helicopter support ship (LPA). (RAN)*

HMAS Anzac *manoeuvring at speed. (RAN)*

The Royal Australian Navy's new minehunter Huon *was launched almost complete on 25 July 1997. (RAN)*

China: The Chinese People's Liberation Army-Navy (PLAN) is reported to be close to starting work on a Project 093 SSBN to succeed the solitary Project 092 'Xia' type, but there is no sign of a successor to the five Project 091 'Han' type SSNs built over a period of more than twenty years. Even the rate of SSK-building is not fast. The first Project 039 'Song' is still not fully operational, despite having started sea trials two years ago. A swathe has been cut through the large fleet of obsolescent Project 033 'Romeos', but the Project 035 'Ming' type has been built at an average rate of one a year (thirteen have been delivered since 1971). Whatever the reason, PLAN has bought two Project 877 'Kilo' type from Russia, followed by the improved variant, Project 636. The latter

will be delivered in September this year and next summer, respectively. Licence-production in a Chinese yard seems likely.

Rumours of the purchase of the incomplete carrier *Varyag* from Ukraine turned out to be false, but plans for two 45,000-ton carriers of some sort are continuing. Western intelligence sources put an in-service date some time in the second decade of the next century.

In January this year the purchase of two incomplete Project 956A *Sovremennyy* class destroyers became public. To quote the editor of *Combat Fleets*, by themselves they will not alter the balance of power regionally, but they will introduce PLAN to a range of weapons far more advanced than anything in the existing inventory. The first of the Project 052 '*Luhu*'-

type destroyers, the *Harbin*, has made a number of foreign visits since last year, culminating in a visit to San Diego, California. She and the *Qingdao* have American LM-2500 gas turbines, but the third ship will have units supplied by Ukraine. These ships have a number of Western systems, including the French Crotale air-defence missile system and the Tavitac combat system, and Italian anti-submarine torpedoes and electronic warfare systems.

In smaller craft PLAN is facing a massive problem of block obsolescence, with large numbers of FACs built to thirty-year-old designs. At the same time it is seriously deficient in such basic skills as air defence, anti-submarine warfare and mine countermeasures.

India: India's dreams of being a regional superpower are taking longer than expected to achieve. The intention to have a new carrier ready for the 50th anniversary of independence has come to nothing, and the old carrier *Vikrant* (ex-HMS *Hercules*) was paid off in January this year without being replaced. The *Viraat* (ex-HMS *Hermes*) is not much younger, but it is hoped to keep her running until 2005. Plans to buy the *Admiral Gorshkov* from the Russian Navy were dropped when it was realised that she would need very extensive repairs following a fire in her engine room in 1991. The latest idea is to build an 'air-defence ship' at Cochin; but on present form she will not be ready in time for the final paying off of the *Viraat* in eight years time.

All three Project 15 *Delhi* class improved '*Kashin*' type air-defence destroyers are afloat, and the *Delhi* herself was commissioned in May this year. Three Project 1135.6 class Improved '*Krivak* III' frigates were ordered from the Northern Shipyard in St Petersburg last year, for delivery in 1999–2000. The first of three Improved *Godavari* class frigates, to be named *Brahmaputra*, is to be launched this year at the Garden Reach yard in Calcutta.

The fifth Project 25 *Khukri* class corvette, to be named *Kora* (P-48?) is expected to be delivered by Garden Reach this year, and the *Kalish* is due to be launched. The *Prahar* (K-83), eleventh of the Project 1241RE *Veer* class ('Tarantul I' type), was commissioned in March this year; the twelfth and final unit (name not yet known) is expected to be completed by the end of next year.

The interest in building an indigenous SSN continues unabated, and funds have been switched from other programmes, but the in-service date of 2004 seems optimistic. Two Project 636 improved '*Kilo*' type SSKs have been ordered from Russia, but plans to build two more IKL Type 1500 boats at Bombay appear to have been dropped. The last of the Project 641 'Foxtrots' have been paid off.

The Russian Zvezda-manufactured Kh-35 *Uran* missile has been bought for the *Delhi* class and the modified '*Krivaks*', and it may replace the obsolete P-20 '*Styx*' in some existing classes. The indigenous *Trishul* air-defence missile system now appears to be ready to enter service after a very lengthy gestation.

Japan: Japan's Maritime Self Defence Force (MSDF) pursues its policy of scrap-and-build, but total strength has been reduced to reflect the reduced threat from the Russian Pacific Fleet.

The submarine *Oyashio* (SS-590), launched in October last year, is the first of a new design different in many respects from the previous series. The *Asashio* (SS-589) was commissioned in March this year, the last of seven *Harushio* class built since 1987. Three more SSKs have been approved, for completion from 1998 to 2001.

The third *Aegis* destroyer, the *Myoko* (DDG-175), was commissioned in March last year; the last, the *Chokai* (DDG-176), was launched the following August and will be commissioned in March next year.

Since the commissioning of the lead-ship *Murasame* (DD-101) in March last year, she has been joined by the *Harusame* (DD-102) exactly a year later. The last, *DD-107*, is to be delivered in 2001. A new class of eight 4,900-ton general-purpose destroyers (DDs) is planned, with funds to be requested for the first in Fiscal Year 1998.

The escort force is being cut as older destroyer escorts (DEs) are paid off. The mine-countermeasures force, in contrast, flourishes. The minehunter *Nagashima* (MSC-680) was commissioned last December, the last of a class of eighteen built since the late 1970s. Three of a new design, *MSC-681–683*, are under construction, and the first will be delivered in 1999.

By far the most controversial ship is the new amphibious assault ship (LPD) *Oosumi*, which was launched last November. Officially listed as a tank-landing ship, she is configured like a small carrier, with a full-length flight deck and island superstructure. Opposition politicians, hostile to anything remotely reminiscent of militarism, claim that she will be able to operate AV-8B *Harriers* in an offensive capacity(!), whereas the MSDF claims that she is merely intended to support peacekeeping operations.

Korea: The Republic of Korea's submarine force is growing, with five IKL Type 1200 SSKs in service. The *Park* was commissioned in January last year, followed by the *Yi Chong-Mu* in August, while the sixth, the *Chong Un-ho*, was launched in May and was commissioned in June this year.

The KDX destroyer programme has been recast, with three KDX-1 destroyers, six larger KDX-2s and a much enlarged KDX-3. The first KDX-1, named *Kwang-gaeto* (971), was launched last October. KDX-3 will have *Aegis* or an equivalent system.

Little can be said about North Korea, whose navy is badly affected by the economic catastrophe overwhelming the country. The grounding of one of its small *Sang-o*-type coastal SSKs in South Korea in September last year gave Western intelligence a useful 'hands-on' view. In July this year it was learned that a new anti-ship missile, known as AG-2, has been fired, but there is no indication of its possible applications.

Malaysia: The Royal Malaysian Navy expects to receive its new frigates KD *Lekiu* (30) and KD *Jebat* (29) in August this year, following a year of integration problems encountered with the Nautis-F combat system. The first pair of an eventual quartet of ex-Iraqi corvettes bought from Fincantieri in Italy, KD *Laksamana Nadim* (F-134) and *Laksmana Tun Abdul Gamil* (F-135) were commissioned in May this year.

The long saga of the New-generation Patrol Vessel (NGPV) programme is still running; three years after the first invitations to tender, no final shortlist has been announced. Nor is there any progress on the acquisition of submarines, although the latest estimate is that an order will be placed sometime between 1998 and 2001. A new class of minehunters is also planned.

New Zealand: The Royal New Zealand's first *Anzac* class frigate, HMNZS *Te Kaha* (F-77), was commissioned in June this year, and her sister *Te Mana* (F-111) was launched in May. The broad-beam *Leander* class *Wellington* and *Canterbury* have been modernised, and now have a Mk15 *Phalanx* CIWS on the hangar

The Japanese Harushio *class diesel-electric submarines have a classic Albacore* hull, *but traditional cruciform rudders. (Ships of the World)*

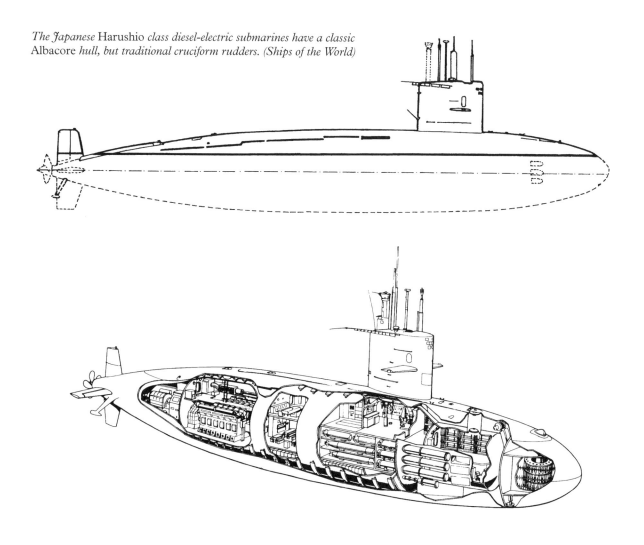

The Malaysian frigate KD Lekiu *on trials. (GEC Marine/Yarrow Shipbuilders)*

roof, as well as a Signaal LW-08 surveillance radar on the mainmast and various other improvements. The older *Leander*, HMNZS *Waikato* remains virtually unaltered, and is used mainly for training.

One of the US Maritime Sealift Command ocean surveillance ships, the former USNS *Tenacious* (T-AGOS-17), was recommissioned in February this year as HMNZS *Resolution* (A-14). She will replace the survey ships *Tui* and *Monowai*.

Pakistan: The Pakistan Navy's first indigenous combatant was launched in November last year, an FAC modelled on the large patrol craft *Larkana*, built at Karachi in the early 1990s. Two more are planned. The Tripartite minehunter *Muhafiz* (M-165) was completed by Karachi Shipyard in May last year, after being assembled with French technical assistance. Her sister *Mujahid* (M-164) was launched in January this year.

Philippines: The Republic of the Philippines has talked a lot about creating a modern navy to deter the Chinese from trespassing in territorial waters, but the large sums required to replace the largely obsolete fleet have not been voted. The first instalment is to include three OPVs, six corvettes, two large patrol craft, six small patrol boats and two minehunters. As an interim measure the three *Peacock* class Hong Kong patrol vessels were bought from the Royal Navy, and were delivered immediately after the British withdrawal at the beginning of June this year.

Singapore: The Republic of Singapore Navy's ex-Swedish SSK RSS *Riken* is expected to arrive later this year from the Baltic, where she has been carrying out intensive training. No decision has been announced about future construction.

The 62-metre *Victory* class corvettes are at last receiving their Israeli Barak air-defence missile systems. The new patrol craft *Gallant* (97), *Daring* (98) and *Dauntless* (99) were commissioned in May this year, completing the first batch of the *Fearless* class. The *Resilience* (83) was launched in November last year, the first of a second batch optimised for

strike warfare. It is hoped to order the first of eight 'new-generation patrol vessels' (in reality 'stealth' missile-armed corvettes) this year or early next year. The design emanates from Kockums in Sweden, and bears a passing resemblance to the new *Visby* design (*see Warship Notes*).

Five 8,500-ton roll-on/roll-off amphibious ships were ordered from Singapore Shipbuilding in the summer of last year. They will replace

Second World War-vintage LSTs acquired from the US Navy.

Taiwan: The Republic of China (Taiwan) Navy continues to make good progress in expanding and upgrading its forces. The fifth *Oliver Hazard Perry*-type frigate *Tzu-I* (1107) was commissioned in January this year, while the *Pan Chao* (1108) was launched in March, and the last of the class, the *Chang Chien* (1109) was

The Taiwanese frigate Yueh Feng *at Simonstown in April 1997. (Antony Preston)*

launched in July. The *Kun Ming* (1205), the third modified *La Fayette* type, was commissioned in February this year, while the *Di Hua* (1207) will be commissioned in December. Three more *Knox* class, the USS *Aylwin* (FF-1081), *Pharris* (FF-1094) and *Valdez* (FF-1096) are to be transferred this year, bringing the total to nine.

Plans to build eleven more *Jin Chiang* class FACs were halted in July last year to allow a government enquiry into accusations of financial impropriety. The small *Hai Ou* type FACs, a combination of the Israeli 'Dvora' hull and the indigenous *Hsiung Feng* missile (itself developed from the Israeli *Gabriel*), may be replaced by a new 'stealth' design.

Thailand: The Royal Thai Navy's new support aircraft carrier, the 12,000-ton *Chakkrinaruebet* (11) was commissioned in March this year. She will operate ex-Spanish Navy AV-8S *Harrier* STOVL aircraft and new S-70B-7 helicopters.

The two ex-*Knox* class frigates *Phutthayotfa Chulalok* (461) and *Phutthaloetla Napalim* (462) arrived from the US this summer. Three 62-metre corvettes have been ordered from Asian Marine (ASIMAR) at Prapadang, outside Bangkok, the first to be delivered next year.

Three 30.1-metre patrol craft were ordered in October last year from a consortium set up by the Australian Submarine Corporation (ASC) and

Silkline International. If successful an order for fifteen more is to follow. Two modified *Gaeta*-type minehunters were ordered from Intermarine in September last year, for delivery in 1999–2000. The 23,000-ton replenishment ship (AOR) *Similan* (871) was delivered by the Chinese Hudong Shipyard in August last year.

Latin American Navies

Argentina: Fears about the vaulting ambitions of the *Armada Republica Argentina* were laid to rest finally at the end of last year, when the Chief of Naval Staff announced major cuts.

These included cancellation of plans

The French SIMBAD launcher and its close-range Mistral missiles provide a cheap defence for small warships. *(Matra BAe Dynamics)*

to complete the re-engining and modernisation of the carrier *Vienticinco de Mayo*, cancellation of the modernisation of the SSK *San Luis*, and deletion of the 20-year-old tank landing ship *Cabo San Antonio*. Also written off were the incomplete corvettes *Robinson* and *Gomez Roca*.

Brazil: In contrast, Brazil has achieved considerable success. The refitted carrier *Minas Gerais* has operated with the Argentines, embarking *Super Etendard* strike aircraft and *Turbo Trackers* for training late last year. Since then she has received surplus SH-3D *Sea King* and new *Super Lynx* helicopters, and may operate refurbished A-4 *Skyhawks*.

Like India, an SSN programme has squandered precious funds, but it was stopped after financial improprieties came to light. In contrast, the SSK programme is producing results. The *Timbira* was delivered in December last year, and work started on the *Tapajo* in March. The improved SNAC-1 design is also in hand, with the *Tikuna* to be laid down next year. The British-built *Oberon* type *Humaíta* was decommissioned in August last year, but her two sisters have been refitted recently.

In April this year the last of four ex-RN *Broadsword* class (Type 22 Batch 1) frigates, BNS *Rademaker* (F-49) was handed over at Devonport. Although details of the modernisation of the *Niteroi* class are settled, the work has been proceeding slowly since December last year. Plans to build more *Barroso* class have been shelved in favour of a large design.

Chile: Chile has agreed to buy the Franco-Spanish 'Scorpéne' SSK design from EN Bazán, but details of a technology-transfer involving ASMAR's Talcahuano yard have not been finalised. The Swedish minelayer *Alvsborg* was bought last year and has been renamed *Almirante Merino*; she will serve as a support ship for FACs and SSKs. The first two of a total of six Type 148 FACs was handed over by the German Navy earlier this year.

Columbia: Last summer the Colombian Navy bought the experimental FAC *Cormorán* from Spanish builders EN Bazán and renamed her *Espartana*.

Mexico: Mexico has been given Congressional approval to receive the *Knox* class frigates *Stein* (FF-1065) and *Marvin Shields* (FF-1066), and will commission them this year.

Venezuela: Venezuela's continuing economic problems have resulted in the cancellation of plans to modernise the six *Lupo*-type frigates.

WARSHIP GALLERY

In this section, we are publishing photographs of warships which are unusual, remarkable as images, mysterious or otherwise of special interest to readers. The section is not intended for standard ship portraits, but for out-of-the-ordinary pictures which illuminate aspects of warships not evident in the usual views. Most of the photographs are from the wide-ranging and largely unknown Conway Picture Library. The editors would be happy to hear from readers with any unusual pictures which might appear in future issues.

HMS Montagu on the rocks on Lundy Island after running aground on 30 May 1906. Attempts to refloat her were unsuccessful, and the wreck was eventually abandoned after her guns were removed. The Duncan class were smaller and slightly faster than the other White-designed 'standard' pre-dreadnought battleships. (CPL)

The battleship Lord Nelson with funnel bands and short funnels, taken between 1909 and 1911. She and her sister Agamemnon had a unique profile, but some features of the Dreadnought can be detected. (CPL)

The Imperial Russian Navy icebreaker Sviatogor was scuttled at Archangel on 3 August 1918, and was seized by a British boarding party. After salvage she was incorporated into the Royal Navy under the same name, and was returned to Russian control on 19 November 1921, after the Intervention War was over. (CPL)

HMS Illustrious at sea during the 'Ocean Wave' deployment in the first half of 1997. Since then the decision has been made to remove the Sea Dart missile system to allow the forward flight deck to be extended. (MOD/HMS Illustrious)

HMS Argus, the Royal Navy's first aircraft carrier with a flush deck and full-length hangar. She is seen shortly after her completion in September 1918, and her small wooden pilothouse can be seen in the raised position. (CPL)

Krupp's Germania shipyard at Kiel in the late 1930s, seen under the bowsprit of the sail training ship Horst Wessel. These buildings were destroyed by Allied bombing during the Second World War. (CPL/Fr. Urbanns)

HMS Hermes, the world's first purpose-built carrier on fire and listing after being hit by Japanese bombers off Trincomalee on 9 April 1942. (CPL)

A narrow escape for the pilot of this Wildcat, which skidded off the deck of the USS Lexington and miraculously came to rest suspended from the flight-deck overhang. (CPL)

Underwater shock test during class trials of the frigate USS Oliver Hazard Perry *(FFG-7). Since the Second World War design-*
ers have paid great attention to shock, which can disable machinery and systems without damaging the hull. (CPL/US Navy)

HMS Thorough paying off at Portsmouth in December 1957. She is a virtually unaltered 'T' class – apart from the removal of the 20mm gun platform – with a shield to the gun and a 'snort' mast added (folded on the port side of the after casing). (CPL/Royal Navy)

INDEX

Page references in *italics* refer to illustrations, and those in **bold** to diagrams, tables and maps.